Cambridge Semitic Languages and Cultures

General Editor: Geoffrey Khan

This is the first Open Access book series in the field; it combines the high peer-review and editorial standards with the fair Open Access model offered by OBP. The series includes philological and linguistic studies of Semitic languages, editions of Semitic texts, and studies of Semitic cultures. Titles cover all periods, traditions and methodological approaches to the field. The editorial board comprises Geoffrey Khan, Aaron Hornkohl, Esther-Miriam Wagner, Anne Burberry, and Benjamin Kantor.

You can access the full series catalogue here:
https://www.openbookpublishers.com/series/2632-6914

If you would like to join our community and interact with authors of the books, sign up to be contacted about events relating to the series and receive publication updates and news here:
https://forms.gle/RWymsw3hdsUjZTXv5

JEROME'S SOURCES IN HIS TRANSLATION OF THE HEBREW BIBLE

Jerome's Sources in His Translation of the Hebrew Bible

Paul Rodrigue

https://www.openbookpublishers.com

©2025 Paul Rodrigue

This work is licensed under an Attribution-NonCommercial 4.0 International (CC BY-NC 4.0). This license allows you to share, copy, distribute, and transmit the text; to adapt the text for non-commercial purposes of the text providing attribution is made to the authors (but not in any way that suggests that they endorse you or your use of the work). Attribution should include the following information:

Paul Rodrigue, *Jerome's Sources in His Translation of the Hebrew Bible*. Cambridge, UK: Open Book Publishers, 2025, https://doi.org/10.11647/OBP.0474

Further details about CC BY-NC licenses are available at http://creativecommons.org/licenses/by-nc/4.0/

All external links were active at the time of publication unless otherwise stated and have been archived via the Internet Archive Wayback Machine at https://archive.org/web

Any digital material and resources associated with this volume will be available at https://doi.org/10.11647/OBP.0474#resources

Semitic Languages and Cultures 38

ISSN (print): 2632-6906	ISBN Paperback: 978-1-80511-637-0
ISSN (digital): 2632-6914	ISBN Hardback: 978-1-80511-638-7
	ISBN Digital (PDF): 978-1-80511-639-4

DOI: 10.11647/OBP.0474

Cover image: Bas-relief of Saint Jerome found in the cave beneath the Chapel of Saint Catherine in Bethlehem (August 2023) ©Paul Rodrigue
Cover design: Jeevanjot Kaur Nagpal

The fonts used in this volume are Charis SIL, SBL Hebrew and SBL Greek.

To my mentor

> *Dixi rigabo meum hortum plantationum*
> *et inebriabo pratus mei fructum*
> Sirach 24.42

> אַל־תִּרְאוּנִי֙ שֶׁאֲנִ֣י שְׁחַרְחֹ֔רֶת שֶׁשֱּׁזָפַ֖תְנִי הַשָּׁ֑מֶשׁ
> בְּנֵ֧י אִמִּ֣י נִֽחֲרוּ־בִ֗י שָׂמֻ֙נִי֙ נֹטֵרָ֣ה אֶת־הַכְּרָמִ֔ים
> כַּרְמִ֥י שֶׁלִּ֖י לֹ֥א נָטָֽרְתִּי׃
> Song of Songs 1.6

CONTENTS

Preface xi

Abbreviations xv

1. Introduction 1
   1.0. A Map of the Argument 1
   2.0. Before the Vulgate 2
   3.0. Preliminary Notes on Jerome's Linguistic
        Background 24
   4.0. The Creation of a New Latin Version
        of Scripture 27
   5.0. An Appreciation of Jerome's Agenda
        through His Reception and Treatment
        of the Hebrew Book of Genesis 43
   6.0. A Point of Terminology 55
   7.0. Some Observations on Jerome's
        Relationship with the LXX 76
   8.0. Jerome's Conception of Translation
        and His Translation Method 89
   9.0. The Purpose of This Monograph 101

2. The Translation of the Joseph Story
   (Gen 37–50) 107
   1.0. Textual History 107
   2.0. The Case Studies 108
      2.1. Thirty Pieces of Silver and Twenty
           Pieces of Gold 109
      2.2. An Independent Departure from the
           Hebrew 113
      2.3. A Case of Hybrid *sensus de sensu*
           Translation 120
      2.4. The Complex Case of Gen. 41.43a–b 129
      2.5. Certain Departures from the Hebrew
           in the Vulgate 146

3. The Translation of the Book of Daniel 155
   1.0. Textual History 155
   2.0. The Case Studies 180
      2.1. The Translation of a Rare Hebrew
           Word: פרתמים 181
      2.2. The Translation of the Word צבי 203
      2.3. A Case of *hebraica veritas* Underlain by
           Jerome's Care for the Latin Version
           of the LXX 212

2.4. "Each was drinking according to his age" in Vulg. Dan. 5.1–2a 219

2.5. The Rendering *collega* in Vulg. Dan. 4.5 234

4. The Translation of the Book of Esther 241

1.0. Textual History 241

2.0. The Case Studies 258

2.1. Paraphrases Reflecting Some Reliance on the Greek and Old Latin Versions in the Vulgate 259

2.2. Paraphrases of the Hebrew that Jerome Produced Mostly Independently of the Other Sources 271

2.3. Two Verses Representative of the Most Common Type of Paraphrase in Vulg. Est. 294

2.4. A Paraphrase of Origen's Edition of the LXX 302

5. Conclusion 309

1.0. A Summary of Jerome's Sources 309

2.0. Jerome's Techniques of Translation and Some Concluding Remarks 311

Bibliography 315
  Primary Sources 315
  Secondary Sources 320
Index 347

PREFACE

The present monograph is based on a doctoral thesis submitted to the University of Cambridge in 2024. While some corrections and alterations have been made, the gist of my thesis is unchanged.

The ideas posited here arose from a twofold frustration. Firstly, early on in my studies I realised that Jerome had relied on sources other than the Hebrew Bible in the production of the Vulgate: a comparative reading of the relevant Bible versions makes it immediately visible. Yet, in my view, this facet of the Vulgate remains insufficiently explored in modern biblical scholarship. Secondly, on a more general level, the fields of Patristics and Hebrew studies are traditionally kept separate. Today's biblicists, however, would considerably benefit from the bridging of these disciplines.

In this monograph, I have endeavoured to describe the historical and linguistic context in which the Vulgate came into existence, and to enrich our understanding of the work of a pivotal figure of Late Antiquity. It was, in fact, demonstrated centuries ago that Jerome resorted to various texts and traditions in order to translate the Hebrew Bible into Latin: he himself admitted it in his letters and commentaries. I have set out to investigate this matter in depth by analysing his translation technique in verses adduced from three books of the Vulgate. On the whole, my aim has been to shed further light on a crucial facet of the Vulgate and to propose a way to fruitfully develop Vulgate and Bible studies in the future.

This enterprise of mine would not have been conceivable without the direction of my teachers and the support and patience of my peers and friends. First, I am greatly indebted to Monsieur Régis Courtray, who helped me delve into the life and works of Jerome and who answered all my emails for four years. I am grateful to Madame Mireille Hadas-Lebel, who spent time and shared her experience and wisdom with me. I owe a lot to Madame Claudine Cavalier, too, who offered me her commentary on the Septuagint of Esther and who always replied to my questions. Monsieur Thomas Römer took me on his team in an archaeological mission in Kiryath Ye'arim in the summer of 2019. I am grateful to him for continuing to support me since then. In 2021, Frère Olivier-Thomas Venard welcomed me with open arms in the BEST project (La Bible en ses Traditions) at the École biblique et archéologique française de Jérusalem. Our weekly meetings on Nablus Street, in the old city of Jérusalem, have significantly contributed to my flourishing as a PhD candidate. Thanks to Frère Olivier-Thomas, I also met Father Kevin Zilverberg, a thorough and conscientious scholar, who taught me a class on the Vetus Latina at the École biblique in 2022, and who continuously engaged in long discussions with me afterwards. I should also like to thank Monsieur Olivier Munnich, who helped me better understand minute aspects of many Greek texts; as well as Professor Noam Mizrahi, whose advice at the beginning of my PhD and throughout my studies has been very stimulating. Likewise, I express my thanks to Dr Stéphanie Binder, who kindly assisted me when necessary. Finally, I am very grateful to the Rothschild Foundation for trusting me with the Hanadiv Fellowship during my doctoral studies, and to the Polonsky Foundation for supporting the publication of this book.

Several excellent scholars enabled me to be as thorough as possible in my research by letting me consult with them as often as I needed. I would therefore like to express my gratitude to Dr Aaron Hornkohl, Dr Theodor Dunkelgrün, and Monsieur Jean-Claude Haelewyck. I have been fortunate to be taught, in particular, by two exceptional scholars, to whose generosity and patience I am indebted. Professor Nicholas de Lange is one of them; being exposed to his teaching as a Bible student has been a privilege. The second one was Dr James Aitken ('Jim'), my late advisor at Cambridge and a pillar of my postgraduate studies. I thank them both.

Other people helped me find the strength within myself to persevere throughout my studies. I extend a special thanks to Docteur Aldo Naouri, whose wisdom is comparable to Nestor's; my friend Sam Swire; Arlette Gordon; Dr Vanessa Paloma Elbaz; Dr José Martínez Delgado ('Pepe'); Dr Leonardo Cohen; Jacqueline Lustman; Docteur Mireille Karsenty; Professor Raymond Scheindlin and his wife Janice; Charles Meyer; David Ratiney; Tim Lee; Agnès Delarive; Théo Touaty; and Dr Matteo Poiani. I am also grateful to Dr Judith Bunbury, my tutor at St Edmund's College in Cambridge, with whom I have had delightful conversations for six years; and to Dr Krisztina Szilágyi, who took great care of my book as my copy editor. Moreover, I would like to thank Hagar Ben-Zion, who is so dear to me, as well as her mother Varna and her father Itsik, z"l. My gratitude finally goes to Rav Mordechai Zeller for his counsel.

I dedicate this book to my mentor, Professor Michael Rand, z"l, under whose supervision I conducted my MPhil and PhD projects from October 2018 to November 2022. From November 2022 to January 2024, Professor Geoffrey Khan took over as my PhD supervisor. At the end of my PhD, he further offered me to publish this revised version of my thesis in his prestigious series, Cambridge Semitic Languages and Cultures. I therefore dedicate it to him, too, as a token of my gratitude and admiration.

I seize this opportunity to express my love for my grandparents, Alexandre and Sylvie Nissen; for my late half-brother, Emmanuel Rodrigue; for Alessia Fontanella, a promising scholar; and for my mother.

Paris
May 2025   Paul A. I. Rodrigue

ABBREVIATIONS

Abbreviations of Bible Versions

LXX	Septuagint
MT	Masoretic Text
VL	Vetus Latina
Vulg.	Vulgate

Abbreviations of Biblical Books

Acts	Acts of the Apostles
Bel and the Dragon	The Fables of Bel and the Dragon
1–2 Chron.	1–2 Chronicles
1–2 Cor.	1–2 Corinthians
Dan.	Daniel
Deut.	Deuteronomy
Eccl.	Ecclesiastes
Est.	Esther
Exod.	Exodus
Ezek.	Ezekiel
Gen.	Genesis
Hab.	Habakkuk
Hos.	Hosea
Isa.	Isaiah
Jac.	James
Jer.	Jeremiah
Judg.	Judges

1–2 Kgs	1–2 Kings
Lam.	Lamentations
Matt.	Matthew
Phlm.	Philemon
Prov.	Proverbs
Ps.	Psalms
1–2 Sam.	1–2 Samuel
Song	Song of Songs
The Prayer	The Prayer of Azariah and the Song of the Three Children
Zech.	Zechariah

Abbreviations of Series and Reference Works

BHS	*Biblia Hebraica Stuttgartensia* (see bibliography under 'Primary Sources', 'MT')
CCSL	Corpus Christianorum: Series Latina. Turnhout: Brepols, 1953–present.
Epist.	*Letter* (e.g., Basil of Caesarea, *Epist.* 197)
LCL	Loeb Classical Library
PG	Patrologiae Cursus Completus: Series Graeca, edited by Jacques-Paul Migne, vols 1–162. Paris: Migne, 1857–1866.
PL	Patrologiae Cursus Completus: Series Latina, edited by Jacques-Paul Migne, vols 1–221. Paris: Migne, 1844–1864.
SC	Sources Chrétiennes

Abbreviations of Primary Sources

Ambrose	*Fid.*	*De fide*
Augustine	*Conf.*	*Confessions*
	Doctr. chr.	*De doctrina christiana*

Epiphanius	*Pan.*	*Panarion*
Eusebius	*Dem. ev.*	*Demonstratio evangelica*
Herodotus	*Hist.*	*Histories* (LCL 117)
Jerome	*Comm. Abac.*	*Commentary on Habakkuk*
	Comm. Eccl.	*Commentary on Ecclesiastes*
	Comm. Ezech.	*Commentary on Ezekiel*
	Comm. Isa.	*Commentary on Isaiah*
	Comm. Jer.	*Commentary on Jeremiah*
	Comm. Os.	*Commentary on Hosea*
	Comm. Phlm.	*Commentary on the Epistle to Philemon*
	Comm. Soph.	*Commentary on Zephaniah*
	Comm. Zach.	*Commentary on Zechariah*
	Nom. hebr.	*On Hebrew Names*
	Pelag.	*Against the Pelagians*
Josephus	*Ag. Ap.*	*Against Apion* (LCL 186)
	Ant.	*Jewish Antiquities* (LCL 242 and 326)
Justin	*Dial.*	*Dialogue with Trypho*
Origen	*Sel. Gen.*	*Selecta in Genesim*
Philo	*Ios.*	*On Joseph* (LCL 289)
	Migr.	*On the Migration of Abraham* (LCL 261)
	Mos.	*On the Life of Moses* (LCL 289)
	Somn.	*On Dreams* (LCL 275)
Rufinus	*Apol. Hier.*	*Apology against Jerome*
[Talmud]	b. Megillah	Babylonian Talmud, Tractate Megillah
Xenophon	*Cyr.*	*Cyropaedia* (LCL 52)

Other Abbreviations

All the abbreviations of primary sources that are not mentioned here are referenced in the bibliography. Titles of modern scholarly works, when long, are generally abbreviated in the footnotes to their initial words; the same abbreviations are used throughout the monograph.

In the English translations of primary sources that I produce and employ in the monograph, I regularly add, in parentheses, "(i.e., …)," which is meant to clarify an element in the original, and "(lit., …)," which stands for 'literally'. Brackets either mean that I have added material to the text that is being translated "[added material]" or that I have skipped a part thereof "[…]." The slash introduces an alternative rendering for a word or a phrase: "rendering A / rendering B." Finally, the more important parts of the source text are quoted in the original language next to my translation thereof, in parentheses, so that the reader may be able to check and compare. In the case studies, however, the verses that I analyse are always fully quoted in the original languages.

1. INTRODUCTION

1.0. A Map of the Argument

At the end of the fourth century CE, Jerome of Stridon, a Latin scholar, theologian and priest, set out to translate the Hebrew Bible—that is, the Hebrew-Aramaic version of Scripture—into Latin. This Latin version of Scripture is now referred to as the Vulgate. In this monograph, I endeavour to identify the sources on which Jerome might have relied in his translation of the Hebrew Bible.

Before this may be delved into, his background and the context in which the Vulgate enterprise took place have to be introduced. Therefore, I first address the following points in my introduction: the translations of Scripture that existed before the Vulgate (section 1.2); biographical information about Jerome's education (section 1.3); the context in which he took the decision to create a new version of Scripture (section 1.4); his treatment of the Book of Genesis (section 1.5); the different meanings that he ascribed to the terms 'Hebrews' and 'Jews' (section 1.6); his relationship with the authoritative version of the Old Testament in the Church (section 1.7); his translation technique (section 1.8). This introduction serves as the basis for the theory that we posit, namely, that Jerome's sources in his translation of the Hebrew Bible are not just the Hebrew Bible.

In order to demonstrate this theory, we explore a series of verses adduced from the so-called Joseph story (Gen. 37–50) (chapter 2), the Book of Daniel (chapter 3), and the Book of Esther (chapter 4). The reasons why these books provide us with case studies that are most relevant to our research are explained at the end of the introduction (section 1.9). All English translations of primary sources have been produced by me.

2.0. Before the Vulgate

2.1. The Septuagint

The first known translation of the Hebrew Bible is the Greek version commonly called Septuagint (LXX).[1] The story of its origin is recounted in the *Letter of Aristeas*, a Greek work composed in the second century BCE.[2] According to this legendary tale, the LXX was produced in Pharos, an island off the coast of Alexandria,[3] by seventy-two elders of the Jewish community: six men from each of the twelve tribes of Israel sent by Eleazar, the High Priest of the Jews at Jerusalem.[4] This operation was requested by

---

[1] Swete, *An Introduction*, pp. 1–10.

[2] On the *Letter of Aristeas*, see Hadas' introduction (pp. 1–90). See also Jobes and Silva, *Invitation to the Septuagint*, pp. 17–23; De Crom, 'The Letter of Aristeas'; Barthélemy, 'Pourquoi la Torah', pp. 23–29. For an in-depth discussion of the story of the creation of the Septuagint and a survey of the early Jewish and Christian sources that deal with it, see Veltri, *Libraries*, pp. 27–77.

[3] *Letter of Aristeas*, 4–5 (p. 94) and 301 (pp. 216–18). See Hadas' observations in the footnotes ibid.

[4] *Letter of Aristeas*, 11 (p. 98); 32–33 (pp. 110–12); 47–50 (pp. 118–20). 'Septuagint' is the English form of the Latin word *Septuaginta*, which

the king, at the suggestion of his librarian Demetrius of Phalerum, so as to complete the royal library:

> 'O King, [...] I have been informed that the laws of the Jews are also worthy of a transcription (καὶ τῶν Ἰουδαίων νόμιμα μεταγραφῆς ἄξια) and of being part of your library.' 'What is it that prevents you from making it happen then, [the king] said? Indeed, everything is at your disposal for this task.' But Demetrius said 'We need an interpretation / a translation [first] (ἑρμηνείας προσδεῖται). For they use their own script (lit., their own characters) in the [land] of the Jews [...] and they have their own tongue.'[5]

According to the *Letter of Aristeas*, the king was then the son of "Ptolemy son of Lagus,"[6] that is, Ptolemy II, who ruled from 285 to 247 BCE. Therefore, if the story is to be taken at face value, the beginning of the translation of the Hebrew Bible into Greek should be dated to the first half of the third century BCE.[7] The books of the Bible were certainly not translated all at once: the original interpreters were probably commissioned to deal with

---

renders οἱ Ἑβδομήκοντα ('the Seventy'), probably in reference to the seventy-two elders from the *Letter of Aristeas* (50; p. 120). For further discussion of the origin of this term, see Jobes and Silva, *Invitation to the Septuagint*, p. 17 and pp. 23–24.

[5] *Letter of Aristeas*, 10–11 (p. 96). See also ibid., 28–32 (pp. 108–10); 38–39 (p. 114); 45–46 (p. 118).

[6] *Letter of Aristeas*, 12–13 (pp. 98–100).

[7] Jobes and Silva, *Invitation to the Septuagint*, pp. 18–20; De Crom, 'The Letter of Aristeas', p. 129; De Troyer, 'The Septuagint', pp. 272–74.

the Torah, i.e., the first five books of the Hebrew Bible.[8] Subsequent Greek interpreters then undertook the translation of the remaining books: LXX translations were produced gradually until the first or second century CE.[9]

In the first centuries of our era, "Greek was the common language spoken in the Mediterranean world"[10] and the primary language employed by the earliest Christian communities.[11] Therefore, as Christians read Scripture in Greek, the LXX became

---

[8] This is what is suggested in the *Letter of Aristeas* by 'the laws / customs of the Jews' (τῶν Ἰουδαίων νόμιμα; 10 [p. 96]), 'the books of the Law of the Jews' (τοῦ νόμου τῶν Ἰουδαίων βιβλία; 30 [p. 110]), and 'the Law' (τὸν νόμον; 46 [p. 118]). See also Jobes and Silva, *Invitation to the Septuagint*, pp. 19–20; and Tov, 'The Septuagint Translation of Genesis'. As shown by Tov, however ('The Septuagint Translation of Genesis', p. 504, fn. 3), there are dissenting views about the hypothesis that the Torah was translated first.

[9] Aitken, 'The Social and Historical Setting of the Septuagint', p. 73; Tov, *Textual Criticism*, pp. 128–32; Jobes and Silva, *Invitation to the Septuagint*, pp. 34–35. A loose use of the word 'Septuagint' in modern scholarship can misrepresent the complex history of the earliest Greek translations of the Hebrew Bible by suggesting an idea of unity. For a discussion of the meaning of the word 'Septuagint', see Jobes and Silva, *Invitation to the Septuagint*, pp. 14–17. It is not the purpose of my monograph to discuss the history of its use; for the sake of conveniency, the term shall be consistently applied to all the translations that Jerome himself considered as part of the Septuagint.

[10] Bogaert, 'The Latin Bible', p. 505.

[11] Graves, 'The Septuagint in the Latin World', p. 605.

the authoritative version of the Old Testament in the Church.¹² It was long assumed that, by the second century, the LXX had begun to fall into disuse among Jews as a result of its appropriation by Christians and under the influence of the Rabbis.¹³ This theory has not stood the test of time.

On the whole, little is known about the reception and the transmission of Greek Bible versions by Greek-speaking Jews in Late Antiquity. Although the LXX was eventually condemned by the rabbinic movement—albeit at a late stage¹⁴—probably as a

---

¹² Tov, *Textual Criticism*, p. 133; Bogaert, 'The Latin Bible', p. 505. For a discussion of the reception and status of the LXX in early Christendom, see also Kamesar's remarks in *Jerome*, pp. 29–34. For an assessment of the Jewish and Christian views on the story of its composition, see Braverman, *Jerome's Commentary*, pp. 16–17, fn. 5.

¹³ See, for instance, Swete, *An Introduction*, p. 30. For an in-depth discussion of the history of this theory, see de Lange, *Japheth in the Tents of Shem*, pp. 1–4; for a discussion of Swete's approach, see de Lange, ibid., pp. 18–20.

¹⁴ According to Fernández Marcos, "there are no signs that there was any rejection of […] the Septuagint among the rabbis before the sixth century" (Fernández Marcos, 'Non placet', p. 41; see also Hadas-Lebel, 'Qui utilisait la LXX', pp. 44–45 and p. 48; and Veltri, 'The Septuagint in Disgrace'). See for example *Soferim* 1.7–8. In this rabbinic text, whose composition is generally not dated earlier than the eighth century, the day when the LXX was created is described as having been 'hard for Israel' (והיה היום קשה לישראל) as the Torah could not be translated appropriately. A passage of the Šulḥan 'Aruk also establishes the anniversary of the creation of the LXX dated 8th of Tevet as a fasting day because of the "three days of darkness on earth" that followed (*'Oraḥ Ḥayyim* 580.1–2).

response to the way Christians had exploited it to found their own exegesis, there is no reason to believe that those of the Jews that had relied on it in the Diaspora, as well as in Judea,[15] banned it from their synagogues after the birth of Christianity. The fact that there were discrepancies between the LXX and a Hebrew text of the second century that had become the standard version in rabbinic circles no doubt could serve as an excuse to undermine the authority of the former in light of the latter.[16] Indeed, as is shown below, the Rabbis ended up promoting the then current Hebrew version and new Greek translations thereof, those of Aquila and Symmachus (see section 1.2.2 below).[17]

However, Rajak is also right in criticising the "assumptions that Jews chose to discard the Greek Scriptures (i.e., the LXX) [...] when Christians adopted them, and that they equipped themselves with different versions once, and because, Christians

---

[15] See Hadas-Lebel, 'Qui utilisait la LXX', p. 45.

[16] It is not only plausible but likely that, by the second century CE, the Rabbis had more or less unanimously adopted a fixed form of the Hebrew text as the standard version of Scripture: this version, often referred to as a 'proto-Masoretic text', was one of several different Hebrew streams. The LXX, in this regard, represented to some extent—beyond the translators' departures and potential scribal corruptions—another Hebrew tradition, one that differed from the so-called 'proto-Masoretic text' (see Tov, *Textual Criticism*, p. 128 and *The Text-Critical Use*, pp. 5–12 and pp. 216–23). Indeed, Second Temple textual pluriformity was confirmed by the discovery of the Dead Sea Scrolls (see de Lange, *Japheth in the Tents of Shem*, pp. 4–5), among which both proto-Masoretic and proto-LXX Hebrew text types seem to have been present.

[17] See de Lange, *Japheth in the Tents of Shem*, p. 46.

had appropriated the old ones."[18] Church Fathers were actually responsible for disseminating this belief (the Rabbis also played a part in this respect, though later than Christian authorities). In the middle of the second century, Justin Martyr—the earliest preserved Christian author to write on the story of the creation of the LXX[19]—attested, from a Christian point of view, to the Christian appropriation of the LXX, as he posited in his *Dialogue with Trypho* that Jews were no longer worthy of this version of Scripture. He justified this view by claiming that they had either been incapable of properly understanding the content of the LXX, or that they had been reluctant to acknowledge the Christ through it. While relying on passages of the Bible, which he cited in his conversation with Trypho, a 'Hebrew from the circumcision' (Ἑβραῖος ἐκ περιτομῆς),[20] that is, a Jew, he argued the following:

> Since I gave [you] both the proofs and the teachings, [not only] from the Scriptures but also on the basis of the facts, do not delay, do not hesitate to trust me, although I am uncircumcised. You have little time left to come over [to our side] (Βραχὺς οὗτος ὑμῖν περιλείπεται προσηλύσεως χρόνος). If ever the Christ arrives before (ἐὰν φθάσῃ ὁ Χριστὸς ἐλθεῖν), in vain will you repent, in vain will you cry.[21]
>
> Are you familiar with these [words which I have just quoted], Trypho? They are laid down in your writings, or,

---

[18] Rajak, 'Theological Polemic', p. 127.

[19] Graves, 'The Septuagint in the Latin World', p. 606.

[20] *Dial.* 1 (PG 6, p. 473B). On the nature of Justin Martyr's work, see Rajak's article, 'Theological Polemic'; and den Dulk, *Between Jews and Heretics*, pp. 43–88.

[21] *Dial.* 28 (PG 6, p. 536A).

rather, not in yours but in ours. For we abide by them, but you, while you read them, you do not mind the meaning in them.[22]

Furthermore, so as to persuade you that you did not understand anything about the Scriptures, I shall remind you of another psalm of David that was dictated by the Holy Spirit. You say that it was meant for Solomon, who was your king, too, but it was also meant for our Christ himself. But you [prefer to] fool yourselves through the ambiguity of certain phrases [in the Scriptures] (ὑμεῖς δὲ ἀπό τῶν ὁμωνύμων λέξεων ἑαυτοὺς ἐξαπατᾶτε).[23]

In summary, Christians had ascribed a new meaning to the content of the Old Testament, one that predicted the coming of the Christ. This entailed a fundamental disagreement with the traditional Jewish understanding of Scripture, which no doubt affected the attitudes of non-Christian Jews to the LXX. However, as De Troyer remarks, Justin Martyr's text actually implies "that both Jews and Christians were [...] using the Septuagint."[24] In this sense, Justin Martyr's claim to exclusive ownership of the LXX should be regarded as an attempt to present the LXX as the Christians' spoils of war: as Rajak argues, his "work is itself part of the process of appropriation."[25]

---

[22] *Dial.* 29 (PG 6, p. 537). The last clause contains a *figura etymologica* based on the root of the word 'mind' (ὑμεῖς [...] οὐ νοεῖτε τὸν [...] νοῦν, lit., 'you do not perceive the mind / the sense'), which I have endeavoured to imitate by rendering it as 'you do not mind the meaning'.

[23] *Dial.* 34 (PG 6, pp. 545C–548A).

[24] De Troyer, 'The Septuagint', p. 279.

[25] See Rajak, 'Theological Polemic', p. 129.

Scholars have established that there already were attempts to revise the LXX towards a proto-Masoretic text before Christianity existed.[26] It is possible, nonetheless, that the way Christians were interpreting and using the LXX provided those of the Jews that condemned the LXX, that is, the rabbinic movement in Palestine, with an incentive to translate the standard Hebrew text afresh. However, regardless of the Christian treatment of the LXX, it was the promotion of Hebrew as the Holy Language (לשון הקדש), the one in which the world was believed to have been created, that fundamentally justified the production of new Greek translations.[27] The need for these translations was rooted in the fact that the status of Hebrew confirmed the primacy of the Hebrew text in itself:

> The emergence of these new versions should be seen as a reaction to new developments in the ever-changing textual reality of Palestine. Thus, when the LXX was brought from Egypt to Palestine, it was soon recognized that the content of that translation differed considerably from the then current Palestinian Hebrew text. As a consequence, in the strict religious climate of Palestine from the first century BCE onwards, it became important for religious leaders to discontinue the use of the O[ld] G[reek] translation. The adherence to the then current Hebrew/Aramaic text involved the creation of new Greek versions reflecting that text. This

---

[26] See de Lange, *Japheth in the Tents of Shem*, p. 5; and Fernández Marcos, '*Non placet*', pp. 39–40.

[27] See de Lange, 'The Revival of the Hebrew Language', pp. 357–58; and Schwartz, 'Language, Power and Identity', pp. 32–33. On the notion of 'Holy Language', see Smelik, *Rabbis, Language and Translation*, pp. 42–58 and pp. 89–99.

factor was apparently more instrumental in the creation of the new Greek versions than others mentioned in the scholarly literature. At a later stage, the frequent use of the LXX by Christians did indeed cause Jews to dissociate themselves from that translation, but the OG had already been revised before the birth of Christianity.[28]

In Tov's view, the Rabbis did not strictly speaking reject the LXX: they had disregarded it from the beginning in their exegetical treatment of Scripture.[29] Beyond the question of the reception of the LXX by the early Rabbis, one can hardly imagine that the Jewish communities of Egypt, among whom the LXX—once celebrated, according to Philo[30]—enjoyed an authoritative status, suddenly abandoned this time-honoured tradition in favour of alternative Greek forms. The Rabbis had indeed endeavoured to expose various types of perceived inaccuracies and alterations in the LXX in light of their standard Hebrew text.[31] At the same

---

[28] Tov, 'The Evaluation of the Greek Scripture Translations', p. 369. See also ibid., p. 365 and p. 375; and Jobes and Silva, *Invitation to the Septuagint*, pp. 25–26.

[29] Tov, 'The Evaluation of the Greek Scripture Translations', pp. 371–72. Aitken makes a compelling case for the opposite view, as he argues, with regard to the Book of Proverbs, that some rabbinic readings might reflect familiarity with the LXX version ('The Jewish Use of Greek Proverbs', pp. 65–77).

[30] Philo, *Mos.*, 2.41.

[31] See b. Megillah 9a. This passage of the Talmud describes the story of the creation of the LXX in a positive light by presenting it as the fruit of divine inspiration; it goes on to list in a neutral way modifications that the LXX translator introduced. In Tov's view ('The Evaluation of the

time, they endorsed new translations thereof, ones that could reflect the content of their exegesis, in contrast with the LXX, and help Greek-speaking Jews understand it.[32] Even if the Rabbis had the power to impose these translations beyond Palestine on com-

---

Greek Scripture Translations', pp. 374–75), this list of alterations underlined the discrepancies between the LXX and the Hebrew in order to convey a policy of disparagement of the LXX. One could arguably disagree with Tov as the text does not explicitly accuse the author of the LXX translation of anything; I agree on this point with Veltri's remark that the tradition in b. Megillah 9a is either positive or neutral ('The Septuagint in Disgrace', p. 143). On the other hand, the negative rabbinic view on the creation of the LXX was couched in clear terms in the post-Talmudic tractate *Soferim* 1.7–8. As Zeitlin argues, the two opposite stances contained in rabbinic literature reflect different historical stages in the Rabbis' evaluation of the LXX, the positive stance being the earlier one (see Hadas' edition of the *Letter of Aristeas*, p. 81, fn. 110).

[32] See de Lange, 'The Revival of the Hebrew Language', p. 357; and Graves, 'Midrash-Like Word Plays', pp. 68–86. Alexander, who also addresses this point, overestimates the importance of the LXX and of its adoption by Christians in the Rabbis' decision to endorse new Greek translations (Alexander, 'The Cultural History', pp. 85–86). De Lange argues that "it is a plausible supposition (although impossible to prove) that in synagogues of Greek-speaking Jews where the reading of Scripture in Hebrew had begun to take hold under rabbinic influence, Akylas's (i.e., Aquila's) translation was read out after the Hebrew reading, as a kind of *targum*, and was cited in Greek prayers and homilies" (*Japheth in the Tents of Shem*, p. 57). See also Smelik, *Rabbis, Language and Translation*, pp. 185–90. For a critical approach to the theory that Aquila's translation was meant to serve as a base text for the teaching of rabbinic exegesis, see Grabbe, 'Aquila's Translation and Rabbinic Exegesis'.

munities where the LXX was in use, the response of these communities to adapt their habits followed a process of reception and transmission of new Bible versions that was neither simple nor quick. Surviving texts have confirmed the existence of Jewish Greek Bible versions containing renderings derived, *inter alia*, from the LXX, from Aquila's translation and from that of Symmachus: the fact that Greek-speaking Jews relied on versions that could be made with a certain fluidity from different ancient translations attests to the reality that Jewish textual traditions evolved in an organic way.[33] At any rate, as Aquila's version was being actively circulated, the reliance of Greek-speaking synagogues on the LXX did not have to come to an end either.[34]

Ultimately, the status of the LXX cannot have evolved in a uniform way across all Jewish communities. For instance, Justinian's Novel 146 sheds light on a tension between the LXX and Aquila's version in an eastern Jewish community of the sixth century CE,[35] presumably that of Constantinople: the time when this

---

[33] See Ceulemans, 'Greek Christian Access', pp. 185–86.

[34] See de Lange, *Japheth in the Tents of Shem*, pp. 53–67. Salvesen makes an interesting point: "Evidently Aquila's translation was regarded by some Christians as a Jewish challenge to the primacy of the Septuagint. Yet that does not mean that the Septuagint had disappeared overnight from Jewish communities, who may have already been using scrolls incorporating revisions of the Septuagint towards the emerging Masoretic Hebrew text, and who would have found replacement copies costly to obtain" ('Did Aquila and Symmachus', p. 123). See also Aitken, 'The Jewish Use of Greek Proverbs', p. 68.

[35] As demonstrated by de Lange, in permitting the use of Aquila's version instead of the LXX in Greek-speaking synagogues, Justinian was

piece of imperial legislation was issued matches the dating of the earliest attested rabbinic condemnations of the LXX, between the sixth and eighth centuries CE.[36] This might give us an indication of a transitional stage where the LXX, while losing ground in certain Greek-speaking Jewish communities, was still revered among others.[37] To be sure, Aquila's version, which was "recognised by Christians as the main Jewish version and approved by the rabbis,"[38] was gradually adopted by Byzantine Jewry, for whom it eventually achieved high status.[39] Until, and beyond, the fall of Constantinople, Jewish Greek Bible versions that were derived from ancient translations, while mostly imbued with Aquila's, still exhibited the enduring influence of certain LXX readings.[40]

---

making a concession to the Hebraist party (*Nov.* 146, I, 1; p. 716), that is, to those of the Jews who promoted Hebrew Scripture and advocated an alternative Greek translation thereof against the LXX (see de Lange, 'Hebraists and Hellenists', p. 223 and p. 225).

[36] See fn. 14.

[37] See de Lange, *Japheth in the Tents of Shem*, p. 66; and Hadas-Lebel, 'Qui utilisait la LXX', pp. 48–49.

[38] Aitken, 'The Jewish Use of Greek Proverbs', p. 53. See also Salvesen, 'Did Aquila and Symmachus', p. 107.

[39] De Lange, 'The Greek Bible Translations of the Byzantine Jews'; Salvesen, 'Did Aquila and Symmachus', pp. 122–23.

[40] See de Lange's concluding remarks in *Japheth in the Tents of Shem*, pp. 80–81, pp. 90–91, p. 117 and p. 136; Salvesen, 'Did Aquila and Symmachus', pp. 123–24; and Boyd-Taylor, 'Afterlives of the Septuagint'.

2.2. The Hexapla

In the Hexapla, a work of the middle of the third century CE, Origen, a Christian scholar, presented six versions of the text of the Old Testament in the form of six columns: the Hebrew text, a Greek transliteration of the Hebrew, Aquila's Greek translation of the Hebrew text, that of Symmachus, the LXX, and Theodotion's Greek translation of the Hebrew.[41] Often referred to as the *recentiores* or 'the Three', Aquila, Symmachus and Theodotion were three Jewish translators of the second century CE who disagreed with the way the Hebrew Bible had been reflected in the LXX. Their new translations had different purposes: Aquila, known for his extremely literal style, attempted to reflect the grammar of the Hebrew word for word; Symmachus, whose "task [...] was to aspire to a dignified position among the Greek literary authors of his time,"[42] more generally rendered the meaning of a unit as a whole;[43] as for Theodotion, whose style can be recognised, for

---

[41] Nautin claims that Origen's Hexapla did not contain the Hebrew text in Hebrew letters (*Origène*, pp. 314–15). See also Estin, *Les Psautiers*, p. 22; de Lange, *Japheth in the Tents of Shem*, p. 47; and Stemberger, 'Exegetical Contacts', pp. 578–79. For a different view, see Dorival, 'Les Hexaples d'Origène', p. 523; and Grafton and Williams, *Christianity and the Transformation of the Book*, pp. 90–95.

[42] Fernández Marcos, '*Non placet*', p. 41.

[43] The name Aquila is directly mentioned in the Palestinian Talmud (for a discussion of the Rabbis' attitude to Aquila, see de Lange, *Japheth in the Tents of Shem*, p. 46, p. 57 and p. 66; see also Smelik, *Rabbis, Language and Translation*, pp. 434–42). Symmachus, on the other hand, has been associated with Sumkhos, who is cited in rabbinic literature as the disciple of Rabbi Meir (see Barthélemy, 'Qui est Symmaque?'). On the

instance, from his transliterations of rare Hebrew words, scholars tend to argue that he operated more as a reviser of the LXX.[44] All three translators' works were compiled by Origen as the third, fourth and sixth columns of his Hexapla, respectively. As he undertook to resolve the textual discrepancies that existed between the various manuscripts of the LXX in circulation, he endeavoured to make his own revision of the LXX on the basis of a textual witness which he must have believed represented it best.[45]

---

relationship between the Rabbis and Aquila and Symmachus, see also Salvesen, 'Did Aquila and Symmachus'.

[44] In modern scholarship, the *recentiores*' new versions can be presented as revisions or as translations. As noted by Jobes and Silva, the distinction between the revision of an existent translation of a text and a new translation of the same text can be difficult to establish. See their remarks in *Invitation to the Septuagint*, pp. 35–39. On Jerome's conception of his work as a reviser, as opposed to his work as a translator, see for instance Estin's remarks in *Les Psautiers*, pp. 28–29. For a more comprehensive discussion of the *recentiores*' identity and respective translation methods, see Field's preface to the Hexapla (referenced in my bibliography under 'Primary Sources', 'Origen', 'Hexapla'), I, pp. xvi–xlii; Swete, *An Introduction*, pp. 29–53; Fernández Marcos, *Introducción*, pp. 119–62 and '*Non placet*', pp. 40–42; Bogaert, 'Septante et versions grecques', pp. 559–65 and p. 569; de Lange, *Japheth in the Tents of Shem*, pp. 45–49. For further discussion of Aquila's and Symmachus' translations and their place in Origen's work, see Nautin, *Origène*, pp. 340–42; on Theodotion, see Barthélemy, *Les Devanciers d'Aquila*, pp. 144–57.

[45] Jerome argued in the preface to the Vulgate Book of Chronicles that, out of three coexisting LXX forms, Origen selected as his base text the version represented by the "Palestinian manuscripts" (Vulg., p. 546); this passage is translated and discussed in my fn. 216. Each of the pref-

Ultimately, the purpose of this enterprise was to reconstruct the original Hebrew text in Greek. Indeed, in this revision of the LXX, Origen signalled, by means of an obelus, those passages in the LXX that he did not find in the Hebrew, and added, with an asterisk, passages that did not feature in the LXX but did in the Hebrew.[46] He did not rely on the Hebrew text *per se*, but on the

---

aces that Jerome wrote for his Vulgate translations can be found in Weber and Gryson's edition of the Vulgate (see bibliography under 'Primary Sources', 'Jerome', 'Vulgate and Its Prefaces'), prefixed to the translation.

[46] See Origen's explanatory remarks in *Comm. Matt.* 19.16–30 (XV, 14; pp. 387–88) and *Ep. Afr.*, 6–7 (pp. 530–32). See also Jerome's description of Origen's enterprise in the preface to the Vulgate Book of Chronicles. According to Jerome, Origen "not only collated the texts of four versions (i.e., the LXX and the three *recentiores*) by recording each word in a single row (so that any [translator] who differed might be immediately distinguishable from those who agreed [*ut unus dissentiens statim ceteris inter se consentientibus arguatur*]), but, more audaciously, he mixed Theodotion's version with the Septuagint by pointing out with asterisks what might be missing and with affixed slashes what could seem to be superfluous" (Vulg., p. 546). See also Jerome's preface to the Vulgate of the Pentateuch (Vulg., p. 3) and *Epist.* 112.19 (VI, pp. 38–39). On the significance of the obelus in Origen, see Field's preface to the Hexapla, I, pp. lii–lx; de Lange, 'The Letter to Africanus', pp. 242–47; Bogaert, 'Septante et versions grecques', pp. 572–73. On the production of the Hexapla and Origen's goal, see Field's preface, I, pp. xlvii–li; Jobes and Silva, *Invitation to the Septuagint*, pp. 39–46; Dorival, 'Les Hexaples d'Origène', pp. 521–24 and pp. 528–31; Barthélemy, 'Origène et le texte de l'Ancien Testament'; Schaper, 'The Origin', pp. 3–6; Gentry, 'Origen's Hexapla', p. 553 and pp. 562–66; Braverman, *Jerome's Commentary*, pp. 15–25; Nautin, *Origène*, pp. 343–53; Olariu,

recentiores, and mostly on Theodotion, whose versions, when coinciding, could show him the structure of the Hebrew.[47] While the fifth column has been surmised to contain his revision of the LXX, Bogaert, among others, has attempted to demonstrate that it is more likely to have actually displayed the text of the LXX that Origen selected as the most reliable recension, and upon which his revision was based.[48] Should it be the case, his revision may have been produced as a separate work for which the Hexapla served as a preparatory phase.[49]

'From Suspicion to Appreciation', pp. 54–57; Grafton and Williams, *Christianity and the Transformation of the Book*, pp. 107–32.

[47] Fernández Marcos, *Introducción*, p. 213. Jerome said that Origen had relied specifically on Theodotion's version, more so than on the two other *recentiores*' versions (see Vulg., p. 546 [the passage is translated in fn. 46]). See Barthélemy, *Les Devanciers d'Aquila*, p. 148; Olariu, 'From Suspicion to Appreciation', pp. 56–57; and Munnich, 'Origène, éditeur'.

[48] Bogaert, 'Septante et versions grecques', p. 570. See also Jobes and Silva, *Invitation to the Septuagint*, p. 41 and pp. 43–46; Estin, *Les Psautiers*, pp. 22–23; and Fernández Marcos, *Introducción*, pp. 217–19. Certain scholars still claim that the fifth column contained Origen's revision. See Nautin, *Origène*, pp. 456–57; Munnich, 'Les révisions juives de la Septante', pp. 181–85; Dorival, 'Les Hexaples d'Origène', p. 523; Schaper, 'The Origin', pp. 6–10. Jerome's description of Origen's work in his preface to the Vulgate Book of Chronicles (Vulg., p. 546), as well as his remarks in *Epist.* 106.2 (V, pp. 105–6), though vague, could indicate that he was consulting Origen's revision from the Hexapla, and not as a separate work.

[49] Scholars tend to refer to the fifth column as the 'Hexaplaric recension' without making it clear in the first place whether this points to Origen's revision or to his base text. As this terminology can be misleading, the

2.3. The Vetus Latina

While Greek dominated in the east, in Egypt and Cyrenaica, as a common language, Latin was gaining ground in the west.[50] Indeed, by the second century CE, it had begun to coexist with Punic in *Africa Proconsularis*,[51] the Roman province of Africa which extended from Numidia, in the west, to Cyrenaica, and which corresponds roughly to modern-day Tunisia and to parts of Algeria and Libya. It is likely that the growth of Latin as a vernacular among the Christian communities of *Africa Proconsularis* prompted the first translations of the LXX into Latin.[52]

---

term 'Hexaplaric' will not be applied to Origen's revision in my monograph. If necessary, I shall use the adjective 'Origenic' in order to refer to Origen's revision.

[50] Wilhite, *Ancient African Christianity*, p. 2.

[51] Wilhite, *Ancient African Christianity*, pp. 52–56.

[52] Bogaert, 'The Latin Bible', p. 505; and Houghton, 'The Earliest Latin Translations of the Bible', pp. 3–4. For a general discussion of African Christianity, see Wilhite, *Ancient African Christianity*, pp. 1–10 and pp. 15–19. Bogaert argues that Christian Latin writers were still rare in the third century, and that Greek remained the main language of Roman Christianity until the middle of the fourth century ('The Vetus Latina [Old Latin]', p. 626). Likewise, according to Houghton, the replacement of Greek by Latin, which was already employed in the Church at the beginning of the third century, was a gradual process that lasted at least a century (*The Latin New Testament*, pp. 14–19). In Zelzer's view, though, while Latin had been used as early as the second century in many communities, the Roman Church "officially" employed Greek until the middle of the third ('La *Vetus Latina*', p. 399). An official date—should there be one—such as the middle of the third century seems too early. More generally, trying to establish an exact date for the end of

The first attested mention of Scripture in Latin literature is in 180 CE, in *The Acts of the Scillitan Martyrs*. In this short account of a trial set in Carthage, certain parts of the Greek New Testament were named directly in Latin: "Saturninus, the proconsul, said: 'What have you got in that bookchest of yours?' Speratus

---

bilingualism in the Latin Church seems problematic in itself, given the lack of early evidence and a potentially still active use of Greek, albeit rare, at a late stage in certain Latin Church Fathers. At the end of the fourth century, for instance, Ambrose of Milan was known for his command of Greek: he quoted Scripture in Greek (*Epist.* 29.1; PL 16, p. 1054B), he could derive his biblical exegesis from a Greek word (*Epist.* 45.5; PL 16, pp. 1142C–1143A), a theological point could be based on a Greek concept (*Fid.* 1, 19, 128–29; PL 16, pp. 557C–558A), and he had perhaps corresponded in Greek with Basil of Caesarea, who wrote to him in Greek (see Basil's *Epist.* 197; PG 32, p. 663A). The work of Victorinus of Poetovio, at the end of the third century, also attests to this bilingual reality (see Houghton, *The Latin New Testament*, p. 16). On the whole, in the second half of the fourth century, most of the Fathers born into a Latin-speaking environment did not master or even understand Greek anymore, even though they had probably studied it in school: Augustine is a famous example (*Conf.* 1, 13–14 [PL 32, pp. 670–71]; 7, 9 [PL 32, p. 740]). Jerome (who, as discussed below and in my fn. 65, perfected his knowledge of the language in his late twenties), Rufinus of Aquileia and Ambrose should be considered as exceptions to this rule. Rufinus' and Jerome's efforts to translate ancient Greek works into Latin actually make it clear that, by their time, Greek was not accessible for the Latin Christian audience. Noteworthy in this regard is that Jerome specified that he translated Eusebius' *Chronicon* into Latin not only to "exercise his genius," as Cicero did when translating Greek works (*Chron.*, 1; p. 56), but above all for his Christian readership, who could not read Greek: "this intricate narrative contains […] matters unknown to the Latins" (*Chron.*, 5; p. 58).

said: 'Books and epistles of Paul, a righteous man' (*Libri et epistulae Pauli viri iusti*)."[53] It has been posited that the first written Latin translations of the Greek Bible were preceded by informal renderings, probably oral ones in a liturgical context: during homilies, as early as the beginning of the second century CE, Christian Latin congregants who did not understand Greek may have expected an *ad hoc* Latin interpretation of Greek pericopes.[54]

Written translations of the Greek New Testament and of the LXX of Psalms were produced in Carthage, where Tertullian, the earliest Christian Latin author whose work is still extant, operated between the end of the second century CE and the beginning of the third. His Latin quotations of Scripture varied, as the same

---

[53] *The Acts of the Scillitan Martyrs*, 12 (p. 88). The fact that portions of the Greek New Testament were named in Latin does not necessarily mean that there were Latin translations. According to Houghton, the texts that were being referred to may have been Greek (*The Latin New Testament*, p. 5). On the other hand, in Bogaert's view, on account of the location of the trial, they must have been Latin translations ('The Latin Bible', p. 505).

[54] See Zelzer, 'La *Vetus Latina*', p. 399; and Houghton, 'Scripture and Latin Christian Manuscripts', pp. 17–18, and *The Latin New Testament*, pp. 7–8. There has been no direct transmission of the earliest Latin renderings of Greek pericopes which occurred in liturgy. Salmon agrees that they were meant mostly for congregants in a liturgical context. However, he also argues that they were not always composed in a Latin accessible to all: rather, their style was imbued with "une langue populaire," "des vulgarismes accessibles à la masse du peuple," and at the same time with calques of Greek (and of Hebrew, through the Greek of the LXX) and with neologisms only intelligible to elites and polyglots (Salmon, 'Introduction', pp. 12–13).

verse could appear in different forms across his work: to account for these variations in his scriptural citations, it was surmised that he had been potentially translating on the basis of different Greek manuscripts, and that he had perhaps relied on extant Latin renderings, too. A few decades after Tertullian, Cyprian's consistency in his Latin quotations of Scripture indicates his reliance on a fixed Latin version.[55] Citations of most books of the Bible are attested in his work *Ad Quirinum testimonia adversus Judaeos*, written in 250 CE.[56]

In the fourth century, a variety of Latin versions of Scripture circulated in the form of fragmentary quotations scattered across the works of Christian writers (Lucifer of Cagliari, for example, is one of many that drew their quotations from already extant Bibles). Different Greek models arguably underlay these versions, which were made in various places, around the same time.[57] Once they had been disseminated, some of them could be

---

[55] On Tertullian and Cyprian, see Houghton, *The Latin New Testament*, pp. 5–14; Zelzer, 'La *Vetus Latina*', pp. 400–1; and Capelle, *Le Texte du psautier latin en Afrique*, pp. 1–50. See also Zilverberg, *The Textual History of Old Latin Daniel*, pp. 49–91 and pp. 126–59, where attestations of the VL of Daniel in Tertullian and in Cyprian are investigated.

[56] This does not necessarily indicate that these books had been entirely translated into Latin by the middle of the third century. Indeed, fragmentary citations are representative of the type of work that Latin translators could perform, that is, informal and *ad hoc* renderings. Therefore, fragments of biblical books could also exist on their own without having been adduced from complete translations.

[57] According to Zelzer, Latin translators operated independently of each other ('La *Vetus Latina*', p. 403). Gryson argues the opposite: in his view,

amended and revised on the basis of different criteria.[58] At the end of the fourth century, Augustine commented on the diversity of the Latin versions that were coexisting:

> Latin-speaking people [...] certainly need two other [languages]—Hebrew, to be sure, and Greek—in order to know the Holy Scriptures [well] and to resort to the source texts (in case the endless variety of Latin translators causes some uncertainty) (*latinae quidem linguae homines* [...] *duabus aliis ad scripturarum divinarum cognitionem opus habent, hebraea scilicet et graeca, ut ad exemplaria praecedentia recurratur, si quam dubitationem attulerit latinorum interpretum infinita varietas*). [...] As it has been said, because of the translators' disagreements (*propter diversitates interpretum*), the knowledge of these languages is necessary. For those who have rendered the Scriptures from the Hebrew language into the Greek one can be numbered, but the Latin translators [cannot] by any means. For, in the early days of the faith, as soon as a Greek manuscript came into the hand of anyone who believed himself to have the slightest command of both languages (i.e., Greek and Latin), he ventured a translation.[59]

---

in most cases, each Latin version represents a different revision of the same initial translation (cf. Gryson's edition of the Vetus Latina of Isaiah [referenced in my bibliography under 'Primary Sources', 'VL', 'Book of Isaiah'], *Esaias*, II, p. 1650).

[58] Zelzer, 'La *Vetus Latina*', pp. 400–3.

[59] *Doctr. chr.* 2, 11, 16 (CCSL 32, p. 42). This passage of *De doctrina christiana* is always quoted in modern scholarship to illustrate the state of the Latin translations of the Bible in Augustine's time. Less famous are the lines that follow, which show that Augustine was not condemn-

1. Introduction

These various translations, though often disagreeing to some extent with each other, represented the LXX for the first Latin-speaking Christian communities. The term *Vetus Latina* (VL), 'Old Latin', is commonly employed to refer in the singular to all Latin translations of the LXX: one must bear in mind that it points to a plural reality, which VL scholars sometimes express through the use of the plural form *Veteres Latinae*.[60]

---

ing, but actually praising the diversity of the Latin translations in existence (unlike Jerome, as we shall see). It was the 'carelessness' of the readers that was at fault in his view: "This state of affairs (*quae res*) has certainly helped to understand [the Scriptures] more than it has hindered... if only readers (*legentes*) were not careless (*neglegentes*)! Actually, examining multiple manuscripts has often [enabled me to] clarify some very obscure sentences" (*Doctr. chr.* 2, 12, 17; CCSL 32, p. 42). After demonstrating his point with a couple of examples adduced from the Book of Isaiah, both of which are presented in two different translations, Augustine added the following remark: "Which of the [translators] may have followed the [original] words, unless the source texts (lit., the texts of the previous language) can be read, it is uncertain. But still from each of them something great is imparted to those who read carefully (*scienter*). In fact, [even when] translators happen to differ a great deal, it is difficult for them not to find common ground (*difficile est enim ita diversos a se interpretes fieri, ut non se aliqua vicinitate contingant*)" (ibid., p. 43).

[60] Two groups of VL texts are now distinguished in modern scholarship on the basis of the provenance of the witnesses: the African group and the European one (see Zelzer, 'La *Vetus Latina*', p. 399). The European group is generally divided into several subgroups represented by different extant Patristic texts. The investigation of the developments of the African and European groups has shed light on the overall history of the

3.0. Preliminary Notes on Jerome's Linguistic Background

Jerome was born in Stridon, a Roman province in the area of the modern-day north-east border of Italy,[61] near the end of the first half of the fourth century CE.[62] According to Cavallera, his native tongue no doubt was Latin;[63] his training in Latin grammar and literature began at an early age in school.[64] To gain a strong command of Greek, he had to wait until his trip to Chalcis, south of Antioch, in 375, where he attended the lessons of Apollinaris of Laodicea, a Christian scholar who conducted his lessons in Greek.[65]

---

reception and transmission of the Bible among Latin audiences (for further discussion, see Zelzer, 'La *Vetus Latina*', pp. 398–403).

[61] Jerome, *Vir. ill.*, 135 (p. 56). See also Cavallera, *Saint Jérôme*, II, pp. 67–71. There is no consensus on where exactly the town of Stridon was located.

[62] The date of his birth is disputed (Cavallera, *Saint Jérôme*, II, pp. 1–12). According to Booth's computations, it corresponds to 347 or 348 ('The Date of Jerome's Birth', p. 353).

[63] Cavallera, *Saint Jérôme*, II, p. 71.

[64] Cavallera, *Saint Jérôme*, I, pp. 6–7. In his preface to the Vulgate of Job, Jerome mentioned a memory of one of his earliest Latin classes: "I have learned, in part, the Hebrew tongue, and almost from the cradle I have been rubbing shoulders in Latin with grammarians, rhetoricians and philosophers" (Vulg., p. 732).

[65] *Epist.* 84.3 (IV, p. 127). In *Epist.* 17.2 (I, p. 52), Jerome spoke of himself as "a man most eloquent in Aramaic and Greek," though in a self-mocking tone in context. See also Cavallera, *Saint Jérôme*, I, p. 7, especially fn. 4, and p. 42. On Apollinaris, see ibid., p. 56.

His initiation into Hebrew probably took place in Chalcis, too, under a Jew who had converted to Christianity: after much toil, as Jerome himself suggested, he persevered and his apprenticeship was eventually crowned with success.[66] During his stay in Rome in the early 380s, he was in contact with the local Jewish community.[67] In 386, he settled in Bethlehem.[68] As he engaged with the translation of the Hebrew Bible in the 390s, he got into the habit of consulting with Hebrew teachers from his Palestinian milieu.[69] Among these, a certain Baranina seems to have played an important part in his learning of Hebrew.[70]

---

[66] See *Epist.* 125.12 (VII, pp. 124–25); *Epist.* 108.26 (V, p. 195); and *Comm. Isa.* 22.15–25 (CCSL 73, p. 306). Modern scholars have pursued a critical approach to Jerome's actual ability to translate Hebrew on his own. See Rebenich, 'Jerome: the "vir trilinguis"', pp. 56–63; Burstein, 'La compétence de Jérôme'; Barr, 'St. Jerome's Appreciation'; Stemberger, 'Exegetical Contacts', p. 582; and Bardy, who questions Jerome's claims about his encounters with Hebrew instructors ('Saint Jérôme et ses maîtres hébreux'). Nautin has gone as far as to dismiss Jerome as a plagiarist, hardly capable of translating Hebrew by himself (*Origène*, pp. 326–28; and 'Hieronymus', p. 309). Other scholars have stood up for his competence in Hebrew: see Graves, *Jerome's Hebrew*, pp. 2–12 and pp. 88–97, and 'Latin Texts', p. 235 and pp. 238–40; Kamesar, *Jerome*, pp. 41–49; Braverman, *Jerome's Commentary*, pp. 3–6; Jay, *L'Exégèse*, pp. 39–43.

[67] See, for example, *Epist.* 36.1 (II, p. 51).

[68] Cavallera, *Saint Jérôme*, I, pp. 123–29.

[69] Some are mentioned, for example, in his prefaces to the Vulgate of Daniel (Vulg., p. 1341) and of Job (Vulg., p. 731). Jerome's relationship with his Hebrew instructors is investigated below in section 1.6.

[70] *Epist.* 84.3 (IV, p. 127).

Aramaic generally gave him trouble. Jerome began to study it alongside Greek and Hebrew during his trip to Chalcis.[71] This first experience was not sufficient to allow him to translate Aramaic into Latin. As late as 399, when working on the Book of Tobit,[72] he himself asserted that he had to collaborate with "a speaker most proficient in [Hebrew and Aramaic]" who translated the book from Aramaic into Hebrew for him, and that it was on the basis of that Hebrew translation that the Vulgate of Tobit was produced.[73] In the preface to the Vulgate Book of Daniel, he also confessed how difficult translating the Aramaic portions of the original had been for him, although, in this case and in that of Judith, he did not mention the help of an intermediary.[74]

---

[71] See Barr, 'St. Jerome's Appreciation', pp. 286–88; King, 'Vir Quadrilinguis?', p. 210; and Graves, *Jerome's Hebrew*, pp. 85–86. See also *Epist.* 17.2 (I, p. 52).

[72] In this monograph, unless specified otherwise, all the dates of composition for Jerome's biblical prefaces and translations are based on Canellis' computations in *Préfaces*, pp. 93–98.

[73] *Vulg.*, p. 676. As a general rule, one should not uncritically accept Jerome's claims about the language or languages of his *Vorlagen*. However, that he gained access to an Aramaic copy of the Book of Tobit is perfectly plausible. According to Gallagher, although the textual history of the Book of Tobit is particularly complex, "there is in fact little reason to doubt that a Jewish community in Jerome's day had in its possession a reworked Aramaic copy of Tobit" (Gallagher, 'Why Did Jerome', p. 363). On the textual history of Tobit, see Gallagher, 'Why Did Jerome', p. 360.

[74] See *Vulg.*, p. 1341 and p. 691, respectively.

Jerome ultimately had the opportunity to hone his competence in Aramaic when he moved to Bethlehem.⁷⁵

4.0. The Creation of a New Latin Version of Scripture

In 382, Jerome travelled back to Rome after a two-year trip to Constantinople. Soon after, Pope Damasus commissioned him to produce a stylistic revision of the Latin versions of the Gospels, and one of the VL of Psalms.⁷⁶ When addressing the Pope in the preface to his version of the Latin Gospels, Jerome explained at length why his goal was to return to the Greek source in his revision of the Latin New Testament:

> You urge me to make a new work from the old one (*novum opus facere me cogis ex veteri*), so that I may sit in judgement, as it were, on the [Latin] versions of the Scriptures, now that they are scattered all over the globe (*ut post exemplaria Scripturarum toto orbe dispersa quasi quidam arbiter sedeam*); and, because they differ from one another, so that I may determine which are those that agree with the Greek truth (*quae sint illa quae cum graeca consentiant*

---

⁷⁵ See Millar, 'Jerome and Palestine', pp. 62–65. For a detailed introduction to Jerome's life, see Kamesar, 'Jerome', pp. 653–59.

⁷⁶ Cavallera, *Saint Jérôme*, I, pp. 82–84. Estin argues that the story according to which the Pope requested a revision from Jerome is based on an 'apocryphal' epistolary exchange and that the context in which Jerome made his first revision cannot be established (Estin, *Les Psautiers*, p. 26).

veritate decernam).[77] It is a pious endeavour, but a perilous presumption for someone who is himself to be judged by all to act as a judge with others, and to change the language of an old man and bring back an aging world to the babies' first steps. Indeed, whether learned or unlearned, which man, after taking [this] volume into his hand and realising that what he has been reading [in it] disagrees with the flavour that he has once tasted, would not immediately let out a scream, claiming that I am a forger and a desecrator, I who dare to add, alter, and correct [things] in the old books? Against such jealousy, I take comfort in two facts: firstly, you [Pope Damasus], who are the Supreme Priest, command that [this] be done (*quod et tu qui summus sacerdos es fieri iubes*); secondly, [the reality] that truth does not vary (lit., that what varies is not true) (*et verum non esse quod variat*) is even confirmed by the testimony of those who slander [me] (*etiam maledicorum testimonio conprobatur*). Indeed, if we are to trust the Latin versions (*si enim latinis exemplaribus fides est adhibenda*), let them answer which ones: there are almost as many [versions] as there are manuscripts (*tot sunt paene quot*

---

[77] Jerome often introduced his work in this manner in the prefaces to his Vulgate translations. See for example the preface to the Vulgate Book of Chronicles: "Now, in fact, since different versions, varying from region to region, are in circulation (*pro varietate regionum diversa ferantur exemplaria*), and since this genuine and ancient translation has been corrupted and violated, you think that it is up to us either to determine which one might be the true one out of [so] many, or to compose a new work [which might replace] the old work (*novum opus in veteri opere condere*)" (Vulg., p. 546).

codices).⁷⁸ If, however, the truth is to be sought from many, why not correct what has been either wrongly rendered (lit., produced) by bad translators, even more poorly edited by presumptuous ignoramuses, or added or altered by dozy secretaries, by returning to the Greek source (*ad graecam originem revertentes*)? [...] Therefore, the present little preface promises no less than the four Gospels, whose order is as follows: Matthew, Mark, Luke, John. They have been amended through a comparison of Greek manuscripts, of the early ones, that is (*codicum graecorum emendata conlatione sed veterum*). So that they might not be [too] much at odds with the Latin reading to which we are accustomed (*a lectionis latinae consuetudine*), I have controlled my reed pen in such a way that those of the things that seemed to alter much of the meaning have been corrected, [and] I have permitted the rest to remain as it has been.⁷⁹

Jerome's decision to revise the Latin Gospels towards Greek sources was motivated by a thirst for scriptural truth: that same thirst for scriptural truth also eventually led him to treat the VL Old Testament. In his first reworking of the Latin Psalter, which

---

⁷⁸ In the preface to the Vulgate of Joshua, Jerome made a very similar remark about the books of the Old Testament: "Among the Latins, there are as many versions as there are manuscripts (*apud Latinos tot sint exemplaria quot codices*), and everyone either added or deleted what he pleased, as he saw fit: assuredly, what is true cannot vary (lit., what disagrees cannot be true) (*utique non possit verum esse quod dissonet*)" (Vulg., p. 285).

⁷⁹ Vulg., pp. 1515–16.

version is now lost,[80] his task was limited to stylistic emendations. While he arguably corrected, for instance, his predecessors' use of neologisms, or certain unidiomatic turns, his aim must have been to harmonise the Latin versions of the Psalter in light of the LXX.[81] After setting out for Bethlehem in the mid-380s, he decided to undertake another revision of the Latin Psalter, one that would be based on Origen's corrected edition of the LXX.[82]

---

[80] The version of the Latin Psalter that is commonly called *Psalterium Romanum* was formerly assumed to correspond to Jerome's first revision. However, this hypothesis has been widely contested: according to Estin, beyond the fact that the *Psalterium Romanum* cannot be ascribed to Jerome, his first revision of the Psalter has never been identified (*Les Psautiers*, pp. 25–28). There seems to be a consensus that the *Psalterium Romanum* actually represents "the Old Latin base text which [he] corrected" (Tkacz, 'Labor tam utilis', p. 49). See also Kelly, *Jerome*, p. 89; Rebenich, 'Jerome: the "vir trilinguis"', p. 52; and Thibaut, 'La révision hexaplaire', p. 108.

[81] Salmon, 'Introduction', p. 13. As Braverman argues, Jerome's "first revision of the Old Latin Psalter [...] did not take Origen's *Hexapla* into consideration" (*Jerome's Commentary*, pp. 26–27).

[82] Bogaert, 'The Latin Bible', p. 515; Salmon, 'Introduction', p. 13. In this context, scholars often speak of the 'Hexaplaric' recension of the LXX, or of the LXX of the Hexapla, without specifying what this actually points to. As noted in fn. 48, while many scholars now believe the fifth column of the Hexapla to have displayed the uncorrected LXX text that served Origen as his base text for a separate amended edition, some still argue that the Hexapla in fact contained Origen's amended edition. Therefore, one should always clarify their stance, as it is often impossible to infer from context what 'Hexaplaric' implies. De Sainte-Marie shows in his paper that, in the context of Jerome's second revision of

This revision, which Jerome presented in his preface as *iuxta Septuaginta interpretes* ('in accordance with the Seventy translators'),[83] is referred to as the *Psalterium Gallicanum*.[84]

The earliest manifestation of Jerome's interest in Hebrew and, at the same time, in the Hebrew Bible is contained in the preface to his translation of Eusebius' *Chronicon*, which he produced in 380. As he laid down a few basic rules in the field of translation, he also shared his views on certain biblical and non-biblical translations; some of his remarks introduce the principles of what was to become his agenda in the creation of the Vulgate project ten years later:

> The holy books [...] that were produced by the Seventy translators do not retain the same flavour in the Greek lan-

---

the Book of Psalms, it is also essential to make this matter clear from the beginning (see de Sainte-Marie, 'Le Psaume 22', p. 151).

[83] Jerome's preface to this revision of the Psalter can be found in Weber and Gryson's edition of the Vulgate, in Vulg., p. 767.

[84] According to Estin, this revision was produced between 389 and 392 (*Les Psautiers*, p. 28). For an investigation of Jerome's style in this revision, see Thibaut's analysis of Ps. 24 in the *Psalterium Gallicanum* in 'La révision hexaplaire'. Noteworthy is that Jerome extended his revision of the VL based on Origen's edition beyond the Book of Psalms, but not to the entire Old Testament (see de Bruyne, 'Une nouvelle préface', pp. 229–30). His remarks on his own work are also important to bear in mind: according to his testimony, his treatment of Origen's edition represented his first actual translation of Scripture; then came his translation of the Hebrew (see *Epist.* 112.19; VI, pp. 38–39). For further discussion of Jerome's work on the Latin Psalter, see Norris, 'The Latin Psalter', pp. 71–74.

guage [as in the Hebrew]. For this reason, Aquila, Symmachus and Theodotion were incited to publish works that were somewhat different [although they were based] on the same work (i.e., the Hebrew text) (*incitati diversum paene opus in eodem opere prodiderunt*): the first one endeavoured to render word for word (*nitente verbum de verbo exprimere*); the second one, to seek rather the meaning (*sensum potius sequi*); the third one, not to depart too much from the old [translators] (i.e., the LXX) (*non multum a veteribus discrepare*). [...] And, as a result, the Holy Writings (*Sacrae litterae*) can sound less neat or melodious, as articulate men who do not know that they were translated from Hebrew perceive the surface and not the marrow, and they dread the filthy aspect (lit., cloak) of the speech (*vestem orationis sordidam perhorrescant*), as it were, before they might discover the beautiful body of the things underneath. In the end, what is more tuneful than a psalter that sometimes runs in iambic metre, in the style of our Horace and of the Greek Pindar,[85] or that resounds with

---

[85] In *Epist.* 22.30 (I, pp. 144–46), written in 384, Jerome recounted a dream that he had while on his way to Jerusalem from Rome, in which he was judged for being a sinful "Ciceronian" and not a Christian. He explained in this letter that the dream allowed him to redeem his former taste for pagan literature and to finally make a pledge to only read the Holy Scriptures from then on. Noteworthy is that he repudiated Horace in a way that implicitly disavowed what he had written in the preface to his translation of Eusebius' *Chronicon*, four years earlier: "What does Horace do with a psalter? What about Virgil with the Gospels? Or Cicero with the Apostle? Is the brother not scandalised if he sees you reclining in an idol-temple? [...] We should not drink [out of] the chalice of Christ and at the same time [out of] the chalice of demons. I shall tell you the story of my misadventure" (*Epist.* 22.29; I, p. 144). In my monograph, all dates for Jerome's letters are based on Labourt's edition (see

Alcaic metre, or that swells with the Sapphic one, or that is presented with verses of six feet? What is more beautiful than the singing of Deuteronomy and of Isaiah? What is more solemn than Solomon? What is more perfect than Job? All these compositions circulate in hexameters and pentameters among their own [people] (i.e., in Hebrew), as Josephus and Origen write.[86] When we read them in Greek, they sound somewhat different; when in Latin, they are utterly discordant. And if anyone does not think that the charm of a language is altered when translated, let them recite Homer word for word (*ad verbum*) in Latin; I

---

the first footnote to each letter in *Saint Jérôme: Correspondance* [cf. in my bibliography under 'Primary Sources', 'Jerome', '*Epist.*']).

[86] According to Gray, Jerome did not literally mean that these Hebrew texts were composed in hexameters and pentameters (*The Forms of Hebrew Poetry*, pp. 13–14 and pp. 16–17). Indeed, Gray argues: "Jerome's views of the nature of Hebrew poetry [...] are a reproduction of the statements of Josephus, or deductions made by Jerome himself from or in the spirit of Josephus' statements. [...] Josephus, in commending Hebrew poetry to his Greek readers, followed his usual practice of describing things Jewish in terms that would make a good impression on them" (ibid., pp. 14–16). Ehlers, Fieger and Tauwinkl agree with Gray's hypothesis: in their view, Jerome probably meant to "paint aspects of biblical literature in bright colours for the Greek and Roman readers." They add the following: "if [Jerome's translation of the Book of Job] is examined attentively, certain turns of phrase proper to Latin poetry may be noticed. It is therefore possible that his intention was to convey, to a certain degree, to the reader the same impression made by reading a classical epic poem" ('Some Notes about Jerome, pp. 50–51). This last point, while tantalising, is unsubstantiated: in-depth literary and comparative analyses would be required in order to check whether Jerome responded differently to a Hebrew text that he considered poetry, that is, as opposed to one that he would have considered prose.

will even say, let them translate him into their own language with prose words: they shall realise (lit., see) that the wording (*ordinem*) [sounds] ridiculous, and that the most eloquent poet can hardly speak.[87]

At this early stage, Jerome still expressed ideas in their infancy. Two years later, in a letter addressed to Damasus, he further showed his interest in the use of Hebrew, particularly through the agency of Aquila's work, in his exegetical interpretation of the words *seraphim* and *sabaoth* in VL Isa. 6.1–9, and of VL Exod. 4.10:

> *Seraphim*, as we find it in the *Interpretation of Hebrew Names* (*in interpretatione nominum Hebraeorum*),[88] are translated

---

[87] Jerome's preface to *Chron.* (3–4; pp. 56–58). On the date of composition, see Jeanjean and Lançon's introduction (*Chron.*, pp. 19–26). See also Kamesar's discussion of this preface in 'Jerome and the Hebrew Scriptures', pp. 59–63.

[88] This Hebrew and Greek lexicon of biblical names, to which Jerome referred here as the *Interpretatio Nominum Hebraeorum*, arguably served as his base text in the composition of his own glossary in the late 380s (see Kelly, *Jerome*, pp. 153–55; and below, section 3.2.1.2). The *Interpretatio Nominum Hebraeorum* was well known among exegetes like Origen who were used to consulting it (see Nautin, 'Le "De Seraphim"', p. 269). Nautin attempts to demonstrate that here, in *Epist.* 18, Jerome relied exclusively on the Greek part of the lexicon and that he misconstrued the etymology of the word *seraphim* as a result. His explanation is that Jerome's rendering *principium oris eorum* 'the beginning of their speech (lit., of their mouth)' corresponds, in the lexicon, to a construal of the word שְׂרָפִים as derived from the roots שַׂר 'prince' and פִּיהֶם 'their mouth': only, Nautin argues that *principium* reflects ἀρχή (i.e., the Greek part of the lexicon) and not שַׂר, as שַׂר cannot mean 'beginning'. He concludes that, since Jerome's whole interpretation in the letter was based

either as 'the burning' (*incendium*) or as 'the beginning of their speech' (*principium oris eorum*). [...] As for the [reading] that indeed follows—'the beginning of their speech'—how could it be related to the Scriptures? I am afraid that if we undertook to say [it], we would not seem to act as translators but as violators of the Scriptures. The origin of speech and of common discourse (*initium oris et communis eloquii*), as well as everything that we utter (*et hoc omne quod loquimur*), [is] the Hebrew language, in which the Old Testament was written: [this is what] the whole of antiquity has transmitted. [...] 'And they said: holy, holy, holy Lord, God *sabaoth*.' [...] Our saviour is also called *sabaoth*, take this example from Psalm 23 [...]: 'The Lord of virtues himself is the king of glory', which is written in Hebrew [as] 'the Lord *sabaoth*'. And it should be known that wherever the Seventy translators said 'the Lord of virtues' and 'the almighty Lord', in Hebrew it was phrased as 'the Lord *sabaoth*', which Aquila translates as 'the Lord of the militias'. [The word] 'Lord' itself here is also [composed] of four letters, which is a characteristic way of calling God (*quod proprie in Deo ponitur*): *iod he iod he*, that is, twice *IA*, which twofold [expression] constitutes this unspeakable and glorious name of God.[89]

[Moses] apologised by saying: 'please, Lord, I am not worthy', instead of which the Hebrew reads 'I do not have circumcised lips'. The Seventy translators express the sense

---

on the notion of 'beginning', he must not have known Hebrew (Nautin, 'Le "De Seraphim"', p. 269). Without delving too much into this matter, I shall simply note that Nautin does not seem to realise that *principium* may be a Latin pun based on a word that shares the same root: *princeps* 'prince'.

[89] *Epist.* 18.6–7 (I, pp. 60–63).

[of the text] more so than a word-for-word [version thereof] (*sensum potius quam verbum de verbo exprimentibus*).⁹⁰

According to Jerome, Hebrew was not only the language in which the Old Testament had been written, but also the first language of humanity (*initium oris et communis eloquii*). As will be discussed in the following section, this belief underlay both his conception of the Hebrew text as the original text and his text-critical approach to the LXX. In 383, we learn from his letter to Damasus that he considered the Hebrew Bible to be the most essential hermeneutic tool, as he suggested that 'the truth has now to be extracted from the Hebrew books' (*nunc ex hebraeis codicibus veritas exprimenda est*).⁹¹ This return to the Hebrew was presented as a reaction to the existence of different VL versions of Scripture: he called them a *tertius gradus*, a 'third step', that is, the translations of a translation.⁹² He was indeed not only aware but critical of the fact that they were translations of different Greek manuscripts which were supposed to have originated from the LXX, that is, from a uniform Greek translation of the Hebrew text. On the whole, Jerome complained that the textual corruptions that had contaminated the Old Latin manuscripts, as well

---

⁹⁰ *Epist.* 18.15 (I p. 72).

⁹¹ *Epist.* 20.2 (I, p. 79). In *Epist.* 32.1 (II, pp. 37–38), composed in 384, Jerome mentioned that he had been working with the Hebrew scrolls 'for a long time already' (*iam pridem*).

⁹² Jerome's preface to his revision of the Latin Gospels (Vulg., p. 1515).

as the Greek ones on which they were based, resulted in the unreliability of the Latin versions of the Bible in circulation.[93]

His philological and hermeneutic interest in the Hebrew text is what gradually led him to work with the version of Scripture employed by many Jews:[94] in it lay what he called the *hebraica veritas*, the 'Hebrew truth'.[95] The Hebrew text was, in his eyes, the 'fountainhead' (*fons*) from which flowed the original and true meaning of Scripture, as opposed to the 'rivulets' (*rivuli*), i.e., to any other version, whether Greek or Latin, that had strayed from it. For example, in *Epist.* 28, after discussing the

---

[93] As is shown in section 1.7, the copyists were often blamed for the corruption of the manuscripts, but Jerome's criticisms also targeted the LXX translators and, through them, the LXX translation itself.

[94] Tov established that the Hebrew text that underlay the Vulgate was close to the fixed medieval Masoretic Text (*Textual Criticism*, p. 153). It should be borne in mind that Jerome's Hebrew *Vorlage* or *Vorlagen* were consonantal texts, i.e., they did not include vowels. On his knowledge of Hebrew vocalisation, see Barr, 'St Jerome and the Sounds of Hebrew', pp. 4–36 and 'St. Jerome's Appreciation', pp. 293–94 and pp. 300–1; Sutcliffe, 'St. Jerome's Pronunciation of Hebrew'; and Graves' observations in *Jerome's Hebrew*, pp. 108–11. For further discussion of Jerome's Hebrew *Vorlagen*, see my fn. 218, as well as Graves' remarks in 'Vulgate', pp. 285–87.

[95] The reader will find this expression in Jerome's preface to his commentary on Genesis (QHG, p. 3), but also scattered across his *œuvre*, for example in *Epist.* 57.7 (III, p. 64) or, in the context of his commentary on Daniel, in *Comm. Dan.* 3.91a (p. 206). The *hebraica veritas* is discussed at greater length in the next two sections. On Jerome's growing curiosity for the Hebrew text, see Kamesar, *Jerome*, pp. 41–49.

word סלה and its translation in the LXX and in the *recentiores*, he argued that he

> extracted [his knowledge] from the bottom of the Hebrews' fountainhead (*de intimo Hebraeorum fonte libavimus*), by not following rivulets of conjectures (*non opinionum rivulos persequentes*) and by not dreading the diversity of errors with which the whole world has been filled, but by desiring to both know and teach what is true.[96]

By 390–392, he had produced a new Latin translation of the Book of Psalms on the basis of the Hebrew and in consultation with the versions of Aquila and Symmachus. This Psalter, often called *Psalterium Hebraicum* ('Hebraic Psalter') or *iuxta Hebraeos* ('in accordance with the Hebrews'), "represented one part of his great endeavour to translate the entire Old Testament from the Hebrew."[97] Finally, in the late 390s, in the Vulgate preface to the Pentateuch, Jerome explained that his eagerness to translate the Hebrew into Latin was triggered by the text-critical work of Origen and by the example of the authors of the New Testament:

> I have received the desired letters of my Desiderius […], who beseeches me to transmit to our audience a Pentateuch translated into the Latin tongue from the Hebrew language. A perilous work, for sure, open to the barking of

---

[96] *Epist.* 28.5 (II, p. 21). The term *fons* can also be found, for example, in *Epist.* 20.2 (I, p. 79), *Epist.* 34.4 (II, p. 46), *Epist.* 106.2 (V, p. 105) or in the preface to *Comm. Eccl.* (CCSL 72, p. 249). For other occurrences of the term *rivuli*, see *Epist.* 20.2 (I, p. 79) or *Epist.* 106.2 (V, pp. 105–6). See also the discussion in Kamesar, *Jerome*, pp. 44–46.

[97] Bogaert, 'The Latin Bible', p. 515. See also Salmon, 'Introduction', pp. 13–14.

my detractors, who assert that I am fashioning something new to replace the old [texts] and insult the Seventy translators (*qui me adserunt in Septuaginta interpretum suggillationem nova pro veteribus cudere*).[98] [...] But I would not have dared, had it not been for Origen who stimulated me with his zeal: he [indeed] mixed Theodotion's translation with the ancient edition by marking the entire work with asterisks and obeli (i.e., with stars and broaches),[99] [that is,] by either making what was previously missing glitter, or by smothering and thrusting whatever was superfluous. And above all [I am indebted to] the authority of the Evangelists and of the Apostles, in whom we read many things from the Old Testament which are not contained in our manuscripts.[100]

---

[98] Jerome suggested twice in the preface to the Vulgate of Chronicles that he composed a "new work" which could replace the "old one" (Vulg., p. 546).

[99] Jerome could write 'broach' (*veru*) instead of obelus: see for example the Vulgate preface to the Pentateuch (Vulg., p. 3); the introductory annotation at Vulg. Est. 10.3 (Vulg., p. 724) (translated in the introduction to chapter 4 of this monograph); or *Epist.* 106.7 (V, p. 108). He could also refer to it as a 'slash' (*virgula*): see the preface to the Vulgate Book of Chronicles (Vulg., p. 546); *Epist.* 112.19 (VI, p. 38); the preface to the Psalter *iuxta Septuaginta interpretes* (Vulg., p. 767); or that of his revision of the VL of Job (edited by Canellis in *Préfaces*, p. 390).

[100] Vulg., p. 3. Both Braverman (*Jerome's Commentary*, p. 26) and Kamesar (*Jerome*, p. 64) have spoken of an "apostolic approval." This phrase was derived from an incidental remark that Jerome made in the preface to his revision of the Latin Gospels (Vulg., p. 1515), in reference to the version of the Old Testament which he believed the authors of the Gospels had employed (see my fn. 125): *sit illa vera interpretatio quam Apostoli probaverunt* ('Let the translation that the Apostles approved of be the

In the preface to the Vulgate Book of Job, Jerome further argued that resorting to his new translation would not be inconsistent with the Church's usual practice to employ the *recentiores'* versions in homilies. Not only that, the *recentiores* were "Jews" and "heretics," while he at least was a Christian:

> If, among the Greeks, after the production of the Septuagint, now that the Gospel of the Christ shines, Aquila, a Jew, and Symmachus as well as Theodotion, Judaising heretics (*iudaizantes heretici*), have been accepted—they who conceal many of the Saviour's mysteries with their deceitful translation and yet who are [read] in the churches through the Hexapla (εχαπλοις, *sic*) and upon whom churchmen elaborate (*explanantur ab ecclesiasticis viris*)[101] —how much more I, a Christian, of Christian parents, bearing the standard of the cross on my forehead, I whose endeavour has been to fetch what is missing, to rectify what has been distorted,[102] and to open the sacraments of the

true one'). As shown below, Jerome did rely on certain passages of the Gospels to justify the promotion of the Hebrew text as the original source of Scripture. However, the phrase 'apostolic approval' is misleading when used to describe the role that these texts played in the formation of his agenda, as the Apostles, who lived over three centuries before Jerome, could not have given their approval to his undertaking. Rather, he approved of them (see below).

[101] Jerome made the same point in *Epist.* 112.19 (VI, p. 39) and in *Comm. Ezech.* 33.23–33 (CCSL 75, p. 475). See also his preface to the Vulgate Book of Ezra (Vulg., p. 639) and his final remarks in *Ruf.*, II, 33 (p. 194).

[102] As indicated above in fn. 84, before setting out to translate the Hebrew Bible, Jerome endeavoured to translate the LXX on the basis of Origen's edition (see Canellis, *Préfaces*, p. 385, fn. 4). According to his remarks in his preface to his translation of Origen's edition of the LXX

Church with a pure and faithful language, [how much more] should I not be condemned by either hateful or malicious readers? Let those who please have the old books (i.e., the VL), whether copied on purple parchments with gold and silver, or with uncials, as they commonly say—[a pile of] bricks (lit., loads) engraved with letters rather than [real] manuscripts (*litteris onera magis exarata quam codices*)[103]—as long as they permit me and my [friends] to have

---

of Job, he employed the same editorial markers as Origen, i.e., the asterisk and the obelus: "O Paula and Eustochium, [...] rejoice that Job, the happy one who until now was lying in manure among the Latins, and who was swarming with worms of errors, [is] intact and spotless. [...] I am therefore warning you, as well as each and every reader, through this customary preface and, as I always attach the same [information] to the beginnings of [my] books, I ask you to know that, wherever you see introductory slashes (i.e., obeli) (*praecedentes virgulas*), what has been appended [to it] (*ea quae subiecta sunt*) is not contained in the Hebrew scrolls. On the other hand, where the shape of a star (i.e., asterisk) glitters, [you will find] what has been added from Hebrew in our tongue" (my translation of the Latin preface edited by Canellis in *Préfaces*, pp. 388–90). See also Jerome's comments in *Ruf.*, II, 24 (pp. 168–70).

[103] Jerome seems to have blamed a certain trend, which consisted of collecting expensive editions of biblical books, for contributing to the dissemination of Old Latin texts and encouraging their preservation against more accurate, new translations. This matter was addressed in a similar tone in the preface to his revision of the VL of Job, in which these luxurious editions are accused of reinforcing collectors' attachment to their flawed Bible versions: "Familiarity with an old thing (*vetustatis consuetudo*) is indeed so [strong] that flaws, even when acknowledged, [remain] pleasant to most people, so long as they prefer to own pretty manuscripts rather than corrected ones" (my translation of the

poor little pages and manuscripts [that are] not as pretty as [they are] correct (*non tam pulchros codices quam emendatos*). Both editions, the Septuagint according to the Greeks, and my [version] according to the Hebrews, [are available] in Latin: I have translated both, by the sweat of my brow. Let each and every one select what they please and prove themselves committed rather than malevolent.[104]

Through his knowledge of four languages, Latin, Greek, Hebrew and Aramaic, which he must have known to be a unique asset among the Church Fathers,[105] Jerome eventually aspired to give the Christian Latin readership access to the entire Old Testament as it was represented in the Hebrew version of his time, which he considered to be the original form of the text. Therefore, he undertook its translation into Latin, but he also consistently resorted to the *recentiores*' translations throughout this work.[106]

Until the sixteenth century, the phrase *editio vulgata*, that is, the edition in common use,[107] referred mostly to the LXX and sometimes to the VL, although it could also involve both the LXX

Latin preface edited by Canellis in *Préfaces*, p. 388). On the trend targeted by Jerome's criticism, see Canellis, ibid., fn. 1 and 2, and pp. 404–5, fn. 1 and 2; and Williams, *The Monk and the Book*, pp. 181–88.

[104] Vulg., p. 732.

[105] See my fn. 52.

[106] Braverman, *Jerome's Commentary*, pp. 25–30; and Tov, *Textual Criticism*, p. 153.

[107] *Vulgata* is the feminine singular form of the perfect passive participle of *vulgo*, which means 'to publish, spread, make known'; here, it agrees with the feminine noun *editio*. The phrase *editio vulgata* is traditionally translated as 'common edition'.

and the VL, without distinguishing one from the other. At the beginning of the sixteenth century, the expression *editio vulgata* started to be frequently employed to refer to the received edition of Jerome's version of the Bible. The modern sense of the term Vulgate was only firmly established after the Council of Trent, held in the mid-sixteenth century, and the publication of the Clementine edition at the end of the same century.[108]

5.0. An Appreciation of Jerome's Agenda through His Reception and Treatment of the Hebrew Book of Genesis

Years before translating the Hebrew of Genesis for the Vulgate project, Jerome had already begun to actively engage with it. Indeed, in his philological and theological commentary on Genesis, *Quaestiones Hebraicae in Genesim* (QHG), dated generally between

---

[108] Sutcliffe, 'The Name "Vulgate"', pp. 347–52. In the middle of the eighteenth century, Sabatier still called Jerome's version *Vulgata nova*, 'the new Vulgate', and the VL *Versio antiqua*, 'the ancient version' (see Sabatier's edition of the Vetus Latina, under 'Primary Sources', 'VL', in my bibliography). Furthermore, the name 'Vulgate' has come with time to imply both Jerome's translation of the Hebrew Old Testament and the Latin New Testament: the latter is placed after the former in Weber and Gryson's edition of the Vulgate. It is unlikely, however, that Jerome's work on the New Testament extended beyond his revision of the Gospels in the early 380s. All other New Testament books contained in any edition of the Vulgate should therefore not be considered as the result of his work (see Bogaert, 'The Latin Bible', pp. 517–18; Parker, 'The New Testament Text and Versions', p. 421; and Graves, 'Vulgate', pp. 279–80).

389 and 393,[109] he reproduced Latin extracts rendering the LXX version of the book, each of which serves as a lemma in the commentary.[110] When commenting on these lemmas, in case of discrepancies between the LXX and the Hebrew, Jerome routinely

---

[109] Kamesar's computation of the publication date, between 391 and 393, is compelling (*Jerome*, pp. 74–76). See also Hayward, *Saint Jerome's Hebrew Questions*, pp. 23–27; and Nautin, 'L'Activité littéraire', pp. 253–56.

[110] See Duval, *Comm. Jon.*, pp. 42–43 [cf. in my bibliography under 'Primary Sources', 'Jerome']. The exact origin of the lemmas employed in QHG is difficult to establish. It is noteworthy that Jerome discussed some of the revisions that he performed on them. In QHG 37.36 (pp. 57–58), for example, he openly revised the lemma towards the Hebrew: it reads *Phutiphar* (cf. MT Gen. 37.36 לְפוֹטִיפַר), "not *Petefre*, as it was written in Latin," attested Jerome in the body of the text (QHG 37.36 [p. 58]). Accordingly, the LXX reads Πετεφρη, which was represented by *Petefre* in the VL manuscript that he corrected (for another example of the same type, see QHG 35.27 [p. 55]). At times, he could also fail to inform the reader: in QHG 41.50 (p. 61), a portion of the lemma reads *antequam venirent anni famis* 'before the years of famine might come', whereas LXX Gen. 41.50 runs πρὸ τοῦ ἐλθεῖν τὰ ἑπτὰ ἔτη τοῦ λιμοῦ 'before the coming of seven years of famine'. Jerome's omission of the word 'seven', as well as the syntax in his quotation of the verse, causes the lemma to echo the Hebrew in MT Gen. 41.50 בְּטֶרֶם תָּבוֹא שְׁנַת הָרָעָב 'before the year of famine came', against the LXX version. On the whole, the lemmas in QHG may go back to VL renderings that Jerome transcribed from memory, to ones that he revised to a certain extent, or to his own *ad hoc* renderings (see Remley's remarks in 'The Latin textual basis', p. 180; and Bogaert's in 'De la *vetus latina*', p. 223). Billen argues that Jerome's quotations of the Heptateuch (all seven books from Genesis to Judges), which frequently agree with those of Tertullian, often stemmed from "the use of primitive Old Latin Texts," that is, from already existing Latin versions (*The Old Latin Texts of the Heptateuch*, p. 5

adduced the Hebrew to highlight them and correct the Greek: he did so by translating, transliterating or paraphrasing into Latin the Hebrew passage corresponding to the lemma. The purpose of QHG was couched in clear terms in its preface: it was to explain the actual meaning of Scripture, by means of the Hebrew of Genesis, to a Latin readership, and to ultimately prove the LXX wrong through the authority of the Hebrew. In this sense, QHG can be regarded as an explanatory preamble to Jerome's overall project of a Latin translation of the Hebrew version of Scripture:

> It shall be my endeavour both to rebut the errors of those who assume various things about the Hebrew books, and to restore to their proper authority those things which seem to abound in the Latin and Greek manuscripts.[111]

Slightly later in his career, towards the end of the 390s, Jerome took on the Vulgate of Genesis, that is, the translation of the Hebrew version of the book into Latin.[112] Therefore, on a formal

---

and p. 77). At any rate, the reader is regularly faced in QHG with a direct comparison, made by the author, of a Latin translation of the LXX with a quotation of the Hebrew.

[111] Jerome's preface to QHG (p. 2). The sense of his undertaking in this work is discussed at great length by Kamesar throughout his monograph on QHG (see, for example, *Jerome*, pp. 76–81). See also Hayward, *Saint Jerome's Hebrew Questions*, pp. 1–14; and Cavallera, *Saint Jérôme*, I, pp. 144–47.

[112] The Vulgate translation of Genesis is generally dated between 398 and the beginning of the 400s. This dating has been disputed by multiple scholars who have tentatively argued that Jerome's translation of the Pentateuch went back to 393. For an overview of the matter, see Canellis, *Préfaces*, pp. 93–97 (cf. especially the comparative chart on 97).

level, his first translation of Genesis from the Hebrew was not in the Vulgate but in QHG, taking the form of fragmented renderings and of paraphrases of variable length.[113] His reason for endeavouring to consult the Hebrew text had been stated as a principle at least six to ten years before the production of QHG, in his epistolary exchanges with Pope Damasus: "the Old Testament, which was translated by the Seventy elders into the Greek language, reached us third-hand" (*tertio gradu ad nos usque pervenit*; lit., 'in the third step', i.e., through the VL, the Latin translation

---

[113] Jerome's way of referring to his translation of the Hebrew Bible as a finished project (*vetus iuxta hebraicum transtuli*) in his work *On Illustrious Men* of 392-393 was rhetorical, and not to be taken at face value (*Vir. ill.*, 135 [p. 57]; on the dating of *Vir. ill.*, see Kamesar, *Jerome*, pp. 73-74). Indeed, it is established that Jerome completed the Vulgate project around 406 (see Canellis, *Préfaces*, pp. 97-98). If *On Illustrious Men* is composed of short biographies written in the past tense (the last of which is Jerome's autobiography), his suggestion that he had already translated the entire "Old Testament according to the Hebrew" (*transtuli*) in 392-393 should actually be understood as a projection on his part (see Bogaert's comments in 'The Latin Bible', p. 517; and Kedar-Kopfstein's in 'The Vulgate as a Translation', pp. 46-55). Kamesar further argues: "the translation of Genesis appeared only years after *QHG* [...]. Indeed, it is well known that Jerome published the volumes of *IH* [*Iuxta Hebraicum*, i.e., his translation of the Hebrew Bible] not according to the biblical order, but translated different books in the order in which they were requested by his friends" (*Jerome*, p. 78). The order in which Jerome translated the books of the Hebrew Bible is a complex matter, but the Pentateuch is generally not considered one of the earlier ones (see my fn. 112; Kamesar, *Jerome*, pp. 73-74; Gribomont, 'The Translations: Jerome and Rufinus', pp. 224-26; and Jay, 'La datation').

of the LXX translation);[114] "The truth," wrote Jerome, "has now to be extracted from the Hebrew manuscripts" (*nunc ex hebraeis codicibus veritas exprimenda est*).[115] By the early 380s, he was challenging the VL versions in circulation, and he probably considered eventually replacing them with a uniform Latin translation of the LXX corrected towards the Hebrew. With QHG, he affirmed even more clearly that the Hebrew text was the most fundamental source for understanding the Bible, thus preparing the reader for the upcoming Vulgate. The phrase *hebraica veritas* was then taking on its full meaning.[116] At the same time, one could hardly

---

[114] Jerome's preface to his revision of the Latin Gospels (Vulg., p. 1515). This preface was written in 383–384. In the Vulgate preface to what he called the "Books of Solomon" (i.e., Proverbs, Ecclesiastes, Song of Songs, Wisdom of Solomon, and Sirach), Jerome spoke of the VL in similar terms: "If anyone is actually more pleased with the edition of the Septuagint interpreters, he has it, as it was once corrected by me (i.e., Jerome's revision of the VL is to be understood); and, in fact, I do not make a new [edition] so as to wipe out the old [one] [...]. But still, [...] my [new translation] (i.e., the Vulgate) has not been adulterated by being poured into a third vat (*in tertium vas*) (i.e., like the LXX into the VL), but it will have retained its flavour by being entrusted to a most pure vessel straight out of the press (*statim de praelo*; i.e., the 'press' is the original text, that is, the Hebrew version)" (Vulg., p. 957).

[115] *Epist.* 20.2 (I, p. 79). This letter, in which Jerome already showed himself confident about the relevance of the Hebrew, was written as early as the preface to his revision of the Latin Gospels. Both belong to his second Roman period, starting in the early 380s, after the trip undertaken to Chalcis in 375, and before the departure for Bethlehem, around 385.

[116] QHG, p. 3 (see my fn. 95). According to Hayward, the first occurrence of the phrase *hebraica veritas* probably was in QHG (Hayward, *Saint Jerome's Hebrew Questions*, p. 93, fn. 19). The slightly different

have expected the people concerned by this undertaking—most Latin-speaking worshippers and Church exegetes, such as Augustine—to renounce their old version of Scripture and to accept a new translation without questioning it. They could not engage either in a close scrutiny of the Hebrew material that Jerome purported to be translating in the Vulgate, for lack of the required knowledge and of access to the texts and services of Hebrews that he himself had got at a cost (see below, in section 1.6).[117] Therefore, the recurring assertion that, before him, the 'Evangelists and Apostles' themselves consulted and employed the Hebrew Bible allowed him, through the authority of the first authors of the New Testament, to reassure his readership of the validity of his stance. This was a way to justify a project that was not to be taken as an attack on the LXX but, rather, as a part of the most ancient hermeneutic tradition in the history of Christendom:

---

wording *iuxta sensus Hebraici veritatem* ('according to the truth of the Hebrew sense') occurred in Jerome's 388–389 commentary on Ecclesiastes (*Comm. Eccl.* 8.13; CCSL 72, p. 319), that is, arguably one to five years before QHG. In 407, Jerome also referred to the 'Aramaic truth' (*chaldaica veritas*) with respect to the Aramaic portion of the Book of Daniel (*Comm. Dan.* 5.11a, p. 250), and in 383–384 he spoke of the 'Greek truth' (*graeca veritas*) in relation to the original New Testament texts (Vulg., p. 1515 [see my translation in section 1.4]).

[117] On Jerome's access to Hebrew manuscripts, read Sutcliffe, 'St Jerome's Hebrew manuscripts'; and Williams, *The Monk and the Book*, pp. 147–54. For a discussion of the Rabbis' role in the works of the Church Fathers, read Krauss, 'The Jews in the Works of the Church Fathers'; and Kamesar, 'Rabbinic Midrash and Church Fathers'.

> What then? Are we condemning the ancients? Not in the least! [...] Listen then, O rival, pay attention, O detractor: I do not condemn the Seventy, I do not criticise them, but I confidently prefer the Apostles to them all (*sed confidenter cunctis illis Apostolos praefero*). Christ calls me through their mouths (I read that they have been placed before the prophets in the spiritual gifts, among which the translators hold almost the last position [*in quibus ultimum paene gradum interpretes tenent*]). Why are you tormented with envy? Why do you stir up unskilled souls against me? If anywhere I seem to you to be mistaken in [my] translation, ask the Hebrews! Consult the teachers of the various cities! What they have on Christ, your manuscripts do not.[118]

> The pupils of the Apostles (*apostolici viri*) resort to the Hebrew Scriptures. It is obvious (*perspicuum est*) that the very Apostles and Evangelists did so [too]. Wherever the Lord and Saviour mentions the Old Testament, he adduces excerpts (*ponit exempla*) from the Hebrew books [...]. I am not saying this because I [want to] tarnish the Seventy translators, but on account of the fact that the authority of the Christ and of the Apostles is greater (*sed quo apostolorum et Christi sit maior auctoritas*). Wherever the Seventy do not disagree with the Hebrew, the Apostles drew excerpts from their translation; where, on the other hand, the [former] are at odds, the [latter] laid down in Greek what they learned among the Hebrews. Therefore, just as I indicate that many [writings] laid down in the New Testament on the basis of the books of the Old one are not contained in the Septuagint, and as I show that they are written in the Hebrew, let the accuser point the same way to anything that was written in the New Testament on the basis of the

---

[118] Vulg., p. 4.

> Seventy translators[' version], anything that is not contained in the Hebrew, and the dispute is settled.[119]
>
> To be sure, the Apostles and the Evangelists were familiar with [the work of] the Seventy translators, but from where were they [supposed] to quote those things which the Septuagint does not have? Christ, our God, [is] the founder of both Testaments [...]. Assuredly, what the Saviour attests to be written, is written. Where is it written? The Septuagint does not have it, the Church does not know [these] apocryphal [writings]; therefore we must return to the Hebrews[' version], from which both the Lord speaks and the disciples (i.e., the Apostles and the Evangelists) select [their] examples in the first place (*ad Hebraeos igitur revertendum est, unde et Dominus loquitur et discipuli exempla praesumunt*).[120]

In the preface to the Vulgate Book of Chronicles, Jerome further presented the Apostles' authority as even "more important" than that of the Hebrews (see section 1.6 below):

> While leaving the previous edition (i.e., the LXX) unviolated, I have composed a new one (i.e., the Vulgate) (*qui inviolata editione veteri ita novam condidi*) so as to make my work worthy of the Hebrews and, more importantly, of the authorities, [i.e.,] the Apostles (*ut laborem meum Hebraeis et, quod his maius est, Apostolis auctoribus probem*).[121]

---

[119] *Ruf.*, II, 34 (pp. 196–98).

[120] Vulg., pp. 546–47.

[121] Vulg., p. 546. See also Vulg., p. 638 and p. 768; *Epist.* 20.2 (I, p. 79) and 57.9–11 (III, pp. 68–71); and the preface to QHG (p. 2). See Cameron's discussion of Jerome's use of the New Testament within the context of the *hebraica veritas* in 'The *Vir Triculutus*', pp. 203–42.

Jerome's comments often suggested that the superiority of the Hebrew text was proved by the way the Apostles had used it. However, for him, the idea that it represented the original version of Scripture was not proved, but rather corroborated by the role that it had supposedly played in the authors of the Gospels. Firstly, it has been demonstrated that Jerome had to select specific passages to claim that the Apostles and the Evangelists had relied on the Hebrew Bible: he exploited the fact that these passages arguably agreed with the Hebrew against the LXX to affirm that the former was the original text. This reasoning has been questioned and partly invalidated by modern scholarship. According to Braverman,

> it is indeed true [...] that the apostles did cite *some* OT (i.e., Old Testament) verses which were found only in the Hebrew text and not in the LXX. However, even a cursory examination of all the OT passages cited in the NT clearly shows that the LXX and not the Masoretic Hebrew text is the principal source for these quotations. In fact, Justin, almost 250 years before, had employed the direct opposite of Jerome's argument. Based on the available LXX text, he had accused the Jews of removing many words and phrases from the Hebrew text. Jerome must have been aware that his argument was sheer rationalization, necessary in order not to offend the Church in its sanction of the LXX.[122]

---

[122] Braverman, *Jerome's Commentary*, p. 32. See also Kamesar, *Jerome*, p. 64; Kato, 'Hebrews, Apostles, and Christ', pp. 430–39; and Canellis, *Préfaces*, pp. 106–7.

Had Jerome wished to make the opposite point, namely, that the authors of the New Testament relied on the LXX more so than on the Hebrew text, he could have posited, like Justin, as Braverman relevantly points out, that certain passages in the LXX that alluded to the Christ had been removed from the Hebrew text.[123] The New Testament, to be sure, was a most compelling authority to invoke before the Christian community if one wished to promote the primacy, and therefore the supremacy, of the Hebrew text. It is almost certain, though, that Jerome was not "aware" of what he was doing, despite what Braverman has argued. Indeed, I contend that he appealed to the authors of the New Testament in good faith, being genuinely convinced that they, too, had considered the Hebrew text as the original form of Scripture against the LXX.[124] In the preface to his revision of the Latin Gospels, while introducing his work on the New Testament, he incidentally observed that the true version of the Old Testament should be the one "approved" by the Apostles:

> But no, I am not discussing the Old Testament (*neque vero ego de Veteri disputo Testamento*) which, after being translated by the Seventy elders into the Greek language, reached us third-hand. I do not wonder (*non quaero*) what Aquila or Symmachus thinks, [or] why Theodotion steers a middle course between the new [translators] and the old ones: let the translation that the Apostles approved of be

---

[123] See Justin, *Dial.* 68 (PG 6, p. 636A–C), 71–73 (PG 6, pp. 641–649A).

[124] See Jerome's comments in *Comm. Isa.* 6.9–10 (CCSL 73, p. 92); and Jay, *L'Exégèse*, pp. 90–91.

the true one (*sit illa vera interpretatio quam Apostoli probaverunt*).[125]

Resorting to citations of the New Testament was above all a way to prove the importance of the Hebrew text in the eyes of the Christian community. However, for Jerome, the fact that there was a correspondence between these citations and the Hebrew text was not in itself the proof that it was the original text: the Hebrew text was the original text, regardless of external authorities, because Hebrew was, as he claimed in *Epist.* 18, the first language of humanity (*initium oris et communis eloquii*), "in which the Old Testament was written."[126] Another remark that he made around 392 in his commentary on the Book of Zephaniah also presents Hebrew as the language from which all other languages originated: 'The Hebrew language is the source of all languages' (*linguam Hebraicam omnium linguarum esse matricem*).[127] Jerome

---

[125] Vulg., p. 1515. With the phrase 'the translation that the Apostles approved of', Jerome alluded to the version of the Old Testament which the authors of the Gospels had allegedly relied on and cited across their works. In the present context, he clearly indicated that he did not wish to engage in a philological comparison between the Hebrew text, the LXX and the Apostles' citations of the Old Testament (*neque vero ego de Veteri disputo Testamento; non quaero*), as this would have forced him to digress from the topic of the preface: 'I am talking about the New Testament now' (*de Novo nunc loquor Testamento*) (Vulg., p. 1515). However, as seen above, he firmly believed that the Apostles had given precedence to the Hebrew form of the Old Testament over the LXX version.

[126] *Epist.* 18.6 (I, p. 61).

[127] *Comm. Soph.* 3.18 (CCSL 76A, p. 708). For the date of composition of the commentary, see Kelly, *Jerome*, p. 160 and p. 290.

was, in this respect, fundamentally rabbinic. Indeed, in the early third century CE, the Rabbis had campaigned to promote Hebrew as the language of the creation of the world, and as the one in which Scripture had originally been composed.[128] Jerome was not the first Church Father whose beliefs agreed with the ideas diffused by this movement: Origen said in one of his homilies that he regarded Hebrew as 'the language originally given through Adam' (*lingua per Adam primitus data, ut putamus Hebraea*).[129] He was, as de Lange argues, "entirely convinced of the primacy of the Hebrew Bible,"[130] and the belief in the divine relation between Hebrew, the creation of the world and the writing of Scripture underlay this conception. Unlike Jerome, however, Origen did not go as far as to publicly support a *hebraica veritas* against the Christian Bible tradition, which he continuously defended.[131] Jerome was convinced of the primacy of the Hebrew Bible for the same reason as Origen, whose work he knew, but he, unlike Origen, gradually adopted an openly critical, and text-critical, approach to the LXX in light of the *hebraica veritas* principle.[132]

---

[128] See my fn. 27.

[129] *Hom. Num.* XI, 4 (p. 84). For a discussion of this passage, see de Lange, 'The Revival of the Hebrew Language', pp. 351–54.

[130] De Lange, 'The Revival of the Hebrew Language', p. 358.

[131] See Origen, *Ep. Afr.*, 3–11 (pp. 524–38); and also de Lange, 'The Letter to Africanus'.

[132] See Munnich's observations in 'Les révisions juives de la Septante', pp. 170–75.

6.0. A Point of Terminology

In QHG, Jerome argued that one's understanding of Genesis should be based on the Hebrew, as per the *hebraica veritas* agenda; to support this claim, he invoked, continuously throughout his commentary, the traditions of people whom he called "the Hebrews."[133] As his storehouse of scriptural expertise, when quoted against rival sources, he generally made them triumph over adverse interpretations of the Bible; their function in the theory of translation and exegesis underlying QHG was to be right against other traditions. Although most often the term 'Hebrews' points to Jewish informants of his time, their identity is not as clear as the name suggests; indeed, Jerome systematically called these informants 'Hebrews' (*Hebraei*) as opposed to 'Jews' (*Judaei*). De Lange remarks that in Greek, as a general rule, "the ancient Israelites were *Hebraioi*, contemporary Jews *Ioudaioi*."[134] In Jerome, it could be the opposite: the Hebrews generally were

---

[133] The identity and role of these Hebrews have received some attention in modern scholarship. See Bardy, 'Saint Jérôme et ses maîtres hébreux'; Rebenich, 'Jerome: the "vir trilinguis"', pp. 55–63; Condamin, 'L'influence de la tradition juive', pp. 1–6; Gordon, 'Rabbinic exegesis', pp. 384–87 and pp. 415–16; Millar, 'Jerome and Palestine', pp. 65–69; Kamesar, 'Rabbinic Midrash and Church Fathers', pp. 35–36; Kraus, 'Rabbinic Traditions in Jerome', pp. 539–46, and the references ibid. in fn. 1; Cameron, 'The Rabbinic Vulgate?', pp. 122–25; and Weigert, *Hebraica Veritas*, pp. 68–82.

[134] De Lange, *Origen and the Jews*, p. 29.

his contemporaries and the Jews often, though not always, figures of the past.[135] De Lange further notes that "although *Ioudaioi* in various places and periods was neutral in its connotations it did easily tend to take on derogatory overtones, in which case *Hebraioi* became the polite word for the Jews."[136] The caveat that overtones were involved allows us to better appreciate the reversal in Jerome's conception of Jews. When quoting the traditions of 'Hebrews' against the LXX translators, as was his wont in QHG, he could refer to the latter, *inter alia*, and with no sense of contradiction, as 'the Jews'.[137] The exegesis of these Hebrews served

---

[135] It was more uncommon for him to use the name 'Hebrew' for characters of the past. He did so when speaking of the 'true Hebrew' (*verus Hebraeus*) who embodied the entire Israelite people in *Epist.* 78.2 (IV, p. 55) and 78.33 (IV, p. 80). In the preface to the Vulgate of the Pentateuch, he spoke of the Israelites as 'Hebrews', too (Vulg., p. 3). He also presented Matthew the Apostle as 'a Hebrew from the Hebrews' (*Hebraeus ex Hebraeis*) (*Epist.* 121.2; VII, p. 15); and he called Paul the Apostle the same way: "Certainly a Hebrew from the Hebrews, [Paul] was trained at the feet of Gamaliel, a man most learned in the Law" (*Epist.* 121.10; VII, p. 47). This is a direct quotation of Acts 22.3 where Paul introduces himself as a 'Jewish man' (Ἐγώ εἰμι ἀνὴρ Ἰουδαῖος): it is meaningful here that Jerome amended 'Jewish' to 'Hebrew'.

[136] De Lange, *Origen and the Jews*, p. 29.

[137] In the preface to the Vulgate of the Pentateuch, the LXX translators are the "Jews" who "deliberately" (*prudenti consilio*) hid from Ptolemy the allusions made to "the Father, the Son and the Holy Spirit" in the Hebrew Old Testament; by contrast, the "Hebrews" are described as a community of teachers (*diversarum urbium magistros*) who, through the Hebrew text, can offer access to information "about the Christ" which Christians will not find in the LXX (*quod illi habent de Christo, tui codices*

to correct or refine the interpretations of someone like Aquila,[138] though a Jewish "proselyte,"[139] or a "Jew" along with the two other *recentiores* Symmachus and Theodotion, who moreover were "Judaising heretics,"[140] "Jews and Ebionites"[141] and "Jews and semi-Jews."[142] Thanks to these Hebrews, Jerome also found opportunities to prove Aquila and Symmachus wrong,[143] although he could resort to the *recentiores*' expertise alongside the LXX, too, when in doubt regarding the etymological interpretations of Josephus, a Jew.[144]

Jerome's Hebrews were mostly anonymous, but it is clear that the term generally referred not only to the Jews of his time but possibly to those of his nearby environment, whether in Chalcis, in Rome, in Jerusalem, or in Bethlehem. Given the diversity

---

non habent; Vulg., pp. 3–4). This example shows that, in a specific context, Jerome could make a clear distinction between Jews and Hebrews.

[138] QHG 29.34 (pp. 44–45).

[139] *Epist.* 57.11 (III, p. 71); *Comm. Isa.* 8.11–15 (CCSL 73, p. 116).

[140] Vulg., p. 732. For a discussion of the term 'Judaising' in Jerome, see Newman's paper 'Jerome's Judaizers'.

[141] Vulg., p. 639. See also section 3.1.2.

[142] In *Comm. Isa.* 2.22 (CCSL 73, p. 40), Jerome alluded to the *recentiores* (*ceteri*, 'the others'), arguing that they did not believe in Christ and that they were 'Jews or semi-Jews, that is, Ebionites' (*Iudaei aut Semiiudaei, id est Ebionitae*). He also depicted Aquila on multiple occasions as a champion of the Synagogue (which in Jerome implied an innate hatred for the Christ); see *Epist.* 32.1 (II, p. 38) and 36.13 (II, p. 60).

[143] QHG 41.43 (p. 60). This passage is discussed at length in section 2.2.4 of this monograph.

[144] QHG 32.28–29 (p. 51).

of Judaism in his time, the exact affiliation of those whom he identified as Jews or Hebrews is not always certain. Salvesen argues that "there is little to indicate that Christian writers were able to distinguish between non-rabbinic and rabbinic Jews. [...] They seem unaware of any different groups within Judaism apart from Jewish or Judaising Christians."[145] Indeed, Jerome sometimes presented his Hebrew teachers as Jewish converts to Christianity.[146] However, he also shows in his way of referring to the

---

[145] Salvesen, 'Did Aquila and Symmachus', p. 113.

[146] See my discussion below and in fn. 163. It should be borne in mind that the Jewish diaspora with which Jerome engaged in Rome, in the early 380s, was probably different from the Palestinian community of Bethlehem, where he moved in 386 (see Weigert's remarks in *Hebraica Veritas*, pp. 76–79). Stemberger's suggestion that "the role of Jewish or Judaizing Christians may have been greater than that of educated Jews" in his learning of Jewish exegesis is tantalising but unsubstantiated (Stemberger, 'Exegetical Contacts', p. 583). While it is certainly the case that Jewish converts to Christianity played their part (as is shown in *Epist.* 125.12 [VII, pp. 124–25] cited below), as well as Christian Jews, the fact that in most cases Jerome did not specify whether his Hebrew teacher was also a Christian—a detail upon which he would not have hesitated to pride himself—weakens Stemberger's point. The only reason why he could have remained silent about the Christian background of an informant was if he was one of his 'Judaisers', i.e., an originally non-Jewish man, potentially a Christian proselyte drawn towards Jewish thought (see Newman, 'Jerome's Judaizers', p. 424). It is noteworthy that, when Christian detractors doubted, criticised or condemned Jerome's translation of Scripture, he, on the other hand, consistently replied that they should check for themselves by "asking the Hebrews" (see below): this may have been a diplomatic way to recommend the expertise of Jews who precisely were not Christian.

recentiores that he had a sense that other types of Jews could exist. Judaism was not uniform at the beginning of the fifth century, and among all the Jewish communities of the Mediterranean region the rabbinic movement did not represent a norm.[147] Rabbis were certainly present in the life of Jerome,[148] and many of the contemporary Jewish figures to whom he alluded probably corresponded, unless explicitly stated otherwise, to those whom we would now describe as rabbinic Jews. Famous in this regard is the passage of a letter in which he called contemporary Jewish traditions δευτερώσεις—a plural noun derived from the word δεύτερος ('second')—in Greek:

> How numerous the Pharisees' traditions are! Nowadays (*hodie*) they call them δευτερώσεις. [...] Jewish precepts pass for reason and for human wisdom among the ignorant and the low populace. This is why the [Jews'] teachers (*doctores eorum*) are called σοφοί, that is, 'sages' (*sapientes*). And when on certain days they set forth their traditions, they

---

[147] According to Schwartz, it is only by the sixth century that the rabbinic movement, which had then extensively grown, began to establish to some extent its authority by influencing the structure of Judaism and of Jewish life ('Rabbinization', p. 69). Schwartz also claims that the importance of rabbis in the late fourth and early fifth centuries was still limited in Palestine (ibid., p. 61). According to Boustan, the increasing influence of rabbis could be dated to the late fifth century ('Afterword: Rabbinization', pp. 436–38).

[148] For the opposite view, see Stemberger, according to whom "Jerome probably had no contacts [with rabbis] at all" ('Exegetical Contacts', p. 583).

are wont to say to their students: οἱ σοφοὶ δευτεροῦσιν, i.e., 'the sages teach traditions' (*sapientes docent traditiones*).[149]

Jerome explained his understanding of the δευτερώσεις through his translation of the verbal form derived from it, δευτεροῦσιν, which he construed as the act of 'teaching traditions'.[150] In this sense, the term δευτερώσεις, which could also be rendered as 'second traditions', but also as 'repetitions' or 'rehearsals', is the Greek equivalent for משניות, the plural of Mishna.[151] Indeed, the

---

[149] *Epist.* 121.10 (VII, pp. 53–54). Jerome occasionally made mention of Jewish sages. Newman argues that, in Jerome, prominent Jewish figures were usually cited as instructors or as spiritual leaders, while their political or administrative status was generally not touched upon ('Jerome and the Jews', pp. 41–42). See also *Comm. Eccl.* 4.13–16 (CCSL 72, p. 288) where Jerome referred to 'Baracchiba', whom Braverman identifies as Rabbi Akiba ben Joseph, the *tanna* of the end of the first century CE (*Jerome's Commentary*, pp. 6–7). According to Newman, however, the identity of Baracchiba is not certain ('Jerome and the Jews', p. 201). See also *Epist.* 121.10 (VII, p. 53) and *Comm. Isa.* 8.11–15 (CCSL 73, p. 116), where Jerome named other illustrious rabbinic figures of the past.

[150] See also Jerome, *Comm. Isa.* 8.11–15 (CCSL 73, p. 116); and *Comm. Matt.* 22.23 (II, p. 150). Eusebius (e.g., *Dem. ev.* 6, 18; PG 22, p. 461B) and Epiphanius (e.g., *Pan.* 33, 9; PG 41, p. 572A) had also employed the word δευτερώσεις, but there is no reason to think that Jerome did not learn it by himself. Nearly a century and a half after his time, Justinian utterly banned the δευτέρωσις (in the singular) from Greek-speaking synagogues (*Nov.* 146, I, 2; p. 716). On Justinian's Novel 146, see de Lange, 'Hebraists and Hellenists'; Smelik, 'Justinian's Novella 146 and Contemporary Judaism'; Juster, *Les Juifs dans l'Empire romain*, I, pp. 369–74.

[151] See Kamesar's observations in 'Rabbinic Midrash and Church Fathers', pp. 20–21.

word 'Mishna' comes from the Hebrew verb שנה, 'to repeat'. While it originally points to a rabbinic method for teaching the oral traditions and laws by recitation, it also came to designate these very traditions and laws, and eventually their compilation in a written form attributed to Rabbi Yehuda ha-Nasi around the end of the second century CE: this collection of texts constitutes a fundamental piece of rabbinic literature. By extension and in a broader sense, the term 'Mishna' has also come to refer to the entire Jewish oral Law. Jerome did not comment at great length on what the δευτερώσεις exactly were to him or on those who imparted them, the δευτερωταί.[152] He said that 'Jews place all the wisdom in the δευτερώσεις' (*Iudaei vocant* δευτερώσεις [...] *in quibus universam scientiam ponunt*);[153] that they were 'Jewish fables' (*iuxta iudaicas fabulas, quas illi* δευτερώσεις *appellant*),[154] and 'fables for old women' (*aniles fabulae*).[155] He called them 'traditions of men' (*traditiones hominum*) and argued that Jews followed them 'while scorning the Law of God' (*contemnentes legem Dei*);[156] and that they "love useless things in caring about the traditions

---

[152] The same way as δευτέρωσις corresponds to the word משנה in Hebrew, the δευτερώτης—δευτερωταί in the plural—is the equivalent of the תנא in Aramaic, from the same root as שנה in Hebrew. The *tannaim* were instructors of the oral law whose teachings have been recorded in the Mishna.

[153] *Epist.* 18.20 (I, p. 76).

[154] *Comm. Ezech.* 36.1–15 (CCSL 75, p. 500).

[155] *Epist.* 121.10 (VII, p. 53).

[156] *Comm. Isa.* 59.12–15 (CCSL 73A, p. 685). See also *Comm. Abac.* 2.9–11 (CCSL 76A, p. 606).

of men and the illusions of the δευτερώσεις (δευτερωσέων *somnia diligentes*)."¹⁵⁷ He also claimed to have heard a "fable" told by "someone from the Hebrews in Lydda, who, as one of their sages, was also called a δευτερώτης;"¹⁵⁸ and that the "δευτερωταί had been fooling the people with the most vicious of traditions (*illudebant populo traditionibus pessimis*)."¹⁵⁹ There could be a giveaway on the identity of the δευτερωταί in *Epist.* 121.10: de Lange observes that

> Jerome's expression *hoi sophoi deuterōsin* closely resembles the common rabbinic formula *tᵉnō rabbanan*, 'our rabbis teach' (always used to introduce a tannaitic teaching). This suggests that *sophos* translates the Hebrew term *rabbi*. It is worth pointing out, however, that more literally *sophoi* translates ḥakamim (sic), which (together with *talmidei ḥakamim*, 'disciples of the sages') is the common designation of Jewish scholars in the rabbinic literature.¹⁶⁰

These Jewish authorities who taught traditions (δευτεροῦσιν / *docent traditiones*) and whom Jerome has portrayed as teachers (*doctores*) and sages (σοφοί / *sapientes*) are usually left unnamed.

---

¹⁵⁷ *Comm. Os.* 3.1 (CCSL 76, p. 33).

¹⁵⁸ *Comm. Abac.* 2.15–17 (CCSL 76A, p. 610). See also *Comm. Isa.* 3.13–14 (CCSL 73, p. 53).

¹⁵⁹ *Comm. Isa.* 29.17–21 (CCSL 73, pp. 379–80). It seems to have been common practice among the Church Fathers to disparage the δευτερώσεις (see Kamesar, 'Rabbinic Midrash and Church Fathers', pp. 33–34).

¹⁶⁰ De Lange, *Origen and the Jews*, p. 35.

While they may not all have represented the rabbinic class of his time (*hodie*),[161] there is no doubt that they included rabbis.[162]

Although, in general, Jerome did not explicitly distinguish Hebrews and Jews as two different groups of people, most of the time these terms had two different meanings for him. This use of the terminology is noticeable across his entire *œuvre*, as the people who passed on Jewish traditions to him were never named 'Jews' but always 'Hebrews'. Aside from the numerous citations of these 'Hebrews' in QHG, Jerome mentioned in a letter, for instance, in a neutral way, that the 'brother' who taught him Hebrew in Chalcis 'used to be a believer among the Hebrews'

---

[161] *Epist.* 121.10 (VII, pp. 53–54).

[162] In Schwartz's view, although the word δευτερώσεις has clear rabbinic associations, it should not be understood as reflecting exclusively the teaching or the activity of rabbis: "That Jerome [...] can use rabbinizing language to describe Jewish religious experts may inform us that rabbis and rabbi-types were becoming important in Jewish religious life by the middle and later fourth century, especially in Palestine, but it may be significant that in only one of his many discussions of the *deuteroseis* does Jerome describe their expositors as important communal functionaries [...]. We should not suppose that they all had strong connections to the rabbinic movement, though some did" (Schwartz, 'Rabbinization', p. 65). See also ibid., pp. 61–65; Lapin, *Rabbis as Romans*, pp. 158–59; Kamesar, 'Rabbinic Midrash and Church Fathers', pp. 33–34; Newman, 'The Normativity of Rabbinic Judaism', pp. 169–70 and 'Jerome and the Jews', pp. 49–51 and p. 201; and Weigert, *Hebraica Veritas*, pp. 79–82.

(*cuidam fratri, qui ex Hebraeis crediderat*), that is, a Jew who converted to Christianity.[163] In the preface to the Vulgate of Job, he also claimed that the man from Lydda whose lesson he bought "for no small amount"—so that he might help him understand the Book of Job—was 'an instructor who was thought to have the highest of ranks among the Hebrews' (*lyddeum quemdam praeceptorem qui apud Hebraeos primas habere putabatur*).[164] In his commentary on the Book of Ecclesiastes, a man whom he claimed to 'often cite' he called 'my Hebrew' (*Hebraeus meus, cuius saepe facio mentionem*).[165] In the preface to his revision of the VL Book of Chronicles, he said that "the most learned Hebrews" and, in particular, "an expert in the Law from Tiberias who was held in high esteem by the Hebrews," had been his assistants in the undertaking of amending the VL version of Chronicles: "if anyone wishes to find fault with this translation on any account, let him

---

[163] *Epist.* 125.12 (VII, pp. 124–25) (see Newman's observations in 'Jerome and the Jews', p. 52). Jerome also alluded to a teacher of his who seems to have been a Christian held in very high regard among Jews for his proficiency in Hebrew: "But there is someone from whom I am personally happy to have learned a great many things, and who has honed [his] Hebrew so much that he is regarded as a Chaldean among their scribes" (*Epist.* 18.10; I, p. 65).

[164] Vulg., p. 731. Krauss claims to have identified this instructor (whose name he believed to be 'Lyddaeus') in several other passages where Jerome cited a teacher of his (Krauss, 'Jerome', p. 116). However, in none of these passages did Jerome name the Hebrew on whom he was relying.

[165] *Comm. Eccl.* 4.13–16 (CCSL 72, p. 288).

ask the Hebrews!"¹⁶⁶ It is worth raising the question of how Jerome communicated with these teachers, and with his informants in general. A comment that he made in 407, in his commentary on the Book of Daniel, on וּשְׁחִיתָה ('fault') in Dan. 6.5, may indicate that his exchanges with his Hebrew instructors in Bethlehem were carried out in Greek:

> Instead of 'suspicion' (*pro suspicione*), Theodotion and Aquila have rendered ἀμβλάκημα (i.e., a fault), which in Aramaic is called *essaitha* (i.e., וּשְׁחִיתָה). But as I asked from a Hebrew what it meant, he answered that the sense of the word signified (*vim verbi sonare*) δέλεαρ, which we can call 'an enticement' (*illecebram*), or σφάλμα, that is, 'an error' (*errorem*).¹⁶⁷

In his commentary on Ezekiel, he made a similar remark about the word קֶסֶת ('inkhorn') in Ezek. 9.3:

> Aquila [...] and Theodotion said κάστυ, instead of which in Hebrew it is written *cesath*. When I asked the Hebrew what it meant, he answered me: 'In the Greek tongue, it is called καλαμάριον (i.e., a reed-pen case) (*graeco sermone appellari* καλαμάριον): [it was named] after the thing in which reed-pens (*calami*) are sheathed.'¹⁶⁸

---

¹⁶⁶ My translation of the preface edited by Canellis in *Préfaces*, pp. 340–46. See also Jerome's preface to his commentary on Hosea (*Comm. Os.*; CCSL 76, p. 5); and *Epist.* 73.9 (IV, p. 25).

¹⁶⁷ *Comm. Dan.* 6.4c (p. 264).

¹⁶⁸ *Comm. Ezech.* 9.2–3 (CCSL 75, p. 105). Graves also argues that Jerome is likely to have communicated with his Hebrew teachers and to have been taught Hebrew in Greek (Graves, *Jerome's Hebrew*, pp. 84–85). See also Stemberger, 'Exegetical Contacts', p. 582.

When Jerome employed the term 'Jew', whether for contemporaries or figures of the past, it usually had very derogatory connotations and it was frequently associated with blameworthy behaviour and with evil traits, such as the propensity for proselytising. For example, in *Epist.* 112, Jews, not Hebrews, were portrayed in colourful ways:

> But if we are forced to receive the Jews with their principles (*cum legitimis suis*), and if they are permitted to observe in the churches of the Christ [the rules] that they have been following in the synagogues of Satan, I shall tell you how I feel: they will not become Christians, but they will make us into Jews (*non illi Christiani fient, sed nos Iudaeos facient*).[169]

Likewise, in *Epist.* 121, Jerome described the Pharisees and their successors, the Jews of his time, as 'a hostile race' (*gentis inimicae*) of people who appointed 'most wise men' (*sapientissimos quosque*) to their synagogues to taste the blood of maidens and check its purity.[170] In *Epist.* 84, by way of justification for having mingled with Baranina, a 'Jew', he also explained that this man happened to be his master in Jerusalem and in Bethlehem. He added that his Hebrew lessons came at a price for him (*quo pretio*),[171] but also for the instructor himself who dreaded the reaction of his coreligionists. He concluded as follows:

---

[169] *Epist.* 112.13 (VI, p. 32).

[170] *Epist.* 121.10 (VII, p. 53). On this passage, see Newman, 'Jerome and the Jews', pp. 41–42.

[171] See also *Ruf.*, II, 35 (p. 198).

> If it is expedient to loathe men and to detest a certain people, [then] I shun the circumcised (*circumcisos*) with the utmost hatred. Indeed, up to this day, they persecute our Lord, Jesus Christ, in the synagogues of Satan... [Given my stance,] if I had a Jewish man (*hominem Judaeum*) as a teacher, could anyone question my motives?[172]

Less common in Jerome was the use of the term 'Jews' to refer to the ancient Israelites from the Old Testament.[173] On the rare occasions when he cited both Hebrews and Jews interchangeably within a short compass, it was in a way that spared the former and stressed the immorality of the latter.[174] When speaking of Paul the Apostle, he exceptionally happened to use the terms 'Hebrew', 'Israelite' and 'Jew' in a synonymous way.[175] Finally, his

---

[172] *Epist.* 84.3 (IV, p. 127). See also Condamin, 'L'influence de la tradition juive', pp. 3–4.

[173] See for example *Comm. Isa.* 22.15–25 (CCSL 73, p. 305), or *Comm. Dan.* 2.48 (p. 182) and 4.24b (p. 232). While still employing the word *iudaeus*, Jerome may have made a tacit distinction between Jews and Judeans in certain contexts: in *Comm. Dan.* 9.24a (p. 398) for example, he clearly associated Jews / Judeans with the land of 'Judea' (*Iudaea*). This is perhaps illustrated, too, in the Vulgate Book of Esther, in which he consistently translated the word יהודי 'Jew / Judean' with *iudaeus* (see for instance Vulg. Est. 2.5 or 4.7).

[174] See, for instance, *Epist.* 112.20–22 (VI, pp. 41–43).

[175] *Comm. Phlm.* 23–24 (CCSL 77C, pp. 103–4): '[Paul] testified about himself: 'They are Hebrews, so am I; they are Israelites, so am I; they are the seed of Abraham, so am I'. And again elsewhere [he said] '[I am] a Hebrew from the Hebrews', as well as other things that indicate that he was a Jew more than a man of Tarsus' (*de se ipse testatur*: '*Hebraei sunt, et ego; Israhelitae sunt, et ego; semen Abrahae sunt, et ego*'; *et rursum*

calling Philo 'the most eloquent man among the Jews' (*vir disertissimus Iudaeorum*), without any derogatory connotations, is one of a few exceptions.[176] Even though in most cases it seems that he could have acknowledged that Hebrews and Jews corresponded to the same people, he often employed the former term for those of his contemporaries who could speak the holy language, and occasionally for the ancient Israelites and for those whom he considered to be their true successors, i.e., the Apostles (who not only shared the Israelites' tongue but who had lived in accordance with their principles).[177] The term 'Jews', when not applied to the Israelites, he confined to what he regarded as a community of immoral individuals who had failed to acknowledge the Christ, and whose beliefs and practices insulted the dogmas of Christians and threatened the stability of church life.[178]

---

alibi: '*Hebraeus ex Hebraeis*', *et cetera quae illum Iudaeum magis indicant quam Tharsensem*).

[176] See *Comm. Ezech.* 16.10b (CCSL 75, p. 171); and the preface to *Nom. hebr.* (CCSL 72, p. 59).

[177] As shown in *Epist.* 121.2 (VII, p. 15) and in *Epist.* 121.10 (VII, p. 47), Jerome preferred calling the Apostles 'Hebrews' rather than 'Jews' (see my fn. 135).

[178] See for example *Comm. Eccl.* 4.13–16 (CCSL 72, p. 290). Jerome's conception of Jews and Hebrews probably depended to some extent on Origen's (de Lange, *Origen and the Jews*, pp. 29–33) and Eusebius' (Weigert, *Hebraica Veritas*, pp. 69–71). De Lange argues (*Origen and the Jews*, p. 30): "With [Origen's] use of *Hebraioi* we may contrast that of *Ioudaioi*. If the connotations of *Hebraioi* are philological, those of *Ioudaioi* are polemical." See also Courtray's understanding of this distinction in Jerome's terminology, in *Prophète*, pp. 234–35.

It is noteworthy that the traditions of Jerome's Hebrews occasionally agree with material that has reached us in various Midrashim and Targumim (see 2.2.4 below). In QHG, the material that he quoted in the name of Hebrews was brought to his attention by informants, often described as acquaintances and instructors.[179] Accordingly, his conception of a 'Hebrew truth' was a method of scriptural hermeneutics that adduced material not just from the Hebrew Bible, but from Hebrew sources in the more general sense. The fact that these sources should not be viewed as Jewish but, more specifically, as Hebraic, is particularly noticeable in an exchange with Augustine. In a letter addressed to Jerome, Augustine told of a bishop of the city of Oea, modern Tripoli, who, by reading Jerome's translation of the Hebrew Book of Jonah in church and by giving a sermon based on it, caused a

---

[179] In QHG, the circumstances in which Jerome gained access to Jewish traditions are never specified. They are unlikely to have reached him through compendia like today's editions of Midrashim and Targumim. See Cameron, 'The Rabbinic Vulgate?', p. 126; Kraus, 'Rabbinic Traditions in Jerome', p. 540, and the literature cited ibid. in fn. 2; and Hayward, 'Saint Jerome and the Aramaic Targumim', pp. 120–23. Alexander points out that "we need not suppose that Jerome himself would have had access directly to a written copy of the Targum, which in his day would have circulated primarily in oral form" (Alexander, 'The Cultural History', p. 93). He further argues that the fact that much of the Jewish exegesis reflected in the Vulgate Book of Lamentations conforms with the Midrash rather than with the Targum suggests that the latter did not exist yet in Jerome's time: "If a Targum of the book was extant, it is hard to see why [Jerome's informants] would not have known it [...] given the Targum's role in Jewish liturgy and education" (Alexander, 'The Cultural History', pp. 93–94).

commotion among the congregants. The congregation was said to have reacted with vehement opposition to a particular passage in Jerome's translation because it differed from the version to which they were accustomed. When the bishop called on Jews to adjudicate the dispute, wrote Augustine, these concluded, obviously not "out of ignorance or malice," that the Greek and Old Latin versions agreed with the Hebrew text: in other words, Jerome's translation, which had been proved wrong by Jews, was necessarily faulty.[180] "Won't we be able to find any [Jew] who might have some knowledge of the Hebrew tongue?" replied Jerome, "Or will they all imitate these Jews who were found, as you say, in a little town in Africa, and who conspired to defame me?"[181] In his view, it was precisely out of "malice or ignorance" that 'Augustine's Jews' (*Iudaei vestri*) claimed that the original Hebrew scrolls and the Greek and Old Latin codices agreed against his new translation of the Hebrew. Indeed, for him, it was evidence either that these Jews could not read Hebrew (*manifestum est eos aut Hebraeas litteras ignorare*), or that they lied to the bishop of Oea so as to make fun of his community and their

---

[180] *Epist.* 104.5. This passage of Augustine's letter can be found in Labourt's edition of Jerome's correspondence (*Saint Jérôme: Correspondance*, V, pp. 98–99).

[181] *Epist.* 112.21 (VI, p. 41). For Jerome, who reproached Augustine for not pointing out the exact passage which he had allegedly mistranslated, the cause of this strife was his rendering of קִיקָיוֹן as *hedera* ('ivy') in Vulg. Jonah 4.6 (*Epist.* 112.22; VI, p. 42). The Hebrew was rendered as κολοκύνθη 'gourd' in the LXX, and accordingly as *cucurbita* in the VL.

translation of Jonah (*aut ad inridendos cucurbitarios voluisse mentiri*), or that Augustine had fabricated the story (*ut ipse adseris*).¹⁸² At any rate, Jerome's response showed that he had no interest in the opinion of Jews who might not know Hebrew.¹⁸³ He was offering a specific definition of the *hebraica veritas* to his readership in this regard: those who could read and understand Hebrew (and Aramaic) knew best how to interpret Scripture through the Hebrew Bible, as opposed to most Church exegetes operating through the LXX or the VL. He openly communicated this belief at the outset of the Vulgate project, in his preface to the Pentateuch.¹⁸⁴ In the preface to the Vulgate of Ezra, he further asserted that, beyond the LXX, even the Greek translations found in the Hexapla would be potentially misleading to anyone who did not have a good command of Hebrew:

---

¹⁸² *Epist.* 112.22 (VI, pp. 42–43).

¹⁸³ Latin was then the vernacular of African Jews. There is now a consensus that they probably did not know Greek or Hebrew; and if they did, it must have been to a very limited extent. On the languages used by the Jewish communities in Roman Africa, see Blondheim, *Les parlers judéo-romans*, pp. XXVIII–XXX; Le Bohec, *Les Juifs dans l'Afrique romaine*, pp. 86–87; Kraus, 'Hebraisms in the Old Latin', pp. 511–13; Binder and Villey, 'Jewish Communities in North Africa', pp. 529–30. Juster also argues that it was probably mandatory for Jews who were Roman citizens to know Latin (*Les Juifs dans l'Empire romain*, I, p. 366, fn. 2). On the use of the VL among Latin-speaking Jews, see also Kraus, 'Hebraisms in the Old Latin', pp. 511–13; and Houghton, 'Scripture and Latin Christian Manuscripts', pp. 19–20.

¹⁸⁴ Vulg., pp. 3–4. I have partly translated this preface in section 1.4. See also my fn. 137.

Firstly, the potential acquisition of all the [Hexapla] versions (*exemplaria omnia*) actually comes at a great cost and with infinite difficulty;[185] secondly, those who will have acquired [them], but who do not know the Hebrew tongue, will err all the more because they do not know which of the several [translators] may have spoken more truthfully (*quis e multis verius dixerit*).[186] This even happened not so

---

[185] Jerome occasionally alluded to the expensiveness of the Hexapla: see for example the passage from *Ruf.*, II, 34 (p. 194) translated in my fn. 186. In the preface to the Vulgate Book of Joshua, he even presented this financial argument as a significant incentive for the Christian audience to buy his translation instead of a variety of different Bible versions: "I offer to men of my language [...] [the opportunity] to own my edition, instead of the Greeks' Hexapla, which require both a great deal of money and a lot of work" (Vulg., p. 285). Jerome's hostility towards a certain traffic in luxurious editions of the Bible is reminiscent of this point (see my fn. 103). His statements also shed light on the transmission history of the Hexapla, each of whose translations may have circulated as single, separate versions, rather than in pandects. For a discussion of Jerome's access to the Hexapla, see Williams, *The Monk and the Book*, pp. 147–54 and p. 175; Grafton and Williams, *Christianity and the Transformation of the Book*, pp. 178–84; and Ceulemans' remarks in 'Greek Christian Access', pp. 181–83.

[186] Jerome's way of referring to the translators (*e multis*) whose versions were found in the Hexapla points to the *recentiores* but also to alternative interpreters. He generally presented these interpreters as anonymous Jews whose translations constituted additional columns in Origen's compilation. See, for example, the preface to his translation of Eusebius' *Chronicon*: "The holy books [...] that were produced by the Seventy translators do not retain the same flavour in the Greek language [as in the Hebrew]. For this reason, Aquila, Symmachus and Theodotion were incited to publish works that were somewhat different [although they were based] on the same work [...]. As for the fifth, the sixth, and

1. Introduction

long ago to a certain man [known for being] most wise among the Greeks,[187] who went as far as to follow the erring of some translator—who knows which one (*uniuscuiuslibet interpretis sequeretur errorem*)—while occasionally leaving aside the sense of Scripture! I, on the other hand, at least have a slight knowledge of the Hebrew language, and my Latin is not lacking by any means: I am more capable of settling [the disputes among] the alternative [translators] (lit., the others) (*de aliis magis possumus iudicare*)[188] and of expressing those of the things that I understand [from Hebrew] in my [own] language.[189]

---

the seventh edition, although we do not know who their authors are supposed to be, still, they differ [from one another] to such a remarkable extent (*ita probabilem sui diversitatem tenent*) that they have earned [their] nameless authority" (Jerome's preface to *Chron.*, 3; p. 56). See also *Ruf.*, II, 34 (p. 194): "You have bought at a great cost, as I know, [the translations of] Aquila, Symmachus and Theodotion, as well as [those of] the Jewish translators of the fifth and sixth editions (*quintaeque et sextae editionis iudaicos translatores*)." For further discussion of the additional columns in Origen's work, see Field's preface to his edition of the Hexapla, I, pp. xlii–xlvi; and Grafton and Williams, *Christianity and the Transformation of the Book*, p. 89.

[187] According to Canellis, this is an allusion to Apollinaris of Laodicea (*Préfaces*, p. 366, fn. 2). See Jerome's remarks on Apollinaris in *Ruf.*, II, 34 (p. 196).

[188] The expression 'the others' (*de aliis*) had a precise meaning: it is a technical term that points to the Greek translators that are found in the Hexapla and who are not the Septuagint ones, i.e., generally the *recentiores*, here the *recentiores* together with the anonymous Jewish interpreters (see fn. 186).

[189] *Vulg.*, p. 639. See also Jerome's preface to the Vulgate Book of Joshua: "Among the Latins, there are as many versions as there are

Those whom Jerome called 'the Hebrews' played a fundamental part in his advocacy of the Hebrew language and of the Hebrew text. As he was consistently reproached, throughout his entire career and by various opponents, for opposing the LXX in his translation of the Hebrew Bible, his defence could go as follows: "If anywhere I seem to you to be mistaken in [my] translation, ask the Hebrews! Consult the teachers of the various cities!"[190] He expressed himself in similar terms in his response to Augustine's accusations:

> But what kind of interpretation should be followed in the Holy Scriptures? The book that I wrote *On the Best Method of Translating* as well as all the tiny prefaces to the divine volumes that I have prefixed to my edition explain this.[191] [...] And if, as you say, you accept my way of amending the New Testament, [...] likewise, you must have believed

manuscripts (*apud Latinos tot sint exemplaria quot codices*), and everyone either added or deleted what he pleased, as he saw fit: assuredly, what is true cannot vary (lit., what disagrees cannot be true) (*utique non possit verum esse quod dissonet*)" (Vulg., p. 285). These excerpts show that Jerome's attitude to the coexistence of different biblical versions was the opposite of Augustine's: "[The existence of different Old Latin versions] has certainly helped to understand [the Scriptures] more than it has hindered. [...] Actually, examining multiple manuscripts has often [enabled me to] clarify some very obscure sentences. [...] From each [translator] something great is imparted to those who read carefully" (Augustine, *Doctr. chr.* 2, 11–12, 16–17 [CCSL 32, p. 42]).

[190] Vulg., p. 4.

[191] The 'book' in question, *On the Best Method of Translating*, corresponds to a letter that Jerome addressed to Pammachius in 395–396: *Epist.* 57 (III, pp. 55–73). See my discussion in section 1.8 below.

1. Introduction

> in the same integrity regarding [my rendering of] the Old Testament (*eadem integritatem debueras etiam in veteri credere testamento*), namely, that I have not fabricated my own [interpretations], but as I have found them in the Hebrews, so have I translated these holy matters (*divina*). If ever you doubt it, ask the Hebrews![192]

Equally noteworthy, on other occasions, he argued the following:

> By all means, if you are not convinced, read the Greek manuscripts and the Latin ones and compare them with these opuscules [of mine], and wherever you may see that they are at variance with each other, ask anyone among the Hebrews in whom you feel like placing your trust.[193]

> So wherever my work might disagree with the ancient ones (i.e., the LXX translators), ask any of the Hebrews and you will clearly realise that I am abused by rivals for no reason.[194]

Jerome could also rely on the authority of the *recentiores* to further defend and promote that of the 'Hebrews' among Latin Christians:

> Our Latins, envious Christians really, [...] bark at us: why should we discuss [these matters] according to the Hebrew [...]? If they do not place their trust in me, they certainly read the other editions: those of Aquila, Symmachus and Theodotion. Let them ask the Hebrews (not just from one place—lest they start telling that these ones were bought off by me—but from a variety of provinces)! And when they see that all [the Hebrews] agree with my 'error' and

---

[192] *Epist.* 112.20 (VI, pp. 40–41).

[193] Vulg., pp. 365–66.

[194] Vulg., p. 768.

my 'ignorance', then let them understand that they themselves are far too intelligent, and that they desire to sleep, more so than to learn.[195]

The principle according to which the authority of 'Hebrews', beyond the Hebrew text itself, underlies the *hebraica veritas*, was clearly articulated in QHG:

> Because this little work of ours is, once again, a collection of Hebraic inquiries or traditions (*vel quaestionum hebraicarum vel traditionum congregatio est*), let us therefore adduce what the Hebrews think about this (*quid Hebraei de hoc sentiant*).[196]

7.0. Some Observations on Jerome's Relationship with the LXX

In the preface to the Vulgate Book of Job, Jerome said: "I am forced, through each and every book of holy Scripture, to respond to the slanders of objectors, who accuse my translation of being a reproof of the Seventy translators."[197] In the same vein, in the preface to the Vulgate Book of Kings, he asked his reader to trust that he did not mean to disparage the LXX translators: "I beseech you, O reader, do not take my work as a reproof of the ancient ones!"[198] Rufinus' charge against Jerome's position shows well

---

[195] *Comm. Ezech.* 33.23–33 (CCSL 75, p. 475).

[196] QHG 14.18–19 (p. 24).

[197] Vulg., p. 731.

[198] Vulg., p. 365. Relevant, too, are Jerome's prefaces to QHG (pp. 1–3), to the Vulgate of Chronicles (Vulg., pp. 546–47), to the Vulgate of Ezra (Vulg., pp. 638–39), and to the Vulgate of Job (Vulg., p. 732), as well as *Epist.* 57.9–11 (III, pp. 67–71), his response to Augustine (*Epist.*

how close it came to being seen as an act of heresy.[199] At least as early as 383, Jerome said that he conceived of the Hebrew text as a "fountainhead" that conveyed the original and true meaning of Scripture,[200] which can explain in itself why he later became the target of many persisting polemics. Although he consistently denied ever doubting the authority of the LXX, his actual stance on the matter was not always plain or coherent: it could be difficult to disentangle and somewhat fluctuating. As a matter of fact, from the late 380s on, Jerome began to advance theories which openly questioned the accuracy or the quality of the LXX as a translation of the Hebrew, and which routinely presented it as a deceitful version of Scripture in light of the Hebrew truth.[201] In the early 390s, for instance, in the preface to QHG, he overtly argued that the LXX translators had introduced, on purpose, blatant inaccuracies into their work. They sought, in his view, to

---

112.19–22; VI, pp. 38–43), and his remarks in *Comm. Ezech.* 33.23–33 (CCSL 75, p. 475).

[199] See Rufinus, *Apol. Hier.*, II, 39 (CCSL 20, p. 114). Jerome pleaded his case in the *Apology against Rufinus* (*Ruf.*, II, 33; pp. 192–94). These exchanges are introduced and addressed at greater length in the introduction to chapter 3 of this monograph.

[200] See *Epist.* 20.2 (I, p. 79).

[201] Before the second half of the 380s, it does not seem that Jerome had expressed any doubt yet about the reliability or the validity of the LXX. I agree to this extent with Schwarz (*Principles and Problems of Biblical Translation*, p. 28) and Braverman (*Jerome's Commentary*, p. 26, fn. 41), according to whom, in 384, Jerome probably still had not made up his mind about the significance of the differences between the LXX and the Hebrew text.

hide the 'mysteries' (*mystica*) announcing the coming of the Christ in the original Hebrew text.[202] This was done to ensure that Ptolemy who, as "a follower of Plato, thought highly of the Jews for worshipping one single god," would not see them as worshippers of a second god in the Christ.[203]

Between the late 380s and the end of his career in the 410s, however, Jerome could refine his views on the LXX in making a distinction between the original work of the translators and what the text itself had become in his time. Indeed, if he blamed the translators for their omissions, he also frequently accused the copyists of having corrupted the manuscripts. In the preface to his revision of the VL of Chronicles, around 386–389, he declared that,

> in the Greek and Latin manuscripts (*in Graecis et in Latinis codicibus*), this book of names is corrupt (*vitiosus est*), so much so that it should not be considered as a list of Hebrew names, but of barbarous and Sarmatian (*Sarmatica*) ones. The Seventy translators are not to blame for this: filled with the Holy Spirit (*Spiritu Sancto pleni*), they translated things that were true. No, [in fact,] it is the fault of the scribes (*sed scriptorum culpae adscribendum*), who copy out

---

[202] See also *Epist.* 57.7 (III, pp. 64–65). Jerome's conception of the 'mysteries' of the Old Testament is further addressed in the next section of this monograph (section 1.8).

[203] QHG, p. 2. This view was repeated in the Vulgate preface to the Pentateuch. In this preface, Jerome also suggested that the LXX translators may not have been deceitful but simply ignorant, since they translated the Old Testament "before the coming of the Christ" (Vulg., pp. 3–4; see my translation below). See Kamesar's remarks on Jerome's treatment of this subject in *Jerome*, pp. 64–66.

incorrect [writings] from incorrect [manuscripts] (*de inemendatis inemendata scriptitant*).²⁰⁴

Similarly, in the early 390s, in the preface to the Vulgate Book of Job, Jerome's attempt to justify the condemnation of the LXX and of the VL targeted above all the scribes' work and, by extension, the transmission process. The LXX translation itself, though not entirely spared, was presented in a comparatively milder way:

> Let my dogs hear that I have toiled over this volume, not to criticise the old translation (i.e., the LXX) (*non ut interpretationem antiquam reprehenderem*), but so that those things in it that are either obscure (*obscura*) or missing (*omissa*), or certainly (*certe*) those that have been distorted as a result of the scribes' corruption (*scriptorum vitio depravata*), might become more visible through our translation (i.e., the Vulgate).²⁰⁵

Jerome used this preface to repeat that he did not mean "to criticise" the LXX, and he indeed softened his usual criticisms of the Greek text: in comparison with what could have been "either ob-

---

[204] My translation of the preface edited by Canellis in *Préfaces*, p. 342. The variant *de emendatis* 'from correct [manuscripts]' was proposed by Migne, instead of *de inemendatis* 'from incorrect [manuscripts]' (PL 29, p. 402A). In either case, the conclusion is the same. Indeed, Canellis' version indicates that scribes 'reproduced' (*scriptitant*) 'incorrect' readings from manuscripts that were already contaminated with scribal inaccuracies. Likewise, Migne's variant signifies that the scribes are responsible for introducing incorrect readings, while their *Vorlage* was not initially flawed (i.e., it contained the accurate, original LXX translation). Either way, the scribes are at fault, not the translators.

[205] Vulg., p. 732.

scure or missing" in it, the distortions due to the "scribes' corruption" were 'certain' (*certe*). To be sure, here, as in his other prefaces, his priority was the advocacy of his own work, which he tried to pursue without sounding overly controversial: ascribing errors or corruptions to those who had been in charge of transmitting the text was less polemical, in this sense, than attacking the original translation frontally. However, when criticising the textual transmission of the LXX, Jerome did not always make it clear whether he meant the Greek chain or the Old Latin one, or both; whether he had the copyists in mind, or the VL translators and revisers, was not necessarily plain either. As seen above, in the context of his revision of the VL of Chronicles, he simply spoke of "the scribes," without specifying which ones (*scriptorum culpae*): after mentioning the Seventy translators, he may have meant to decry the Greek scribes, but it is also possible that the work of the Old Latin ones was equally condemned (*in Graecis et in Latinis codicibus*). In the preface to his revision of the VL Books of Solomon, written in the late 380s, he preferred to put the emphasis on the role of the Old Latin translators, whom he disparaged for being 'inexperienced' (*imperiti translatores*) and for having 'poorly rendered the Greek' (*male in linguam nostram de Graeco sermone verterant*).[206] In the mid-390s, in his preface to the Vulgate of Ezra, he argued that the LXX of Ezra varied so much across the multitude of manuscripts in circulation that the text

---

[206] This preface is edited by Canellis in *Préfaces*, pp. 422–24. The so-called 'Books of Solomon' correspond to the Books of Proverbs, Ecclesiastes, Song of Songs, Wisdom of Solomon, and Sirach. Here, Jerome meant the Latin translators of the first three LXX books.

which they were supposed to display had to be "mutilated and ruined" (*Septuaginta [...] interpretes, quorum exemplaria varietas ipsa lacerata et eversa demonstrat*). Earlier in the same preface, however, the Greek and Old Latin scrolls were mentioned alongside each other (*graeca et latina volumina*), which may indicate that Jerome's remark was in fact directed both at the LXX manuscripts and at the VL ones.[207] In the late 390s, in the preface to the Vulgate Book of Chronicles, he accused "the scribes" again, i.e., without naming the Greek or the Old Latin ones (*quae scriptorum confusa sunt vitio*); the fact that he had also extensively discussed the reception and transmission history of the Greek text, though, could suggest that he was thinking of the Greek scribes.[208] On the other hand, around 405, in the preface to the Vulgate Book of Joshua, he attacked the Old Latin chain of Scripture transmission: "Among the Latins, there are as many versions as there are manuscripts (*apud Latinos tot sint exemplaria quot codices*), and everyone either added or deleted what he pleased, as he saw fit (*unusquisque pro arbitrio suo vel addiderit vel subtraxerit quod ei visum est*)."[209] By choosing to attribute mistakes to the

---

[207] Vulg., p. 638.

[208] Vulg., pp. 546–47. The LXX translation was described here as originally 'pure' when the translators 'rendered [the Hebrew] into Greek' (*pura [...] ab eis in graecum versa est editio*); at the same time, Jerome argued that the LXX translators also omitted a number of passages from the Hebrew. The preface to the Vulgate Book of Chronicles is partly translated in section 1.5 and in fn. 216 of this monograph. See also *Epist.* 112.19 (VI, p. 39).

[209] Vulg., p. 285. Technically, by 'everyone', Jerome could have meant the VL interpreters just as much as the VL scribes. However, in this case,

scribes (whether the Greek or the Old Latin ones) or to the VL translators and revisers—rather than to the LXX translators—Jerome probably hoped to appease, to some extent, the Christian readership with regard to what he depicted as corruptions or inaccuracies in the text. He certainly endeavoured to advance the idea that many errors were due to the incompetence of the copyists and of the VL translators and revisers. Yet he was wont to assert that the LXX translators, too, were responsible for certain departures (which, by contrast, he often presented as theologically or politically motivated). Even at a very late stage in his career, though, Jerome still adopted, from time to time, an intermediate approach, not knowing whether to blame the LXX translators for their omissions or the scribes for their mistakes. In 414, in his commentary on Ezekiel, he wrote:

> First, it should be known that more or less eight verses from this passage [...] are not contained in the Septuagint: [the translators] have omitted (*praetermiserunt*) them as well as many others; unless things that were translated by

---

he may have had the latter group in mind: indeed, the scribes could be accused of 'deleting' (*subtraxerit*) portions of the text (see below) but also of 'adding' (*addiderit*) material to it (see Jerome's preface to his revision of the Latin Gospels [Vulg., p. 1515], partly translated in section 1.4). Here, the vagueness of Jerome's remark may ultimately reflect an inability to ascertain who, in the transmission process, was to be held accountable for textual alterations. See also his preface to the Vulgate of Job (Vulg., p. 731).

them were removed (*sublata sunt*) little by little (*paulatim*) through the corruption of scribes (*scriptorum vitio*).[210]

Here, with this late remark, Jerome confirmed that he was not always able to make up his mind on the origin of what he perceived as omissions or corruptions in the LXX.

It is noteworthy that, while openly addressing the inaccuracies of the LXX, he could also attempt to explain why this version had been uninterruptedly employed in the Church:

> It would take a long time to enumerate now all the things that the Seventy [translators] added and omitted on their own initiative, [and] which have been marked with obeli and asterisks in the copies of the Church. [...] But how shall we deal with the authentic books [then], which do not contain these additions [...]? If we were to endeavour to spell it out, it would take [us] countless books. Furthermore, as I said, the asterisks [already] attest to all their omissions, and so does our translation (should it be compared with the old version by a careful reader). Nonetheless, the Septuagint edition has rightfully prevailed in churches (*et tamen iure Septuaginta editio obtinuit in ecclesiis*), either because it is the first one and it was (lit., is) produced before the coming of the Christ (*vel quia prima est et ante Christi fertur adventum*), or because the apostles made use of it (*vel quia ab apostolis usurpata*), at least in the passages where it is not at variance with the Hebrew edition.[211]

---

[210] *Comm. Ezech.* 33.23–33 (CCSL 75, p. 475). For the date of composition of the commentary, see Kelly, *Jerome*, p. 306.

[211] *Epist.* 57.11 (III, pp. 70–71).

After having actively undermined the credibility of the Seventy translators, Jerome could still declare that the LXX had "rightfully (*iure*) prevailed in churches." This was not so much a way of recanting his stance, however, as a diplomatic answer to detractors whom he meant to soothe: "The edition of the Seventy translators, which has been strengthened by the seniority of its readers (*quae legentium vetustate firmata est*), is useful to the Churches (*utilem esse Ecclesiis*)."[212] To be sure, Jerome did not consider the LXX a divinely inspired work: his defence of its use was mostly based on the longevity of the practice, not on the accuracy of the text. In 395–396, for instance, he suggested, by way of a citation of the Epistle of James, that the Seventy translators should not be "repudiated" but "forgiven," as they were no more than "men:" 'we all make a lot of mistakes' (*multa peccamus omnes*) (Jac. 3.2).[213] Likewise, in the late 390s, a decade after saying that the Seventy, "filled with the Holy Spirit, translated things that were true" (see above), he called into question their sacred status and their reputation as 'prophetic' authors:

> I do not know which author, with his lie[s], first fabricated the [so-called] 'seventy cells of Alexandria' (*septuaginta cellulas Alexandriae mendacio suo extruxerit*), in which [the LXX translators] [are supposed to] have been scattered and [to] have written down identical things (*quibus divisi eadem scriptitarint*). [...] Aristeas [...] and, long after, Josephus reported nothing of the sort, but wrote that [the LXX translators], while gathered in a single basilica, had compared [their work], not that they had prophesied (*contulisse, non*

---

[212] Jerome, *Ruf.*, II, 35 (p. 198). See also *Epist.* 106.46 (V, p. 125).

[213] *Epist.* 57.7 (III, p. 64).

prophetasse). For it is one thing to be a seer (*vatem*), it is another thing to be a translator (*interpretem*): in the former case, the spirit predicts things to come; in the latter, education and a rich vocabulary communicate whatever they [can] grasp... unless, of course, Cicero should have been regarded as inspired by the spirit of rhetoric (*afflatus rethorico* [sic] *spiritu*) when translating the *Oeconomicus* of Xenophon, the *Protagoras* of Plato, and *For Ctesiphon* by Demosthenes! Or [is it that] the Holy Spirit wove together attestations of the same books in a certain way through the Seventy translators, [and] in another through the Apostles? Thus the former remained silent about something [but] the latter could assert falsely that it was written (*ut quod illi tacuerunt, hii scriptum esse mentiti sint*)? [...] [The Seventy] translated before the coming of the Christ: what they could not have known (lit., what they did not know) they expressed in doubtful terms (*dubiis protulere sententiis*).[214]

Finally, around 400, after claiming in a letter to resort to the "Hebrew truth" in case of "disagreement between the Greek and Latin" texts, Jerome established a hierarchy between two types of Greek textual traditions and the original Hebrew version of Scripture. From least to most reliable, they were the following: the edition that "all Greek authors call Κοινή (*sic*)"—meaning 'common' (*communis*) or 'spread' (*vulgata*)[215]—which "many now

---

[214] Vulg., pp. 3–4. On the legend of the cells in which the LXX translators were said to have operated, see Wasserstein and Wasserstein, *The Legend of the Septuagint*, pp. 106–25.

[215] The singular form *vulgata* here functioned as a synonym for *communis*; Jerome employed it to refer to the LXX (see fn. 107).

name Λουκιάνειος (sic),"²¹⁶ corresponds to the 'old edition' (*vetus editio*) of the LXX which was corrupted from place to place, over the course of time, as the scribes pleased (*pro voluntate scriptorum*); the original translation of the LXX interpreters, which is displayed in the Hexapla, 'is preserved uncorrupted and untainted in the books of scholars' (*in eruditorum libris incorrupta et inmaculata*); and finally the 'authority of the Hebrews' (*Hebraeorum auctoritas*), i.e., the Hebrew text, is the 'fountainhead' of the

---

²¹⁶ Jerome mentioned the 'Lucianic' edition in the preface to the Vulgate Book of Chronicles, as he identified three types of LXX recensions in circulation (among which the one associated with Palestinian manuscripts was supposed to have served as Origen's base text). He called this phenomenon the *trifaria varietas*: "Now, in fact, since different versions, varying from region to region, are in circulation (*pro varietate regionum diversa ferantur exemplaria*), and since this genuine and ancient translation has been corrupted and violated, you think that it is up to us either to determine which one might be the true one out of [so] many, or to compose a new work [which might replace] the old work (*novum opus in veteri opere condere*) [...]. Alexandria as well as Egypt praise Hesychius as the author of their Septuagint; Constantinople, through to Antioch, approve the versions of Lucian the martyr; the provinces in the middle, those between these [regions], read the Palestinian manuscripts (*palestinos codices*), which Eusebius and Pamphilius published after Origen worked on them. And all [the regions of] the world compete with one another on account of this threefold diversity (*hac trifaria varietate*)" (Vulg., p. 546). Jerome also mentioned the Lucianic and Hesychian editions in his preface to his revision of the Latin Gospels (Vulg., p. 1515). On the *trifaria varietas*, see Canellis, *Préfaces*, pp. 65–66; Kreuzer, 'Old Greek, *kaige* and the *trifaria varietas*', pp. 74–76 and pp. 84–85; Barthélemy, *Les Devanciers d'Aquila*, pp. 126–27; Gentry, 'Pre-Hexaplaric Translations', pp. 232–35.

truth, from which the Greek and Latin versions (referred to as 'rivulets') have diverged.[217] Jerome brought this explanation to a close by concluding that whatever disagreed with the original LXX translation (*quicquid* [...] *ab hac discrepat*) no doubt (*nulli dubium est*) would disagree (*discordet*) with the Hebrew, too. In other words, for him, the Hebrew text upon which the LXX interpreters had based their translation was necessarily the same as his Hebrew recension.[218] As a matter of fact, this theory had already been hinted at by Jerome in 380, in the preface to his translation of Eusebius' *Chronicon*:

---

[217] *Epist.* 106.2 (V, pp. 105–6). For further occurrences of the terms 'fountainhead' and 'rivulets', see fn. 96.

[218] The French scholar Jean Morin posited in 1633, in his *Exercitationes biblicae*, that Jerome had relied on different Hebrew texts over the course of his career (see *Exercitationes biblicae*, pp. 298–300; on Morin's work, see Hardy, *Criticism and Confession*, pp. 264–74). This proposition has stood the test of time (see Kedar-Kopfstein, 'Divergent Hebrew Readings in Jerome's Isaiah'; 'Textual Gleanings from the Vulgate to Jeremiah'; and 'The Vulgate as a Translation', p. 71). Jerome, however, does not seem to have realised, or acknowledged, that variant Hebrew readings existed (see the two potential exceptions pointed out by Graves in 'Latin Texts', p. 236, fn. 31); at any rate, this reality never urged him to adopt a text-critical approach to the Hebrew-Aramaic version of Scripture. To be sure, the idea that different forms of the Hebrew Bible had existed (see my fn. 16; and Scheck's comments in his introduction to Jerome's commentary on Ezekiel [*St. Jerome*, pp. 12–13]), or that the Hebrew-Aramaic text could have undergone, to any extent, alterations or corruptions over time, was incompatible with the principle of 'Hebrew truth'.

> The holy books [...] that were produced by the Seventy translators do not retain the same flavour in the Greek language [as in the Hebrew]. For this reason, Aquila, Symmachus and Theodotion were incited to publish works that were somewhat different [although they were based] on the same work (i.e., the Hebrew text) (*incitati diversum paene opus in eodem opere prodiderunt*).[219]

On the whole, Jerome's attitudes to the LXX are complex and, to some extent, inconsistent. While he had placed his trust in the Hebrew text, he continually questioned the quality of the LXX, despite recurring protestations. Whether he actually believed that there once was an original LXX that faithfully represented Scripture (i.e., that matched the Hebrew text of his time) cannot be established beyond doubt; in what cases exactly he held the Seventy translators responsible for the discrepancies between the LXX and the Hebrew, while the Greek and the Latin scribes, as well as the VL interpreters, were said to be the ones at fault in other cases, it is not clear either.[220]

---

[219] Jerome's preface to *Chron.*, 3 (p. 56).

[220] For further discussion of Jerome's views on the LXX, see Braverman, *Jerome's Commentary*, pp. 25–34 and pp. 43–52; Kamesar, *Jerome*, pp. 41–49 and pp. 58–72; Hayward, *Saint Jerome's Hebrew Questions*, pp. 94–96; and Graves, 'Latin Texts', pp. 240–44.

8.0. Jerome's Conception of Translation and His Translation Method: Paraphrase and *sensus de sensu*

Not only did Jerome present the Vulgate as an accurate translation of the Hebrew text, he also showed himself most assertive about the importance of his Hebrew associates in this undertaking. In QHG, he occasionally described their teachings as 'true' (*verus*), a meaningful choice of words in the context of the *hebraica veritas*.[221] The premise, though, that his translations in the Vulgate always bear the stamp of their traditions in case of disagreement with other versions should be taken with a pinch of salt. Other interpretations of Scripture, over which the interpretations of the Hebrews prevailed in QHG, appear nonetheless in the Vulgate. Also surprising is that the syntax of the Vulgate can at times be closer to the LXX than to the Hebrew, when the latter two happen to differ from each other and the Latin could have followed the Hebrew syntax rather than the Greek one.[222] In this regard, some of Jerome's protestations against charges of misrepresentation of the original Hebrew Scriptures can strike the reader as suspicious. Indeed, around 390–392, in the preface to his translation of the Hebrew Book of Psalms, Jerome acknowledged

---

[221] See, for example, QHG 12.4 (pp. 19–20), *vera est igitur illa Hebraeorum traditio* ('therefore, that tradition of the Hebrews is true'); or QHG 19.30 (p. 30), *respondebimus veram esse illam Hebraeorum coniecturam* ('we shall reply that that inference of the Hebrews is true').

[222] These last two points will be demonstrated later in this monograph through a variety of case studies.

that a non-Hebrew reader would not be able to check the Hebrew for himself so as to compare the content of the VL of Psalms, to which he was accustomed, with that of the new Vulgate version. Knowing that his objectors would immediately criticise his work, Jerome formulated his defence as follows: 'As far as I am aware, I have not swerved in any manner from the Hebrew truth [in my translation of the Psalms]' (*me nihil dumtaxat scientem de hebraica veritate mutasse*).[223] Again, around the same date, in the preface to the Vulgate Book of Kings, he mentioned the possibility that a reader unfamiliar with Hebrew, after reading his translation of the Hebrew text and finding something different from what the LXX or the VL had taught him, might 'ungratefully' (*ingratus*) regard him as a loose 'paraphrast' (παραφραστής, *sic*) rather than as a real translator. In anticipation of this accusation of having misrepresented the original in his Latin, he reasserted his absolute fidelity to the *hebraica veritas* in an emphatically defensive tone: 'I am not conscious / guilty at all of having swerved in any way from the Hebrew truth' (*mihi omnino conscius non sim mutasse me quippiam de hebraica veritate*).[224]

---

[223] Vulg., p. 768.

[224] Vulg., p. 365. The term *conscius* 'conscious' sometimes suggests guilt: see for example the passage in Plautus' *Mostellaria*, 3, 1, *nihil est miserius quam animus hominis conscius* ('nothing is more wretched than a man's guilty mind'). The usage *mihi conscius sum* in particular, which Jerome employed here, can be an idiomatic turn in Latin for the expression of guilt: see 1 Cor. 4.4 (Vulg., p. 1772), *nihil enim mihi conscius sum* ('in fact, I do not have a guilty conscience at all').

1. Introduction

Jerome's way of defending himself was often passionate; the question of his being, in fact, a 'paraphrast' should however be raised. Indeed, the term 'paraphrast' was employed in a derogatory manner in the preface to the Vulgate of Kings, but it also meaningfully echoes another of its occurrences in a mid-390s letter of Jerome's titled *On the Best Method of Translating*. In this letter, Jerome presented paraphrase as an essential component of his method. After being accused of having distorted the original sense of a Greek letter in his Latin translation, he admitted that he was not wont to translate his sources word for word, *verbum e verbo*, but that he rather followed their general sense, *sensus de sensu*.[225] In context, this assessment of his translation technique was first meant for pagan Greek texts, i.e., non-scriptural literature: "In fact, not only do I confess it, but I profess it loud and clear: I do not render word for word (*non verbum e verbo*) in [my] translation of the Greeks, [...] but sense for sense (*sed sensum exprimere de sensu*)."[226] According to Jerome, the translator was not to be concerned with the idioms peculiar to the source language, as they often could not be rendered literally without it being at the cost of the aesthetic pleasantness or of the intelligibility of the translation:

> I have Cicero as a mentor in this field [...]: he [indeed] skipped, added, and altered many things in [his translations] so as to untangle (*explicaret*) the peculiarities of one language (*proprietates alterius linguae*) through those of his.

---

[225] *Epist.* 57.1–5 (III, pp. 55–59).
[226] *Epist.* 57.5 (III, p. 59).

[...] And Horace, too, a sharp and well-read man, prescribed the same thing to the educated interpreter in the *Ars poetica*: 'And you shall make sure, O faithful interpreter (*fidus interpres*), not to translate word for word (*verbum verbo reddere*).'[227] Terence translated Menander, Plautus and Caecilius [dealt with] the old comic [playwrights]: do they cling on to the words (*numquid haerent in verbis*), or do they not rather preserve the charm (*decorem*) and the elegance (*elegantiam*) in their rendering? What you call the 'truth of the translation' (*veritatem interpretationis*), we, educated men, call it κακοζηλίαν (sic) (i.e., a poor pastiche). [...] 'It is difficult for what was well phrased in one language to preserve the same charm (*eundem decorem*) in a translation. [...] If I translate word for word, it will sound like nonsense (*si ad verbum interpretor, absurde resonant*); but if, out of necessity, I [happen to] have changed anything in the order or in the phrasing (*aliquid in ordine, in sermone mutavero*), I will seem to have deserted in my duty as a translator.'[228] [...] Since I was a teenager, it is not the words but the reasonings (*non verba sed sententias*) that I have been translating [...]: 'By producing a word-for-word translation (*ad verbum expressa translatio*) from one language into another, one obscures the meaning (*sensus operit*).'[229]

Jerome went on to proclaim that he would also resort to the *sensus de sensu* translation method in the case of Scripture, 'where

---

[227] See Horace, *Ars poetica*, 133–34.

[228] Here Jerome quoted the preface to his translation of Eusebius' *Chronicon* (see *Chron.*, 2; p. 56).

[229] *Epist.* 57.5–6 (III, pp. 59–61). Jerome drew the last citation of this passage from Evagrius' preface to Athanasius' *Life of Antony* (see PL 73, pp. 125–26).

1. Introduction

the wording is also the mystery' (*scripturis sanctis, ubi et verborum ordo mysterium est*). A thorough understanding of the reason why *mysterium* is to be construed as 'the mystery' and not as 'a mystery' is necessary in this context, as this term is a key notion in Jerome's conception of scriptural translation.

First, Jerome spoke of *verborum ordo*, literally 'the order of the words'. This phrase is not to be understood as 'word order' specifically, which in the study of syntax points to the arrangement of the words in a sentence: here it referred more broadly to the way a sentence was formulated, i.e., to the wording, and, by extension, to the overall sense that it conveyed. Other occurrences of this phrase in similar contexts further indicate that this was the meaning that Jerome attributed to it.[230] He then called the wording in Scripture *mysterium*, a particularly significant term in his œuvre. The majority of scholars assume that, by *scripturis sanctis, ubi et verborum ordo mysterium est*, Jerome meant that the wording of the Bible was 'a mystery', i.e., unintelligible. Jerome did not imply this in the least.[231] On the contrary, for him,

---

[230] See *Epist.* 49.16 (II, p. 142); 112.19 (VI, p. 39). See also the phrase *verborum oridinisque discordia* ('disagreement in words and in order') in *Epist.* 57.8 (III, p. 66).

[231] The fact that the structure of his sentence is ambiguous explains why modern scholars who quote it have misconstrued it. To be sure, this passage has not received enough attention in scholarship (Kamesar seems to be the exception [see his observations in 'Jerome', p. 669]). The full sentence reads *Ego enim non solum fateor, sed libera voce profiteor me in interpretatione Graecorum absque scripturis sanctis, ubi et verborum ordo mysterium est, non verbum e verbo sed sensum exprimere de sensu,*

the *mysterium* was the entity that embodied the divine, and the wording in Scripture, which contained the unfathomable essence of the Christian faith, embodied the *mysterium*. The word *mysterium* comes from the Greek μυστήριον, which is tantamount to a secret rite (the verb μυέω means 'to initiate into a secret rite'): Jerome consistently employed this term when citing passages of the Old Testament which, in his view, alluded to the Christ, and from which Jewish interpreters had allegedly sought to remove key elements in their translations. For example, the *recentiores* in the preface to the Vulgate Book of Job 'conceal many of the Saviour's mysteries with their deceitful translation' (*multa mysteria*

---

which I translate as follows: 'In fact, not only do I confess it, but I profess it loud and clear: I do not render word for word in [my] translation of the Greeks (who do not include [*absque*] the Holy Scriptures, where the wording is also the mystery), but sense for sense'. It could seem at first glance that, with the preposition *absque* ('except'), Jerome was excluding the translation of Scripture from the field of application of the *sensus de sensu* method. The implication would consequently be that he applied the word-for-word method instead, which is most scholars' assumption. The context of *Epist.* 57 makes it clear, however, that his rejection of the word-for-word translation method did not only concern pagan literature ("the Greeks"), but had to do with the translation of Scripture, too: this is shown by many comments that Jerome made throughout the same letter (see below). Therefore, in *Epist.* 57.5, the remark introduced by *absque* should be read as a parenthesis distinguishing Scripture (*scripturis sanctis*) from non-scriptural texts (*Graecorum*), irrespective of the *sensus de sensu*; the point of that distinction was to stress the idea that the wording of Scripture conveyed 'the mystery' (see my explanation below) on top of (*et*) what pagan literature already had to offer.

Salvatoris subdola interpretatione celarunt).²³² In the preface to QHG, when Jerome criticised the work of the LXX translators, the plural *mystica* was employed as a synonym for *mysteria*: "they were unwilling to disclose the mysteries (*mystica*) in the Holy Scriptures to Ptolemy, the king of Alexandria, and, most importantly, those [of the mysteries] that were announcing the coming of the Christ."²³³ The word *arcanum* was also used synonymously in the Vulgate preface to the Pentateuch: "[the LXX translators] did not divulge the secret of the faith" (*arcanum fidei*).²³⁴ His formulation in *Comm. Zach.* 6.9–15 is also interesting in this regard: "I have once set out to present the secrets of the Hebraic learning (*arcana eruditionis Hebraicae*), as well as the hidden teaching of the masters of the Synagogue (*magistrorum synagogae reconditam disciplinam*)—at least in the case of what pertains to the Holy Scriptures—to Latin ears."²³⁵ Finally, the word *sacramenta* had a semantic weight comparable to that of *mysterium*. Indeed, Jerome referred to 'the mysteries of [the Seventy interpreters'] faith' (*fidei suae sacramenta*) in the preface to the Vulgate Book of Isaiah;²³⁶ and in the preface to his commentary on Isaiah he argued the following: "The present [piece of] Scripture contains all the Lord's mysteries (*universa Domini sacramenta*

---

²³² Vulg., p. 732. See also the preface to the Vulgate Book of Isaiah (Vulg., p. 1096).

²³³ QHG, p. 2.

²³⁴ Vulg., p. 3. See Jerome's use of the analogous phrase *in mysterio fidei* ('in the mystery of the faith') in *Epist.* 18.2 (I, p. 56).

²³⁵ *Comm. Zach.* 6.9–15 (CCSL 76A, p. 796).

²³⁶ Vulg., p. 1096.

praesens scriptura contineat) [...]. Whatever is [found] in the Holy Scriptures, whatever the human language can express and the comprehension of mortals can receive, it is contained in this volume."[237] Ultimately, Jerome's way of conceiving of the divine as a mystery that manifests itself through the wording of Scripture is reminiscent of the midrashic notion that associates God's secrets with the Mishna:

מי שמסטורין שלי אצלו הם בני, ואיזו היא, זו המשנה שנתנה על פה
והכל ממך לדרוש

> Those who have my secrets (מסטורין) with them are my sons. But what is it? It is the Mishna, which was given orally: you are to interpret everything [through it].[238]

In conclusion, the segment of Jerome's letter that reads *scripturis sanctis, ubi et verborum ordo mysterium est* should be understood as 'the Holy Scriptures, where the wording is also *the* mystery'. The *sensus de sensu* method evidently applied to it: as will be demonstrated in this monograph, Jerome consistently employed it in his translation of the Hebrew.

As also indicated by a remark that he made in *Epist*. 39.4, this *mysterium* was inextricably intwined with the notion of stylistic simplicity: "I cannot praise enough the mysteries of Scripture (*scripturae mysteria*) and the divine sense that one may

---

[237] Preface to *Comm. Isa.* (CCSL 73, pp. 1–2).

[238] Tanḥuma Buber, *Ki Tissa* 17, 120 (II, נג, א, p. 117). It is noteworthy that the Rabbis used a Greek loanword in their own writings (μυστήρια / מסטורין). For a discussion of the notion of 'mysteries' in the parallel, and rival, chains of scriptural transmission of the Church Fathers and of the Rabbis, see Kamesar, *Jerome*, pp. 29–34.

admire in simple words (*in verbis simplicibus*)."²³⁹ The stylistic simplicity of the Bible, as opposed to the verbosity or preciosity of pagan texts, reflected the holiness of the faith, from which had also originated the purity of the Apostles' lifestyle.²⁴⁰ A sample of remarks adduced from Jerome's letters attests to this conception:

> I will not blame some Christian for expressing himself in an uncouth way (*sermonis inperitiam*) [...], [as] I have always held in high esteem, not wordy rusticity (*verbosa rusticitas*), but holy simplicity (*sancta simplicitas*). He who purports to imitate the apostles in [his] speech, let him imitate [them] in [his] lifestyle first. The greatness of [their] sanctity (*sanctimoniae magnitudo*) accounted for (*excusabat*) their simplicity in [their way of] speaking (*illorum in loquendo simplicitatem*).²⁴¹

> He who discusses Hebrew literature should not strive for arguments [like those] of Aristotle, nor is a [single] rivulet to be diverted from a Ciceronian stream of eloquence, nor are ears to be flattered with the rhetorical flowers and the scholarly declamation of a Quintilian. It requires down-to-earth language (*pedestris oratio*), [a language] similar to the everyday one (*similis cotidianae*) and not smelly like a candlelight, [a language] that might untangle a matter (*quae rem explicet*), disclose the sense (*sensum edisserat*), clarify what is obscure (*obscura manifestet*); [it does] not [require a language] whose structure is convoluted (*non quae verborum conpositione frondescat*). [...] As I myself

---

²³⁹ *Epist.* 39.4 (II, p. 79).

²⁴⁰ See Antin's discussion of Origen's view on the matter ('"Simple" et "simplicité" chez saint Jérôme', p. 372). For a broader discussion of the notion of simplicity in the Church Fathers, see ibid., pp. 372–73.

²⁴¹ *Epist.* 57.12 (III, pp. 72–73).

> happen to discuss the Scriptures, let me imitate the simplicity of the Scriptures.[242]

> I have been a translator of the Apostle more so than a dogmatist (*interpres magis Apostoli quam dogmatistes*), and I have [also] operated as a commentator: should anything not read easily (*quidquid durum videtur*) [in my commentary], let [the blame] be put on the one on whom we have commented, more so than on us who have [simply] commented [on him]... unless it turns out that he said something else! and that we twisted the simplicity of his words (*simplicitatem verborum eius*) with a malicious translation![243]

In Jerome, the wording in Scripture conveyed the *mysterium* through the simplicity of its style.[244] In order to translate it into Latin, he employed the *sensus de sensu*. When he attempted to further demonstrate the validity of this approach, he argued that not only profane but also ecclesiastical authors had resorted to the *sensus de sensu* in the past, like

> Hilary the confessor who rendered homilies on Job and various tractates on Psalms from Greek into Latin, and who did not dozily follow [these texts] to the letter (*non adsedit litterae dormitanti*) nor bend himself to the rotten transla-

---

[242] *Epist.* 36.14 (II, p. 61).

[243] *Epist.* 49.14 (II, p. 136). In this letter, Jerome shared his exegetical interpretations of certain verses adduced from the New Testament, for which he also provided his own Latin translations.

[244] For a detailed discussion of the relationship between stylistic simplicity and the Christian faith in Jerome, see Antin, '"Simple" et "simplicité" chez saint Jérôme'.

tion [method] of the uncouth, but who [instead] transcribed the captured meanings (*captivos sensus transposuit*), as it were, in his own language, as per the right of a victor.[245]

Likewise, Jerome claimed that the LXX translators and, in fact, even the Evangelists and the Apostles themselves did not systematically follow the Hebrew of the Scriptures word for word but, still, that they interpreted it successfully in expressing its meaning:

> It is clearly (*videlicet*) not uncommon (*nec hoc mirum*) for both profane and ecclesiastic men [to employ the *sensus de sensu*], as the Seventy interpreters, as well as the Evangelists and the Apostles, did it in the sacred scrolls (*idem in sacris voluminibus fecerint*).[246]

This point was summarised in a hunting metaphor: "The concern of a follower of the Christ was not to go fowling (*aucupari*) for words and syllables, but to lay down the reasonings of the dogmas (*sententias dogmatum ponere*)."[247] Finally, Jerome brought his demonstration to a close with the following words: "It is not the words that are to be considered in the Scriptures but the sense (*non verba in scripturis consideranda, sed sensum*)."[248] A few lines

---

[245] *Epist.* 57.6 (III, p. 62). In 385, in *Epist.* 34.3 (II, p. 46), Jerome disparaged Hilary's translations on account of his ignorance of Hebrew and of his very slight knowledge of Greek.

[246] *Epist.* 57.7 (III, p. 62).

[247] *Epist.* 57.7 (III, p. 63).

[248] *Epist.* 57.10 (III, p. 70). For further discussion of Jerome's understanding of the word *sensus*, see Kraus, *Jewish, Christian, and Classical Exegetical Traditions*, pp. 45–49.

before reaching this conclusion, he described the preaching method of Paul the Apostle as being 'paraphrastic': when Paul quoted Isa. 64.3 in 1 Cor. 2.9,

> he did not render [the text] word-for-word (*non verbum expressit e verbo*) but in paraphrasing [it] (παραφραστικῶς, sic) he communicated [its] sense (lit., the same sense) with different terms (*eundem sensum aliis sermonibus indicavit*).[249]

Jerome regularly appealed to the authority of the Apostles in order to justify his approach to the Hebrew text.[250] Here, by comparing himself to Paul, whom he clearly portrayed as a paraphrast, he presented himself to some extent as one, too. Therefore, when four to five years earlier he objected to this epithet in the preface to the Vulgate of Kings (see above), it could only be as an anticipatory precaution against his critics, as he was gradually becoming the advocate of the Hebrew truth. When accused of distorting a text in his translation, his defence generally consisted of claiming that, like the Apostles, he had primarily cared about the ideas, without subjecting himself to the original wording. To that extent, the *sensus de sensu* translation method did correspond to a form of paraphrase.[251] In the translation of a Hebrew text, this liberty that Jerome took with the original often manifested itself in a certain flexibility in the selection of his

---

[249] *Epist.* 57.9 (III, p. 68).

[250] See section 1.5 of this monograph.

[251] The case studies investigated in this monograph shall show to what extent this was the case.

sources, as many were at his disposal. In other words, in his translation of the Hebrew Bible, his source was not always the Hebrew Bible. What were Jerome's sources, then, in the composition of the Vulgate? This is the question that we pose in this monograph.

9.0. The Purpose of This Monograph

9.1. Jerome's Inconsistency

While it is widely acknowledged that the Vulgate was not produced solely on the basis of the Hebrew Bible, few modern biblicists have actually devoted in-depth studies to this matter. Yet comparative analyses of the Vulgate and of some of the other versions of Scripture have long revealed this state of affairs. In 1678, for instance, the French scholar Richard Simon adopted a comparative approach when engaging with the Vulgate in his *Histoire critique du Vieux Testament*: this allowed him to realise that Jerome had been somewhat inconsistent with regard to the *hebraica veritas* agenda.[252] Simon recognised indeed that the Hebrew text had served as the textual basis of the Vulgate.[253] At the same time, he adduced a series of verses from the Vulgate of Genesis and went on to compare them, alongside Jerome's statements in QHG, with the other versions: while some Vulgate verses showed that Jerome had followed the Hebrew text in case of dis-

---

[252] For a discussion of Simon's work and contribution to the field of biblical criticism and to early modern biblical scholarship, see Hardy, *Criticism and Confession*, pp. 373–91.

[253] Simon, *Histoire critique*, p. 245.

crepancies, others contained readings that disagreed with it. Simon thus demonstrated that Jerome had occasionally followed the LXX or the *recentiores* against the Hebrew, and that his translations in the Vulgate were not systematically in line with his interpretations in his commentaries.[254] He further concluded that Jerome had reproduced, in the Vulgate, passages from the previous translations—even though he could have also openly dismissed them as erroneous—for the sake of Church audiences who were familiar with the old versions.[255] Jerome himself admitted in 388–389 that a translation of the Hebrew Book of Ecclesiastes which he made in the context of his commentary on the book,[256] i.e., ten years before the Vulgate translation of Ecclesiastes, had been "adjusted to [our] customary use of the Seventy translators (*magis me septuaginta interpretum consuetudini coaptavi*) wherever it did not disagree beyond measure with the Hebrew [text] (*in his dumtaxat, quae non multum ab Hebraicis discrepabant*), [...] so as

---

[254] Simon, *Histoire critique*, pp. 249–57. For example, in his first case study (ibid., pp. 249–50), Simon notices the following: Jerome argued in QHG 1.2 that the reading *ferebatur* 'it was being carried [over]' in VL Gen. 1.2—a straightforward rendering of ἐπεφέρετο in the LXX—should be amended to *incubabat* 'it was lying upon', in accordance with מְרַחֶפֶת 'it was hovering [over]' in the Hebrew text (QHG 1.2 [p. 4]). However, he retained *ferebatur* in the Vulgate version of Gen. 1.2. This is a case of blatant contradiction between the interpretation of a verse in QHG and the rendering of the same verse in the Vulgate.

[255] Simon, *Histoire critique*, pp. 246–48.

[256] On this translation, see Kelly, *Jerome*, p. 110.

not to bewilder (*deterrerem*) the zealous reader with too much novelty (*novitate nimia*)."[257]

9.2. The Idea Explored in This Monograph

Although Jerome vigorously promoted the *hebraica veritas* principle as a straight return to the Hebrew against the LXX and the VL,[258] his Vulgate translations, when analysed in light of other Bible versions, reveal in practice a more complex hermeneutic approach. Our study will not bring a new perspective on his work; on the contrary, our aim here is to explore the idea that Richard Simon already formulated in the seventeenth century, which is not consistently exploited in modern scholarship, and according to which Jerome's sources in his translation of the Hebrew Bible are not always the Hebrew Bible. This monograph shows to what extent, in his Vulgate translations, the LXX as well as its Old Latin translations have been textual resources of his. The Greek Bible versions contained in the Hexapla, i.e., the translations of Aquila, Symmachus and Theodotion, also continued to

---

[257] *Comm. Eccl.* (CCSL 72, p. 249). In 400, Jerome expressed himself in the same terms with regard to his earlier revision of the Latin Psalter towards the Greek (*Epist.* 106.12; V, p. 111). Also similar is his way of describing the manner in which he revised the Latin Gospels towards Greek recensions (Vulg., p. 1515).

[258] In the preface to the Vulgate of Chronicles, Jerome literally spoke of a 'return to the Hebrews': 'we must return to the Hebrews[' version], from which both the Lord speaks and the disciples (i.e., the Apostles and the Evangelists) select [their] examples in the first place' (*ad Hebraeos igitur revertendum est, unde et Dominus loquitur et discipuli exempla praesumunt*) (Vulg., p. 547).

serve him in his interpretation and rendering of Hebrew Scripture. The part that the expertise of his 'Hebrews' played was considerable, too. We further demonstrate that, when divergent interpretations of an obscure passage in the Hebrew existed, Jerome did not systematically favour one over all others in his translation: he could instead conflate several textual traditions, in such a way that the Vulgate version retained different interpretations. Finally, regardless of the clarity of the Hebrew text, he also departed from it for purely stylistic reasons, either by following the other versions, or independently of them. In summary, each of his translations for the Vulgate is underlain by a variety of traditions.

9.3. The Corpus Employed in This Monograph

When translating the Hebrew Bible in the context of the Vulgate project, Jerome was faced with texts that were transmitted in four languages—Hebrew, Aramaic, Greek and Latin—and which involved both Christian and Jewish traditions. In this monograph, we analyse his translation technique in the Vulgate versions of the Joseph story (Gen. 37–50) (chapter 2), of the Book of Daniel (chapter 3) and of that of Esther (chapter 4). Basing our study on this selection of books allows us to explore his responses to works written in Hebrew, in Aramaic, in Greek and in Latin. More broadly, it gives us the opportunity to investigate his relationship with his sources in a chronologically relevant way. Indeed, QHG belongs to the early 390s, and the composition of the

Vulgate Book of Genesis was dated to the end of the 390s;[259] these works are therefore representative of the beginning and of the middle of Jerome's career as a translator of the Hebrew Bible. The Vulgate Book of Daniel and the commentary on Daniel, which have been dated to 392–393 and 407 respectively, correspond to the beginning of his career and to the first year after it ended. Finally, the Vulgate Book of Esther, which was completed in 404–405, is one of his last translations.[260]

The Book of Daniel and that of Esther represent complex traditions. In the former case, the Hebrew version of the story is interwoven with a lengthy Aramaic portion, while the Greek version contains three episodes missing from the Hebrew-Aramaic text, which are known from two different sources, the LXX and Theodotion (as we shall see, Jerome exploited the Greek texts in various ways). In the case of Esther, the book circulated in various forms in the time of Jerome: among the Greek and Latin versions of the story that coexisted,[261] two in Greek and several fragmentary ones in Latin have come down to us. The Vulgate versions of the Joseph story, of the Book of Daniel and of that Esther are, for these reasons, not only adequate but particularly pertinent to focus on.

---

[259] See fn. 109 and fn. 112.

[260] For a detailed discussion of these dates, see my introductions to the relevant chapters.

[261] Jerome referred to one *editio vulgata* of Esther and discussed it at some length (see section 4.1).

9.4. The Methodology

In the introduction to each chapter, we first address the textual history of the work in question. In the case of the Daniel and Esther chapters, we also investigate Jerome's reception and general treatment of these books (this was done for the Vulgate Book of Genesis in section 1.5). Then, in the core of each chapter, in order to demonstrate that Jerome exploited various sources and sometimes incorporated readings that differed from the Hebrew into his translation of the Hebrew text, verses adduced from the relevant Vulgate version are analysed in comparison with all the sources that he potentially had at hand and which are still extant. In each case, we deal with specific aspects of the verse that is being investigated, such as a structure, a phrase, or a term: this takes the form of case studies (each of which is introduced in due course). The verses selected in these case studies permit us to identify patterns in Jerome's translation technique and to thoroughly examine his relationship with his sources. All primary sources are quoted in the original language and rendered into English. The translations have been produced by me. Through my translations, I attempt in each case to highlight and address the elements in the original that are germane to our study. I may occasionally comment on my translations so as to explain or clarify my choices.

2. THE TRANSLATION OF THE JOSEPH STORY (GEN. 37–50)

1.0. Textual History

In this chapter, our investigation of Jerome's treatment of the Book of Genesis focuses on his translation of Gen. 37–50, which portion is commonly referred to as the Joseph story. In the Hebrew version, the composition of this particular episode has recently tended to be dated later than the rest of the Book of Genesis, as today's scholars have endeavoured to make it contemporaneous with post-exilic literature. Whereas, some time ago, the production of the Joseph story was generally dated to the monarchic period,[262] many have now posited a *terminus a quo* from some time before to slightly after the beginning of exilic times.[263] Others locate the text in the Persian period.[264] The end of the

---

[262] Over half a century ago, Vergote argued that the text, while composed around the ninth or eighth century BCE, was based on a story that dated back to a few centuries earlier (*Joseph en Égypte*, pp. 203–13). See also Schulman, 'On the Egyptian Name of Joseph'; Blum and Weingart, 'The Joseph Story'; Joosten, 'The Linguistic Dating'; and Hendel and Joosten, *How Old Is the Hebrew Bible?*

[263] Redford, *A Study of the Biblical Story of Joseph*, pp. 241–53. See also Soggin, 'Dating the Joseph Story'.

[264] Kratz, 'The Joseph Story', pp. 29–32; Schipper, 'Joseph, Ahiqar, and Elephantine'; and Golka, 'Genesis 37–50'. See also Young, Rezetko, and Ehrensvärd's survey of scholarly attempts to date Gen. 37–50 in *Linguistic Dating of Biblical Texts*, II, pp. 7–9.

fourth century BCE, in the early Hellenistic period, with a *terminus ad quem* in the third century BCE for its latest parts, has even been suggested.[265]

2.0. The Case Studies

In our analysis of Jerome's treatment of Gen. 37–50, seven verses are studied: the first one is a case of *hebraica veritas* in which Jerome's correction of a discrepancy in the LXX, though philologically based on the Hebrew text, is presented as theologically motivated by a passage in the New Testament (section 2.1). The second one, in which Jerome also followed the Hebrew text against the LXX—this time by adducing Jewish exegesis—displays a minor, but noticeable, departure from the Hebrew, one that is independent of the other versions (section 2.2). The following two cases show that the meaning of the Hebrew, when obscure, was derived from other sources (sections 2.3 and 2.4).

---

[265] See Römer, 'How "Persian" or "Hellenistic" is the Joseph Narrative?', pp. 43–53 and 'The Role of Egypt', pp. 64–65. Certain scholars contend that attempts to date the composition of the Joseph story should not be based on linguistic analyses of the text; indeed, they dismiss this approach to periodisation as inconclusive, useless, or even irrelevant. See, for instance, Schmid, 'How Old Is the Hebrew Bible?'; Römer, 'How to Date Pentateuchal Texts', pp. 361–63; Young, 'Biblical Texts'; and Ehrensvärd, 'Why Biblical Texts'. For the opposite view, namely, that approaching Biblical Hebrew diachronically can be useful and that the periodisation of Biblical Hebrew texts can benefit from linguistics, see Hornkohl, 'Biblical Hebrew: Periodization', pp. 320–21; Joosten, 'The Linguistic Dating'; Hendel and Joosten, *How Old Is the Hebrew Bible?*; and Redford, *A Study of the Biblical Story of Joseph*, pp. 54–65.

Finally, the last three examples represent sheer departures from the Hebrew text (section 2.5). Verses that have been addressed by Jerome in QHG provide us with more material to understand his course of action in the Vulgate: investigating the discrepancies between his QHG interpretations and his Vulgate renderings will bring to light cases of inconsistency in his employment of his sources. Therefore, the first four case studies of this chapter have been selected in relation to QHG. The last three examples examined in section 2.5 are not based on verses treated in QHG. Beyond the MT, the LXX, the VL and the *recentiores*, and alongside the Vulgate and the lemmas in QHG, rabbinic and targumic sources that are echoed by the traditions that Jerome quoted in QHG are adduced where necessary throughout the chapter.

2.1. Thirty Pieces of Silver and Twenty Pieces of Gold: The *hebraica veritas* of the New Testament in QHG and Vulg. Gen. 37.28

In Gen. 37.28, Joseph is drawn out of the pit where his brothers left him for dead and he is sold to the Ishmaelites for a certain sum of money. The lemma in QHG, which reads *XX aureis*, 'for twenty golden pieces', renders LXX εἴκοσι χρυσῶν, 'for twenty pieces of gold'.[266] Jerome then remarked: "Instead of gold (*pro aureis*), it is silver (*argenteos*) in Hebrew." Indeed, the MT reads: בְּעֶשְׂרִים כָּסֶף. He went on to demonstrate that the LXX translators could not have been right anyway since 'the Lord (i.e., Jesus) was not to be sold for a cheaper metal than Joseph' (*neque viliore*

---

[266] QHG 37.28 (p. 57).

metallo dominus venum dari debuit quam Ioseph), a reference to Matt. 26.15 in which Judas agrees to hand Jesus over to the chief priests for 'thirty pieces of silver' (τριάκοντα ἀργύρια).

In other words, if Jesus was sold for silver, Joseph cannot have been bought with gold. With this justification in hand, Jerome had no interest in explaining what might have motivated a misrepresentation of the original in the LXX.[267] His intention was to prove to his Latin readership, who followed the LXX version of this verse through the VL (*XX aureis*), that it was wrong; not because the word contained in the original was 'silver' and not 'gold', as this was something that they, being unfamiliar with Hebrew, could not check for themselves, but because the Hebrew text or, rather, the Old Testament, prefigured the events of the New Testament, and there could be no incongruence between the selling of Joseph and that of Jesus. In the Vulgate, as expected, Jerome readjusted his translation to the Hebrew: *viginti argenteis* 'for twenty pieces of silver'.

The example of QHG and of Vulg. Gen. 37.28 serves as a twofold illustration of the *hebraica veritas* principle. First, in QHG, Jerome exposed the LXX as inaccurately representing the original: on a strictly linguistic level, by quoting the Hebrew version (with no mention of the Hebrews' expertise); theologically, by

---

[267] According to Lee, cited by Harl (*La Genèse*, p. 262), and with whom Hayward also agrees (*Saint Jerome's Hebrew Questions*, p. 219, fn. 1), the LXX rendering 'gold' must reflect a cultural adaptation that conformed better with the monetary system of the translator's time (Lee, *A Lexical Study*, pp. 64–65). See Josephus, *Ant.*, 2.34.

2. The Translation of the Joseph Story (Gen. 37–50)   111

remarking that an analogous episode in the New Testament necessarily implied consistency. Then, in the Vulgate, he accordingly applied, with a straightforward rendering of the Hebrew, the textual correction that he had introduced in QHG. In 398, in his commentary on Matthew, he confirmed this correction once more:

> Joseph was not sold for twenty pieces of gold, as many think in accordance with the LXX translators (*ut multi putant iuxta LXX interpretes*), but, in accordance with the Hebrew truth (*iuxta Hebraicam veritatem*), for twenty pieces of silver. Indeed (*enim*), a slave could not be more valuable (*pretiosior*) than the Lord.[268]

---

[268] *Comm. Matt.* 26.15 (II, p. 240). Regarding the commentary's date of composition, see Kelly, *Jerome*, p. 222. When Jerome referred to Gen. 37.38 in his commentary on the Epistle to Philemon, it was according to the LXX rendering 'gold', with no allusion to the original, 'silver' (*Comm. Phlm.* 15–16; CCSL 77C, p. 97). According to Kelly's computations, the commentary on the Epistle to Philemon was completed around 387 (*Jerome*, p. 88 and p. 145), only half a decade before QHG but more than a decade before his commentary on Matthew. However, we know that by 383 Jerome was already well-versed in Hebraic research (see section 1.4). Furthermore, in *Comm. Phlm.*, he occasionally engaged in Hebrew onomastics in order to initiate the Latin readership into the interpretation of certain names (*Comm. Phlm.* 1–3 [CCSL 77C, pp. 81–82] and 25 [CCSL 77C, p. 105]), or in the explanation of Hebrew words (*Comm. Phlm.* 20; CCSL 77C, p. 100). That he quoted LXX Gen. 37.28 in *Comm. Phlm.* without adding that the Hebrew did not read 'gold' but 'silver', whereas he did so in *Comm. Matt.*, is undoubtedly meaningful. Indeed, if in 387 Jerome's ambition to promote the study of the Hebrew text as the path to scriptural truth had not spread yet beyond the boundaries of his letters, it may be that he did not want to

Here, again, Jerome first referred to the Hebrew text (*iuxta Hebraicam veritatem*) and then verified its reliability against the LXX version through the authority of the New Testament (*enim*): to that extent, the *hebraica veritas*, as it is presented, is not so much a function of what the Hebrew text contains, as of the inherent logic that makes the events of the Old Testament a preamble to the New. Likewise, a remark that Jerome made around 396–398, in the preface to the Vulgate Book of Chronicles, suggests that the Apostles' authority motivated his quest for truth in the study of the Hebrew text more so than the Hebrew text itself:

> Why should my fellow Latins not accept me? While leaving the previous edition (i.e., the LXX) unviolated, I have composed a new one (i.e., the Vulgate) (*qui inviolata editione veteri ita novam condidi*) so as to make my work worthy of the Hebrews and, more importantly, of the authorities, [i.e.,] the Apostles (*ut laborem meum Hebraeis et, quod his maius est, Apostolis auctoribus probem*).[269]

The way Jerome was purporting to quote the New Testament in relation to the Hebrew text was actually not representative of his ideas: this was only meant for his readers. Indeed, his faith in the

---

expose the wider audience of Latin-speaking Christians to that idea (*Comm. Phlm.*—one of his first biblical commentaries—had been written for them at the request of two of his closest disciples, Paula and Eustochium; see *Comm. Phlm.* 1–3 [CCSL 77C, p. 81], and Kelly, *Jerome*, pp. 144–45). Kelly explains that Jerome had by then lost interest in the task of revising the books of the New Testament, as is suggested by the fact that, in *Comm. Phlm.*, he always attributed the Latin text that he was quoting to other translators, never to himself (Kelly, *Jerome*, p. 88).

[269] Vulg., p. 546.

accuracy of the Hebrew text did not need the validation of the Apostles, as it fundamentally rested on the belief that Hebrew, "in which the Old Testament was written," was "the origin of speech and of common discourse" (*initium oris et communis eloquii*),²⁷⁰ and "the source of all languages" (*omnium linguarum esse matricem*).²⁷¹ In this regard, Jerome trusted in the truth of the Hebrew text in itself, irrespective of other sources.

As explained in the introduction to this monograph (section 1.5), he routinely exploited citations of the Old Testament in the New Testament where they might agree with the Hebrew text against the LXX. In the eyes of the Christian readership, this was supposed to be evidence that the validity of the Hebrew had been acknowledged by the most important Christian authorities, that is, the Apostles; in reality, Jerome used this device to convince Latin Christians.²⁷² Here he exploited the content of Matt. 26.15 and, by extension, the authority of the New Testament, in order to be able to contend, before a Christian audience, that the Hebrew text was right against the LXX.

2.2. An Independent Departure from the Hebrew: Gen. 49.21

In Gen. 49, Jacob gathers his twelve children so as to communicate to each of them his lot. Naphtali's turn comes in Gen. 49.21.

---

[270] *Epist.* 18.6 (I, p. 61).

[271] *Comm. Soph.* 3.18 (CCSL 76A, p. 708).

[272] See section 1.5.

MT

נַפְתָּלִי אַיָּלָה שְׁלֻחָה הַנֹּתֵן אִמְרֵי־שָׁפֶר:

Naphtali [is] a hind set free, he who gives forth words of beauty.

Vulgate

Nepthalim cervus emissus et dans eloquia pulchritudinis.

Naphtali [is] a stag set free and giving forth utterances of beauty.

QHG

Nepthalim virgultum resolutum, dans in generatione pulchritudinem.[273]

Naphtali [is] a thicket let loose, giving forth beauty in [its] production.

LXX

Νεφθαλὶ στέλεχος ἀνειμένον, ἐπιδιδοὺς ἐν τῷ γενήματι κάλλος.[274]

Naphtali [is] a stem let loose, giving forth beauty in [its] production.

VL

Nephtalim codex defectus porrigens in genere speciem (/ arbor remissa proferens in germine decorem).

---

[273] QHG 49.21 (p. 70).

[274] This LXX verse is discussed in Speiser, *Genesis*, p. 367, and in Harl, *La Genèse*, pp. 311–12.

2. The Translation of the Joseph Story (Gen. 37–50) 115

> Naphtali [is] a stump taken off, spreading forth splendour in [its] kin (/ [is] a removed tree producing grace in [its] offshoot).[275]

Aquila

ἔλαφος ἀπεσταλμένος

A dispatched stag...

In QHG, Jerome interpreted the passage as follows:

> In Hebrew, what is written goes thus: 'Naphtali is a watered field (*ager irriguus*), giving forth utterances of beauty (*dans eloquia pulchritudinis*)'. [...] On the other hand, the Hebrews mean (*Hebraei autem volunt*) that a watered field and utterances of beauty are prophesied because of Tiberias, which seemed to have some knowledge of the Law. Furthermore, where we have stated 'watered field' and the LXX στέλεχος [ἀνειμένον], i.e., 'a thicket let loose' (*virgultum resolutum*), in Hebrew it reads *aiala selua*, which can also be translated as 'a stag set free' (*cervus emissus*), showing the promptness of a very fertile land on account of [its] early fruits (*propter temporaneas fruges velocitatem terrae uberioris ostendens*).

Jerome started off here by positing an allegorical reading of אַיָּלָה שְׁלֻחָה as a 'watered field', which he presented as a tradition of the Hebrews (*Hebraei autem volunt*): in the present study, we shall

---

[275] The two readings displayed here represent different Old Latin traditions (see Fischer's edition [referenced in my bibliography under 'Primary Sources', 'VL', 'Book of Genesis'], *Genesis*, p. 512).

focus on his linguistic treatment of the Hebrew.²⁷⁶ As he went on to say in QHG that אַיָּלָה שְׁלֻחָה could be translated as 'a stag set free' (*cervus emissus*), he accordingly applied this rendering in the Vulgate against the LXX and VL versions 'thicket / stem / stump / tree', so as to restore the literal meaning of the original and to convey, at the same time, the exegetical implications suggested by the tradition that he quoted ("the promptness of a very fertile land on account of [its] early fruits"). In short, *cervus emissus* in QHG and Vulg. Gen. 49.21 is a *hebraica veritas* rendering reinforced by the exegesis of the Hebrews.

It is noteworthy, though, that both in QHG and in the Vulgate, Jerome interpreted the animal as being a male (*cervus*), while the MT refers to a female (אַיָּלָה). His transliteration *aiala selua* confirms that he read אילה שלחה, not שלוח איל, which would be the masculine form referring to the male of the hind: his Hebrew *Vorlage* therefore agreed here with the MT. Before Jerome, Aquila rendered it in the masculine, too, as is shown by the masculine participle ἀπεσταλμένος agreeing with the noun ἔλαφος (which form can be either masculine or feminine in Greek and which accordingly refers either to a male or to a female): 'a dispatched stag' (ἔλαφος ἀπεσταλμένος).²⁷⁷ However, further analysis of Jerome's responses demonstrates that, when he rendered אילה

---

²⁷⁶ The tradition that Jerome cited has been addressed and studied at some length. See Weill, 'Notes de littérature judéo-hellénistique', pp. 127–28; Aberbach and Grossfeld, *Targum Onqelos on Genesis 49*, pp. 44–45; and Hayward, *Saint Jerome's Hebrew Questions*, p. 242.

²⁷⁷ Aquila's rendering of Gen. 49.21 is the only one attested among the *recentiores*.

as a male in the Vulgate, he operated independently of the other versions, including Aquila.

Among the ten other passages where the word אילה occurs, in 2 Sam. 22.34 (LXX 2 Kgs 22.34), Ps. 18.34 (LXX and Vulg. Ps. 17.34), 22.1 (LXX and Vulg. Ps. 21.1), 29.9 (LXX and Vulg. Ps. 28.9), Prov. 5.19, Song 2.7 and 3.5, Jer. 14.5, Hab. 3.19, and Job 39.1, the sex of the animal can only be determined in five of the *recentiores*' translations: ἔλαφος is in the feminine three times in Aquila (Ps. 17.34, 21.1 and 28.9), once in Symmachus (Ps. 17.34), and once in Theodotion (Jer. 14.5).[278] Therefore, besides Aquila's translation of Gen. 49.21, אילה is represented by a female in all attested cases. On the other hand, Jerome translated אילה four times with the feminine *cerva* 'hind' (Vulg. Ps. 28.9; Vulg. Jer. 14.5; Vulg. Prov. 5.19; Vulg. Job 39.1), five times with the masculine *cervus* (Vulg. Gen. 49.21; Vulg. Ps. 21.1; Vulg. Song 2.7 and 3.5; Vulg. Hab. 3.19), and twice in a way that cannot be ascertained (Vulg. 2 Sam. 22.34 and Vulg. Ps. 17.34).[279] On the

---

[278] In total, there are seven verses where *recentiores* renderings of אילה have been attested: Gen. 49.21, Ps. 17.34, 21.1 and 28.9, Song 2.7 and 3.5, and Jer. 14.5. Furthermore, while LXX Hab. 3.19 does not contain a word for 'hind' or 'stag', two variant readings in Origen's edition of the LXX do (ἔλαφος); these variants, however, do not reveal the sex of the animal (see Field's Hexapla, II, p. 1011).

[279] It can be observed that, where the gender of the noun is unidentifiable in the Vulgate, it is also in the LXX (there is no extant reading for VL 2 Kgs 22.34). It is interesting in this regard that in the *iuxta Septuaginta interpretes* version of Ps. 17.34 (i.e., in Jerome's revision of the VL of Psalms produced on the basis of Origen's edition of the LXX

four occasions when he followed the feminine gender of the Hebrew, this decision was not prompted by another version but by the context itself, which made it impossible for him to replace אילה with a male.[280] In Vulg. Ps. 21.1, he rendered אילה with the masculine: עַל־אַיֶּלֶת הַשַּׁחַר 'on top of the dawn hind' was translated as *pro cervo matutino* 'before the morning stag'. Therefore, Jerome could employ the masculine instead of the feminine in spite of Aquila (ὑπὲρ τῆς ἐλάφου τῆς ὀρθρινῆς 'on top of the daybreak hind'). Close scrutiny of the LXX and VL responses to the other occurrences of אילה further shows that, in all five cases where it is a

---

[see fn. 84]) the noun appears as a masculine genitive plural form: *cervorum*. Jerome no doubt was following the Old Latin: indeed, in the VL version, *cervi* is masculine too (see also fn. 280). The Psalters *iuxta Septuaginta interpretes* and *iuxta Hebraeos* (which I have here referred to as 'Vulg. Ps.') are displayed side by side in Weber and Gryson's edition of the Vulgate.

[280] In the case of LXX Ps. 28.9, the translators rendered קוֹל יְהוָה ׀ יְחוֹלֵל אַיָּלוֹת 'the voice of the Lord will cause hinds to writhe (i.e., to calve)' in a way that has made it unclear whether the verse was pointing to males or to females: φωνὴ κυρίου καταρτιζομένου ἐλάφους 'the voice of the Lord who arrays hinds / stags'. However, in the *iuxta Septuaginta interpretes* version, Jerome rendered the Greek with the masculine: *vox Domini praeparantis cervos* 'the voice of the Lord who prepares stags'. This translation agrees with the Old Latin. Indeed, in the VL version of Ps. 28.9, the noun is masculine: *cervos* (the reading *cedros* 'cedar-trees' is a corrupted form of *cervos*: see Sabatier's remarks in his edition of the VL [cf. my bibliography under 'Primary Sources', 'VL'], II, p. 56, fn. 9). In his translation of the Hebrew version of the Psalm, Jerome reintroduced the feminine (which can be determined on the basis of the verb that he employed): *vox Domini obsetricans cervis* 'the voice of the Lord which assists hinds in parturition'.

male in the Vulgate, the Greek and the Old Latin did not underlie his choice either: indeed, the fact that there is no rendering for אילה in LXX (or VL) Gen. 49.21, Ps. 21.1, Song 2.7 and 3.5, and Hab. 3.19 confirms that Jerome operated independently of these versions. More importantly, in the case of Vulg. Ps. 21.1, he opted for the masculine (*cervo*) not only against the LXX and the VL but, as seen above, against Aquila.

On the whole, the employment of the masculine to render the feminine seems to have been a translation habit of Jerome's;[281] to be sure, in most cases, it owed nothing to the other versions. We may argue in this sense that *cervus emissus* in Vulg. Gen. 49.21 was not meant as a rendering of ἔλαφος ἀπεσταλμένος against *aiala selua* / אַיָּלָה שְׁלֻחָה; the correspondence between the Vulgate and Aquila would be a coincidence in this regard. The discrepancy in gender between אילה in Gen. 49.21 and *cervus* in the Vulgate should therefore not be regarded as more than an independent departure from the Hebrew occurring in the context of a *hebraica veritas* translation. More so in Gen. 49.21 than anywhere else, Jerome may have thought that the male animal would be a more logical choice than the female, as it symbolised Naphtali, one of Jacob's sons.

---

[281] It should be noted that Jerome was also wont to render איל as a male in the Vulgate, with the masculine *cervus* (Vulg. Deut. 12.15, 12.22, 14.5, 15.22; Vulg. 3 Kgs 4.23 [=MT 1 Kgs 5.3]; Vulg. Song 2.9, 2.17, 8.14; Vulg. Isa. 35.6) (and once exceptionally with *aries* 'ram' in Vulg. Lam. 1.6).

2.3. A Case of Hybrid *sensus de sensu* Translation: The Tunic in Vulg. Gen. 37.3 and Elsewhere

In Gen. 37.3, Jacob is said to have offered Joseph a certain garment as he was his favourite son: וְעָשָׂה לוֹ כְּתֹנֶת פַּסִּים. The LXX has treated כְּתֹנֶת פַּסִּים in this verse as being 'a shimmering / polychrome tunic' (χιτῶνα ποικίλον) which the lemma in QHG reflects accordingly: *et fecit ei tunicam variam* 'and he made him a variegated tunic'.[282] Aquila's and Symmachus' respective translations of כְּתֹנֶת פַּסִּים read χιτῶνα ἀστραγάλων,[283] 'a tunic reaching to (lit., a tunic of) the knuckles / ankles', and χιτῶνα χειριδωτὸν, 'a tunic reaching to the hand (lit., furnished with sleeves)', i.e., a long-sleeved tunic. For their part, the targumic translators (apart from Onkelos) interpreted פַּסִּים as referring to the colourful aspect of the tunic (כְּתֹנֶת), like the LXX interpreters.[284] In either case, the

---

[282] QHG 37.3 (p. 57). See also Philo, *Somn.*, 1.220.

[283] Field addresses the differences in the case ending of ἀστράγαλος between his edition and Lagarde's (Hexapla, I, p. 54, fn. 7).

[284] See the discussion in Harl, *La Genèse*, p. 259; Speiser, *Genesis*, pp. 289–90; and Kedar-Kopfstein, 'The Vulgate as a Translation', pp. 159–60. Hayward's analysis of this passage in QHG must be read with caution. Hayward claims that Aquila's rendering is shared by Targumim Onkelos, Neofiti, Pseudo-Jonathan, and by the Fragment-Targums of the Pentateuch, but it is actually the opposite (see Hayward, *Saint Jerome's Hebrew Questions*, p. 219). Indeed, the contrast between these texts involves two traditions—'a colourful tunic' in the LXX and the VL, 'a long one' in Aquila and Symmachus—and the Targumim agree with the LXX (all have מצייר 'ornamented', or מצוייר in one of the Fragment-Targums [I, p. 60]). Targum Onkelos, on the other hand, does not pick a side and calques the Hebrew: כיתונא דפסי.

translators, who were unclear about the exact meaning of the Hebrew word, operated through inference, by way of an interpretation derived from context. As the Hebrew presumably means that the garment worn by Joseph is characterised by both beauty and majesty, each tradition has attempted, in its own way, to represent an aspect of this. In QHG, Jerome remarked that

> instead of a variegated tunic (*pro varia tunica*) Aquila translated [it] as an 'ἀστράγαλον tunic', that is, an ankle tunic (*tunicam talarem*),[285] and Symmachus as a 'long-sleeved tunic' (*tunicam manicatam*); either because it reached all the way down to the ankles and it was wonderful (*mira*) on account of how colourful its adornment had been made by the hands of the craftsman (*manibus artificis varietate distincta*), or because it had long sleeves (*manicas*).

On the one hand, Jerome's comments on the length of the garment draw on the interpretations of Aquila and Symmachus. On the other, his depiction of it as being colourful represents the LXX, as neither Aquila's rendering nor Symmachus' suggested this. Ultimately, in the exegesis of this passage, Jerome conflated two different traditions that he adduced from three Greek sources to understand the meaning of the Hebrew. Further analysis of the other translations of the word פסים reveals, however, that most of his responses agree with those of the LXX translators.

The rarity of פסים is noteworthy: in the Hebrew part of the Hebrew Bible, it only occurs in the phrase כתנת פסים in Gen. 37.3 and 2 Sam 13.18, or as כתנת הפסים in Gen. 37.23, 37.32, and 2

---

[285] Noteworthy is that, a couple of centuries after Jerome, Gregory the Great employed the phrase *talarem tunicam* twice in reference to Joseph's robe (see Fischer's edition of the VL of Genesis, *Genesis*, p. 382).

Sam. 13.19. The fact that it occurs twice in the Aramaic part, in Dan. 5.5 and 5.24, as פַּס יְדָה and פַּסָּא דִי־יְדָא respectively, where it is associated with the hand, may have led some to render it as 'long-sleeved' or in an equivalent fashion. On the whole, in QHG 37.3, Jerome did not try to ascertain which one, the LXX or the *recentiores*, had the right version, i.e., which one represented the Hebrew truth. Rather, he saw fit to combine the two traditions in order to get closer to what he supposed to be the truth: this hybrid exegetical treatment of the phrase כְּתֹנֶת פַּסִּים in QHG is also reflected in his translations. In Vulg. Gen. 37.3, he first rendered the Hebrew in a way reminiscent of the LXX reading: *fecitque ei tunicam polymitam*. The adjective *polymitus*, a Greek loanword (πολύμιτος), is a compound that means '[woven] with many threads', i.e., embroidered. Jerome also employed *polymitum*, a noun derived from the adjective, in the sense of a fine piece of cloth, to render the uncertain *hapax legomenon* מֶשִׁי in Ezek. 16.13, which seems to have to do with silk.[286] This use of *polymitum* is paralleled by *subtilibus* 'fine things', too, in his translation of the only other occurrence of the same word in Ezek. 16.10.[287] In his commentary on Ezekiel, while discussing the clothes described in

---

[286] In his commentary on Ezekiel, Jerome argued that he followed Symmachus (*nos* [...] *hic iuxta Symmachum 'polymitum' diximus*) in his translation of מֶשִׁי (*Comm. Ezech.* 16.13b; CCSL 75, p. 177). According to Field, Jerome misread Symmachus, who was not rendering מֶשִׁי here but the next word in the verse, רִקְמָה 'a variegated thing' (see Field, Hexapla, II, p. 804, fn. 22 and 23).

[287] See Jerome's remarks in *Comm. Ezech.* 16.10d (CCSL 75, pp. 173–74) and 16.13b (ibid., p. 177).

Ezek. 16, Jerome drew a noteworthy parallel with those worn by Joseph, on which he commented at length as follows:

> These are the variegated clothes (*varia vestimenta*) with which Joseph was dressed, and [his] brothers could not have sold him, had they not stripped [him] of his variegated tunic (lit., of the colourfulness of [his] tunic) (*tunicae varietate nudassent*) in the first place. [...] Surely, if riches, and not holiness and a variety of virtues, were to make the variegated aspect of [one's] clothing (*varietatem vestium*), Pharaoh and Nabuchodonosor would have been described as wearing these clothes, and not Joseph who, with a wanderer and a shepherd for a father, could not have been wearing multicoloured and kingly clothing (*vestes discolores et regias*).[288]

It is clear that in Vulg. Gen. 37.3 *polymitus*, which stresses the shimmering of the fabric, represents the LXX reading ποικίλος.[289]

---

[288] *Comm. Ezech.* 16.10a (CCSL 75, pp. 170–71). In light of the fact that Jerome wrote his commentary at a very late time in his career—it was completed in 414 according to Kelly (*Jerome*, pp. 304–6)—it seems that, beyond the Vulgate and QHG, he never actually incorporated the tradition according to which Joseph's garment was long into his exegesis (see my fn. 289). As demonstrated below, however, and particularly in the Vulgate translation of Gen. 37.23 where the garment is portrayed as both long and shimmering (*tunica talari et polymita*), the two traditions were not mutually exclusive in his eyes.

[289] In his correspondence, Jerome's remarks on Joseph's tunic always agree with ποικίλος. See *Epist.* 130.2 (VII, p. 167), in which he wrote that Joseph's "embroidered garment (*vestis polymita*) was woven with a spectrum of many virtues," a direct translation of Origen's remark in *Sel. Gen.* 37.3 (PG 12, p. 128C; read also Jerome, *Epist.* 49.4–5 [II, p. 124] and 54.11 [III, p. 34]). In *Epist.* 130.2, he also equated Joseph's tunic to

In Vulg. Gen. 37.23b, Jerome opted for a twofold rendering of הַפַּסִּים, a hybrid translation that echoed the LXX and at the same time the *recentiores*, whereby both traditions might be mirrored, as outlined in QHG: *nudaverunt eum tunica talari et polymita*[290] ('they stripped him of the tunic [that was] reaching to the ankles and embroidered').[291]

At first glance, it stands to reason that Jerome endeavoured to be in line with both traditions, that of the LXX and that of the *recentiores*, as per his exegetical analysis of the Hebrew syntagm in QHG 37.3. The following data show, however, that his choices

---

the 'gilded dress' (*vestitu deaurato*) of the queen in Ps. 45.10 (his quotation of the Psalm in the letter corresponds to his translation of LXX Ps. 44.10, ἐν ἱματισμῷ διαχρύσῳ 'in clothing [interwoven] with gold', not to Vulg. Ps. 44.10, in which he rendered בְּכֶתֶם אוֹפִיר 'in Ophir's gold' as *in diademate aureo* 'in a golden diadem'). It is noteworthy in this respect that a similar tradition exists in Leqaḥ Ṭov 94:32 (I, p. 185) which likens פסים in Gen 37.3 to the word פזים 'fine gold', 'glistening gems'.

[290] Both Caesarius of Arles and Isidore of Seville spoke, after Jerome's time, of Joseph's tunic as being *polymita et talari*, in accordance with the reading in Vulg. Gen. 37.23 (see Fischer, *Genesis*, p. 388).

[291] From a technical point of view, employing two adjectives to render הַפַּסִּים was probably a way for Jerome to represent the repetition of כתנת in Gen. 37.23b and to avoid translating it twice with the same word (וַיַּפְשִׁיטוּ אֶת־יוֹסֵף אֶת־כֻּתָּנְתּוֹ אֶת־כְּתֹנֶת הַפַּסִּים אֲשֶׁר עָלָיו). In the case of Vulg. Gen. 37.32, he simply did not render כְּתֹנֶת הַפַּסִּים (the word כתנת occurs a second time in a different construct chain at the end of the verse, הַכְּתֹנֶת בִּנְךָ 'the tunic of your son'; here Jerome rendered it as *tunica*). The phrase was translated as τὸν χιτῶνα τὸν ποικίλον in LXX Gen. 37.23 and 37.32 and as *tunicam variam* in the VL verses, which illustrates to some extent Jerome's independence in his stylistic choices.

2. The Translation of the Joseph Story (Gen. 37–50)

actually followed the LXX. The renderings of Aquila and Symmachus for the other occurrences of פַּסִּים are only attested in 2 Sam. 13.18 (= Hexapla 2 Kgs 13.18): Aquila's version reads καρπωτός 'reaching to the wrist' and Symmachus' χειριδωτός 'reaching to the hand'. In either case, their readings mean that the tunic is long, which is consistent with their translations of Gen. 37.3, in which it is either long-hemmed, as in Aquila, or long-sleeved, as in Symmachus. While the LXX translators consistently rendered פסים as ποικίλος in Gen. 37.3, 23 and 32, it is noteworthy that, in 2 Sam. 13.18 and 19 (= LXX 2 Kgs 13.18–19), their respective renderings are χιτὼν καρπωτός and τὸν χιτῶνα τὸν καρπωτὸν ('a tunic reaching to the wrist'), both of which match the tradition later represented by the *recentiores* (assuming that this passage in the Book of Genesis was translated in the LXX before the *recentiores* treated it) and, more specifically, by Aquila's rendering of 2 Sam. 13.18. Therefore, while the LXX translators followed the same tradition in their rendering of פסים throughout the Book of Genesis, they resorted to a different reading in LXX 2 Kgs, one that is matched by the interpretation of the *recentiores* who, again, for their part, remained consistent.[292] In Vulg. 2 Sam. 13.18–19, Jerome rendered the Hebrew phrase twice as *talari tunica* 'a tunic reaching to the ankles'. If this reflects the same tradition as in the *recentiores*, it also corresponds to the passage in which it is supported by the LXX translators. Therefore, Jerome's translation technique proves to conform, in almost every instance, with the

---

[292] It is plausible that the *recentiores* used the LXX reading in 2 Sam. 13 and applied it in Gen. 37 against the LXX.

renderings of the LXX. He purported in QHG to abide by the interpretations of both groups of translators, which is formally the case, but our analysis shows that his variations in the Vulgate follow those of the LXX, regardless of the *recentiores* (the case of Vulg. Gen. 37.23, which contains both traditions at the same time, is an exception).

One should keep in mind that Jerome said many times that he would employ the *sensus de sensu* method in his translations, i.e., that he would endeavour to express the general sense of his source text, and not render it word for word:[293] in a case like that of כתנת פסים, he could only try to do so, as the exact meaning of the Hebrew was not certain in the first place. Therefore, for him, this syntagm represented two traditions, the conflation of which he trusted would bring him as close as possible to an accurate understanding of the Hebrew.[294] The fact that the rendering of פסים in LXX 2 Kgs 13.18–19 meant 'long-sleeved' may have been,

---

[293] See section 1.8.

[294] This hermeneutic method is reminiscent of Augustine's way of employing different Old Latin Bible versions, as presented in *Doctr. chr.* 2, 12, 17 (CCSL 32, pp. 42–43; see my translation below, at the end of 2.4.2). However, one of the major differences between the Old Latin translators, whom Augustine condemned as hardly capable of understanding Greek (*Doctr. chr.* 2, 11, 16; CCSL 32, p. 42), and Jerome, is that Jerome not only mastered Greek but relied primarily on Greek sources in his interpretation of the Hebrew. Augustine claimed that obscure passages of the Bible could be clarified through "the inspection of multiple [Old Latin] manuscripts," i.e., through Latin Christian versions; comparatively, in Gen. 37.3 and elsewhere Jerome was deriving his understanding of כְּתֹנֶת פַּסִּים from Greek Jewish ones.

in his eyes, a confirmation that the *recentiores*' interpretation was correct; it certainly gave him the incentive to further trust it. In theory, one of the two options (if not both) could have been wrong; however, in doubt, reproducing both gave him a greater chance to represent one that could be right. Following not only the two interpretations offered by the LXX translators, but also the order in which they occurred in the LXX, was therefore the safer path. In the midrashic literature, פסים has been construed as the plural form of the word פס, which may have consequently yielded the sense 'flat of the hand' or 'of the foot', hence 'palm' or 'sole'.[295] As said above, the singular form does not exist in Biblical Hebrew: within the Hebrew Bible, only the context of the two Aramaic passages in which the word occurs could have permitted the inference that פסים had to do with the hand.[296] In this

---

[295] See Gen. Rab. 84:8 (II, pp. 1010–11): according to Rabbi Elazar ben Azaria, the פַּסִים can be, among other things, "what reaches the פַּס of one's hand."

[296] If, in Dan. 5.5, the king is said to see the פס of a hand (פַּס יְדָה) "writing over against the sconce on the plaster of the wall," it seems logical that he should be seeing the back of the hand, rather than the palm, which is supposedly facing the wall while writing. The LXX version only contains a 'hand' (χεῖρα), but Jerome, both in the Vulgate and in his commentary (*Comm. Dan.* 5.5; p. 244), translated פַּס יְדָה as *articulos manus*, 'the joints of the hand', as in VL Dan. 5.5 (see Haelewyck's edition of the VL of Daniel [referenced in my bibliography under 'Primary Sources', 'VL', 'Book of Daniel'], *Danihel*, p. 253). The Old Latin form is following Theodotion, who rendered τοὺς ἀστραγάλους τῆς χειρὸς 'the joints of the hand' (he thus employed the term ἀστράγαλος like Aquila in Gen. 37.3). In Vulg. Dan. 5.24, פַּסָא דִי־יְדָא was translated as *articulus*

regard, Aquila's and Symmachus' translation corresponds as much to a contextual interpretation of the word as the rendering of the LXX translators in Gen. 37.3. By blending two traditions drawn from Greek sources—first and foremost from the LXX, and secondarily from the *recentiores*—Jerome showed that in theory he deemed both traditions equally worthy, albeit different, for representing the meaning of the Hebrew word. In practice, however, this translation technique has demonstrated that the Vulgate agenda—which was based on the *hebraica veritas* principle, according to which the single and true meaning of Scripture was to be attained through the Hebrew text—was not always achievable. Jerome once argued that

> Apollinaris, who endeavoured to sew together (*adsuere*)—no doubt with great zeal but not through a scientific [method] (*non secundum scientiam*)—rags from the translations of all [the interpreters] into a single garment, had fabricated [a version] of Scripture that did not follow the rule of truth but his own judgement (*consequentiam Scripturae non ex regula veritatis, sed ex suo iudicio texere*).[297]

However, Jerome also resorted to a patchwork translation technique in his treatment of כתנת פסים. In Vulg. Gen. 37.23 (*tunica talari et polymita*) in particular, his method has consisted of 'sewing together' different versions. As shown throughout this monograph, the Vulgate is often underlain by traditions that Jerome conflated by 'following his own judgement'.

---

manus 'the joint of the hand', which also conformed with the VL reading, in accordance with Theodotion's version ἀστράγαλος χειρὸς.

[297] *Ruf.*, II, 34 (p. 196).

2.4. The Complex Case of Gen. 41.43a–b

LXX

καὶ ἀνεβίβασεν αὐτὸν ἐπὶ τὸ ἅρμα τὸ δεύτερον τῶν αὐτοῦ, καὶ ἐκήρυξεν ἔμπροσθεν αὐτοῦ κῆρυξ ·

And [Pharaoh] mounted [Joseph] on a chariot, the second [best] of his, and a crier cried aloud before him. / and [Pharaoh] cried aloud before him: "Crier."[298]

QHG

Et clamavit ante eum praeco

And a herald shouted before him. / And [Pharaoh] shouted before him: "Herald."[299]

MT

וַיַּרְכֵּב אֹתוֹ בְּמִרְכֶּבֶת הַמִּשְׁנֶה אֲשֶׁר־לוֹ וַיִּקְרְאוּ לְפָנָיו אַבְרֵךְ

And he had him ride the second [best] chariot of his / the chariot of his second-in-command, and they shouted in front of him: "Avrekh."[300]

---

[298] The Greek syntax, which offers two possible constructions reflected here and subsequently in my translation of QHG, is discussed at greater length below. Furthermore, the noun κῆρυξ, which commonly refers to a 'herald', has been purposely rendered as 'crier' here in order to highlight the fact that the verb employed, ἐκήρυξεν, is derived from the same root.

[299] QHG 41.43 (p. 60).

[300] According to Speiser, in light of 2 Chron. 28.7 (וְאֶת־אֶלְקָנָה מִשְׁנֵה הַמֶּלֶךְ), the noun הַמִּשְׁנֶה refers to Joseph's new rank, not to the chariot (Speiser, *Genesis*, p. 314). In the Hebrew construct chain, indeed, the chariot could belong to Pharaoh's 'second-in-command' (see my translation); however, this is not how the LXX translators understood it, as the neuter

Vulgate

fecitque ascendere super currum suum secundum clamante praecone ut omnes coram eo genu flecterent

And he made [him] mount his second chariot while the herald proclaimed that all should bend the knee in front of him.

Aquila

καὶ ἐβόησεν ἐνώπιον αὐτοῦ γονατίζειν

And he proclaimed in front of him (lit., in his face): "Kneel."

Symmachus

καὶ ἐβόησεν ἔμπροσθεν αὐτοῦ ἀβρήχ

And he proclaimed before him: "*Abrech.*"

---

form τὸ δεύτερον modifies τὸ ἅρμα. Philo frequently confirmed this reading in supplying the word 'chariot' in his paraphrase of the passage: καὶ ἐπὶ δευτερεῖον τῶν ἁρμάτων (*Ios.*, 120); τὸ δευτερεῖον τῶν βασιλικῶν ἁρμάτων (*Ios.*, 148); τὸ δευτερεῖον ἅρμα (*Migr.*, 160–61 and *Somn.*, 2.46). In the Vulgate, even though the accusative *suum secundum* could theoretically be read as a masculine ('his second-in-command'), its position in the sentence makes it clear that Jerome meant it as a neuter: 'his second chariot' (see below). Even more straightforward is the syntax of the Targumim, in which the construct chain בְּמִרְכֶּבֶת הַמִּשְׁנֶה is rendered by a noun and an adjective, both in the determined state (see below). See also Speiser (*Genesis*, p. 314) for the word אַבְרֵךְ. Vergote construes אַבְרֵךְ as a form of proskynesis and dismisses the translation 'Attention!' ('Watch out!' in French) as not tenable (Vergote, *Joseph en Égypte*, pp. 135–41); Severino Croatto favours the reading 'overseer' ("Abrek „Intendant" dans Gén. XLI 41, 43', pp. 113–14).

2. The Translation of the Joseph Story (Gen. 37–50)

Targum Neofiti

וארכב יתיה בארתכא תניינתא דידיה והוון מקלסין קדמוי יחי אבוי דמלכא
דרב בחכמתא וזעיר [בשפר] ורכיך בשנייה

And he had him ride the chariot, the second [best] of his, and they were praising before him: "Long live the father of the king, who is great in wisdom, and young [in beauty], and tender in years."

Targum Pseudo-Jonathan

וארכיב יתיה ברתיכא תנייתא דליה והוו מקלסין לקדמוי דין אבא למלכא
רב בחכמתא ורכיך בשנייה

And he had him ride the chariot, the second [best] of his, and they were praising before him: "This is the father of the king, great in wisdom and tender in years."[301]

Genesis Rabbah

ויקראו לפניו אברך אב בחכמה ורך בשנים

And they shouted in front of him "*Avrekh*:" a father (*av*) in wisdom, and tender (*rakh*) in years.[302]

2.4.1. The Tradition of אַבְרֵךְ

In QHG, Jerome argued the following:

---

[301] This targum is paralleled by the Fragment-Targums (I, p. 63 and p. 153) and by the Genizah manuscripts (I, p. 115). In Targum Onkelos, אַבְרֵךְ is replaced by the phrase 'this is the father of the king', with no further elaboration: וארכיב יתיה ברתיכא תנייתא דיליה ואכריזו קדמוהי דין אבא למלכא 'and he had him ride the chariot, the second [best] of his, and they proclaimed before him: "This is the father of the king"'.

[302] Gen. Rab. 90:3 (III, p. 1102).

Aquila translated 'and he shouted in front of him the kneeling' (*et clamavit in conspectu eius adgeniculationem*).³⁰³ Symmachus, rendering the Hebrew term itself (*ipsum hebraicum sermonem interpretans*), said 'and he shouted before him (*et clamavit ante eum*) abrech'. Therefore, it seems to me that 'a herald' (*praeco*) or 'the kneeling' (*adgeniculatio*) (the latter of which can be taken as a way to greet or beseech Joseph [*quae in salutando vel adorando Ioseph accipi potest*]) should not be understood, so much as what the Hebrews transmit (*non tam [...] intellegenda, quam illud, quod Hebraei tradunt*) when they say that 'a tender father' (*patrem tenerum*) is meant by this term (*ex hoc sermone transferri*). Indeed, *ab* is said as in 'father' (*pater*), *rech* as in 'soft' or 'most tender' (*delicatus sive tenerrimus*), while Scripture indicates that he has been a father to all (*pater omnium*), certainly in respect of shrewdness (*iuxta prudentiam*), but a most tender teenager, [too,] even a boy, in respect of age (*iuxta aetatem tenerrimus adolescens et puer*).³⁰⁴

Along with the etymological construal of אַבְרֵךְ as the compound 'tender father', a hermeneutic tradition that is shared by the Targumim and Genesis Rabbah, Jerome proposed in his exegesis an explanation that was based on Joseph's function in the tale.³⁰⁵

---

³⁰³ With *in conspectu eius*, literally 'at the sight of him', Jerome endeavoured to reflect the etymology of ἐνώπιον αὐτοῦ, through which Aquila imitated that of לְפָנָיו. If Jerome considered that the word *coram* was related to *os*, 'mouth', 'face', the employment of *coram eo* in the Vulgate may have been an attempt to reflect the Hebrew etymology, too.

³⁰⁴ QHG 41.43 (p. 60).

³⁰⁵ It has not been stressed enough, if at all, in recent scholarship, that the interpretation 'father of the king' in the Targumim only becomes clearer once read alongside Gen. 45.8, in which verse God is said to

2. The Translation of the Joseph Story (Gen. 37–50)

Considering what he said about his relations with his informants,[306] with the phrase 'what the Hebrews transmit' he expected his readership to infer that an acquaintance of his had shared with him the tradition that he was citing. A passage of Origen's third-century commentary on Genesis casts doubt on the manner in which this tradition actually reached him:

> 'And a crier cried aloud before him. / And [Pharaoh] cried aloud before him: Crier' (καὶ ἐκήρυσσεν ἔμπροσθεν αὐτοῦ κῆρυξ).[307] The Hebrew has *Abrech* (Τὸ Ἑβραϊκὸν ἔχει Ἀβρὴχ), which means 'tender father' in the proper sense (ὃ κυρίως σημαίνει, 'πατὴρ ἁπαλός'). It is appropriate (Εἰκότως) that [the text] referred to Joseph as a tender father, since he was tender in respect of age (ἐπειδήπερ ἁπαλὸς ὢν κατὰ τὴν ἡλικίαν), [and] like a father he demonstrated a life-saving principle to the Egyptians (σωτήριον ἀρχὴν Αἰγυπτίοις ἐνεδείξατο). But the term indicates nothing other than the kneeling (Δηλοῖ δὲ οὐδὲν ἡ λέξις, ἢ τὸ γονατίζειν). For the message (lit., voice) of the crier (ἡ φωνὴ τοῦ κήρυκος) is clear.[308]

---

have made Joseph 'a father to Pharaoh' (וַיְשִׂימֵנִי לְאָב לְפַרְעֹה). Interpolation or inspiration from an analogous passage is a recognised response among translators who seek to explain the meaning of an obscure or oblique word.

[306] See section 1.6.

[307] This double English rendering of Origen's quotation of LXX Gen. 41.43 does not represent his text, in which a single version of the lemma is discussed. Again, it is my attempt to address the ambiguity introduced in my translations of LXX Gen. and QHG 41.43 at the beginning of this section and below.

[308] *Sel. Gen.* 41.43 (PG 12, pp. 133D–36A). See Kamesar's remarks on this passage in 'Rabbinic Midrash and Church Fathers', pp. 30–31.

Whether Jerome ever checked for himself and learned the Jewish interpretation of the etymology of אַבְרֵךְ through an informant, alongside his reading of Origen, is impossible to determine.[309] De Montfaucon and Bardy identify Origen as his source for this material.[310] Kamesar refines: Jerome's dependency on Origen's exegesis did not fully fashion his own. On the contrary:

> [Origen] cites both the rendering of Aquila and the Jewish interpretation as the correct literal translation of the word 'avrech', rather than presenting them as alternative translations of a difficult word. Nor does he distinguish these interpretations from that of the LXX, which he sews on as the conclusion of his comment. It is therefore difficult to accept the view of B. de Montfaucon and others, who believe that Jerome is here dependent on Origen. In the first place, Origen does not even say that the first interpretation which he cites is of Jewish origin,[311] so from what source

---

[309] See Bardy, 'Saint Jérôme et ses maîtres hébreux', p. 146.

[310] See de Montfaucon's notes on Hexapla Gen. 41.43 (PG 15, p. 301); and Bardy, 'Les traditions juives', p. 230.

[311] Indeed, Origen only showed how to derive it from the etymology of the Hebrew word, a point on which Kamesar agrees with de Lange (*Origen and the Jews*, p. 129). However, if he came to the etymological construal of the Hebrew as 'tender father', it must have been through the insight of a man well-versed in the Hebrew language, or perhaps through a Greek Midrash; the *recentiores*' interpretations did not mirror this etymology, and Origen's Hebrew, if he had any command of it, would not have been sufficient on its own (on Origen's relationship with his Hebrew sources, see de Lange's remarks in *Origen and the Jews*, pp. 51–52 and p. 58; and Kamesar, 'Rabbinic Midrash and Church Fathers',

2. The Translation of the Joseph Story (Gen. 37–50)   135

did Jerome obtain this information? In fact, we should probably see Jerome's comment as an indirect critique of the methods of his predecessor. For the Latin Father generally attempts to interpret the Hebrew text itself by critically employing the *recentiores* and Jewish teachers, not by simply sewing them together.[312]

Origen started off with the idea that *abrech* was to be construed as the compound 'tender father' (πατὴρ ἁπαλός), as it both reflected the reconstructed etymology of the Hebrew (κυρίως) and suited Joseph's background more generally (Εἰκότως). Indeed, on the basis of this etymology, he proposed an allegorical interpretation that explained the function of Joseph in the tale, as in Jerome, albeit with minor differences. Aquila, on the other hand, who understood אַבְרֵךְ as related to the root בָּרַךְ 'to kneel' and to the noun בֶּרֶךְ 'knee', represented it through the verb γονατίζειν 'to kneel', derived from the noun τὸ γόνυ 'knee'. Origen's approval of his rendering as conveying what he presumed to be the meaning of *abrech* in context was couched in clear terms: "But the term indicates nothing other than the kneeling" (Δηλοῖ δὲ οὐδὲν ἡ λέξις, ἢ τὸ γονατίζειν). On the whole, as Kamesar argues, Origen accepted both the compound and Aquila's rendering as correct interpretations, the former as an etymology that befitted the story and the latter as a contextual rendering. By contrast, as Jerome objected to this analysis in his own explanation of the lemma, he may be

---

pp. 30–31, and ibid. fn. 42). Also relevant is the similarity of his wording to that of the Targumim and particularly to the Midrash of Genesis Rabbah.

[312] Kamesar, *Jerome*, pp. 102–3.

said to have displayed a form of independent thinking that was meant to be critical of his predecessor's views.[313]

2.4.2. The Translation of אַבְרֵךְ

According to Hayward, in the Vulgate, Jerome translated אַבְרֵךְ like the LXX as 'herald'.[314] Kamesar suggests that אַבְרֵךְ is rendered twice, that is, through a double rendering whereby *clamante praecone* ('while the herald proclaimed') matches the reading of

---

[313] It is well known that Origen referred to Aquila as a "slavishly literal" translator (δουλεύων τῇ ἑβραϊκῇ λέξει), one on whom he often relied to make sense of the Hebrew (see Origen, *Ep. Afr.*, 4 [p. 526]; see also de Lange, *Origen and the Jews*, p. 58; and Barthélemy, 'Origène et le texte de l'Ancien Testament', p. 259). It should be mentioned that Petit's edition of Origen's text reflects a variant reading, one with a different, though confusing, Greek syntax: Δηλοῖ δ' οὐδὲν ἡ λέξις καὶ τὸ γονατίζειν 'But the expression "the kneeling" is not obvious at all either' (see in my bibliography under 'Primary Sources', 'Catenae on Genesis': *La chaîne sur la Genèse*, IV, p. 252). If this syntax did not seem corrupt, one could believe that Origen was in fact exploiting the Hebrew compound to prove Aquila wrong. Kamesar's point that, unlike Jerome in QHG, Origen admitted the LXX reading at the end of his comment would be further invalidated by another variant reading in Petit, from which the word κῆρυξ is missing: φανερὰ γάρ ἐστιν ἡ φωνὴ 'For the message (lit., voice) is clear'. In summary, Petit's *lectio difficilior*, albeit not *potior* here and very difficult to admit, could suggest that, since Origen in fact preferred the compound over Aquila's rendering, Jerome did not emancipate himself from his thinking in refuting Aquila's version, on the contrary. However, it seems not only likely but logical that Jerome read Origen's text the way it has been represented above, in the body of the text, and understood by Kamesar.

[314] Hayward, *Saint Jerome's Hebrew Questions*, p. 226

the LXX and *genu flecterent* ('bend the knee') that of Aquila: "[Jerome] attempted to maintain the traditional LXX/VL version to a certain degree, and to provide a readable, readily comprehensible text."[315] By all means, in his rendering of the Hebrew, Jerome remained mindful of the habits of the Old Latin version's followers, in a way that also conformed with paraphrase as a translation technique, and more specifically with the *sensus de sensu* method. His remarks in QHG are obviously at odds with his rendering. Indeed, the Vulgate appears to be agreeing with the two readings that were disqualified in QHG, *praeco* and *adgeniculatio*, in favour of the Hebrews' tradition, *pater tener*, which, on the other hand, was not employed in the Vulgate. In modern LXX scholarship, this segment of the verse (καὶ ἐκήρυξεν ἔμπροσθεν αὐτοῦ κῆρυξ) is always understood as 'and a crier cried aloud before him', which would be the most straightforward way to construe it. At the same time, my English translation shows that an alternative is grammatically possible: 'and [Pharaoh] cried aloud before him: "Crier"'. If κῆρυξ is a nominative, as scholars have construed it so far, it is to be read as the subject of the clause.[316] Recourse to a *figura etymologica* in the LXX, whereby two cognates are employed in the same sentence, can also be a way to indicate stylistically that these words operate together within the sentence; accordingly, in Gen. 41.43, the noun κῆρυξ would be the subject of

---

[315] Kamesar, *Jerome*, p. 103, fn. 20.

[316] Harl (*La Genèse*, p. 275) and Hayward (*Saint Jerome's Hebrew Questions*, p. 226) read κῆρυξ as the subject of the sentence without considering any alternative.

the verb ἐκήρυξεν.³¹⁷ However, in theory, without the article ὁ, the form κῆρυξ can also be construed as a vocative. On a strictly grammatical level, it would be acceptable to read it as such; only, in doing so, one obtains a different meaning.

Greek syntax is flexible: it can accommodate different word orders without entailing changes in the meaning of a sentence. In Gen. 41.43 though, the LXX translators' concern to mirror the Hebrew word order in placing the verb at the beginning of the sentence and the noun at the end may be meaningful. It stands to reason that they could not have read אַבְרֵךְ as the subject of וַיִּקְרְאוּ, a plural form, and the mention of multiple Hebrew witnesses to a singular form, וַיִּקְרָא, in the apparatus of BHS does not prove either that they read אַבְרֵךְ as being the subject of the verb. On the contrary, should the verb be a singular, not only could Pharaoh as the last expressed subject be the subject of that sentence, too, but the context would arguably make him an expected candidate for the proclamation: he is indeed the only character to be running Joseph's induction ceremony from Gen. 41.41 to 41.45. This is what Aquila and Symmachus seem to be telling us too: who else could be implied in the third person singular

---

³¹⁷ In the case of LXX Dan. 3.4, for example, the same pair of cognates as the one employed in LXX Gen. 41.43 renders וְכָרוֹזָא קָרֵא: καὶ ὁ κῆρυξ ἐκήρυξε (Theodotion, on the other hand, does not resort to a *figura etymologica* in Dan. 3.4 [καὶ ὁ κῆρυξ ἐβόα]). In MT Dan. 3.4 the Aramaic syntax and context are unambiguous: וְכָרוֹזָא can only be the subject of the sentence. In LXX Dan. 3.4, not only the word order, which in itself leaves no room for doubt, but above all the article ὁ indicates that κῆρυξ is a nominative.

ἐβόησεν, if not Pharaoh?³¹⁸ First of all, in the LXX, the reading of κῆρυξ as the subject automatically deprives the verse of an actual proclamation in direct speech; a verb like κηρύσσω, though, is often employed in the LXX to introduce proclamations in direct speech (cf. Exod. 32.5, 36.6; 2 Chron. 36.22-23; Prov. 1.21-22; Hos. 5.8; Dan. 3.4). Secondly, if κῆρυξ is to be part of a *figura etymologica*, as in ἐκήρυξεν… κῆρυξ, it is also possible to regard it as an addition meant to express the subject implied in וַיִּקְרְאוּ (or to replace Pharaoh as the subject of וַיִּקְרָא), and not as a rendering of אַבְרֵךְ *per se* (which would thus be left untranslated by the LXX interpreters). Thirdly, as indicated above, Pharaoh is the implied subject of a series of sentences in Gen. 41.42-43, all of which start with καί. Reading κῆρυξ as a nominative would not only interrupt this sequence of actions performed by Pharaoh, it would also cause the herald to become the last subject expressed before Pharaoh assigns the land of Egypt to Joseph at the end of Gen. 41.43: καὶ ἐκήρυξεν ἔμπροσθεν αὐτοῦ κῆρυξ· καὶ κατέστησεν αὐτὸν ἐφ' ὅλης γῆς Αἰγύπτου would then read as 'and a crier cried aloud before him; and he (i.e., the crier) appointed [Joseph] to the whole land of Egypt'.³¹⁹ Assuredly, a herald could not be the one appointing Joseph to the administration of the state; the latter part

---

³¹⁸ A shift in subject through the emendation of וַיִּקְרָא, if this was the original reading, to the impersonal plural וַיִּקְרְאוּ may have been prompted by the fact that crying out, as a herald does, was unworthy of Pharaoh's rank. A group of ministers or servants implied in וַיִּקְרְאוּ could perform the declaration without inflecting the sense of the verse. See also fn. 323.

³¹⁹ The finite verb κατέστησεν 'he appointed' here translates the infinitive absolute וְנָתוֹן 'to give', which functions as a substitute for the finite

of the verse should be understood in the following way: 'and he (i.e., Pharaoh) appointed [Joseph] to the whole land of Egypt'. By contrast, construing κῆρυξ as a vocative addressed to Joseph would represent an active response to an obscure term such as אַבְרֵךְ on the part of the LXX translators. The vocative introduced by the verb ἐκήρυξεν is not just conceivable grammatically, it also makes sense in context that Joseph be declared a 'herald' as the new representative of Pharaoh's court (but plausibly as God's envoy, too).[320] In Gen. 41, Joseph shows Pharaoh that, if he has

---

verb: וַיִּקְרְאוּ לְפָנָיו אַבְרֵךְ וְנָתוֹן אֹתוֹ עַל כָּל־אֶרֶץ מִצְרָיִם 'and they shouted in front of him "*Avrekh*", and he was appointed / and [Pharaoh] appointed him to the whole land of Egypt'.

[320] See Gen. 45.5–8, where Joseph says three times to his brothers that God sent him. This passage in particular could have played a part in the LXX translators' interpretation of אַבְרֵךְ (should κῆρυξ refer to Joseph in Gen. 41.43). The occurrence of the word κῆρυξ in the LXX and the Pseudepigrapha is rare enough to be noticed in a context involving Joseph in the *Joseph and Aseneth* novella. In *Jos. Asen.*, 14, when Aseneth has finished praying to God, the morning star rises and becomes 'a messenger and a herald (ἄγγελος καὶ κῆρυξ) of the great day's light'. The heavens break open and a great and unspeakable light appears; Aseneth falls on her face, a man descends from the heavens, one who is 'the general of the Lord God' and 'the commander-in-chief of all the host of the Most High' (cf. Gen. 41.40–43 and 45.8–9). When Aseneth looks up again, she sees him: this man is 'like Joseph in every respect' (καὶ ἰδοὺ ἀνὴρ ὅμοιος κατὰ πάντα τῷ Ἰωσήφ; *Jos. Asen.*, 14 [pp. 58–59]). While one piece of external evidence adduced from a single source is not sufficient to prove that there was a Greek tradition portraying Joseph as a κῆρυξ, a divine messenger, it shows that the parallel at least existed in Jewish Hellenistic literature. See also Philo's description of Joseph in *Ios.*, 93–95 and 116–17.

2. The Translation of the Joseph Story (Gen. 37–50)

been the only one capable of interpreting his dreams, it is only in the name of God and thanks to God (Gen. 41.16, 25, 28, 32): Pharaoh logically starts perceiving him as the man that God chose to deal with the afflictions to come (Gen. 41.38–39). It would be consistent with these passages to read ἐκήρυξεν in LXX Gen. 41.43 as translating the Hebrew verb independently of κῆρυξ, which would in turn be representing the LXX interpretation of Joseph's new status, independently of ἐκήρυξεν. To be sure, κηρύσσω is a conventional rendering for קָרָא and, in an unrelated manner, κῆρυξ could also be how the LXX translators chose to render אַבְרֵךְ: in other words, if they did not really understand the Hebrew word, they may have believed that, at a climactic moment in the story of Joseph, the timing was befitting to call him a herald, a term that illustrated well his repute as God's agent. Should this be the case, the LXX word order may indicate that κῆρυξ was meant as a vocative describing Joseph.

While in QHG Jerome reproduced the syntactical ambiguity of LXX Gen. 41.43 in the word order of his quotation, he may have shown us, at the same time, that he allowed for the possibility that Joseph was being called a herald. Firstly, there is no *figura etymologica* in his lemma (*Et clamavit ante eum praeco*).[321]

---

[321] Relevant are certain VL readings attested in direct textual witnesses which differ from the Latin version cited in QHG. Two paronomasias, *praedicavit praeco* ('the herald proclaimed') found in a European text type and *praecedit praeco* ('the herald precedes') in Isidore of Seville, could represent attempts to form an etymological wordplay. More importantly, Gregory of Elvira, who was Jerome's elder by a couple of decades, used the phrase *praeco praeconavit*, a *figura etymologica* based on the rare verb *praecono* derived from the noun *praeco* (see Fischer,

Also noteworthy is his rendering of the versions of Aquila and Symmachus. Both have *clamavit*, which translates ἐβόησεν, and, unlike the LXX syntax, their constructions are clear: in Aquila, the verb governs the accusative *adgeniculationem*; in Symmachus, the Hebrew word transliterated as *abrech* is introduced in direct speech. Secondly, in the context of Gen. 41.43 in the *recentiores*, there is no potential subject other than Pharaoh, who is by default the only possible subject for *clamavit*; Jerome cannot have construed their versions any differently. In QHG, he equated *praeco* with *adgeniculationem* ("Therefore, it seems to me that 'a herald' or 'the kneeling'…"): since the verb *clamavit* obviously governs *adgeniculationem* in his rendering of Aquila, it could also be construed as introducing *praeco* in the QHG lemma, as a vocative in direct speech.[322] Jerome's phrasing is open to interpretation. In the Vulgate, he seems to have translated אַבְרֵךְ twice, as Kamesar suggested. Yet one could also argue that אַבְרֵךְ was actually treated only once, with *clamante praecone* rendering וַיִּקְרְאוּ or וַיִּקְרָא, and *genu flecterent* אַבְרֵךְ.[323] If indeed the ablative absolute

---

Genesis, p. 429). Billen argued that Jerome knew and relied on a variety of Old Latin versions in his citations of the Heptateuch (Billen, *The Old Latin Texts of the Heptateuch*, p. 77). Given his proficiency in Greek, however, there is no doubt that some of the lemmas of his biblical commentaries also represented his own *ad hoc* renderings of the LXX.

[322] Hayward's one-sided translation of the lemma excludes this possibility: "And a crier shouted before him" (Hayward, *Saint Jerome's Hebrew Questions*, p. 77).

[323] Whether Jerome's Hebrew *Vorlage* read וַיִּקְרְאוּ or וַיִּקְרָא makes no difference. In either case, the introduction of a herald with *clamante praecone* could be supplying a subject (*praeco*), whether for the impersonal

2. The Translation of the Joseph Story (Gen. 37–50)

of the Vulgate, *clamante praecone*, was meant to match just the Hebrew verb, then it is plausible that Jerome read κῆρυξ as a vocative in the LXX. By all means, *clamante praecone* directly echoes the QHG reading *clamavit... praeco*, only it does so by introducing a subordinate clause, the content of which, *ut omnes* [...] *genu flecterent*, no doubt is a translation of אַבְרֵךְ. Accordingly, in Jerome's eyes, ἐκήρυξεν may have been introducing κῆρυξ in direct speech, that is, as a vocative. While he employed the same verb and the same noun as in QHG, he might have left aside the interpretation that it represented in the LXX, i.e., אַבְרֵךְ as κῆρυξ (with which he disagreed in QHG). His translation of אַבְרֵךְ would then correspond exclusively to the command expressed in indirect speech, namely, that all bend the knee before Joseph, as in Aquila (with whom he also disagreed in QHG).

On the whole, it is clear that in Vulg. Gen. 41.43 Jerome intended to echo the LXX wording for those of the Old Latin audience who were accustomed to it, and to include Aquila's interpretation. Whether the word אַבְרֵךְ itself is represented twice therein, through both the interpretation of the LXX and that of Aquila—both of which were equally dismissed in QHG in favour of 'tender father', which 'the Hebrews transmit'—cannot be established beyond doubt. Jerome himself may have been hesitant. However, the fact that two divergent traditions were clearly displayed in the Vulgate, even if only formally, is significant in itself. The method that consists of relying on two different sources

---

implied in the Hebrew plural, or to replace Pharaoh in the making of the declaration. At any rate, Jerome meant to please the audiences of the VL.

or more in the translation of an obscure passage is reminiscent of Augustine's theory on the value of variant versions:

> [The existence of different Old Latin versions] has certainly helped to understand [the Scriptures] more than it has hindered (*plus adiuvit intellegentiam quam impedivit*) ... if only readers were not careless! Actually, examining multiple manuscripts has often [enabled me to] clarify some very obscure sentences (*nonnullas obscuriores sententias plurium codicum saepe manifestavit inspectio*). [...] Which of the [Latin translators] may have followed the [original] words, unless the source texts (lit., the texts of the previous language) can be read, it is uncertain. But still from each of them something great is imparted to those who read carefully. In fact, [even when] translators happen to differ a great deal, it is difficult for them not to find common ground (*difficile est enim ita diversos a se interpretes fieri, ut non se aliqua vicinitate contingant*).[324]

Augustine lauded the exegetical value of the textual diversity that had stemmed from the work of different Old Latin translators. On the other hand, the production and circulation of various versions of the Bible were determining factors in Jerome's decision to undertake his own translation of the Hebrew text, with which he set out to establish a fixed, uniform Latin version of the Old Testament on the basis of a single source. The Vulgate translation of Gen. 41.43 shows that this goal was technically unachievable when a passage of the Hebrew was too obscure. Here Jerome applied an analogous hermeneutic method to the one recommended

---

[324] *Doctr. chr.* 2, 12, 17 (CCSL 32, pp. 42–43).

2. The Translation of the Joseph Story (Gen. 37–50)

by Augustine;[325] only, the fundamental difference is that he could rely both on the Hebrew and on Greek sources. Earlier in the same passage, Augustine criticised the Old Latin translators for endeavouring to translate the Bible from the Greek without actually knowing Greek:

> Latin-speaking people [...] certainly need two other [languages]—Hebrew, to be sure, and Greek—in order to know the Holy Scriptures [well] and to resort to the source texts (in case the endless variety of Latin translators causes some uncertainty). [...] Because of the translators' disagreements, the knowledge of these languages is necessary. For those who have rendered the Scriptures from the Hebrew language into the Greek one can be numbered, but the Latin translators [cannot] by any means. For, in the early days of the faith, as soon as a Greek manuscript came into the hand of anyone who believed himself to have the slightest command of both languages (i.e., Greek and Latin), he ventured a translation.[326]

To that extent, where according to Augustine Old Latin translators had failed, Jerome succeeded: this was the innovation of the Vulgate. Also innovative on Jerome's part was to conflate Jewish traditions and Christian ones in his translation. In the case of Vulg. Gen. 41.43, for instance, the Jewish tradition was represented by Aquila, and the Christian one by the echo of the VL wording accompanying Aquila. Jerome's reliance on the VL in Vulg. Gen. 41.43 also illustrates his willingness to compromise with the Christian audience; at the same time, it attests to the

---

[325] See my remarks at the end of the preceding case study (section 2.3).
[326] *Doctr. chr.* 2, 11, 16 (CCSL 32, p. 42).

impossibility of fulfilling his agenda in the strictest sense, that of "extracting the truth from the Hebrew books."[327] In this respect, the *sensus de sensu* method, which he presented as his translation policy, was supposed to allow him to express the general sense of a Hebrew unit: here he had to resort to additional sources, on top of the Hebrew, to achieve it.

2.5. Certain Departures from the Hebrew in the Vulgate

2.5.1. An Example of Agreement with the LXX: Vulg. Gen. 37.1

MT

וַיֵּשֶׁב יַעֲקֹב בְּאֶרֶץ מְגוּרֵי אָבִיו בְּאֶרֶץ כְּנָעַן׃

And Jacob settled down in the land of his father's sojournings, in the land of Canaan.

LXX

Κατῴκει δὲ Ἰακὼβ ἐν τῇ γῇ, οὗ παρῴκησεν ὁ πατὴρ αὐτοῦ, ἐν γῇ Χανάαν.

Jacob then settled down in the land where his father had dwelt, in the land of Canaan.

Vulgate

habitavit autem Iacob in terra Chanaan in qua peregrinatus est pater suus.

Jacob then dwelt in the land of Canaan, in which his father had sojourned.

---

[327] *Epist.* 20.2 (I, p. 79).

2. The Translation of the Joseph Story (Gen. 37–50)

No difference in meaning can be distinguished between the MT verse and its counterpart in the LXX. A syntactical departure of the latter from the former is reflected in the construction of the English translations above; this departure can be observed in the Vulgate, too. The original unit בְּאֶרֶץ מְגוּרֵי אָבִיו 'in the land of his father's sojournings' is composed of a preposition introducing a chain of three construct nouns, the second of which is a plural noun (מְגוּרֵי), the last a form suffixed with the third person masculine singular pronoun (אָבִיו). In the LXX, this syntagm is paraphrased with a relative clause introduced by a locative, the relative οὗ, referring to the antecedent ἐν τῇ γῇ: 'in the land (ἐν τῇ γῇ) where (οὗ) his father had dwelt'. In this clause, the subject, ὁ πατὴρ αὐτοῦ 'his father', and the finite verb, παρῴκησεν 'he dwelt', translate the last two words of the chain, מְגוּרֵי אָבִיו. It is in this regard that the Vulgate matches the LXX syntax: *in terra Chanaan in qua peregrinatus est pater suus* 'in the land of Canaan, in which his father had sojourned.'[328] Latin syntax could have allowed Jerome to render a long Hebrew construct chain with a series of

---

[328] Jerome also translated the first occurrence of בְּאֶרֶץ 'in the land' in the verse as *in terra Chanaan* in the Vulgate. Making *in terra Chanaan* the antecedent of the clause introduced by *in qua* allowed him to avoid repeating the syntagm 'in the land' at the end of the verse (as in the Hebrew). The VL, which in theory should represent the LXX, seems to agree with the Vulgate in this case; although it may be omitting a large part of the original verse, the reading attested in VL Gen. 37.1 displays a construction analogous to that of Vulg. Gen. 37.1, against the LXX: *habitabat autem Jacob in terra Chanaan* 'Jacob was then dwelling in the land of Canaan'. Whether this Old Latin reading, potentially incomplete, inspired Jerome cannot be ascertained, as it is adduced from a later

genitives;[329] his choice to follow a construction similar to the Greek one, against the Hebrew, was stylistic. It can be further explained by Gen. 35.27:

MT

וַיָּבֹא יַעֲקֹב אֶל־יִצְחָק אָבִיו מַמְרֵא קִרְיַת הָאַרְבַּע הִוא חֶבְרוֹן אֲשֶׁר־גָּר־שָׁם אַבְרָהָם וְיִצְחָק׃

And Jacob came to Isaac, his father, [at] Mamre, the city of Arba / the fourfold city, that is, Hebron, where Abraham had sojourned, as well as Isaac.

Vulgate

venit etiam ad Isaac patrem suum in Mambre civitatem Arbee haec est Hebron in qua peregrinatus est Abraham et Isaac.

He also came to Isaac, his father, in Mambre, the city of Arbee, that is, Hebron, in which Abraham had sojourned, as well as Isaac.

LXX

Ἦλθεν δὲ Ἰακὼβ πρὸς Ἰσαὰκ τὸν πατέρα αὐτοῦ εἰς Μαμβρὴ εἰς πόλιν τοῦ πεδίου (αὕτη ἐστὶν Χεβρών) ἐν γῇ Χανάαν, οὗ παρῴκησεν Ἀβραὰμ καὶ Ἰσαάκ.

---

work by Augustine, *Questions on the Heptateuch*, 122 (PL 34, p. 581). Augustine wrote his *Questions on the Heptateuch* years after Jerome completed the Vulgate: when quoting Gen. 37.1, he could have been the one inspired by the Vulgate, or by a VL manuscript that had been contaminated by it.

[329] In Vulg. Judg. 9.1, for example, the construct chain וְאֶל־כָּל־מִשְׁפַּחַת בֵּית־אֲבִי אִמּוֹ 'and to the entire family of the house of his mother's father' was rendered as *et ad omnem cognationem domus patris matris suae* 'and to all the kin of the house of his mother's father'.

2. The Translation of the Joseph Story (Gen. 37–50) 149

> Jacob then came before Isaac, his father, to Mambre, to the city of the plain (it is the very Hebron), in the land of Canaan, where Abraham had dwelt, as well as Isaac.

MT Gen. 35.27 presents the place 'where Abraham had sojourned, as well as Isaac' in a manner that is analogous to MT Gen. 37.1, though the wording is not exactly the same. In the former case, the verse contains a relative clause introduced by שָׁם [...] אֲשֶׁר; in the latter, a construct chain is introduced by the preposition בְּ. In the LXX, both are translated the same way, with a relative clause introduced by οὗ, and with the same finite verb, παρῴκησεν, purposely repeated to mirror the repetition of the root גור in the Hebrew, finite in MT Gen. 35.27 (גָּר) and nominal in MT Gen. 37.1 (מְגוּרֵי). As Gen. 36 focuses on the descendants of Esau, Jacob's brother, the story of Jacob and of his sons is momentarily interrupted at 35.29. Although the resumption of the narrative in 37.1 was already clearly illustrated in the Hebrew through similar constructions and the repetition of a verbal root, the LXX translators meant to stress it even more. Their translation technique has consisted of further bridging chapters 35 and 37 by imitating the syntax of 35.27 in 37.1. This stylistic device allowed them to circumvent a long chain of genitives and to express in Greek a parallel which they considered to be implied in the Hebrew. Likewise, Jerome treated מְגוּרֵי in Gen. 37.1 like אֲשֶׁר־גָּר־שָׁם in Gen. 35.27 by rendering it as *in qua peregrinatus est*. If he appreciated the twofold value of the Greek translators' paraphrase in LXX Gen. 37.1, he probably saw fit to follow them on a path that neither impaired the original meaning of the verse nor altered the course of the story.

2.5.2. Two Paraphrases Independent of Other Versions

MT Gen. 39.8

וַיְמָאֵן ׀ וַיֹּאמֶר אֶל־אֵשֶׁת אֲדֹנָיו הֵן אֲדֹנִי לֹא־יָדַע אִתִּי מַה־בַּבָּיִת וְכֹל אֲשֶׁר־יֶשׁ־לוֹ נָתַן בְּיָדִי:

But he refused and said to his master's wife: "Behold, with me, my master does not know what is in the house, and all that belongs to him, he puts (lit., gives) in my hand."

Vulg. Gen. 39.8

qui nequaquam adquiescens operi nefario dixit ad eam ecce dominus meus omnibus mihi traditis ignorat quid habeat in domo sua

He, by no means assenting to the nefarious act, said to her: "Behold, as everything has been entrusted to me, my master has no knowledge of what he might have in his own house…"

MT Gen. 39.10

וַיְהִי כְּדַבְּרָהּ אֶל־יוֹסֵף יוֹם ׀ יוֹם וְלֹא־שָׁמַע אֵלֶיהָ לִשְׁכַּב אֶצְלָהּ לִהְיוֹת עִמָּהּ:

And it happened, as she spoke to Joseph, day [after] day, but he would not listen to her, to lie with her, to be with her.

Vulg. Gen. 39.10

huiuscemodi verbis per singulos dies et mulier molesta erat adulescenti et ille recusabat stuprum

And, with words of this sort, each and every day, the woman would be troublesome to the young man, and he would reject debauchery.

In the Vulgate, Jerome altered the two original verses contained in the Hebrew by means of additions, omissions, and paraphrases, none of which agrees with the sources with which his translation has been compared so far (i.e., the LXX, the VL, the *recentiores*, the Targumim and later rabbinic literature). In Vulg. Gen. 39.8, he expanded on the scene by adding the adverb *nequaquam* 'by no means'—thus stressing Joseph's refusal to lie with his master's wife (see Gen. 39.7)—and the mention of a 'nefarious act' nowhere expressed in the MT (וַיְמָאֵן 'but he refused' / *nequaquam adquiescens operi nefario* 'by no means assenting to the nefarious act'); he further added the possessive pronoun *sua* in his rendering of בַּבָּיִת 'in the house' (*in domo sua* 'in his own house').[330] In Vulg. Gen. 39.10, *et mulier molesta erat adulescenti* 'and the woman would be troublesome to the young man' does not represent any element of the original verse. In all cases, Jerome elaborated on the Hebrew, albeit with perfectly harmonious additions in context. In Vulg. Gen. 39.8, אֵשֶׁת אֲדֹנָיו 'his master's wife' was simply rendered as "her" (*eam*); אִתִּי 'with me' was not translated; בְּיָדִי 'in my hand' was reduced to a singular first-person pronoun (*mihi* 'to me'); the unit אֲשֶׁר־יֶשׁ־לוֹ '[all] that belongs to him' was either omitted or combined with the translation of מַה־בַּבַּיִת 'what is in the house' (*quid habeat in domo sua* 'what he might have in his own house'); and the master is no longer presented as the one who entrusts his belongings to Joseph (וְכֹל אֲשֶׁר־יֶשׁ־לוֹ נָתַן בְּיָדִי 'and all that belongs to him, he puts [lit., gives]

---

[330] The definite article in the prefixed preposition בְּ makes it clear that it is the master's house, which the context itself confirms, too. Although the possessive pronoun is also attested in LXX Gen. 39.8 (ἐν τῷ οἴκῳ αὐτοῦ), it was not necessary for Jerome to draw on the Greek to consider adding *sua*.

in my hand' / *omnibus mihi traditis* 'as everything has been entrusted to me'). In Vulg. Gen. 39.10, the *waw*-consecutive verb וַיְהִ֗י 'and it happened', which can be translated as *accidit* 'it happened' in the Vulgate (see for example Vulg. Gen. 39.11), was elided by Jerome; and the clause וְלֹא־שָׁמַ֤ע אֵלֶ֙יהָ֙ 'but he would not listen to her' was left untranslated.[331] Finally, the two infinitive clauses לִשְׁכַּ֥ב אֶצְלָ֖הּ לִהְי֥וֹת עִמָּֽהּ 'to lie with her, to be with her', which are subject to significant exegetical expansions in the Targumim, were here compressed and paraphrased as *et ille recusabat stuprum* 'and he would reject debauchery'.

Paraphrase has been Jerome's watchword in his translation of these two verses. His additions were meant to introduce his own evaluation of the Hebrew, his omissions allowed him to avoid repetitions and to lighten certain turns of phrase. In both cases, his approach operates within the flow of the narration without changing the original sense beyond measure: this is an example of the *sensus de sensu* method. It is significant that, in paraphrasing the Hebrew, Jerome also incorporated to some extent his exegetical interpretations of the verses into his translation (this translation technique is also found in the Targumim, where Hebrew verses can be rendered with substantial midrashic

---

[331] The clause *et mulier molesta erat adulescenti* could also be regarded as a very loose paraphrase of וְלֹא־שָׁמַ֤ע אֵלֶ֙יהָ֙, to the extent that Jerome probably meant to stress how much the master's wife harassed Joseph trying, day after day, to have him listen to her advances. As a matter of fact, Barr argues that Jerome was expressing his own views on women in his paraphrasing of Gen. 39.8 and 39.10 ('The Vulgate Genesis', p. 272). See also Skemp's comments in 'Learning by Example', p. 278.

2. The Translation of the Joseph Story (Gen. 37–50) 153

expansions). That his translation contains exegetical material of this type might indicate that he intended to rely on it in Bethlehem to deliver sermons,[332] the same way as the expansions in the Targumim could be designed for synagogue services. On the whole, his departures from the Hebrew Bible make him a paraphrast of Scripture; his independence of other textual bases makes him the author of his own version of these passages.

---

[332] An extensive exploration of the relationship between Jerome's translations and his homiletic work could provide insight into this matter.

3. THE TRANSLATION OF THE BOOK OF DANIEL

1.0. Textual History

The MT of the Book of Daniel comprises twelve chapters written in Hebrew and Aramaic: chapters 1–2.4a are Hebrew, 2.4b–7 Aramaic, and 8–12 revert to Hebrew.[333] The Hebrew-Aramaic version was probably composed between the fourth and the second century BCE.[334] Alongside the LXX translation, there is an alternative Greek version of the book known as Theodotion's version, which closely follows the MT where the LXX departs from it.[335]

---

[333] On the languages of the Book of Daniel, see Di Lella, *The Book of Daniel*, pp. 10–12 and pp. 14–17; Gzella, *A Cultural History of Aramaic*, p. 96, pp. 205–6, p. 208; Davies, *Daniel*, pp. 35–38.

[334] Di Lella, *The Book of Daniel*, pp. 13–14; Segal, *Dreams*, p. 7; Davies, *Daniel*, pp. 33–34.

[335] For a general discussion of the two Greek versions of Daniel, see Di Lella, 'The Textual History'; and Amara, 'Septuagint'. For an overview of the modern research, see Olariu, 'Textual History', pp. 518–25. The alternative non-LXX version of Daniel has been attributed to Theodotion at least since the first half of the third century by Origen (see Jerome's citation of Origen's lost work, the *Stromata*, in *Comm. Dan.* 4.5a [p. 220], and Origen's remarks in *Ep. Afr.*, 4 [p. 526]). Jerome believed, in accord with Origen, that Theodotion was the author of this version (see Vulg., p. 1341; *Ruf.*, II, 33 [pp. 192–94]; *Comm. Dan.*, p. 132, and 3.91a [p. 206]). However, as it has been established that early Christian writers quoted it before the date that is traditionally attributed to Theodotion (approximately the second half of the second century), it has ceased

Three major Greek expansions, missing from the Hebrew-Aramaic story, exist in two different forms in the LXX and Theodotion: 'Susanna' and 'The Fables of Bel and the Dragon' (Bel and the Dragon) traditionally appear before the first and the last chapters of the MT, respectively, and 'The Prayer of Azariah and the Song of the Three Children' (the Prayer) reads between MT Dan. 3.23 and 3.24 as Dan. 3.24–90.[336] These three episodes were

---

to be considered as his version. Various theories have been proposed. That the non-LXX version of Daniel was produced after the LXX, and in response to it, is a point on which modern scholars almost unanimously agree. On the whole, it could represent a revision of the LXX form towards a Hebrew-Aramaic *Vorlage* close to the MT (or a new Greek translation produced from this *Vorlage* against the LXX). It has also been suggested that this version served as the base text for a later revision made by Theodotion (this hypothesis has been disputed). For an overview of this debate, see Moore, *Daniel, Esther, and Jeremiah*, pp. 30–33; Munnich, 'Daniel, Susanna, Bel and the Dragon', pp. 291–92 and pp. 295–96; Davis Bledsoe, 'The Relationship', pp. 179–80 and pp. 184–86; Di Lella, 'The Textual History', pp. 593–97; Swete, *An Introduction*, pp. 46–49; Collins, *Daniel*, pp. 3–11; Braverman, *Jerome's Commentary*, p. 31, fn. 61; Olariu, 'From Suspicion to Appreciation'; and Haelewyck's preface to his edition of the VL of Daniel, *Danihel*, pp. 23–24. Modern scholars sometimes refer to the non-LXX version of Daniel as 'proto-Theodotion's version'. For the purpose of our study, and because Jerome attributed it to Theodotion, we shall continue to refer to it as Theodotion's version.

[336] The history of the arrangement of the LXX of Daniel and of that of Theodotion's version is complex; their structures can vary from one textual witness to another. See fn. 360.

arguably composed between the late Persian period and sometime in the second half of the Hellenistic one.[337] The existence of two Greek textual traditions for the Book of Daniel entailed two to three types of Old Latin translations, one representing the LXX, one representing Theodotion's version, and one that conflated the two.[338] Jerome completed his translation of the Hebrew-Aramaic version of Daniel in 392–393. He himself claimed that he wrote his commentary on the book "many years" after translating the

---

[337] Moore, *Daniel, Esther, and Jeremiah*, pp. 28–29, pp. 44–48, pp. 91–92, and p. 128. See also Henze, 'Textual History', pp. 133–37.

[338] Burkitt, *The Old Latin*, pp. 6–7. A text mixing both Greek versions has been identified in Cyprian's Latin citations, which led Burkitt to conclude that the transition from the LXX to Theodotion's version took place in Cyprian's time, that is, in the first half of the third century, in Carthage (see also Zilverberg, *The Textual History of Old Latin Daniel*, pp. 157–58). Burkitt also posited that Cyprian relied on a Latin form of the LXX version that had been partly revised towards another Old Latin form which corresponded to Theodotion's version (*The Old Latin*, p. 6 and pp. 27–29): Zilverberg, who disagrees with this hypothesis, argues that the shift had already happened in the Greek, before the process of translation into Latin took place (given the organic nature of VL forms, revisions could have taken place in Latin, too, that is, after the translation process, but to a smaller extent; Zilverberg, *The Textual History of Old Latin Daniel*, pp. 131–34). See also Haelewyck, *Danihel*, p. 49 and p. 72. For a survey of the scholarly research on the extant textual witnesses to the VL versions of Daniel, see Zilverberg, *The Textual History of Old Latin Daniel*, pp. 16–20 (these textual witnesses are introduced ibid., pp. 26–46). For a discussion of the VL types of Daniel, see Haelewyck, *Danihel*, pp. 40–65; on the VL form of the three additional episodes, see Cañas Reíllo, 'Latin'.

book;[339] according to Courtray's computations, this was in 407.[340] He also specified that his commentary would introduce the Latin readership to the versions of the *recentiores*, whom he consistently cited in his interpretations of the biblical text.[341] From a Christian point of view, his thirst for Hebrew truth was polemical in many regards: the position of the Book of Daniel in the Jewish and Christian canons, for example, was in itself a point of contention.

1.1. The Position of Daniel in the Biblical Corpus

In the Christian tradition, the Book of Daniel is placed among the Prophets.[342] In the Hebrew Bible, it belongs to the *Ketuvim* (כתובים), i.e., the Writings, the last of the three sections implied in the acronym 'Tanakh' (תנ"ך). Jerome informed the reader of this difference in the preface to the Vulgate of Daniel: "I warn [the reader] that Daniel is not contained in the Prophets among the Hebrews, but among [the books] that they have titled 'Holy Writings' (*Agiografa*) (i.e., the Writings)."[343] He showed on multiple occasions that he deemed Daniel worthy to be called a

---

[339] *Comm. Dan.*, p. 130.

[340] *Comm. Dan.*, pp. 11–14. See also Courtray, *Prophète*, pp. 23–27.

[341] *Comm. Dan.*, p. 132. See, for instance, *Comm. Dan.* 1.3–4 (p. 142). For a review of Jerome's employment of the *recentiores*' work in his commentary on Daniel, see Courtray, 'Jérôme traducteur', pp. 108–9.

[342] See Canellis, *Préfaces*, p. 128, fn. 5; Olariu, 'Textual History', p. 517; Dorival, 'L'Apport des Pères de l'Église', pp. 84–87 and p. 91; and Bogaert, 'Septante et versions grecques', p. 646.

[343] Vulg., p. 1342.

prophet, though: in the Vulgate preface—whose heading reads "Jerome's preface to Daniel the Prophet (*in Danihele propheta*) begins"—he called Daniel a 'prophet' (*Danihelem prophetam*);[344] in the *Apology against Rufinus*, he stressed the fact that he had straightaway acknowledged Daniel as a prophet in the heading of his preface to the book (*me non negasse eum prophetam quem statim in fronte prologi prophetam esse confessus sum*);[345] in his commentary on the book, not only did he refer to Daniel as a prophet,[346] he asserted that "none of the prophets has spoken so openly about Christ;"[347] in his letter to Paulinus of Nola, he said that Daniel was "the last of the four prophets (i.e., Isaiah, Jeremiah, Ezekiel, Daniel)."[348] In Weber and Gryson's edition of the

---

[344] Vulg., p. 1341.

[345] *Ruf.*, II, 33 (p. 192).

[346] *Comm. Dan.*, p. 124 and p. 134.

[347] Ibid., p. 126.

[348] *Epist.* 53.8 (III, p. 21). Daniel does act as a prophetic character in the story and the fact that Jerome considered him a prophet, as per the Christian tradition, was not at variance with a certain Jewish understanding. Indeed, the Qumran scroll 4Q174 (frag. 19, l. 3) and to some extent the Gospel of Matthew (Matt. 24.15), though not speaking for the tradition supported by the Rabbis in the time of Jerome, reflect a Jewish understanding of Daniel as being a prophet; Josephus, too, seems to have implied that the book was placed among the Prophets in his description of the biblical corpus (*Ag. Ap.*, 1.38–41; for a discussion of these sources in comparison with rabbinic material, see Scheetz, 'Daniel's Position', pp. 179–84). The initial position of the Book of Daniel in the Hebrew canon may have been among the Prophets; according to Dorival, it is very likely that the Rabbis are responsible for its moving to the Writings ('L'Apport des Pères de l'Église', pp. 99–100).

Vulgate, the book is placed among the prophetic books, between Ezekiel and Hosea, the first of the twelve Minor Prophets (which close the Old Testament corpus in that edition, excluding the two Books of Maccabees): from that point of view, the Vulgate does not conform with the Hebrew tradition, in which the Book of Daniel is not part of the *Nevi'im* (נביאים), i.e., the Prophets, the second section of the Tanakh.[349]

In principle, however, the *hebraica veritas* should have involved following the structure of the Hebrew Bible, too: Jerome may have departed from his agenda in this regard by leaving Daniel among the Prophets in his arrangement of the Old Testament corpus, as per the tradition displayed in one LXX manuscript, the Codex Sinaiticus.[350] Repeatedly reasserting that Daniel was a prophet no doubt was a way to please the Christian readership and the defenders of the Christian tradition; placing Daniel in the corpus of Prophets, on the other hand, represented a contradiction with regard to the *hebraica veritas* project. Jerome seems to have deliberately remained ambiguous: beyond the fact

---

[349] See Scheetz, 'Daniel's Position', pp. 189–91 (Scheetz never discusses Jerome's intention but only the order reflected in today's Vulgate edition). For a summary of the different sequences of Old Testament books found in Vulgate manuscripts, see Graves, 'Vulgate', p. 281.

[350] The Vulgate arrangement of the Old Testament is not exactly the same as that of two LXX manuscripts, the Codex Vaticanus and the Codex Alexandrinus, in which Daniel, being placed directly after Ezekiel but also after the Minor Prophets, closes the Old Testament. It matches, however, that of the Codex Sinaiticus, in which the Minor Prophets also come after Daniel (see Andrist, 'La structure des codex *Vaticanus, Alexandrinus,* et *Sinaiticus*', pp. 13–14).

that he openly presented the book as belonging to the Writings among the Hebrews, and not to the Prophets, while still consistently calling Daniel a prophet across his *œuvre*, the reality is that he never clearly stated where the Vulgate of Daniel should be placed in his view.[351] Maintaining an ambiguity probably allowed him to appear less controversial while in the process of promoting the existence of a Hebrew truth. To be sure, valuable information on his treatment of the Hebrew-Aramaic of Daniel is to be found by further delving into his reception of the book. It should be pointed out that, from his vantage point, the Book of Daniel had a special status, both on a canonical level and on a linguistic one. Investigating these two aspects will shed further light on his relationship with his sources.

1.2. The Canonical Status of Daniel

1.2.1. The LXX and Theodotion's Version

While the LXX was the version of Scripture in use in churches, the LXX of Daniel, temporarily authoritative, had, by Jerome's time, been replaced by Theodotion's version. No clear explanation for

---

[351] One should keep in mind that the order represented in current Vulgate editions may not reflect the original order of the corpus as Jerome may have wanted it; also possible is that he never actually figured out this aspect of his project. Given the absence of a clear statement on his part, I am inclined to argue that he deliberately left the position of Daniel in his version of the Old Testament undetermined. Should he have ascribed a position to the book, though, an investigation of the most ancient manuscripts of the Vulgate could permit us to establish what it might have been.

this unique phenomenon in the history of the LXX seems to have been found.³⁵² In his preface to the book, Jerome addressed the issue by venturing several hypotheses; he admitted, at the same time, that he did not know why exactly Theodotion came to supplant the LXX:

> The Churches of the Lord Saviour do not read (*non legunt*) Daniel the Prophet according to the Seventy translators, as they use Theodotion's version (*utentes Theodotionis editione*); and why this happened, I do not know (*et hoc cur acciderit nescio*). Indeed, whether, because it is [in] the Aramaic tongue (*sermo Chaldaicus*) and it disagrees with our way of

---

[352] For a survey of early Church Fathers' comments on the reception of Theodotion's version and on the replacement of the LXX version, see Olariu, 'From Suspicion to Appreciation'. Olariu suggests that "the decision to displace the Old Greek with Theodotion only in the book of Daniel accords well with both the high prophetical status ascribed to this book within the Christian circles, and the necessity of the church to have, as much as possible, a text free of textual discrepancies with the Hebrew text for apologetic reasons" ('From Suspicion to Appreciation', p. 66). Olariu's hypothesis rests on the assumption that this phenomenon is the result of a "decision" (which is also Jerome's assumption, as shown below). However, there is no evidence that the Church ever held a council where an official decision was made, and the fact that the reading of Theodotion's version of the Book of Daniel gradually supplanted that of the LXX version in the Church and among Church Fathers is no proof in this respect. If ever this was the fruit of a decision, Christian communities could remain flexible in their use of coexisting versions anyway. Indeed, there is no doubt that every community enjoyed a certain degree of autonomy; more importantly, the existence of Old Latin texts mixing the LXX of Daniel and Theodotion's version (see fn. 338) shows that these versions were not always regarded as mutually exclusive.

> speaking in some [of its] characteristics (*quibusdam proprietatibus a nostro eloquio discrepat*), the Seventy translators did not want to keep (*servare*) these passages in their rendering; whether the book was produced under their name (*sub nomine eorum*) by someone else—by whom, I do not know—who did not know the Aramaic language [well] enough; or whether there has been some other reason (*aliud quid causae extiterit*) of which I am not aware, I can assert this one thing (*hoc unum adfirmare possum*): [the LXX] is very much at variance with the [Hebrew] truth (*multum a veritate discordet*) and it was the right decision to repudiate it (*recto iudicio repudiatus sit*).[353]

For Jerome, the excessive dissimilarity between the LXX form of the book and the Hebrew-Aramaic version amply justified the rejection of the former from the Church. He reiterated this opinion in 401 in the *Apology against Rufinus*:[354]

> I have informed the reader that the Churches of the Christ read (*legere*) this prophet (i.e., Daniel) according to Theodotion, and not according to the Seventy translators. If, in this book, I have said that their work differed greatly from the [Hebrew] truth (*multum a veritate distare*) and that it had been the right decision on the part of the Churches of the Christ to reject it (*recto Ecclesiarum Christi iudicio reprobatam*), I, who [just] said it, am not at fault, but the readers are.[355]

---

[353] *Vulg.*, p. 1341.

[354] For the date, see Kelly, *Jerome*, p. 254.

[355] *Ruf.*, II, 33 (p. 192). For a discussion of Jerome's view, see Moore, *Daniel, Esther, and Jeremiah*, p. 31, and the literature cited ibid. in fn. 7.

In his 407 commentary on the book, Jerome added the following: "The churches do not read Daniel according to the Seventy translators, but according to Theodotion, who assuredly (*utique*) was a non-believer (*incredulus fuit*) after the coming of the Christ; some may call him an Ebionite, which is a Jew in another way."[356] Whereas his remarks on Theodotion's version and the LXX had been mostly philological, here he expressed for the first time a personal opinion. His tone makes it clear indeed that he was not pleased that the version replacing the previously authoritative text was that of Theodotion, a man who "assuredly was a non-believer after the coming of the Christ," i.e., who had dared to remain a non-Christian Jew (while the LXX translators had at least operated before the birth of Christ).[357] Later in his commentary, in reference to Dan. 4.3–6, which verses are missing in the

---

[356] *Comm. Dan.*, p. 132. Under the entry dedicated to Origen in *Vir. ill.*, Jerome said that Theodotion was an Ebionite without specifying that he was a Jew (*Vir. ill.*, 54; p. 33). In *Epist.* 112.19 (VI, p. 39), however, he called him 'a Jewish man'; and in the preface to the Vulgate Book of Ezra he called Aquila, Symmachus and Theodotion "Jewish and Ebionite translators of the Old Law" (*Iudaeos et Hebionitas legis veteris interpretes*; Vulg., p. 639).

[357] This is one of the reasons that Jerome gave in *Epist.* 57.11 (III, p. 71) to explain why the LXX translation, despite major departures from the Hebrew text, had still 'rightfully prevailed' in the Church (*et tamen iure Septuaginta editio obtinuit in ecclesiis, vel quia prima est et ante Christi fertur adventum*) (see also *Ruf.*, II, 35 [p. 198]). See Olariu's remarks on early Church Fathers' attitudes, especially Jerome's, towards Theodotion, in 'From Suspicion to Appreciation', pp. 61–64. It is also noteworthy that in *Epist.* 112.19 (VI, pp. 38–39) Jerome associated Theodotion's Jewishness with his being a 'blasphemer' (*ex hominis Iudaei atque blasphemi*

LXX, Jerome discussed again the 'decision' to 'repudiate' the LXX of Daniel from the Church:

> If we put aside the Seventy translators (*Exceptis Septuaginta translatoribus*), who have omitted all these [verses] (I do not know for which reason) (*nescio qua ratione*), the three remaining ones (*tres reliqui*, i.e., the *recentiores*) have rendered 'partner' (*collegam*) [here].[358] This is why (*unde*) their version (i.e., the LXX), by the decision of the heads of the church (*iudicio magistrorum ecclesiae*), was repudiated (*repudiata est*) in this volume (i.e., the Book of Daniel), and that of Theodotion, which agrees with the Hebrew and the other translators (i.e., the *recentiores*), is commonly read (*vulgo legitur*). This is also why Origen, in the ninth volume of the *Stromata*, declares that he discusses what follows from this point on in the [Book of the] prophet Daniel, not according to the Septuagint interpreters, who differ a great deal from the Hebrew truth, but according to the version of Theodotion.[359]

Although Jerome was personally offended that the LXX was supplanted by the version of a non-Christian Jew, he came to terms with this state of affairs as his faith in the Hebrew truth and, by extension, in Theodotion's version, persuaded him that it was the fruit of a justified decision.

---

post passionem Christi 'from a Jewish man, a blasphemer after the passion of the Christ').

[358] Jerome also employed the term *collega* in his translation of Dan. 4.5. This rendering constitutes the fifth case study of this chapter (section 3.2.5).

[359] *Comm. Dan.* 4.5a (p. 220).

1.2.2. The Place of the Three Greek Episodes in the Vulgate

Jerome departed from the *hebraica veritas* principle to the extent that the Vulgate of Daniel did not actually follow the structure of the Hebrew-Aramaic version of the book. Indeed, if he translated the twelve chapters common to all versions from the Hebrew-Aramaic text, he also added to the Vulgate, allegedly from Theodotion's version, the three episodes that the Hebrew-Aramaic did not contain: 'The Prayer' was inserted as Vulg. Dan. 3.24–90, 'Susanna' as Vulg. Dan. 13, and 'Bel and the Dragon' as Vulg. Dan. 14. The fact that he placed the Susanna episode after the end of the Hebrew-Aramaic portion, as the thirteenth chapter of the Vulgate book, is noteworthy: this order does not reflect the arrangement of Theodotion's edition but that of Origen's edition of the LXX.[360] In the preface to the Vulgate book, Jerome

---

[360] Jerome specified that he followed Theodotion's edition in his treatment of the Prayer, Susanna and Bel and the Dragon (see below in section 3.1.3). However, in Theodotion's edition, Susanna is placed at the beginning of the book, before the Hebrew-Aramaic portion (see Haelewyck, *Danihel*, pp. 25–27; Ziegler and Munnich's preface to the Göttingen edition of the LXX of Daniel [referenced in my bibliography under 'Primary Sources', 'LXX', 'Book of Daniel'], *Susanna. Daniel. Bel et Draco*, pp. 20–21; and Courtray, *Prophète*, p. 121). A remark that Jerome made in his commentary on the Book of Isaiah, regarding two characters in the story of Susanna, indicates that he knew that Susanna appeared at the beginning, and not at the end, in Theodotion's edition: *Et inueteratos dierum malorum duos presbyteros iuxta Theodotionem in Danielis principio legimus* 'And we read about the two elders who have aged in evil days at the beginning of [the Book of] Daniel according to Theodotion['s edition]' (*Comm. Isa.* 3.2; CCSL 73, p. 43). In Papyrus 967,

acknowledged the importance of the three additional episodes in the Christian world, but he also stressed how indifferent Jews might be to them:

> [This is] the difficulty of [the Book of] Daniel, which, among the Hebrews, does not contain the story of Susanna, nor the Song of the Three Children, nor the Fables of Bel and the Dragon. Because [these episodes] have been spread across the entire world, we have affixed (*subiecimus*)[361] a broach (i.e., the obelus) to them, which dismisses them when it is placed before (*veru ante posito easque iugulante*):[362] this way we should not seem to have edited out a large part of the book in the eyes of the uneducated (*ne videremur apud inperitos magnam partem voluminis detruncasse*). I have myself heard someone among the instruc-

---

the only extant textual witness to the pre-Origenic LXX edition of Daniel, Susanna appears after Bel and the Dragon as the fourteenth chapter. That Jerome is responsible for making Susanna the thirteenth chapter of the Vulgate version, and for placing the Prayer in the third chapter, is confirmed by the arrangement of the book displayed in his commentary (see below).

[361] The full sentence, *veru ante posito easque iugulante subiecimus*, is ambiguous. One of the possible meanings of the verb *subicio* is 'to append'. However, Jerome cannot have meant that he 'appended' the three episodes to the story here, as he did not place the Prayer at the end of the Vulgate edition of the book but in the third chapter, as in his Greek *Vorlage*. For further discussion of the meaning of *subiecimus* in this context, see Haelewyck, *Danihel*, pp. 65–66.

[362] The obelus is the editorial sign that Origen employed in his revision of the LXX to indicate that the passage before which it is placed is not contained in the Hebrew version (cf. Origen, *Comm. Matt.* 19.16–30 [XV, 14; pp. 387–88]; *Ep. Afr.*, 6–7 [pp. 530–32]; see also section 1.2.2).

tors of the Jews (*quendam de praeceptoribus Iudaeorum*) deride the story of Susanna (*Susannae derideret historiam*) and say that it was invented (*esse confictam*) by a Greek man, I do not know who...[363]

Although Jerome's comments provide valuable information on the status of the Prayer, Susanna, and Bel and the Dragon in Christian and Jewish communities, they do not tell us what his personal stance was. When asked to clarify whether he considered them canonical, he gave two contradictory answers. In 401,[364] his friend Rufinus accused him of having amended the LXX of Daniel in his Vulgate translation and of having doubted the canonicity of the three episodes, thus shaking centuries of Christian faith: "So now, after four hundred years, the truth of the Law, which has been bought from the Synagogue at a price, [suddenly] reaches us!"[365] The same year, Jerome cautiously responded to Rufinus that he had never expressed any personal opinion (*non enim quid ipse sentirem*); that he had only told what the Hebrews had been saying against these episodes and indicated that they did not have them in their scrolls.[366]

Then, in 407, his preface to his commentary on the book opened with a direct response to Porphyry's strike against the canonicity of Daniel.[367] Jerome first argued that Porphyry had

---

[363] Vulg., p. 1341.

[364] Kelly, *Jerome*, p. 249.

[365] Rufinus, *Apol. Hier.*, II, 39 (CCSL 20, p. 114).

[366] Jerome, *Ruf.*, II, 33 (pp. 192–94).

[367] Jerome had already mentioned Porphyry in the Vulgate preface to the book (Vulg., p. 1342).

claimed that the entire Book of Daniel had not been written in Hebrew but in Greek (*Graeci sermonis esse commentum*) and that this could be linguistically proven by the presence of two puns located in the story of Susanna.[368] Indeed, as these puns seemed to be peculiar to the Greek language, Porphyry concluded, according to Jerome, that the Book of Daniel could not have been translated from Hebrew. In response, Jerome said that only Susanna and Bel and the Dragon were "not found among the Hebrews" (*non haberi apud Hebraeos*) and that they "offer[ed] none of the authority of holy Scripture" (*nullam scripturae sanctae auctoritatem praebeant*).[369] The implication was that what was found among the Hebrews did offer "the authority of holy Scripture." Therefore, six years after being forced by Rufinus' accusations to assert that he had not doubted the canonicity of the additional episodes, Jerome explicitly dismissed Susanna and Bel and the Dragon as inauthentic as he attempted to invalidate Porphyry's reasoning.[370]

---

[368] See LXX and Theodotion Susanna 54–55 and 58–59.

[369] *Comm. Dan.*, pp. 124–30. Jerome was more consistent here with the *hebraica veritas* principle, with respect to the additional episodes in Daniel, than he had been anywhere else. This conclusion on their status also turns out to be the opposite of that of Origen who, as a supporter of the Christian Bible tradition, defended their value and their authority, that of Susanna in particular, in his letter to Africanus (*Ep. Afr.*, 3–11 [pp. 524–38]; for a discussion of Origen's stance in his letter to Africanus, see de Lange, 'The Letter to Africanus'). See also Jerome's citation of Origen in *Comm. Dan.* 13.54b–55 and 58b–59 (p. 542).

[370] See Courtray, 'Porphyre et le livre de Daniel', pp. 342–43. A remark that Jerome made in his commentary shows that he did not consider

His editorial method was no less confusing. As indicated in the preface to the Vulgate of Daniel (see above), he singled out the three episodes in his translation of the book by inserting them with obeli "that dismiss them." In the preface to his commentary, he further presented the obelus as a device for highlighting portions that are not in the Hebrew-Aramaic text: "Origen, too, [...] prefixed obeli (*obelis praenotavit*) to certain verses, [thus] pointing out (*designans*) whatever was superfluous (*superflua quaeque*) [in the common edition]."[371] By including the Prayer, Susanna and Bel and the Dragon in his version of the Book of Daniel, though, Jerome also meant to show his detractors that he had not disregarded or rejected the Christian textual tradition: it allowed his Christian readership to use his translation without having to forgo passages upon which preachers had been wont to base their

---

the Prayer pertinent to the 'Hebrew truth' either (see *Comm. Dan.* 3.91a [p. 206] translated below, in section 3.1.3). Also noteworthy is that he referred to Susanna as a *historia* 'story' but also as a *fabula* 'fable', and to the Prayer and to Bel and the Dragon as *fabulae* (see for example Vulg., p. 1341; or *Comm. Dan.*, p. 130). Courtray argues that this terminology shows that he distinguished these episodes from the rest of the book (*Prophète*, pp. 122–23). According to Courtray, it may also indicate that he considered them less authentic (see for example Jerome's use of the word *fabula* in *Comm. Dan.* 6.25a [p. 278], which he equated with *deliramentum* 'nonsense'). For further discussion of Jerome's ambiguous statements on the canonicity of the additional episodes in Daniel and on the structure of the Vulgate book, see Courtray, *Prophète*, pp. 38–40, pp. 42–43, pp. 120–28; and Haelewyck, *Danihel*, pp. 65–66.

[371] *Comm. Dan.*, p. 132.

homilies. Applying the obelus to these episodes was the least polemical way of acknowledging that they were simply not in the Hebrew-Aramaic text; as seen above, he had drawn on Origen's editorial method in this regard.[372] However, while Origen never went as far as to promote the superiority of the Hebrew over the LXX,[373] Jerome had made it clear that the former represented the original and true text. Therefore, in imitating Origen, he was taking a step back. Likewise, it was for apologetic reasons that the Books of Tobit and Judith and the additional episodes of the Book of Esther had been added to the Vulgate. In the case of Tobit, Jerome claimed that he translated the book "against the canon of [the Hebrews]" (*contra suum canonem*) because he preferred "to displease the Pharisees' judgement and to serve the commands of the bishops;"[374] in the case of Judith, because "the Nicene Synod is reported to have considered this book to be part of the Holy Scriptures" (*hunc librum sinodus nicena in numero Sanctarum Scripturarum legitur conputasse*).[375] However, Jerome was not consistent in this case, either. In the preface to the Vulgate Book of

---

[372] See Jerome's reference to Origen in the preface to *Comm. Dan.*, p. 130.

[373] De Lange, *Origen and the Jews*, pp. 50–55.

[374] Vulg., p. 676. This statement is reminiscent of Origen's attitude to the Book of Tobit (see *Ep. Afr.*, 19; p. 562). Jerome also alluded to the dubious canonicity of the Book of Tobit in *Comm. Dan.* 8.16 (p. 330).

[375] Vulg., p. 691. For further discussion of Jerome's reception and treatment of Tobit and Judith, see Gallagher, 'Why Did Jerome'; and Canellis, *Préfaces*, pp. 143–48. The Vulgate of Esther is investigated below, in section 4 of this monograph.

Kings, he suggested that Tobit and Judith should be considered 'apocryphal' since they were not part of the Hebrew canon:

> This preface to the Scriptures could suit as a crested introduction (*galeatum principium*) to all the books that we are translating from Hebrew into Latin, so that we may know that whichever [book] is not among those (*quicquid extra hos est*) is to be placed apart among the apocrypha (*inter apocrifa seponendum*). Therefore, [the Book of] Wisdom, which is commonly ascribed to Solomon, and the Book of Jesus son of Sirach, and those of Judith, of Tobias and of the Shepherd are not in the canon (*non sunt in canone*). I have found the first Book of Maccabees in Hebrew; the second is Greek, which can also be demonstrated on the basis of the style itself. As it stands, I beseech you, O reader, not to regard my work as a reproof of the ancients (i.e., the Septuagint translators).[376]

---

[376] Vulg., p. 365. Earlier in the same preface, Jerome described the arrangement of the Hebrews' canon in the following manner: "the five books of Moses, which they specifically call *Thorath* (sic), that is, 'the Law';" the Prophets; and the αγιογραφα (sic), i.e., 'the Holy Writings' (which corresponds to the Writings) (Vulg., pp. 364–65; see also Vulg., p. 1342). The apocrypha are then introduced as a distinct category. That the Book of Tobit and that of Judith were said to be in the *Agiografa* in their Vulgate prefaces (Vulg., p. 676 and p. 691) is probably the result of a textual corruption: it is sensible to amend it to *Apocrypha*, as Canellis does (see Canellis, *Préfaces*, pp. 139–41, p. 368 and p. 372; and also Braverman, *Jerome's Commentary*, pp. 44–45; and Gallagher, 'Why Did Jerome', pp. 370–72). Origen expounded his conception of the corpus that he called 'apocryphal' with more precision than Jerome (see Braverman, *Jerome's Commentary*, pp. 41–43). For a general discussion of Jerome's views on canonicity, see Braverman, *Jerome's Commentary*,

More importantly, in the Vulgate preface to what Jerome called the 'Books of Solomon', he argued the following: "The Church certainly reads the Books of Judith, of Tobit, and of the Maccabees, but it does not accept [them] among the canonical Scriptures" (*sed inter canonicas scripturas non recipit*).[377] In theory, according to the *hebraica veritas* principle, texts that were not found in the Hebrews' canon should have been excluded from the Vulgate. That Jerome incorporated the Prayer, Susanna, and Bel and the Dragon into his version of Daniel, albeit with obeli, disagreed to this extent with his agenda. In his attempt to partly preserve the version of Daniel known to Christians and to keep the trust of the Church, he had departed from the structure of the Hebrew-Aramaic book.[378]

---

pp. 43–52; Canellis, *Préfaces*, pp. 118–48; Lange, 'The Canonical Histories', pp. 26–27; Gallagher, 'The Latin Canon', pp. 172–75. On his description of the tripartite canon of the Hebrews, see Dorival, 'L'Apport des Pères de l'Église', pp. 87–90 and p. 93. For a discussion of Origen's conception of the canon, see Barthélemy, 'La Place de la Septante dans l'Église', pp. 14–18; and Lange, 'The Canonical Histories', pp. 20–21.

[377] Vulg., p. 957.

[378] Again, Jerome's concept of *hebraica veritas* meant by definition that whatever was in the Hebrew text corresponded to the 'true' Old Testament. Accordingly, the parts of the LXX text that were not read by the Hebrews, or which differed from the corresponding passages in the Hebrew text, should not have represented the 'true' content of Scripture. However, was the obelus employed for passages that were to be regarded as 'not true'? Braverman argues that "since [Jerome] accepted the *veritas hebraica* or Hebrew truth with regard to the text, he also refused to accept as inspired or authoritative works not preserved in Hebrew" (*Jerome's Commentary*, pp. 43–44). Braverman's supposition,

1.3. The Linguistic Status of Daniel

The special status of Daniel was also due to the bilingual composition of the story in the Hebrew Bible. In combining the Hebrew-Aramaic text with the Christians' version, Jerome was presenting a Latin translation based on Hebrew, Aramaic, Greek and (Old) Latin sources. The Aramaic portion of the text complicated his task:

> By all means, one should know that [the Books of] Daniel and Ezra were composed with Hebrew letters, but in the Aramaic language (*chaldaico sermone*) mostly; so was a section of Jeremiah. Job also bears a great deal of similarity with the Arabic tongue (*cum arabica lingua*). Then, indeed, as a young lad, after reading Quintilian and Cicero and the flowers of rhetoric, I secluded myself into the drudgery of this language (i.e., Hebrew) and, after much sweat and much time, I barely started to repeat panting and shrill words [in Hebrew] or—as though walking in a crypt—to catch a glimpse of that sparse light from above.[379] Eventually, I bumped into Daniel (i.e., the Aramaic portion thereof) and I was weighed down with so much weariness that, with a sudden despair, I wished to despise all [my] previous effort. But a Hebrew spurred me on by telling me

though logical, should be taken with a pinch of salt, as Jerome never ceased to contradict himself on this point.

[379] Jerome shared his memory of his training in Hebrew on a number of occasions (see *Epist.* 125.12 [VII, pp. 124–25]; and *Epist.* 108.26 [V, p. 195]). The allusion to a 'crypt' is in reference to his initiation into Christianity in his childhood; he elaborated on this episode at greater length in 414 (Kelly, *Jerome*, p. 306) in his commentary on Ezekiel (see *Comm. Ezech.* 40.5–13 [CCSL 75, pp. 556–57]). For further discussion of this passage, see Courtray, 'Saint Jérôme et la conversion', pp. 216–17.

in his tongue, again and again, the following thing: 'An unrelenting effort has everything conquered.'[380] I, who saw myself as a smatterer among these [people], started to be a student of Aramaic again. And, to say the truth, up to this present day, I can read the Aramaic language and understand it better than I can make it sound. This is to show you how difficult Daniel is...[381]

The shift to Aramaic in the Book of Daniel is an element of the narrative. It takes place immediately after Dan. 2.4, where it is introduced as follows: וַיְדַבְּרוּ הַכַּשְׂדִּים לַמֶּלֶךְ אֲרָמִית 'and the Chaldeans spoke to the king in Aramaic'. Although the Vulgate stays in Latin after this verse, Jerome represented this passage as in the original: *responderuntque Chaldei regi syriace* 'and the Chaldeans responded to the king in Syriac'.[382] The transition to Aramaic and

---

[380] Virgil, *Georgics*, 1.145–46.

[381] Vulg., p. 1341. For a discussion of this excerpt from Jerome's preface, see Barr, 'St. Jerome's Appreciation', p. 287; Canellis, *Préfaces*, pp. 84–85. On Jerome's learning of Aramaic, see King, '*Vir Quadrilinguis?*', pp. 209–11.

[382] Jerome could call Aramaic 'Chaldee' (*chaldaicus*) or 'Syrian' (*syrus*) (see *Pelag.*, III, 2 [CCSL 80, p. 99]; *Comm. Dan.* 1.4a and c [p. 144]; and *Epist.* 17.2 [I, p. 52]), as well as 'Syriac' (*syriacus*), as in Vulg. Dan. 2.4a (see also *Comm. Dan.* 2.4a [p. 158] and 7.28b [p. 312]). According to Millar, he did not distinguish different Aramaic dialects, but he restricted his application of the term *chaldaicus* to the parts of the Bible that were written in Aramaic, and that of *syriacus* or *syrus* to spoken Aramaic (Millar, 'Jerome and Palestine', p. 63 and p. 73). There is no evidence that Jerome made this distinction. On the contrary, his use of these terms in *Pelag.*, III, 2, in Vulg. Dan. 2.4a and in *Comm. Dan.* 2.4a and 7.28b (see my translation of the last three passages below), where *chaldaicus* appears next to *syrus* in the first case and next to *syriacus* in

the one back to Hebrew were also pointed out by Jerome in his commentary on the book:

> Up to here, what was read was told in the Hebrew tongue. From this passage until the vision of King Balthasar's third year (i.e., Dan. 8.1), which Daniel saw in Susa, it is written in Hebrew letters, indeed, but in the Aramaic language, which they call Syriac here (*lingua* [...] *Chaldaica, quam hic Syriacam vocant*). (*Comm. Dan.* 2.4a; p. 158)

> Up this point, the Book of Daniel has been composed in the Aramaic and Syriac tongue (*Chaldaico Syriacoque sermone*). We read the rest, which is what follows until the end of the volume, in Hebrew. (*Comm. Dan.* 7.28b; p. 312)

The three additional episodes were inserted in the Vulgate in a specific manner, as Jerome introduced them in the body of the text by means of annotations interspersed in his translation. These annotations consistently remind the reader that the episode is not contained in the Hebrew-Aramaic text:

> I have not found what follows in the Hebrew scrolls (*quae sequuntur in hebraicis voluminibus non repperi*). (Vulg. Dan. 3.23)

---

the latter three, shows that he employed them interchangeably, whether written or spoken Aramaic was being referred to. For further discussion of Jerome's use of this terminology, see Canellis, *Préfaces*, pp. 84–87; Barr, 'St. Jerome's Appreciation', pp. 286–88; King, '*Vir Quarilinguis?*'; Gallagher, 'Why Did Jerome', pp. 365–66; Rebenich, 'Jerome: The "vir trilinguis"', p. 56.

3. The Translation of the Book of Daniel

> Up to here, it is not contained in the Hebrew (*non habetur in hebraeo*), and what we have put down has been translated from Theodotion's version (*quae posuimus de Theodotionis editione translata sunt*). (Vulg. Dan. 3.90)

> Up to here, we read Daniel in the Hebrew scroll. The rest, which follows until the end of the book, has been translated from Theodotion's version (*de Theodotionis editione translata sunt*). (Vulg. Dan. 12.13)

The three episodes were addressed in a similar tone in the commentary:

> The Hebrews read up to here: the middle [part] that follows until the end of the Song of the Three Children (*usque ad finem cantici trium puerorum*) is not contained in the Hebrew. A few words ought to be said on it, lest we seem to have neglected it. (*Comm. Dan.* 3.23; p. 198)

> Up to here, on the basis of Theodotion's translation, we have touched upon a few points in the avowal and praises of the three children (*pauca perstrinximus confessionis et laudum trium puerorum*), which are not contained in the Hebrew. Let us follow the Hebrew truth from then on (*exin sequamur Hebraicam veritatem*). (*Comm. Dan.* 3.91a; p. 206)

> After explaining as I could what is contained in the Book of Daniel according to the Hebrew, I shall briefly lay out what Origen has said, in the tenth book of his *Stromata*, on the Fables of Susanna and Bel. These are his words... (*Comm. Dan.* 13; p. 530)[383]

---

[383] From this point until the end of the commentary, besides certain remarks, Jerome either quoted or paraphrased the work of Origen. On his way of quoting Origen in his exegetical treatment of Susanna and of Bel and the Dragon in the commentary on Daniel, see Courtray, *Comm.*

> [Jerome's citation of Origen:] The Hebrews reject the story of Susanna, as they say that it is not contained in the scroll of Daniel (*dicentes eam in Danielis volumine non haberi*)... (*Comm. Dan.* 13.54b–55 and 58b–59; p. 542)
>
> [idem:] What the writing (*scriptura*) now says, 'He shouted with a loud voice', seems to invalidate the remark that we made not long ago, namely, that 'a loud voice' [could] only [be] found among saints: indeed, [here] it is said about an idolatrous man who ignores / does not know God. This is something that he who will have said that this story (i.e., Bel and the Dragon) is not contained in the Book of Daniel among the Hebrews shall solve easily; but if anyone can prove that it belongs to the canon (*esse de canone*), then we have to wonder what we should respond to him. (*Comm. Dan.* 14.17; p. 546).

Taking for granted that the three additional episodes contained in the Vulgate were translated by Jerome would be uncritical.[384] It is indeed possible that these versions represent Old Latin versions that he revised. While his annotations always indicate the source from which these texts were supposedly translated into Latin, i.e., Theodotion's version, neither in the Vulgate nor in the commentary is it specified by whom.[385] As for the lemmas in the commentary, it has been argued by Courtray that Jerome was responsible for their translation into Latin and that, in the portions common to all versions of the story, he had relied most of

---

Dan., pp. 43–44 and pp. 530–31, fn. 2 and fn. 4, and *Prophète*, pp. 114–15 and pp. 199–203; and Braverman, *Jerome's Commentary*, p. 51.

[384] See, for example, Courtray's remark in *Comm. Dan.*, p. 28.

[385] See Vulg. Dan. 3.90 and 12.13 and *Comm. Dan.* 3.91a (p. 206) cited above.

the time on the Hebrew-Aramaic text rather than on Theodotion or on the LXX.[386] Regarding Susanna and Bel and the Dragon, Jerome presented his exegesis as a quotation, or a paraphrase, of Origen's *Stromata*; however, he did not specify either whether he himself had translated the lemmas adduced from these episodes (or from the Prayer). If the additional episodes displayed in the Vulgate of Daniel were produced on the basis of Old Latin forms, there is no doubt that he at least revised them before inserting them in the Vulgate. As the origin of these versions is not directly relevant to an investigation of Jerome's sources in his translation of the Hebrew Bible, we shall simply keep in mind that he may not have translated them into Latin from scratch.[387]

---

[386] Courtray, *Prophète*, p. 85 and pp. 102–7, and *Comm. Dan.*, pp. 28–32. A VL version could also be used in certain lemmas (see Courtray, *Comm. Dan.*, p. 32, fn. 1).

[387] Thorough stylistic analyses of the Vulgate versions of the additional episodes in comparison with extant VL fragments can shed light on this issue (the same problem arises regarding Jerome's treatment of the expansions to the Book of Esther [see chapter 4]). Zilverberg, for instance, demonstrated that Jerome probably produced a new translation of a Greek recension of Susanna that mainly followed Theodotion's version, perhaps with an Old Latin text at hand (*The Textual History of Old Latin Susanna*, pp. 28–37). In a more recent article that is yet to be published, Zilverberg refines his analysis by arguing that Jerome actively revised an already existing Old Latin version of Susanna before incorporating it into the Vulgate edition of Daniel ('The Greek Loan Word *Presbyteri*').

2.0. The Case Studies

The verses that we adduce from the Vulgate of Daniel, in comparison with other versions, give us a glimpse of the extent to which Jerome relied on sources other than the Hebrew-Aramaic form of the story; they also reveal independent departures which shed light on his translation technique and on his style. In the first case study (section 2.1), we investigate his treatment of a rare Hebrew word (פרתמים) across works that he composed throughout the entire course of the Vulgate project. Then we turn our attention to his responses to the syntagm ארץ הצבי and to different occurrences of the word צבי (section 2.2): the *recentiores* played an essential role in his understanding of this term, but he still preserved a certain autonomy in the employment of his sources. We then address a particular case of *hebraica veritas* (section 2.3): while Vulg. Dan. 3.16 reflects the syntax of the Aramaic of Dan. 3.16 against that of the LXX version, in the commentary, Jerome tried to justify the LXX reading, probably with the VL readership in mind. The last two case studies deal with two types of departures from the Hebrew-Aramaic of Daniel. The first one (section 2.4) hypothetically represents a case of interpolation in the Vulgate translation of Dan. 5.1; the second one (section 2.5) reveals Jerome's exclusive reliance on the *recentiores*: the suggestion that he did not check the Aramaic in this passage explains how he came to render וְעַד אָחֳרֵין 'and eventually' as *donec collega* 'until a partner' in Vulg. Dan. 4.5.

2.1. The Translation of a Rare Hebrew Word: פרתמים

The term פרתמים occurs three times in the Hebrew Bible: in Dan. 1.3, and in Est. 1.3 and 6.9. It is an originally Persian loanword which only occurs in its plural form, and which has been interpreted as meaning 'noblemen'. When rendering it in the Vulgate, Jerome employed two different words: the noun *tyrannus* 'ruler' in Vulg. Dan. 1.3 and Vulg. Est. 6.9, and the adjective *inclitus* 'renowned' in Vulg. Est. 1.3. His way of discussing it in his exegetical and hermeneutic works sheds light on the sources that he used in his interpretation of the Hebrew text. Likewise, the lexical variation exhibited in the Vulgate, *tyrannus* on the one hand and *inclitus* on the other hand, appears to have been inspired by different sources.

2.1.1. The Treatment of פַּרְתְּמִים in Vulg. Dan. 1.3

MT Dan. 1.3–4a

וַיֹּאמֶר הַמֶּלֶךְ לְאַשְׁפְּנַז רַב סָרִיסָיו לְהָבִיא מִבְּנֵי יִשְׂרָאֵל וּמִזֶּרַע הַמְּלוּכָה וּמִן־הַפַּרְתְּמִים:

יְלָדִים אֲשֶׁר אֵין־בָּהֶם כָּל־מְאוּם

And the king told Ashpenaz, his chief eunuch (lit., of eunuchs), to bring from the children of Israel and from the seed of royalty and from the noblemen / youths in whom there was no blemish.

Vulg.

et ait rex Asfanaz praeposito eunuchorum suorum ut introduceret de filiis Israhel et de semine regio et tyrannorum / pueros in quibus nulla esset macula...

And the king said to Asfanaz, the leader of his eunuchs, that he should bring in, from the sons of Israel and from the kingly seed and [that] of rulers / children in whom there might be no blemish.

In 407, some fourteen years after the Vulgate translation, while Jerome could have presented a different version of the verse in his commentary, the lemma on which he relied to discuss the passage matched exactly the wording in Vulg. Dan. 1.3–4a:

> *Et ait rex Asphanez praeposito eunuchorum suorum ut introduceret de filiis Israel et de semine regio et tyrannorum pueros in quibus nulla esset macula.*[388]

The way פַּרְתְּמִים has been treated in the LXX, in Theodotion and in the VL shows that Jerome did not rely on any of these three versions when rendering the word in the Vulgate. Indeed, it was translated as ἐπιλέκτων 'chosen ones' in the LXX, transcribed as φορθομμιν in Theodotion, and in the VL it is not represented:

LXX

καὶ εἶπεν ὁ βασιλεὺς Αβιεσδρι τῷ ἑαυτοῦ ἀρχιευνούχῳ ἀγαγεῖν αὐτῷ ἐκ τῶν υἱῶν τῶν μεγιστάνων τοῦ Ισραηλ καὶ ἐκ τοῦ βασιλικοῦ γένους καὶ ἐκ τῶν ἐπιλέκτων / νεανίσκους ἀμώμους...[389]

---

[388] *Comm. Dan.* 1.3–4a (p. 142). In the next lemma, on the other hand, Jerome introduced an alternative reading as he cited Dan. 1.4a again: *pueros* (*sive 'iuvenes'*) *in quibus nulla esset macula* 'children (or 'youths') in whom there might be no blemish' (*Comm. Dan.* 1.4a; p. 144). While the main portion of this lemma matches Vulg. Dan. 1.4a and the lemma in *Comm. Dan.* 1.3–4a (*pueros* [...] *in quibus nulla esset macula*), the variant *iuvenes* reflects the Old Latin reading of Dan. 1.4a: *et ex iuvenibus in quibus nulla sit vituperatio* 'from youths in whom there might be no fault'.

[389] Munnich's edition of the LXX of Daniel is based on the only extant textual witness to the pre-Origenic form of the book (see Munnich, 'Daniel, Susanna, Bel and the Dragon', pp. 292–93). When quoting the LXX

And the king told Abiesdri, his own arch-eunuch, to bring him from the sons of the grandees of Israel and from the kingly race and from the chosen ones / blameless (lit., blemishless) youths…

Theodotion

καὶ εἶπεν ὁ βασιλεὺς Ασφανεζ τῷ ἀρχιευνούχῳ αὐτοῦ εἰσαγαγεῖν ἀπὸ τῶν υἱῶν τῆς αἰχμαλωσίας Ισραηλ καὶ ἀπὸ τοῦ σπέρματος τῆς βασιλείας καὶ ἀπὸ τῶν φορθομμιν / νεανίσκους οἷς οὐκ ἔστιν ἐν αὐτοῖς μῶμος…

And the king told Asfanez, his arch-eunuch, to introduce from the sons of the captivity of Israel and from the seed of royalty and from the *forthommin* / youths who had (lit., to whom there is) no blemish in them…

VL

et dixit rex Asphanes spadoni sui qui erat super spadones eius ut introduceret de filiis captivitatis Israhel et de regis semine et ex iuvenibus in quibus nulla sit vituperatio…[390]

And the king said to Asphanes, his castrate who was above his castrates, that he should bring in [some] of the sons of

---

text of Daniel, I shall employ his edition rather than Rahlfs and Hanhart's edition of the Septuagint. I shall also use Ziegler's edition of Theodotion's version of Daniel, which is published in *Susanna. Daniel. Bel et Draco* alongside Munnich's edition of LXX Dan. (see in my bibliography under 'Primary Sources', 'LXX').

[390] This VL form follows Theodotion's version of Daniel rather than the LXX (for example, *de filiis captivitatis Israhel* translates ἀπὸ τῶν υἱῶν τῆς αἰχμαλωσίας Ισραηλ; the noun 'captivity' is not in the LXX). This version represents a European textual tradition attested by three fragmentary manuscripts and dated to the first half of the fourth century (Haelewyck, *Danihel*, pp. 54–60): as shown below in section 2.1.2, it is likely that Jerome was familiar with it.

the captivity of Israel and of the seed of the king and from youths in whom there might be no fault...

In his commentary, Jerome first compared the sources with which he worked, thus showing that the choice of *tyrannorum* to render פַּרְתְּמִים was not motivated by the *recentiores*' versions or the LXX. However, as he went on to specify the origin of *tyrannorum*, his remarks became more obscure. It is indeed not clear whether he meant to refer to a source other than the Hebrew text, or to his own reading of the Hebrew text:

> Instead of *Asphanez* in the common edition (*in editione vulgata*) I have found *Abiesdri* written,[391] and instead of *porthommim*, which Theodotion put down, the Seventy (*Septuaginta*) and Aquila rendered 'the chosen ones' (*electos*), [and] Symmachus 'Parthians' (*Parthos*),[392] [thus] con-

---

[391] The phrase *editio vulgata* generally refers to the LXX (see my fn. 215). Here though, after mentioning the *editio vulgata*, Jerome went on to cite the LXX under the name *Septuaginta*. According to Courtray, who cites Jay (*L'Exégèse*, pp. 113–14), this *editio vulgata* corresponded to the so-called Lucianic edition of the LXX (see my fn. 216)—which Jerome considered a corrupt version of the text (see section 1.7)—and the *Septuaginta* to the edition of the LXX found in the Hexapla (Courtray, *Comm. Dan.*, pp. 142–43, fn. 3). Courtray and Jay have not made it entirely clear whether, in their view, the fifth column of the Hexapla contained Origen's revised edition of the LXX or his base text (see my fn. 48, 49 and 82); however, the former is arguably to be assumed.

[392] Accordingly, as shown in Field, Aquila's version reads ἐκλεκτῶν and Symmachus' Πάρθων. The fact that Jerome attributed *electos*, rather than ἐπιλέκτων (see above), to the LXX, too, could be evidence that he was quoting an Origenic edition of the LXX corrected on the basis of Aquila's version (see my fn. 391; and Munnich's observations in 'Origène,

3. The Translation of the Book of Daniel

> struing the name of a people (*nomen gentis intellegens*) instead of a word that we, according to the Hebrews' edition (*iuxta editionem Hebraeorum*), which is read with accuracy (*quae* κατὰ ἀκρίβειαν [sic] *legitur*), have translated as 'rulers' (*in tyrannos vertimus*), above all because (*maxime quia*) [the phrase] 'from the kingly seed' (*de regio semine*; i.e., וּמִזֶּרַע הַמְּלוּכָה) precedes [it in the verse].[393]

Here, by claiming that he translated פַּרְתְּמִים "according to the Hebrews' edition," Jerome sought to explain to the reader how the Vulgate rendering *tyrannorum* originated. However, the expression "the Hebrews' edition" may have had a different meaning from the one expected, as he also added that "it is read κατὰ ἀκρίβειαν." Field and others before him believed that by the phrase κατὰ ἀκρίβειαν—which I have attempted to render word for word as 'with accuracy'—Jerome was alluding to another translation produced by Aquila.[394] This theory was based on a passage in his commentary on Ezekiel, in which he referred to "Aquila's second edition (*Aquilae* [...] *secunda editio*), which the

---

éditeur', pp. 216–17). One may also wonder whether Πάρθων stemmed from a misreading of what initially was a transliteration of פַּרְתְּמִים (see the various spellings in Ziegler's apparatus and in Field; see also Field's citation of Theodoret in the Hexapla, II, p. 908, fn. 7).

[393] *Comm. Dan.* 1.3–4a (pp. 142–44).

[394] See Field, Hexapla, I, pp. xxiv–xxvi; and Hexapla, II, p. 908, fn. 7. See also the marginal note, *Altera versio Aquilae erat* 'There was another translation of Aquila', in Martianay's edition of Jerome's *Comm. Dan.* 1.3–4a (*Divina Bibliotheca*, III, p. 1075).

Hebrews call κατὰ ἀκρίβειαν (*quam Hebraei* κατὰ ἀκρίβειαν *nominant*)."[395]

Jerome sometimes hinted at the existence of this second version of Aquila's translation in his commentaries, on which he seems to have relied alongside the first one.[396] However, Aquila had already been explicitly mentioned in *Comm. Dan.* 1.3–4a (*electos*); it is striking that in this case the theory of Aquila's second edition has not been challenged or even investigated (at least not to my knowledge) in modern scholarship.[397] Although it is possible that Aquila's second translation was being implied, this is not the more straightforward way of understanding Jerome's remarks in *Comm. Dan.* 1.3–4a. Whether an alternative version of Aquila's work existed is not relevant to the present discussion: we shall simply observe that Jerome is telling us that, when translating פַּרְתְּמִים as *tyrannorum*, he followed "the Hebrews' edition," and that this edition was read "κατὰ ἀκρίβειαν." Firstly, he knew Aquila's reputation for being a "slavishly literal translator" and shared this view on his translation style: "[he] is a most careful unraveller (*diligentissimus explicator*) of Hebrew words."[398] Accordingly, the word ἀκρίβεια may have been a nickname for

---

[395] *Comm. Ezech.* 3.14b–15 (CCSL 75, p. 37).

[396] See for example *Comm. Ezech.* 20.5b–6 (CCSL 75, p. 257). See also Jay's remark in *L'Exégèse*, p. 103, fn. 243.

[397] In his LXX critical apparatus, with regard to Dan. 1.3, Ziegler simply mentions the hypothetical second version of Aquila in parentheses. He makes no comment on it (*Susanna. Daniel. Bel et Draco*, p. 234).

[398] *Epist.* 28.2 (II, p. 19). See also Jerome's remarks in *Epist.* 57.11 (III, p. 71); and my fn. 313.

Aquila, in which case κατὰ ἀκρίβειαν could have meant "according to the stickler (lit., according to 'minuteness')."

At the same time, had Jerome wanted to indicate that he believed Aquila to be responsible for the "Hebrews' edition" from which originated *tyrannorum*, and that he agreed with it against *electos*, which he had already ascribed to Aquila ("Aquila rendered 'the chosen ones' [*electos*]"), it stands to reason that he would have explicitly cited his name or his second edition here. The hypothesis that he autonomously chose the word *tyrannorum* 'rulers' is actually suggested by the following statement: "[I] translated [פַּרְתְּמִים] as 'rulers' (*tyrannos*), above all because [the phrase] 'from the kingly seed' precedes [it]." Here Jerome, who was presenting this interpretation as logical in context (*maxime quia*), exhibited independent reasoning. Secondly, by κατὰ ἀκρίβειαν, he may have meant that he himself read the Hebrew text with more accuracy, as it were, than his Greek predecessors, whose versions he had introduced in the first place.[399] To be sure, he was implicitly promoting a form of *hebraica veritas*.

On the other hand, it was very unusual for Jerome to use the collocation *editio Hebraeorum* 'the Hebrews' edition' when referring to the Hebrew text. This may have been a metonymy for a scroll that he employed, in which a Greek note could have been left in the margin by an anonymous scholar; this note would have

---

[399] The reading *tyrannos*, coming last in Jerome's comparison of versions, is implicitly presented as the best rendering for פַּרְתְּמִים against the three readings that were introduced before. See also Courtray, who argues that Jerome meant to "correct" Theodotion's transcription of פַּרְתְּמִים ('Jérôme traducteur', p. 111).

run as the genitive plural τυράννων, or as the nominative plural τύραννοι, represented in the commentary by *tyrannos*.[400] By adding "above all because [the phrase] 'from the kingly seed' precedes [it]," Jerome would have then meant to share his own view on this marginal note, with which he personally concurred. On the whole, the origin of *tyrannorum* in Vulg. Dan. 1.3 cannot be determined beyond doubt, but it is clear that he meant to justify this choice as the most accurate rendering for פַּרְתְּמִים on the basis of the *hebraica veritas* principle.

2.1.2. The Treatment of פַּרְתְּמִים in Jerome's Other Works

Jerome quoted Dan. 1.3 on multiple occasions throughout his career. To begin with, he translated from Greek some of the so-called paschal letters which Theophilus, bishop of Alexandria, had been writing to announce and celebrate Easter. Once his translations were completed, Jerome would send the paschal letters back to Theophilus in Latin. In 404, he translated one in which Dan. 1.3–4a had been paraphrased:

---

[400] While *porthommim* stands in the commentary as a Latin transliteration of φορθομμιν from Theodotion's version, *tyrannos* should not be read as a transcription of the nominative singular Greek form τύραννος but as the accusative plural form of the Latin *tyrannus*: this can be deduced from the fact that *electos* can only correspond to the accusative plural masculine of the Latin word *electus* (ἐκλεκτός, in the nominative singular, which is the corresponding Greek term, would have been transcribed as *eclectos*). Likewise, *Parthos* represents the accusative plural of *Parthus*, not a transcription of the nominative singular Πάρθος.

> *Praeceperat quippe rex Nabuchodonosor eunuchorum principi, ut de filiis captivitatis Israhel et de regio semine pueros, in quibus nulla esset macula [...] introduceret palatium...* [401]
>
> Indeed, king Nabuchodonosor had ordered the eunuchs' chief to bring into the palace, from the sons of the captivity of Israel and from the kingly seed, children in whom there might be no blemish...

It is noteworthy that Jerome's version of Theophilus' paraphrase reflects a combination of the Vulgate translation and the known VL form. It agrees with Vulg. Dan. 1.3–4a against the VL to the extent that it contains the word *eunuchus* 'eunuch', not the synonym *spado* 'castrate'; *de regio semine* instead of *de regis semine*; and more strikingly *pueros, in quibus nulla esset macula* rather than *ex iuvenibus in quibus nulla sit vituperatio*. It also incorporates elements of the VL, such as *de filiis captivitatis Israhel* (which translates Theodotion's version). More importantly, the word פַּרְתְּמִים is not represented, which is peculiar to the VL. The original Greek letter is no longer extant,[402] but, regardless, given the fact that the Latin paraphrase of Dan. 1.3–4a noticeably follows some of the Vulgate version, that Jerome applied a personal touch to his translation of the letter is hardly questionable. In light of the *sensus de sensu* translation policy, too, it would not be surprising that he took the liberty of adapting the letter; a certain margin of stylistic adjustment is even suggested in the introductory letter that he wrote to Theophilus:

---

[401] Jerome, *Epist.* 100.7 (V, p. 77).

[402] Migne indicates that it is only attested in Jerome's translation (PG 65, pp. 53–54).

> I have made a sustained effort in the translation of [your letter] in order to render every sentence in an equally beautiful way, and so that the Latin phrasing might echo, to some extent (*aliqua ex parte*), Greek eloquence (*et Graecae eloquentiae Latinum [...] responderet eloquium*).[403]

In another letter addressed to Theophilus, Jerome also argued that in his translation he strove to "counterbalance the expressiveness of the Greek language with the poverty of the Latin one (*facundiam graecam latinae linguae [...] paupertate pensare*)," and that, "as well-spoken translators do, [he] did not render word for word (*neque [...] verbum verbo reddidi*) [...] so that nothing might be missing in the sense, in case anything is missing from the words (*ut nihil desit ex sensibus, cum aliquid desit ex verbis*):" "Therefore, receive your book, or rather mine, and, to speak more truly, ours."[404] By not including a rendering for פַּרְתְּמִים in his translation of Theophilus' paraphrase of Dan. 1.3—whereas the rest of his translation followed, to some extent, the wording in Vulg. Dan. 1.3—Jerome was making a concession to the communities accustomed to the Old Latin version. Indeed, as Theophilus had his paschal letters translated into Latin so that they might be disseminated in the west afterwards, Jerome knew that his translations would reach an audience whose knowledge of Scripture was deeply rooted in the reading of the VL:

> I have translated your letter into Latin and I have placed it at the beginning of this volume so that all those who will

---

[403] Jerome, *Epist.* 99.1 (V, p. 67).
[404] *Epist.* 114.2 (VI, p. 45).

read it might know that it is not out of boldness or talkativeness, but on the instructions of your Beatitude, that I have undertaken a task beyond my strength.[405]

Jerome therefore tried to avoid as much as possible accusations of distortion or falsification in his translation. When writing to two of his closest correspondents, Pammachius and Marcella, he attached the Greek original to one of his translations of Theophilus' letters and said:

> You, lights of the Christian senate, receive the letter of this year, both in Greek and in Latin, so that heretics might not falsely allege in return that it is filled either with additions or with alterations on our part.[406]

Also interesting is Jerome's quotation of Dan. 1.3–4 in *Against Jovinian*, where פַּרְתְּמִים appears as a Latin transliteration (*porthommin*)[407] of Theodotion's transcription of the Hebrew, φορθομμιν:

> *Et dixit rex Asphanez principi eunuchorum ut introduceret de filiis captivitatis Israel et de semine regio et de porthommin pueros, in quibus non esset macula...*[408]

Here, the quotation of Daniel disagrees with the paraphrase in the translation of Theophilus' letter to the extent that it follows Theodotion's transcription where the known VL version elides it. This choice is all the more noteworthy in that *Against Jovinian*

---

[405] Jerome, *Epist.* 114.2 (VI, p. 45).

[406] *Epist.* 97.3 (V, p. 34).

[407] As shown below, the spelling of this transliteration can vary. Spelling variations have to do with the transmission of the texts.

[408] *Against Jovinian*, I, 25 (p. 324).

was produced in the same period as the Vulgate translation of Daniel (*tyrannorum*), i.e., around 393.[409] As demonstrated in the previous chapter of this monograph (sections 2.2.3 and 2.2.4), Jerome's hermeneutic method could consist of relying on different sources to derive the meaning of a word. In *Comm. Dan.* 1.3–4a, as argued by Courtray, he rather meant to "correct" Theodotion's transcription of פַּרְתְּמִים by rendering it with a proper Latin word, *tyrannos*.[410] On the other hand, the use of a transliteration such as *porthommin* in *Against Jovinian* shows that he was more naturally reading Scripture from the Greek than from the Hebrew, and from Theodotion's version rather than from a VL form that did not contain a term representing פַּרְתְּמִים. Jovinian was a monk who had expressed extremely polemical ideas in a theological treatise. Jerome, who was called upon by a group of Christian friends to refute and dismantle these theories, set out to dedicate a two-volume work against him.[411] When appealing to passages from the Book of Daniel, the most straightforward course of action for him was indeed to directly translate Theodotion into Latin:[412] given the transmission history of Daniel in the Church,

---

[409] For the date of composition of *Against Jovinian*, see Kelly, *Jerome*, p. 182.

[410] See my fn. 399.

[411] On the story of the composition of *Against Jovinian*, see Savoye's preface to her edition of *Against Jovinian* (pp. 9–60); and Kelly, *Jerome*, pp. 180–86.

[412] Not only the transliteration of φορθομμιν, but the general wording of his citation of Dan. 1.3–4 in *Against Jovinian* shows that he translated Theodotion instead of following the known VL version. For example, the phrase *principi eunuchorum* 'to the chief of the eunuchs' is close

it made no sense to cite this version from the LXX, and Jerome would have had no interest either in employing the Vulgate rendering *tyrannorum* in this context.

Also possible is that the transliteration *porthommin* implicitly conveyed a Hebrew interpretation of the word פרתמים. Indeed, in 389–391, Jerome provided a definition for *forthommim* in his glossary *On Hebrew Names*: *Forthommim divisio perfecta populi gloriosi* '*Forthommim*: a perfect fraction of the glorious people'.[413] *Divisio* ('fraction') is the noun derived from the verb *divido* 'to break apart', 'to divide', and *perfecta* ('perfect') is the feminine singular form of the perfect participle of the verb *perficio* 'to carry out', 'to complete'. It could be that, by being ascribed to the word פרתמים / *forthommim*, the phrase *divisio perfecta* was meant to reflect the Hebrew roots פרר 'to break' (*divisio*) and תמים 'complete' or תם 'to be complete' (*perfecta*).[414] The correspondence between 'a perfect fraction' and the hypothetical Hebrew compound that I propose here could be a coincidence, too, as the term פרתמים systematically points in context to a select group of people anyway: it has this meaning in the Book of Daniel (cf. Aquila's rendering in Dan. 1.3, ἐκλεκτῶν, and the LXX one, ἐπιλέκτων, which both mean 'the chosen ones', as well as the reading τῶν εὐγενῶν

---

enough a rendering of Theodotion τῷ ἀρχιευνούχῳ αὐτοῦ 'to his arch-eunuch' in comparison with VL *spadoni sui qui erat super spadones eius* 'to his castrate who was above his castrates'.

[413] *Nom. hebr.*, under 'Book of Daniel', entry *Forthommim* (CCSL 72, p. 129). For the date of composition of this work, see Kelly, *Jerome*, p. 153.

[414] Wutz has proposed the roots פרר, תמם, and עם 'people' (see *Onomastica sacra*, I, p. 201 [under 'Primary Sources' in my bibliography]).

'of the well-born' anonymously attributed to Ὁ Ἑβραῖος 'the Hebrew man')[415] and in that of Esther (see section 2.1.3 below). However, it is not unlikely either that Jerome actually derived his interpretation of *forthommim* from a Hebrew etymology. First of all, it is sensible to imagine that he believed that every word should be treated as tracing back to a Hebrew origin as, in his view, "the origin of speech and of common discourse (*initium oris et communis eloquii*), as well as everything that we utter (*et hoc omne quod loquimur*), [is] the Hebrew language, in which the Old Testament was written,"[416] and which is "the source of all languages" (*linguam Hebraicam omnium linguarum esse matricem*).[417] Furthermore, it is in a book on "Hebrew names" that Jerome set out to discuss the meaning of *forthommim*. Accordingly, as set forth in the preface to the book, his goal was to propose an 'etymology' for these 'Hebrew names':

> It is also established by the testimony of Origen that Philo, the most eloquent man among the Jews, published a book of Hebrew names (*edidisse librum hebraicorum nominum*) in alphabetical order, and that he appended their etymologies (*eorumque etymologias*) next to them. I had an interest in translating this book, which it is common for the Greeks to own, and with which the libraries of the world have been overflowing. However, the copies that I found were so much at variance with one another, and the order was so

---

[415] See Dan. 1.3 in Field's Hexapla and in Ziegler's LXX apparatus. On the meaning of Ὁ Ἑβραῖος, see Ceulemans, 'Greek Church Fathers', pp. 757–58.

[416] *Epist.* 18.6 (I, p. 61).

[417] *Comm. Soph.* 3.18 (CCSL 76A, p. 708).

confused, that I judged it more suitable to remain silent than to write anything blameworthy. But I was spurred on by [the fact that] this work [would be] of use; and accordingly, on the instruction of my brothers Lupulus and Valerianus, who thought that I had made some progress in my knowledge of the Hebrew language, I scoured each and every volume of the Scriptures in sequence. After restoring an old edifice with a new care (*vetus aedificium nova cura instaurans*), I believe that I have produced something worth rushing for, even among the Greeks.[418]

On the whole, it is possible that Jerome simply followed the definition of *forthommim* from the original Greek glossary, perhaps without even noticing that a Hebrew compound was underlying it; he may also have found the Hebrew compound on his own, in which case he created his own definition of *forthommim*; or an informant may have taught him this Hebrew reconstruction. To be sure, the etymology פרר-תמים resembles a midrashic pun: should it be that *divisio perfecta* was not in the original glossary and that Jerome added it to his 'restored' Latin version, this definition of *forthommim* could betray a rabbinic source or reflect a lost tradition.[419] While the definition *divisio perfecta populi gloriosi*

---

[418] *Nom. hebr.* (CCSL 72, p. 59). See also the preface to QHG (p. 2). Fragments of the original Greek lexicon of Hebrew etymologies mentioned by Jerome in *Nom. hebr.* (*librum hebraicorum nominum*) have come down to us (see Wutz, *Onomastica sacra*, I, pp. 1–316). For further discussion of his glossary *On Hebrew Names*, see Kelly, *Jerome*, pp. 153–55.

[419] I have not found an etymological construal equivalent to פרר-תמים in rabbinic literature; neither is there, in the Greek lexicon, an extant definition of Φορθομμήν or Φορθομμιν that reflects this understanding. It is

was supposed to provide an etymological interpretation for פרתמים, it was also designed to shed light on *tyrannorum* in Vulg. Dan. 1.3. As will be shown below (see section 3.2.1.3), these two readings worked together: for Jerome, a Hebrew word could therefore be interpreted in different ways without necessarily entailing an erroneous translation. In this respect, the definition *divisio perfecta populi gloriosi* can be considered as a form of *hebraica veritas*, too, even though it is semantically as compatible with the interpretation of the LXX translators and of Aquila ('the chosen ones') as it is with Jerome's in Vulg. Dan. 1.3 and in *Comm. Dan.* 1.3–4a ('rulers').

2.1.3. The Translation of פרתמים in Vulg. Est. 1.3 and 6.9

Jerome's treatment of פרתמים in the Vulgate of Esther tells us a little bit more about his translation method. His translation of the Book of Esther, being dated to 404–405, represents one of his last translations for the Vulgate project; it should therefore be kept in mind that it was produced approximately twelve years after the Vulgate of Daniel and two years before the commentary.

---

noteworthy, however, that, in the New Testament section of Jerome's glossary, under 'Acts of the Apostles', the entry *Parthi* reads as follows: *Parthi dividentes perfecte* 'Parthians: those who divide perfectly' (*Nom. hebr.*; CCSL 72, p. 147). Also relevant is the definition attributed to Πάρθοι in the Greek lexicon: Πάρθοι· διακοπῆς τελείας· ἢ διακόπτοντες τελείως 'Parthians: of a perfect fraction; or those who divide perfectly' (*Onomastica sacra*, II, p. 682; see also ibid., I, p. 535). After checking in the original glossary what Symmachus may have meant by Πάρθων / *Parthos* in Dan. 1.3 (see above), Jerome could have drawn on a construal of Πάρθοι in his way of defining *forthommim* in his own glossary.

3. The Translation of the Book of Daniel

MT Est. 1.3

בִּשְׁנַת שָׁלוֹשׁ לְמָלְכוֹ עָשָׂה מִשְׁתֶּה לְכָל־שָׂרָיו וַעֲבָדָיו חֵיל ׀ פָּרַס וּמָדַי הַפַּרְתְּמִים וְשָׂרֵי הַמְּדִינוֹת לְפָנָיו׃

In the third year of his being king, [king Ahasuerus] made a feast for all his princes and servants, the army, [that of] Persia and [of] Media, the noblemen, and the princes of the provinces in front of him.

Vulg. Est. 1.3

Tertio igitur anno imperii sui fecit grande convivium cunctis principibus et pueris suis fortissimis Persarum et Medorum inclitis et praefectis provinciarum coram se

Then, in the third year of his reign, [king Ahasuerus] made a great feast for all his chiefs and slaves, for the strongest [subjects] of the Persians and of the Medes, for the renowned ones and the governors of the provinces in front of him.

LXX Est. 1.3

ἐν τῷ τρίτῳ ἔτει βασιλεύοντος αὐτοῦ, δοχὴν ἐποίησεν τοῖς φίλοις καὶ τοῖς λοιποῖς ἔθνεσιν καὶ τοῖς Περσῶν καὶ Μήδων ἐνδόξοις καὶ τοῖς ἄρχουσιν τῶν σατραπῶν

In the third year of his being king, [king Ahasuerus] gave (lit., made) a reception for his friends, for the remaining nations, for the illustrious among the Persians and the Medes, and for those who rule over the satraps / for the leaders of the satraps.

A-Text Est. 1.3

καὶ ἐποίησεν ὁ βασιλεὺς πότον τοῖς ἄρχουσι τῆς αὐλῆς Περσῶν καὶ Μήδων, καὶ οἱ ἄρχοντες τῶν χωρῶν κατὰ πρόσωπον αὐτοῦ

And the king gave (lit., made) a drinking party for those who rule over the court of the Persians and of the Medes; and those who rule over the lands [were] in front of him.

VL Est. 1.3

(Et) in anno duodecimo (/ tertio) regni sui fecit convivium omnibus principibus qui erant circa territorium regni eius[420]

(And) in the twelfth (/ third) [year] of his reign, [king Ahasuerus] made a feast for all the chiefs who were around the domain of his kingdom.

MT Est. 6.9a

וְנָתוֹן הַלְּבוּשׁ וְהַסּוּס עַל־יַד־אִישׁ מִשָּׂרֵי הַמֶּלֶךְ הַפַּרְתְּמִים

And let the clothing and the horse be given to the hand of one of the king's princes, [one of] the noblemen...

Vulg. Est. 6.9a

Et primus de regis principibus ac tyrannis teneat equum eius

And let the first of the king's princes and rulers hold his horse...

LXX Est. 6.9a

καὶ δότω ἑνὶ τῶν φίλων τοῦ βασιλέως τῶν ἐνδόξων

And let [the king] give [these things] to one of the king's friends, [one] of the illustrious ones...

A-Text Est. 6.11c (= Est. 6.9a)

καὶ εἷς τῶν ἐνδόξων, τῶν φίλων τοῦ βασιλέως, λαβέτω ταῦτα

And let one of the illustrious, [one] of the king's friends, take these things...

---

[420] The readings in parentheses represent variants attested in Haelewyck's edition of the VL of Esther, which I employ in this monograph (cf. *Hester* in my bibliography, under 'Primary Sources', 'VL', 'Book of Esther').

VL Est. 6.9a

Et unus de gloriosis (/ gloriosis amicis) regis

And one of the king's glorious [subjects] (/ glorious friends)...

While in Vulg. Est. 6.9 Jerome rendered הַפַּרְתְּמִים with the same word as in Vulg. Dan. 1.3, *tyrannis* (the ablative plural form of *tyrannus* 'ruler'), in Vulg. Est. 1.3 he translated הַפַּרְתְּמִים as *inclitis*, which corresponds in context to the dative masculine form of the adjective *inclitus* 'renowned'. The fact that there are two extant Greek traditions of Esther, the LXX and the A-Text, shall be properly discussed in the following chapter (section 4): for the time being, we should simply observe that in LXX Est. 1.3 הַפַּרְתְּמִים was translated with ἐνδόξοις, the dative plural form of ἔνδοξος 'of high repute', 'illustrious', and similarly in LXX Est. 6.9 and in A-Text Est. 6.9 with ἐνδόξων.[421] There is no rendering for הַפַּרְתְּמִים in A-Text Est. 1.3 ('those who rule over the court of the Persians and of the Medes' stands for 'all the king's princes and servants, the army, [that of] Persia and [of] Media' in the Hebrew); likewise, the word is not represented in VL Est. 1.3. In VL Est. 6.9, it is represented by *gloriosis*, the ablative plural form of *gloriosus* 'glorious', which translates ἐνδόξων; the position of *gloriosis* in the VL verse agrees with the word order of A-Text Est. 6.9

---

[421] No *recentiores* rendering is attested for פרתמים in Est. 1.3 and 6.9. See my fn. 488.

against that of the LXX version: we are therefore faced with a VL form that represents the A-Text.[422]

There are indications that, in Vulg. Est. 1.3, Jerome drew his inspiration from the LXX version when translating הַפַּרְתְּמִים with the word *inclitus* instead of *tyrannus*. First of all, the word *inclitus* agrees semantically with ἔνδοξος against *tyrannus*, and LXX Est. 1.3 reads ἐνδόξοις. In *Comm. Dan.* 1.3–4a, Jerome claimed that he translated פַּרְתְּמִים with *tyrannus* in Vulg. Dan. 1.3 "above all because (*maxime quia*) [the phrase] 'from the kingly seed' (*de regio semine*) precedes [it]." It cannot be argued, though, that he rendered הַפַּרְתְּמִים differently in Vulg. Est. 1.3 because it was not preceded by the same phrase as in Dan. 1.3, מִזֶּרַע הַמְּלוּכָה 'from the seed of royalty': הַפַּרְתְּמִים in Est. 6.9 was not preceded by it either, and he still translated it with *tyrannis*. It would be tempting to posit that *inclitus* was semantically as close as *tyrannus* to the definition ascribed to *forthommim* in the glossary—*divisio perfecta populi gloriosi* 'a perfect fraction of the glorious people'—and that Jerome, being fond of lexical variation, seized the opportunity of the occurrence of this rare word in Est. 1.3 to propose an alternative rendering, irrespective of the LXX reading ἐνδόξοις. However, the definition from the glossary cannot have underlain the use of *inclitis*, as הַפַּרְתְּמִים in Est. 1.3 is in fact not compatible with it. Indeed, here, those referred to as הַפַּרְתְּמִים are only presented as the king's noblemen, with no specific ethnic identity:

---

[422] The LXX and A-Text of Esther have been edited by Hanhart and published alongside each other in *Esther* (cf. in my bibliography under 'Primary Sources', 'LXX', 'Book of Esther'). I employ this edition in my monograph.

3. The Translation of the Book of Daniel

in other words, they do not represent 'the glorious people' (*populi gloriosi*), i.e., the children of Israel, as opposed to the פַרְתְּמִים in Dan. 1.3.[423] The correspondence between ἐνδόξοις and *inclitis* is therefore not a coincidence: the LXX reading did play a part in Jerome's way of translating הַפַּרְתְּמִים in Vulg. Est. 1.3. There is no doubt that his taste for lexical variation also motivated the use of a term other than *tyrannus*. The word הַפַּרְתְּמִים is not represented in VL Est. 1.3 (the only extant VL version agrees with the A-Text), but the fact that Jerome employed the term *inclitus* and not *gloriosus*, which is found in VL Est. 6.9, could suggest that he followed the LXX in Vulg. Est. 1.3 without paying attention to the Old Latin version.

The history of the treatment of פרתמים in Jerome reveals, in itself, a good deal about his translation method, but also about the limits of the *hebraica veritas* principle. In *Comm. Dan.* 1.3–4a, Jerome started off introducing the three different ways פַּרְתְּמִים in Dan. 1.3 had been translated in Theodotion, in the LXX and Aquila, and in Symmachus; he went on to explain that his rendering in Vulg. Dan. 1.3, *tyrannorum*, had stemmed from a close scrutiny of what he called "the Hebrews' edition," but also from his own understanding of the context. Citing "the Hebrews' edition" no doubt was tantamount to invoking the "authority of the Hebrews,"[424] i.e., the *hebraica veritas*. The absence of פַּרְתְּמִים in his translation of Theophilus' paraphrase showed that, in that

---

[423] Those whom Haman calls הַפַּרְתְּמִים in Est. 6.9 do not belong to 'the glorious people' either. To that extent, Jerome's definition of *forthommim* applied exclusively to the פַּרְתְּמִים in Dan. 1.3.

[424] *Epist.* 106.2 (V, p. 106).

case, he did not consider it necessary to alter the VL version: he indeed adapted his translation to suit the expectations of the targeted audience, i.e., Latin-speaking Christians. The term *porthommin* in *Against Jovinian* was a transliteration of Theodotion's transcription of the Hebrew. At the same time, it is possible that it was underlain by the definition of פרתמים / *forthommim* which Jerome proposed in his glossary *On Hebrew Names*: the way he defined it, *divisio perfecta*, may reflect a compound based on Hebrew etymology, פרר-תמים. While not mentioning the Hebrew truth, he explicitly argued in the preface to the glossary that the names that were being dealt with were Hebrew. In endeavouring to read פרתמים on an etymological level, while *tyrannos* was an interpretation derived from both an authoritative source and an autonomous understanding of the context, Jerome demonstrated that he could interpret passages from the Hebrew Bible on different planes. This method is reminiscent of that of Origen, who exploited different levels of understanding when reading Ἀβρὴχ in Gen. 41.43.[425] In other words, the renderings 'rulers' and 'a perfect fraction of the glorious people' did not contradict each other; on the contrary, they could complete each other. Therefore, when departing from the Vulgate rendering in *Against Jovinian* and in *On Hebrew Names*, Jerome was not departing from the Vulgate agenda: rather, he demonstrated that he could be flexible when applying his hermeneutics to a rare and somewhat obscure Hebrew word. By contrast, with *inclitis* in Vulg. Est. 1.3

---

[425] *Sel. Gen.* 41.43 (PG 12, pp. 133D–36A). See section 2.2.4.

he aligned himself with the LXX version; likewise, the absence of rendering in *Epist.* 100.7 conformed with the VL.

2.2. The Translation of the Word צבי

2.2.1. Jerome's Reliance on Aquila in His Treatment of צבי in Dan. 11.16, 11.41 and 11.45

In Vulg. Dan. 11.16, Jerome rendered the noun צבי 'beauty', 'honour' in וְיַעֲמֹד בְּאֶרֶץ־הַצְּבִי 'and he shall stand in the land of beauty / honour', with the adjective *inclitus* 'renowned': *et stabit in terra inclita* 'and he shall stand in the renowned land'.[426] In *Comm. Dan.* 11.15–16, where the lemma matches the Vulgate verse perfectly, *et stabit in terra inclyta*,[427] he openly stated that he followed Aquila in his translation of the word:

> [The angel] mentioned the following: 'He shall stand in the renowned land (*in terra inclyta*)' […]. 'The renowned land' or, as the Seventy [translators] have rendered it, 'of will' (*voluntatis*), that is, 'which may please God' (*quae complaceat Deo*) […]. Instead of 'renowned land' (*terra inclyta*), which is how it was rendered by Aquila, whom we have followed in this passage (*quem nos in hoc loco secuti sumus*), Theodotion put the Hebrew term itself, *sabir*,[428] instead of

---

[426] The 'land of beauty / honour' is traditionally associated with the land of Israel.

[427] *Inclytus* (or *inclutus*) and *inclitus* are different spellings of the same word.

[428] The attested VL form of Dan. 11.16 contains a transliteration of Theodotion's transcription of the Hebrew: *et stabit in terra sabir*.

which Symmachus translated 'land of strength' (*terram fortitudinis*).[429]

As noted by Jerome, the LXX reads ἐν τῇ χώρᾳ τῆς θελήσεως 'in the country of will', Aquila ἐν γῇ ἐνδόξῳ 'in the illustrious land', Theodotion ἐν τῇ γῇ τοῦ σαβιρ 'in the land of the *sabir*',[430] and Symmachus ἐν τῇ γῇ τῆς δυνάμεως 'in the land of might'. In specifying that he "followed Aquila in this passage," Jerome tells us that his translation in Vulg. Dan. 11.16 was influenced to some extent by Aquila's interpretation.[431] Besides, of all four translators quoted by him, Aquila is the only one who, like him, rendered ארץ הצבי with a noun and an adjective, rather than with two nouns. We know that Jerome consistently consulted the *recentiores* in his translation of the Hebrew Bible: Vulg. Dan. 11.16 illustrates how he could employ Aquila's version as a hermeneutic and stylistic reference.

---

[429] *Comm. Dan.* 11.15–16 (p. 446).

[430] As is shown below, the transcription σαβιρ is one of several Greek spellings of the same word found across the manuscripts. While the letters σαβ- are stable (the *šewa* is often represented by the letter *alpha* in Greek transcriptions), the variations in the ending have to do with the textual transmission of Theodotion's version.

[431] On a stylistic level, with regard to the previous case study (section 2.1), it is interesting that Jerome translated צבי here and פרתמים in Vulg. Est. 1.3 with the same word, *inclitus*; these two terms have also been rendered with ἔνδοξος in the LXX (in LXX Est. 1.3 and 6.9 in the case of פרתמים and in LXX Isa. 13.19 in that of צבי). While the opposite translation technique—the recourse to lexical variation in the translation of the same term—is a recognised feature of Jerome's style, it is shown here that he could also render two different terms with the same word in the Vulgate.

The syntagm ארץ הצבי also occurs in Dan. 11.41: וּבָא בְּאֶרֶץ הַצְּבִי 'and he shall come into the land of beauty / honour'. Noteworthy is the lexical variation in Jerome's response to this occurrence of צבי: in Vulg. Dan. 11.41, he translated *et introibit in terram gloriosam* 'and he shall go into the glorious land'; so did he in the lemma of *Comm. Dan.* 11.40–41a. As he further discussed the meaning of צבי and compared the *recentiores*' versions in the body of the text, he surreptitiously amended *terram gloriosam* to *terram inclytam*, in accordance with *Comm. Dan.* 11.16 and Vulg. Dan. 11.16:

> Antiochus [...] would have arrived to the 'renowned land' (*veneritque ad terram inclytam*), that is, Judea, which Symmachus rendered as 'land of strength' (*terram fortitudinis*), instead of which Theodotion put the Hebrew term itself, *sabai*.[432]

When rendering ἔνδοξος from Aquila's version, Jerome also employed the adjectives *inclitus* and *gloriosus* interchangeably, as synonyms: this is shown by his translation of Aquila Dan. 11.45 in the commentary on Daniel, where μεταξὺ τῶν θαλασσῶν ἐν ὄρει ἐνδόξῳ καὶ ἁγίῳ 'between the seas in the illustrious and holy mountain' (which stands for בֵּין יַמִּים לְהַר־צְבִי־קֹדֶשׁ 'between the seas and the holy mountain of beauty / honour' in the MT) is represented by *inter maria in monte glorioso et sancto* 'between the seas in the

---

[432] *Comm. Dan.* 11.40–41a (p. 494). As in VL Dan. 11.16, Theodotion's transcription of the Hebrew (τοῦ σαβαιν) was transliterated in VL Dan. 11.41: *et introibit in terram Sabain* 'and he shall go into the land of Sabain'. It should be noted that, apart from the way צבי was treated, the renderings for וְיַעֲמֹד בְּאֶרֶץ־הַצְּבִי in Vulg. Dan. 11.16 and for וּבָא בְּאֶרֶץ הַצְּבִי in Vulg. Dan. 11.41 conform with the Old Latin.

glorious and holy mountain'.⁴³³ The Hebrew is then rendered with *inclitus* in the Vulgate of Dan. 11.45: *inter maria super montem inclitum et sanctum* 'between the seas, on top of the renowned and holy mountain'. Jerome resorted to lexical variation for stylistic purposes; he arguably applied this translation technique independently of other sources, as neither the LXX, nor Aquila's version, Symmachus', Theodotion's or the VL form exhibits a similar pair of synonyms for these two occurrences of the word צבי. Although he did not cite Aquila's version in *Comm. Dan.* 11.40–41a (which is not attested in Field's Hexapla either), the syntagm *in terram gloriosam* in Vulg. Dan. 11.41 undeniably reflects his understanding of צבי in Dan. 11.16 (ἐν γῇ ἐνδόξῳ) as much as *in terra inclita* in Vulg. Dan. 11.16 does. While stylistically autonomous in his use of a synonym, Jerome remained hermeneutically dependent on Aquila here.

2.2.2. A Case of Potential Reliance on Theodotion in Dan. 8.9

Jerome consistently used Theodotion's text as a point of reference when interpreting the Hebrew of Daniel: he generally approved of this Greek version and trusted it against the LXX one.⁴³⁴ His method resembled Origen's in this sense, as Theodotion's version

---

[433] *Comm. Dan.* 11.44–45 (p. 506). As Jerome went on to discuss this passage at some length, he consistently represented צבי with *inclytus* (ibid., pp. 498–506). His citations of Symmachus' and the LXX translators' renderings of צבי in *Comm. Dan.* 11.44–45 match those he recorded in *Comm. Dan.* 11.16. Theodotion reads *Saba* (see ibid., p. 506).

[434] See his remarks in Vulg., p. 1341 and in *Comm. Dan.* 4.5a (p. 220).

had been his port of call, too, in the production of a new edition of the LXX in line with the Hebrew text of his time.[435] For the sake of convenience, and because he arguably read from the Greek more naturally than from the Hebrew, it is plausible that, at times, Jerome consulted Theodotion's text without checking the Hebrew.[436] In Vulg. Dan. 8.9, he translated וְאֶל־הַצֶּבִי 'and towards the beauty / honour' as *et contra fortitudinem* 'and against the force'. Jerome could have read צָבָא 'army' instead of צְבִי, either from a different Hebrew *Vorlage*, or by analogy with Dan. 8.10–13, where the former term occurs five times: four times he translated it with the word *fortitudo* (twice in Vulg. Dan. 8.10, once in Vulg. Dan. 8.11, once in Vulg. Dan. 8.13), and once with the synonym *robur* (Vulg. Dan. 8.12). It seems more likely, though, that, regardless of the state of his Hebrew *Vorlage* or of his reading thereof, he simply aligned his translation with Theodotion's version, where Dan. 8.9 וְאֶל־הַצֶּבִי is rendered as καὶ πρὸς τὴν δύναμιν 'and against the might' and Dan. 8.10 עַד־צְבָא הַשָּׁמַיִם as ἕως τῆς δυνάμεως τοῦ οὐρανοῦ 'up to the might of the sky'. In Ezek. 20.6, Theodotion also translated צְבִי with δύναμις: when Jerome addressed this reading in his commentary on Ezekiel, he rendered δύναμις with *fortitudo*, too.[437] Also worth keeping in mind is Symmachus' translation of בְּאֶרֶץ־הַצֶּבִי in Dan. 11.16, ἐν τῇ γῇ τῆς

---

[435] See section 1.2.2, especially fn. 47.

[436] See below, section 3.2.5.

[437] *Comm. Ezech.* 20.5b–6 (CCSL 75, pp. 256–57). In this case, Jerome's translation of צְבִי in the Vulgate did not match that of Theodotion, as it was rendered with the word *egregius* 'extraordinary', which reflects צְבִי and not צָבָא (Vulg. Ezek. 20.6 is discussed below).

δυνάμεως 'in the land of might', which interpretation is recorded by Jerome in the commentary: "Instead of 'renowned land', [...] Symmachus translated 'land of strength' (*terram fortitudinis*)."[438]

In short, Jerome could have interpreted וְאֶל־הַצֶּבִי as *et contra fortitudinem* in Dan. 8.9 by analogy with the verses that followed; the existence of a variant Hebrew version is not to be ruled out either (in which case Theodotion, too, may have relied on a text containing צָבָא and not צְבִי in Dan. 8.9).[439] However, on the

---

[438] *Comm. Dan.* 11.15–16 (p. 446). See also his translation of Symmachus Dan. 11.41 and 11.45 in *Comm. Dan.* 11.40–41a (p. 494) and 11.44–45 (p. 506), respectively.

[439] Theodotion transcribed צְבִי in Greek in Dan. 11.16 and 11.41, and he translated it as though it were צָבָא in other passages of the Bible. This variant reading could be conceivable in certain contexts—for example in Dan. 8.9 or in Isa. 4.2—whereas in other passages, as in Ezek. 20.6 and 20.15, it fits less well. The versions of the other *recentiores* should be taken into account, too, in this regard: indeed, צבי was translated as στάσις—which can mean 'a spot', 'a position' or 'a military faction'—in Aquila's so-called 'first edition' of Ezek. 20.6 and in Ezek. 20.15; it was also one of the two readings attributed to Symmachus in Ezek. 20.6 (see Field's Hexapla, II, pp. 816–17, fn. 11 and fn. 12). This rendering is somewhat reminiscent of δύναμις, often found in Theodotion for צבי. In *Comm. Ezech.* 20.5b–6 (CCSL 75, p. 257), Jerome's translation of στάσις from Aquila's first edition of Ezek. 20.6, *firmamentum* 'a support', also has military overtones. In summary, the *recentiores* often translated צָבָא where our text reads צְבִי. The orthographic proximity of the two words perhaps played a role in this state of affairs; however, it should be borne in mind that צָבָא and צְבִי occurred in contexts where they could be seen as semantically interchangeable, too. Therefore, the tension between two types of rendering in the Greek versions could reflect a translation habit or the existence of a different *Vorlage*.

whole, it seems more plausible that he routinely followed the *recentiores*' versions in the Vulgate—and particularly that of Theodotion for the Book of Daniel—regardless of the Hebrew.

2.2.3. Jerome's Responses to a Few Other Occurrences of the Word צבי: His Flexibility in the Employment of His Sources and Lexical Variation as an Essential Component of His Style

Jerome's recourse to synonyms of *inclitus* or to words belonging to a close semantic field in his responses to other occurrences of the word צבי attests to his penchant for lexical variation. In Vulg. Jer. 3.19, he rendered נַחֲלַת צְבִי 'a heritage of beauty / honour' as *hereditatem praeclaram* 'a remarkable heritage';[440] in Vulg. Isa.

---

[440] The full phrase is a long construct chain that reads נַחֲלַת צְבִי צִבְאוֹת גּוֹיִם 'a heritage of the nations' beauty of beauties / of the nation's honour of honours'. The plural construct form of צְבִי (צִבְאוֹת) is similar to the plural construct form—and to the absolute when unvocalised—of צָבָא, hence Jerome's translation in Vulg. Jer. 3.19: *hereditatem praeclaram exercituum gentium* 'a remarkable heritage of the nations' hosts' (this rendering matches the corresponding lemma in his commentary on Jeremiah [*Comm. Jer.* 3.19; CCSL 74, p. 37]). Noteworthy in this regard is the LXX reading, in which נַחֲלַת צְבִי צִבְאוֹת גּוֹיִם was translated as κληρονομίαν θεοῦ παντοκράτορος ἐθνῶν 'a heritage of God Almighty of the nations', probably by analogy with the collocation יהוה צְבָאוֹת 'Lord of hosts'. The reading that Jerome ascribed to Theodotion in his commentary is interesting, too, as it conflates two renderings, one for צְבִי and one for צָבָא: *hereditatem inclytam fortitudinis robustissimi gentium* 'a renowned heritage of the nations' strongest force' (*inclytam* stands for צְבִי and *fortitudinis robustissimi* for צָבָא) (*Comm. Jer.* 3.19; CCSL 74, p. 37). Finally, it should be observed that Jerome did not employ *praeclarus*, as

4.2, לִצְבִי וּלְכָבוֹד 'for beauty and for honour' as *in magnificentia et in gloria* 'in magnificence and in glory';[441] in Vulg. Isa. 13.19, בָּבֶל צְבִי מַמְלָכוֹת 'Babylon, the beauty / honour of the realms' as *Babylon illa gloriosa in regnis* 'Babylon, that glorious [city] among the realms';[442] in Vulg. Ezek. 7.20, וּצְבִי עֶדְיוֹ 'and the beauty / honour

in Vulg. Jer. 3.19, in his translation of Theodotion Jer. 3.19, but the synonym *inclytus*. *Inclytus* was the term used in Vulg. Dan. 11.16.

[441] The corresponding lemma in Jerome's commentary on Isaiah (*in magnificentia et in gloria*) matches the Vulgate and agrees with the Hebrew against the LXX, ἐν βουλῇ μετὰ δόξης 'in counsel with repute', and the VL, *in consilio cum maiestate* 'in counsel with majesty' (*Comm. Isa.* 4.2–3; CCSL 73, p. 60). More importantly, it does not follow the *recentiores*, as both Aquila and Theodotion translated εἰς δύναμιν καὶ δόξαν 'towards the might and the repute'.

[442] As the verse further reads בָּבֶל צְבִי מַמְלָכוֹת תִּפְאֶרֶת גְּאוֹן כַּשְׂדִּים 'Babylon, the beauty / honour of the realms, the glory of the Chaldeans' majesty', it is interesting that Jerome rendered the noun תִּפְאֶרֶת, 'beauty', 'glory', a synonym of צְבִי which also stands in apposition to 'Babylon' in the verse, with *inclita* in the Vulgate: *Babylon illa gloriosa in regnis inclita in superbia Chaldaeorum* 'Babylon, that glorious [city] among the realms, renowned in the pride of the Chaldeans'. Also noteworthy is that, while both *incluta* and *gloriosa* occur in Jerome's translation of the corresponding LXX lemma in *Comm. Isa.* (*Babylon, quae vocatur incluta gloriosa regis Chaldaeorum* 'Babylon, which is called the renowned, the glorious [city] of the Chaldeans' king' [*Comm. Isa.* 13.19–22; CCSL 73, pp. 233–34]), in the LXX only one adjective was employed, ἔνδοξος, to render the two Hebrew nouns (צְבִי and תִּפְאֶרֶת): Βαβυλών, ἣ καλεῖται ἔνδοξος ὑπὸ βασιλέως Χαλδαίων 'Babylon, which is called illustrious by the king of the Chaldeans'. No VL form of this passage is attested before Jerome's translation in his commentary. In short, in his commentary, Jerome either employed a variant Greek (Origenic) text, or he translated צְבִי and תִּפְאֶרֶת

of its ornaments'[443] as *et ornamentum monilium suorum* 'and the ornament of their necklaces'; in Vulg. Ezek. 20.6, צְבִי הִיא לְכָל־הָאֲרָצוֹת '[this land] is the beauty / honour of all the lands' as *quae est egregia inter omnes terras* '[this land] which is extraordinary among all lands';[444] and in Vulg. Ezek. 20.15, the same Hebrew phrase was translated as *praecipuam terrarum omnium* 'the principal [land] of all lands'.[445]

---

in the Hebrew instead of ἔνδοξος from the LXX, thus revising the LXX lemma towards the Hebrew.

[443] The emendation of the suffixed singular pronoun in עֶדְיוֹ to the plural form עדים 'their ornaments' is suggested in the critical apparatus of BHS. This reading is indeed more likely in context.

[444] While צְבִי is also represented by *egregia* in the corresponding lemma in the commentary on Ezekiel, Jerome's translation of Aquila's so-called 'second edition' contains *inclytum*. Later under the same lemma he argued that the word *inclytus* 'literally' translated the Hebrew: *Iuxta litteram vero inclytam esse terram Iudaeae et cunctis terris fertiliorem* 'According to the literal [meaning], the land of Judea truly is "renowned" and more fertile than all lands' (*Comm. Ezech.* 20.5b–6; CCSL 75, pp. 256–57). The adjective *egregius* can convey a meaning similar to that of *inclytus*, such as 'distinguished'. Therefore, in rendering Aquila Ezek. 20.6 with *inclytum* in the commentary and in opting for *egregia* in Vulg. Ezek. 20.6, Jerome showed again his fondness for lexical variation.

[445] Here the LXX is at odds with the Hebrew: אֶל־הָאָרֶץ אֲשֶׁר־נָתַתִּי זָבַת חָלָב וּדְבַשׁ צְבִי הִיא לְכָל־הָאֲרָצוֹת 'to the land which I gave [them], flowing with milk and honey, which is the beauty / honour of all the lands' was rendered by the LXX translators as εἰς τὴν γῆν, ἣν ἔδωκα αὐτοῖς, γῆν ῥέουσαν γάλα καὶ μέλι, κηρίον ἐστὶν παρὰ πᾶσαν 'to the land which I have given them, a land pouring milk and honey: it is a honeycomb beyond any land'. The word 'honeycomb' probably stemmed by analogy with וּדְבַשׁ (for the LXX, the צבי of 'the land flowing with honey' represented its

Our investigation of Jerome's treatment of the word צבי has first shed light on his active reliance on Aquila's version, which he employed as an exegetical authority in Vulg. Dan. 11.16, 11.41 and 11.45, against the other *recentiores*' versions and the LXX. On the other hand, our analysis of his translation in Vulg. Dan. 8.9 revealed the potential influence of Theodotion. While his hermeneutic method showed his dependence on Greek sources in his understanding of the Hebrew, his recourse to a pair of synonyms to render צבי in Vulg. Dan. 11.16 and 11.41, independently of all other versions, reflected his stylistic autonomy. Our inspection of his responses in the Vulgate to other occurrences of צבי further demonstrated that lexical variation was a characteristic feature of his translation technique.

2.3. A Case of *hebraica veritas* Underlain by Jerome's Care for the Latin Version of the LXX: The King in Dan. 3.16

After king Nebuchadnezzar set up a statue and threatened to cast whoever would not worship it into a furnace of burning fire, a group of Chaldean men approached him to accuse Daniel's three

---

best part, hence 'honeycomb'). In his exegesis of Ezek. 20.15, it is interesting that Jerome tried to reconcile his Vulgate rendering of צבי with the LXX understanding by conflating the two translations in a rewriting of the verse: 'the land which I have promised them, flowing with milk and honey, which is "the principal [land] of all lands," or "a honeycomb"' (*terram quam eis pollicitus sum fluentem lacte et melle, quae praecipua terrarum omnium est—sive favus*) (*Comm. Ezech.* 20.15-17; CCSL 75, p. 262).

3. The Translation of the Book of Daniel

companions of disobedience and of irreverence towards the king's gods (Dan. 3.1–12). When the king summoned Daniel's friends, he reminded them of the punishment, should the accusation be true; he then asked: "And who is the god that shall deliver you from my hands?" (Dan. 3.13–15), to which they responded:

> MT Dan. 3.16
>
> עֲנוֹ שַׁדְרַךְ מֵישַׁךְ וַעֲבֵד נְגוֹ וְאָמְרִין לְמַלְכָּא נְבוּכַדְנֶצַּר לָא־חַשְׁחִין אֲנַחְנָה עַל־דְּנָה פִּתְגָם לַהֲתָבוּתָךְ׃
>
> Shadrach, Meshach, and Abed-Nego answered and said (lit., saying) to the king: "O Nebuchadnezzar, we are not required to reply to you on this matter / on this instruction."

In the Book of Daniel, when the kings' subjects address him in direct speech, it is always by his title:[446] here, it is significant that the three Judeans start off by omitting it.[447] In Jerome's commentary on Daniel, however, the corresponding lemma includes the king's honorific:

> *Nabuchodonosor rex, non oportet nos de hac re respondere tibi*
>
> O King Nabuchodonosor, it is not necessary for us to answer you on this thing.[448]

This reading corresponds to the LXX version, in which the word for 'king' is expressed in the vocative in direct speech. Theodotion agrees with the Aramaic in this respect:

---

[446] See for instance Dan. 3.9, 3.10 or 3.12.

[447] They resume calling the king by his title in Dan. 3.17.

[448] *Comm. Dan.* 3.16b (p. 190).

LXX Dan. 3.16

ἀποκριθέντες δὲ Σεδραχ, Μισαχ, Αβδεναγω εἶπαν τῷ βασιλεῖ Ναβουχοδονοσορ Βασιλεῦ, οὐ χρείαν ἔχομεν ἀποκριθῆναί σοι ἐπὶ τῇ ἐπιταγῇ ταύτῃ·

But Sedrach, Misach [and] Abdenago, having answered, said to king Nabuchodonosor: "O King, we have no obligation (lit., necessity) to answer you on this instruction."

Theodotion Dan. 3.16

καὶ ἀπεκρίθησαν Σεδραχ, Μισαχ, Αβδεναγω λέγοντες τῷ βασιλεῖ Ναβουχοδονοσορ Οὐ χρείαν ἔχομεν ἡμεῖς περὶ τοῦ ῥήματος τούτου ἀποκριθῆναί σοι·

And Sedrach, Misach, Abdenago answered, saying to king Nabuchodonosor: "We have no obligation (lit., necessity) to answer you about this word / matter."

Under the lemma, Jerome informed the reader that the word 'king' was not contained "in Hebrew" (i.e., in the Aramaic). He then ventured an explanation: according to him, the absence of Nebuchadnezzar's title from the Judeans' answer was a deliberate omission on their part.

> In Hebrew, there is no 'king' (*non habet regem*), lest [Sedrac, Misac and Abdenago] might have seemed to revere an impious man, or to call 'king' one who would have encouraged wrongdoings (*iniqua*).[449]

---

[449] *Comm. Dan.* 3.16b (p. 190). The reasoning behind Jerome's explanation resembles the interpretation found in Tanḥuma Yelammedenu. According to this tradition, the characters also deliberately avoided calling Nebuchadnezzar 'king' as, by asking them to worship his idols, he was "denying" their God: 'And they did not say to him "O king", but they said to him: "Nebuchadnezzar, we are not required to reply to you on

3. The Translation of the Book of Daniel

In following the LXX version of the verse in the lemma and in immediately citing the Aramaic afterwards, Jerome meant to correct the former in light of the latter.[450] The vocative *rex* had been accordingly removed from Vulg. Dan. 3.16 as a result of the application of the *hebraica veritas* principle:

> Vulg. Dan. 3.16
>
> *Respondentes Sedrac Misac et Abdenago dixerunt regi Nabuchodonosor non oportet nos de hac re respondere tibi*
>
> Sedrac, Misac and Abdenago, answering, said to the king: "O Nabuchodonosor, it is not necessary for us to answer you on this thing."

In the commentary, after citing the Aramaic, Jerome went on to explain how the LXX reading (Βασιλεῦ 'O King') could be interpreted in this context:

> And if an obstinate man has been reading 'king', too (*quod si quis contentiosus regem quoque legerit*), let us say (*dicamus*) that [Sedrac, Misac and Abdenago] would not [mean to] insolently push the king to shed their blood, but that they would be duly paying homage to the king, in such a way

---

this matter / on this instruction. [...] By denying the Holy one, blessed He be, you are [just] Nebuchadnezzar [to us].'" (ולא אמרו לו מלכא אלא אמרו לו נבוכדנצר לא חשחין אנחנא על דנא פתגם להתבותך [...] לכפור בהקב"ה אתה נבוכדנצר) (Tanḥuma Yelammedenu, *Noah*, ב, ג).

[450] Courtray suggests that an exhaustive inspection of the manuscripts could permit us to completely rule out the possibility, though small already, that the word *rex* was inserted in Jerome's lemma as a result of a scribal mistake (*Prophète*, p. 88, fn. 96; see also ibid., pp. 103–4).

that the worship of God would not be profaned [either] (*ita [...] ut Dei cultus non laedatur*).⁴⁵¹

By the time of the production of the Vulgate, the LXX version of Daniel had arguably fallen into disuse in the Church—to what extent and among which communities exactly it is not known—in favour of Theodotion's version (see section 3.1.2.1). Yet, here, the "obstinate man" who "has been reading 'king'" clearly represents the Christian community that still expects the LXX version of the story, according to which the three Judeans address the king by his title. It is striking in this regard that Jerome proposed a contextual interpretation of this reading (*dicamus*) whereby he defended, to some extent, the LXX of Dan. 3.16. More specifically, as his commentary targeted a Latin readership,⁴⁵² he was defending the Latin form of LXX Dan. 3.16.⁴⁵³ This could be the sign that, at the beginning of the fifth century, while Theodotion's version of Daniel dominated among Greek-speaking communities, the Old Latin of the LXX, on the other hand, had to

---

⁴⁵¹ *Comm. Dan.* 3.16b (pp. 190–92).

⁴⁵² It should also be noted that Jerome dedicated his commentary to Marcella and Pammachius (*Comm. Dan.*, p. 128) who both lived in Rome. On Marcella and Pammachius, see Courtray, *Comm. Dan.*, p. 19; and Cavallera, *Saint Jérôme*, I, p. 85 and II, pp. 96–97.

⁴⁵³ In this respect, the 'obstinate man' from the commentary was not being called 'obstinate' because he rejected the Aramaic directly but in relation to Theodotion's version, or to its Latin translation rather. Jerome cited the Aramaic text ("In Hebrew, there is no 'king'") as an authority that could corroborate Theodotion in the eyes of the users of the (Old) Latin version of the LXX.

some extent more successfully stood the test of time than its parent text.[454] So far, the VL verses of Daniel adduced in this chapter have conformed mostly with Theodotion's version.[455] Interesting is that, in the case of Dan. 3.16, among the different attested versions, one that represents the ancient African form partly follows the LXX:[456]

> *responderunt autem Sedrac Misac Abdenago et dixerunt regi Nabuchodonosor rex non opus est nobis de hoc verbo respondere tibi*

---

[454] Zilverberg demonstrates that some mid-third-century Old Latin forms that conflate the LXX of Daniel and Theodotion's version were probably produced on the basis of texts that were already composite in Greek. According to him, revisions of the LXX of Daniel towards Theodotion's version mostly happened in the Greek (Zilverberg, *The Textual History of Old Latin Daniel*, pp. 131–34; see also my fn. 338). While Theodotion's version began to supersede the LXX relatively early on in Greek—which phenomenon most likely took the form of gradual revisions of the latter towards the former—the three types of Old Latin versions of Daniel (the LXX, Theodotion, and the hybrid form), as a result of a greater stability and level of embeddedness, may have coexisted longer and more independently of one another among Latin-speaking Christian communities. For an overview of the textual developments of the VL forms of Daniel, see Haelewyck, *Danihel*, pp. 72–73.

[455] See fn. 390 and section 3.2.2.1, and also section 3.2.4.1 below.

[456] This VL form, which conflates the two Greek versions, corresponds to the Carthaginian tradition attested in Cyprian in the mid-third century (see Haelewyck, *Danihel*, pp. 47–50).

> But Sedrac, Misac [and] Adbenago answered and said to king Nabuchodonosor: "O King, it is not incumbent on us to answer you on this word / topic."[457]

When Jerome said in the commentary that "in Hebrew, there is no 'king'," it is possible that he meant to compare the Aramaic to this VL tradition; he arguably reproduced the reading 'O King Nabuchodonosor' (*Nabuchodonosor rex*) in his lemma in reference to it, too. This situation certainly illustrates how, in 407, he could still pay attention to the LXX of Daniel and devote some of his exegesis to it. An element of contempt as well as a certain disapproval, not of Theodotion's version, but of his profile and background, can further explain why Jerome did not completely disregard the LXX in this case. After mentioning that "the churches do not read Daniel according to the Seventy translators, but according to Theodotion,"[458] he also argued that "after the coming of the Christ, [Theodotion] assuredly was a non-believer, [...] [maybe] an Ebionite, which is a Jew in another way."[459] According to him, while the Vulgate was "nothing but the translation of

---

[457] The word order of this VL verse can follow that of the LXX (ἀποκριθέντες δὲ / *responderunt autem*) where Theodotion's version departs from it (καὶ ἀπεκρίθησαν). However, the phrase *de hoc verbo*, which is a little unclear in context, seems to correspond to Theodotion (περὶ τοῦ ῥήματος τούτου 'about this word / matter') rather than to the LXX (ἐπὶ τῇ ἐπιταγῇ ταύτῃ 'on this instruction'). *Verbum* is also the word employed to render λόγος in the Latin of John 1.1: it could therefore represent its own internal tradition in the VL.

[458] Vulg., p. 1341.

[459] *Comm. Dan.*, p. 132. See section 3.1.2.1.

a Christian man" (*Christiani homini interpretatiunculam*), comparatively, Theodotion's version was the translation of "a Jewish man," of "a blasphemer after the passion of the Christ."[460] In summary, despite the application of the *hebraica veritas* principle in Vulg. Dan. 3.16, Jerome's exegesis reflects his care for the version in use among Latin-speaking Christians: his attempt to justify the LXX reading of Dan. 3.16 in context could attest to his hostility towards Theodotion and to the somewhat continuous and active use of the Old Latin version of the LXX of Daniel.

2.4. "Each was drinking according to his age" in Vulg. Dan. 5.1–2a: A Plausible Case of Expansion on the Aramaic, Independent of the Greek, by Means of an Interpolation

2.4.1. The Vulgate, the Greek and the Old Latin Translations

In Dan. 5, Belshazzar is the king of Babylon. At the beginning of the chapter, he "makes a great feast" to which he invites a thousand of his most eminent subjects.

MT Dan. 5.1–2a

בֵּלְשַׁאצַּר מַלְכָּא עֲבַד לְחֶם רַב לְרַבְרְבָנוֹהִי אֲלַף וְלָקֳבֵל אַלְפָּא חַמְרָא שָׁתֵה׃
בֵּלְשַׁאצַּר אֲמַר ׀ בִּטְעֵם חַמְרָא לְהַיְתָיָה לְמָאנֵי דַהֲבָא וְכַסְפָּא

Belshazzar the king made a great feast for a thousand of his lords and in front of the thousand he was drinking

---

[460] *Epist.* 112.19 (VI, p. 39).

wine. /[461] Belshazzar ordered (lit., said), under the influence of the wine,[462] that the vessels of gold and silver be brought in...

While in his cups (בִּטְעֵם חַמְרָא), Belshazzar orders in Dan. 5.2 that the vessels that were stolen from the temple in Jerusalem by Nebuchadnezzar, his father, be brought in, so that he and all the guests might drink from them; before the order is given, it is said in Dan. 5.1b that he is 'drinking wine before a thousand [of his lords]' (וְלָקֳבֵל אַלְפָּא חַמְרָא שָׁתֵה). In Jerome's version of Dan. 5.1b, however, it is not he, Belshazzar, who drinks the wine but his guests, 'each according to his age', which expands on the original:

---

[461] The Masoretic accents, which mark, *inter alia*, semantic and syntactic units in the verse, offer one particular exegetical reading of the text (see Khan, *A Short Introduction*, pp. 37–41). Here, they present the segment וְלָקֳבֵל אַלְפָּא חַמְרָא שָׁתֵה as an independent unit ending the verse (as reflected in my translation). Beyond the reading conveyed by the accents, however, there can be different ways of construing the syntax in the transition from Dan. 5.1 to Dan. 5.2: this factor partly explains the divergent interpretations of the Greek and Latin translators (see below).

[462] The syntagm בִּטְעֵם חַמְרָא, literally 'in the tasting of the wine', has been interpreted by the LXX translators and by Jerome as indicative of the king's state: the LXX paraphrased it with ἀνυψούμενος ἀπὸ τοῦ οἴνου καὶ καυχώμενος 'elated with wine and boastful' and ἀνυψώθη ἡ καρδία αὐτοῦ 'his heart was elated'; Jerome paraphrased it with a single adjective and an adverb, *iam temulentus* 'just inebriated'. On the other hand, Theodotion calqued the Aramaic expression in his translation of the verse, ἐν τῇ γεύσει τοῦ οἴνου 'in the tasting of the wine' (which the VL follows, *in gustu vini*): this rendering does not establish the drunkenness of the king as plainly as the LXX and Vulgate versions. For further discussion of the meaning of the Aramaic syntagm, see Hartman's comments in *The Book of Daniel*, pp. 183–84.

3. The Translation of the Book of Daniel

Vulg. Dan. 5.1–2a

Balthasar rex fecit grande convivium optimatibus suis mille et unusquisque secundum suam bibebat aetatem / praecepit ergo iam temulentus ut adferrentur vasa aurea et argentea...

Balthasar the king made a great feast for a thousand of his aristocrats and each [of them] was drinking according to his age.[463] / He then commanded, just inebriated, that the golden and silver dishes be brought in...

The LXX version does not contain this departure from the Aramaic text. The opening lines of LXX Dan. 5 first provide a rough summary of the whole chapter by way of introduction:

LXX, introduction to Dan. 5 (lines 1–4)

Βαλτασαρ ὁ βασιλεὺς ἐποίησε δοχὴν μεγάλην ἐν ἡμέρᾳ ἐγκαινισμοῦ τῶν βασιλείων αὐτοῦ καὶ ἀπὸ τῶν μεγιστάνων αὐτοῦ ἐκάλεσεν ἄνδρας δισχιλίους. / ἐν τῇ ἡμέρᾳ ἐκείνῃ Βαλτασαρ ἀνυψούμενος ἀπὸ τοῦ οἴνου καὶ καυχώμενος...

Baltasar the king gave (lit., made) a great reception on the inauguration day of his palace / on the consecration day of his reign, and he summoned two thousand men from his noblemen. / On that day, Baltasar, elated with wine and boastful...

Then the course of the narrative as represented in the MT resumes:

---

[463] The term *unusquisque* 'each' was not meant to involve the king. Indeed, Jerome paraphrased this verse in his commentary on Daniel and, as shown below, *unusquisque* corresponds to 'each of the summoned chiefs' (*unusquisque autem principum vocatorum*), i.e., to the guests.

LXX Dan. 5.1–2a

Βαλτασαρ ὁ βασιλεὺς ἐποίησεν ἑστιατορίαν μεγάλην τοῖς ἑταίροις αὐτοῦ. / καὶ ἔπινεν οἶνον, καὶ ἀνυψώθη ἡ καρδία αὐτοῦ καὶ εἶπεν ἀνενέγκαι τὰ σκεύη τὰ χρυσᾶ καὶ τὰ ἀργυρᾶ...

Baltasar the king made a great feast for his companions. / And he was drinking wine, and his heart was elated, and he ordered (lit., said) that the golden and silver vessels be brought up...

In the opening lines of LXX Dan. 5, the portion in which the king is supposed to be drinking in front of his guests is missing: he is directly presented as "elated with wine." LXX Dan. 5.1–2a, on the other hand, conforms with the version contained in the MT to the extent that it portrays Belshazzar in the act of drinking: the scene, however, is not taking place 'in front of the guests'.[464] In his translation, Theodotion construed the Aramaic verse differently, albeit in a way that still presented the king as performing the act of drinking.

Theodotion Dan. 5.1–2a

Βαλτασαρ ὁ βασιλεὺς ἐποίησε δεῖπνον μέγα τοῖς μεγιστᾶσιν αὐτοῦ χιλίοις, καὶ κατέναντι τῶν χιλίων ὁ οἶνος. / καὶ πίνων Βαλτασαρ εἶπεν ἐν τῇ γεύσει τοῦ οἴνου τοῦ ἐνεγκεῖν τὰ σκεύη τὰ χρυσᾶ καὶ τὰ ἀργυρᾶ...

Baltasar the king made a great supper for a thousand of his noblemen, and the wine [was] in front of the thousand. / And, [as he was] drinking, Baltasar, in the tasting of the

---

[464] In the MT, the king is said to be drinking in Dan. 5.1b and then to be drunk in Dan. 5.2a. In the LXX, both happen in Dan. 5.2a. See also Theodotion's version below.

3. The Translation of the Book of Daniel

wine, ordered (lit., said) that the golden and silver vessels
be brought up...

In this version, וְלָקֳבֵל אַלְפָּא חַמְרָא was understood as an independent unit meaning 'and in front of the thousand [there was] the wine' (καὶ κατέναντι τῶν χιλίων ὁ οἶνος). The active participle שָׁתֵה was consequently construed without an object and in agreement with the word בֵּלְשַׁאצַּר in the following verse: καὶ πίνων Βαλτασαρ ('and, as he was drinking, Baltasar...'). Theodotion probably added the conjunction καὶ to facilitate the transition from Dan. 5.1 to 5.2. The VL, which follows his translation rather than the LXX, also describes Belshazzar as being in the act of drinking. It is striking however that the Old Latin departs from our edition of Theodotion in a way that more accurately represents the syntax of the Aramaic: while in the Greek the wine is said to be in front of the guests and Belshazzar is drinking, in the VL the king is "drinking in front of a thousand men." This reading agrees with the Aramaic as we understand it from the MT (in accordance with the reading conveyed by the Masoretic accents):

VL Dan. 5.1–2a

Balthasar rex fecit cenam magnam principibus suis mille et in conspectu mille hominum / bibens Balthasar dixit in gustu vini profer[r]entur vasa aurea et argentea...

Balthasar the king made a great supper for a thousand of his chiefs and in front of a thousand men,[465] / [while]

---

[465] An alternative construction is grammatically possible, albeit less conceivable: 'Balthasar the king made a great supper for a thousand of his chiefs and in front of a thousand men. / [While] drinking, Balthasar, in the tasting of the wine...'

drinking, Balthasar, in the tasting of the wine, said that the golden and silver dishes should be brought before [him]...

Of all extant versions, the VL is the one that matches the syntax of the Aramaic best in the coordination between Dan. 5.1 and 5.2 וְלָקֳבֵל אַלְפָּא חַמְרָא שָׁתֵה: בֵּלְשַׁאצַּר אֲמַר / *et in conspectu mille hominum / bibens Balthasar dixit*. One must not infer, though, that this is a case of a VL text revised towards the Hebrew Bible (as it can sometimes be suggested in modern scholarship): the hypothesis that there were contacts between the Old Latin and the Hebrew texts before Jerome's time is unsubstantiated.[466] As a general rule, if one of the translations was revised towards the Hebrew, it was the Greek one, not the Old Latin. When a VL form seems to depart from its Greek parent text and to better conform with the Hebrew (or with the Aramaic), the existence of a different Greek *Vorlage* is to be suspected. For instance, in the case of Dan. 5.1–2, Ziegler's apparatus points to manuscripts in which the reading καὶ is missing from Theodotion Dan. 5.2a. It is therefore probable that the Old Latin translators relied on a *Vorlage* of Theodotion's version in which there was no καὶ, that is, where the syntax said that the king was "drinking wine in front of the thousand": καὶ κατέναντι τῶν χιλίων [τὸν] οἶνο[ν] / πίνων Βαλτασαρ

---

[466] See Kraus, 'Hebraisms in the Old Latin'; Cañas Reíllo, 'The Latin Bible and the Septuagint', pp. 29–31; and Graves, 'Latin Texts', pp. 231–34. The VL form quoted here represents the European tradition of the first half of the fourth century (see Haelewyck, *Danihel*, pp. 54–60).

εἶπεν...⁴⁶⁷ As the word for 'wine' occurred four times in Theodotion Dan. 5 (Dan. 5.1, 2, 4, 23), specifying in Dan. 5.1 that it was wine that the king was drinking may have been viewed as redundant by the Old Latin translators, all the more so in the context of a banquet. As a matter of efficiency—and because 'wine' occurred another three times in the chapter—they could have decided to elide it in their translation of Theodotion Dan. 5.1 (VL Dan. 5.2, 4, 23 still contain the word for 'wine'). In summary, as a result of the absence of καὶ in the Old Latin translators' Greek *Vorlage*, the VL form seems closer to the Aramaic than our edition of Theodotion: likely is that VL Dan. 5.1–2a attests to a different version of Theodotion's translation, and at the same time to the translation technique of its author (or authors) through the omission of the word for 'wine'.

2.4.2. Jerome's Understanding of the Aramaic

In Jerome's commentary on Daniel, the two lemmas corresponding to Dan. 5.1 and to Dan. 5.2a perfectly match the Vulgate

---

⁴⁶⁷ This is my reconstruction of the Old Latin translators' hypothetical *Vorlage* of Theodotion Dan. 5.1b–2a. Unless the extant VL form is incomplete, the translators cannot have read 'wine' in the nominative, as in our edition of Theodotion (ὁ οἶνος). Indeed, the finite verb in the Old Latin clause is *dixit* (*et in conspectu mille hominum / bibens Balthasar dixit* 'and in front of a thousand men, / drinking, Balthasar said'), whereas in Theodotion, irrespective of the conjunction καὶ, the verb 'to be' is implied in the use of the nominative (καὶ κατέναντι τῶν χιλίων ὁ οἶνος. / [καὶ] πίνων Βαλτασαρ εἶπεν 'and the wine [was] in front of the thousand. / [And,] Drinking, Balthasar said'). I therefore propose the accusative [τὸν] οἶνο[ν] in my reconstruction.

verses.[468] More importantly, in *Comm. Dan.* 5.1, Jerome paraphrased Vulg. Dan. 5.1b and a Greek version of the verse alongside each other:

> *Unusquisque autem principum vocatorum iuxta suam bibebat aetatem, sive, ut ceteri interpretes transtulerunt, bibebat ipse rex vinum coram cunctis principibus quos vocaverat.*[469]

> 'And each of the summoned chiefs was drinking in accordance with his age' or, as the other interpreters translated, 'the king himself was drinking wine before all the chiefs that he had summoned'.

The Vulgate translation of וְלָקֳבֵל אַלְפָּא חַמְרָא שָׁתֵה as 'and each [of them] was drinking according to his age' was already confirmed by the lemma in the commentary: in the passage translated above, Jerome further proposed a paraphrase of his version whereby he reaffirmed his way of understanding the Aramaic and of expanding on it (*iuxta suam bibebat aetatem*) in the Vulgate. In theory, those he named the "other interpreters," whom he presented as unanimous in their treatment of the Aramaic (*ut ceteri interpretes transtulerunt*), should have pointed to the *recentiores* against the LXX translators. However, the only attested *recentiores* version, that of Theodotion, disagrees with the reading according to which 'the king himself was drinking wine before all the chiefs that he had summoned' (see above). It is probable that Jerome's paraphrase, which matches the Aramaic verse as we interpret it, attests to Aquila's and Symmachus' versions, and perhaps even to

---

[468] *Comm. Dan.* 5.1–2a (pp. 238–40).
[469] *Comm. Dan.* 5.1 (p. 240).

a version of Theodotion reflected by the Old Latin text.[470] An element of his paraphrase of their version indicates that he intended to stress the contrast between their depiction of the scene and his: the use of the word *ipse* 'himself' in *bibebat ipse rex vinum* is there to highlight the fact that it is the king that is drinking in their version, while it is the guests in his (*Unusquisque* [...] *principum vocatorum* [...] *bibebat*). Staying elliptical in this comparison enabled Jerome to leave room for interpretation. Meaningful in this respect is that he did not assert that the Vulgate proposed the correct reading, nor gave any explanation for the discrepancy between the "other interpreters'" translation and his, although he was citing the two of them alongside each other

---

[470] According to Courtray, there is no doubt that the phrase *ut ceteri interpretes transtulerunt* was referring to Aquila's and Symmachus' versions (*Prophète*, p. 90; Courtray also numbered the LXX among them, surely by accident: as shown above in my translation, Jerome's paraphrase of the "other interpreters" does not match the LXX reading). Field, too, seems to suggest that Jerome was citing the *recentiores*: "Jerome [...] does not cite the [exact] words of the other [interpreters], but just the sense (*sed sensum tantum afferens*)" (my translation of Field, Hexapla, II, p. 919, fn. 2). In Field's edition of Theodotion's version, though, as in Ziegler's, the word for 'wine' is in the nominative and there is the conjunction καί at the beginning of Dan. 5.2: καὶ κατέναντι τῶν χιλίων ὁ οἶνος. / καὶ πίνων ('and the wine was in front of the thousand. / And, as he was drinking [Baltasar]...'). As this reading did not match Jerome's paraphrase of the Greek version, Field—like Courtray—must have excluded Theodotion from the group of "other interpreters" that were being cited in the commentary. However, as demonstrated in this case study, Jerome's remark may have involved Theodotion, too.

(*sive*). This state of affairs has puzzled scholars,[471] who do not know how Jerome's interpretation of the verse originated, as none of the other extant versions reflects the same departure as his. I shall therefore endeavour to propose a tentative way of explaining how he came to the translation 'and each [of them] was drinking according to his age' in Vulg. Dan. 5.1b.

So as to venture the following hypothesis, the correspondence between the components of the Aramaic verse (וְלָקֳבֵל אַלְפָּא חַמְרָא שָׁתֵה) and those of the Vulgate (*et unusquisque secundum suam bibebat aetatem*) has to be established first. The word חַמְרָא 'wine' was elided from Jerome's translation. This omission can be explained by the fact that חַמְרָא occurs four times in the chapter, and that three of these occurrences are found within a short compass (Dan. 5.1, 2, 4, 23): thus, for Jerome, the verb *bibebat* sufficed to imply חַמְרָא in Vulg. Dan. 5.1b. Jerome is indeed likely to have preferred avoiding the repetitions of the Aramaic, all the more so in the present context, where specifying more than once that, at the king's banquet, the beverage was wine must have seemed redundant to him.[472] On a stylistic level, his fondness for lexical variation manifests itself, too, as is shown by his rendering of בִּטְעֵם חַמְרָא in Dan. 5.2 as *iam temulentus* 'just inebriated'. In the end, out of its four occurrences, the term חַמְרָא was only rendered twice with *vinum* 'wine' in the Vulgate, in Vulg. Dan. 5.4

---

[471] See for example Courtray, 'Jérôme traducteur', p. 116.

[472] Jerome's translation technique is reminiscent of that of the VL translators in this regard (see above). Like the LXX translators, he also further elided the second occurrence of the name of the king in Vulg. Dan. 5.2a.

3. The Translation of the Book of Daniel 229

and in Vulg. Dan. 5.23.⁴⁷³ In the Aramaic version, it is also repeatedly indicated that the king is drinking or has drunk: twice in a row on his own (Dan. 5.1b, 5.2a), and then three times along with his guests (Dan. 5.2c, 5.3c, 5.4a). In his effort to avoid repetitions in his translation—the repetition of the king drinking in this case—Jerome may have decided to construe אַלְפָּא as agreeing with the participle שָׁתֵה. Indeed, in his version of Dan. 5.1b, the guests are the ones drinking, as *unusquisque* is the subject of *bibebat*.

There are, moreover, two reasons why the word אַלְפָּא, which in the original presents the guests as a whole, could have been rendered in a way that represents them individually in the Vulgate (*unusquisque*). First, the word for 'a thousand' was already expressed once in Dan. 5.1a (בֵּלְשַׁאצַּר מַלְכָּא עֲבַד לְחֶם רַב לְרַבְרְבָנוֹהִי אֲלַף) and Jerome had already employed the word *mille* to translate it in the Vulgate (*Balthasar rex fecit grande convivium optimatibus suis mille*): his preference for lexical variation urged him to look for a rendering that could convey a synonymous meaning in context. The addition of a genitive in his paraphrase of Vulg. Dan. 5.1b in his commentary stresses all the more that *unusquisque* corresponds to each of the thousand guests (*unusquisque* [...] *principum vocatorum* 'each of the summoned chiefs'). Jerome's understanding of וְלָקֳבֵל may have also inspired him to portray the guests individually through *unusquisque*. In theory, the syntagm וְלָקֳבֵל 'and in front of', being the last element left of

---

⁴⁷³ In his commentary, Jerome expressed the word for 'wine' in his paraphrase of the "other interpreters'" version of Dan. 5.1 (*bibebat ipse rex vinum*).

Dan. 5.1b, is represented by *et* [...] *secundum suam* [...] *aetatem* 'and according to his age' in the Vulgate version. The course of action that Jerome pursued to come to this understanding of לְקָבֵל, and more broadly to an overall different depiction of the scene in Dan. 5.1, may be explainable. The preposition לקבל, which is composed of the root קבל and of the preposition ל 'to', 'for', 'with regard to' prefixed to it, literally means 'in front of' (Dan. 3.3, 5.1). From this basic historical meaning, it has also sometimes been used in the figurative sense of 'on account of' (Dan. 5.10). Furthermore, in Biblical Aramaic, the noun קבל, which theoretically means 'front', is never employed on its own: it is always suffixed to one or two prepositions so as to form compounds which function as prepositions, like לקבל or כָּל־קֳבֵל 'on account of' (Dan. 2.12).[474] When followed by די 'that', 'which', 'as', these prepositions form subordinating conjunctions, such as לְקֳבֵל דִּי (Ezra 6.13) or כָּל־קֳבֵל דִּי (Ezra 4.14), both of which can mean 'because', 'inasmuch as', or 'according to that which'. Jerome was aware that לקבל meant 'in front of' in certain contexts, as shown in Vulg. Dan. 2.31 (*contra te*), 3.3 (*in conspectu statuae*), 5.5 (*contra candelabrum*). In Vulg. Dan. 5.1 though, unlike Theodotion, he did not read לְקָבֵל this way, as he opted for the preposition *secundum* 'according to', which corresponds to its figurative sense. His response to other occurrences of the Aramaic phrase shows that it was not unusual for him to employ the word *secundum* to render כלקבל or לקבל as part of subordinating conjunctions introduced by די. Where in Dan. 2.41 it is said כָּל־קֳבֵל

---

[474] The phrase כָּל־קֳבֵל in the MT probably represents a misreading of כְּלָקֳבֵל, composed of the prepositions כ 'as', 'according to' and ל.

דִּי חֲזַיְתָה פַּרְזְלָא מְעָרַב בַּחֲסַף טִינָא 'inasmuch as you saw the iron mixed with clay of mud', in the Vulgate it reads *secundum quod vidisti ferrum mixtum testae ex luto* 'in accordance with [the fact] that you saw the iron mixed with pottery [made] of clay' (*secundum* corresponds to כָּל־קֳבֵל and *quod* to דִּי). Likewise, *secundum quod* renders כָּל־קֳבֵל דִּי in Vulg. Dan. 2.45 and לָקֳבֵל דִּי in Vulg. Ezra 6.13. In Vulg. Dan. 5.1, we have established that *unusquisque* represents אַלְפָּא in agreement with שְׁתֵה: according to this reading, Jerome could not construe לָקֳבֵל as a preposition anymore, as there was no object to govern.

I therefore argue that he possibly read לָקֳבֵל adverbially, in the sense of 'accordingly'.[475] From this point on, he could have

---

[475] Joubert conjectured that Jerome read קָבֵל in לָקֳבֵל as a noun derived from the root קבל 'to receive' and construed it as 'scope' or 'capacity': according to this theory, he interpreted וְלָקֳבֵל אַלְפָּא חַמְרָא שָׁתֵה as 'and each [of the guests] was drinking wine according to [his] capacity' (Joubert, *Explication*, V, p. 357). I agree with the idea that Jerome construed לָקֳבֵל as 'according to' a portion of a certain type. However, in Vulg. Dan. 5.1, the guests' portions are defined on the basis of their age (*unusquisque secundum suam bibebat aetatem*): I endeavour to demonstrate below that Jerome incorporated this notion into the verse by drawing on similar banquet episodes of the Bible, through a process of interpolation. As for the hypothesis that he understood קָבֵל as a noun derived from the root that means 'to receive', it seems untenable. Firstly, although there is a noun in later rabbinic literature, קִיבּוּל, that means 'receiving' or 'acceptance', קבל as a noun does not have this meaning in the Biblical Aramaic corpus (see above). Secondly, where the verb קבל 'to receive' occurred, Jerome translated it in a straightforward manner, as in Dan. 2.6 (תְּקַבְּלוּן 'you shall receive' / *accipietis* 'you shall receive'); and when he ascribed the meaning of the verb קבל (i.e., 'to receive') to the prepositional לקבל, he also treated the preposition as

drawn on material from analogous banquet scenes in the Bible, on the basis of which he might have worked out what לְקָבֵל implied and expanded on Dan. 5.1 in a relevant manner. For instance, the idea that the guests are considered individually (*unusquisque*), and not as a group (אֲלַפָּא), and that everyone's share of drinks depends on a specific protocol presided by the king, is suggested in the Book of Esther. In the first chapter, king Ahasuerus makes a lavish feast in his castle for all his subjects, 'both great and small' (לְמִגָּדוֹל וְעַד־קָטָן; Est. 1.5), where he serves wine as he sees fit (וְיֵין מַלְכוּת רָב כְּיַד הַמֶּלֶךְ; Est. 1.7), and where the guests drink 'according to the law' (וְהַשְּׁתִיָּה כַדָּת) and 'each and every man' acts, in accordance with the king's decree, 'as per their will' (יִסַּד הַמֶּלֶךְ עַל כָּל־רַב בֵּיתוֹ לַעֲשׂוֹת כִּרְצוֹן אִישׁ־וָאִישׁ; Est. 1.8).[476]

Interestingly, the notion that, at a banquet, portions are distributed among the guests in accordance with their age also represents a significant aspect of the reunion scene in the Joseph story. When Jacob's sons return to Egypt from Canaan so as to buy food from their brother Joseph (whom they have not recognised yet), he, Joseph, sees that their youngest brother Benjamin came with them: he therefore decides to make a feast (Gen. 43.1–

---

though it were a verb (see Ezra 7.17: כָּל־קֳבֵל דְּנָה 'because of this' / *libere accipe* 'receive freely'). As our investigation of Jerome's responses to the occurrences of לקבל shows above, it was actually usual for him to render this construction with the preposition *secundum*.

[476] In the Vulgate, Jerome translated the expression אִישׁ־וָאִישׁ 'each and every one' with *unusquisque* (*ut sumeret unusquisque quod vellet* 'so that each [of the guests] might take what he wanted'). This verse is discussed at length in section 4.2.2.1.

16). As the banquet begins, it is said that Joseph's brothers select seats in front of him, from oldest to youngest: 'and they sat in front of [Joseph], the firstborn according to his birthright, and the young[est one] according to his youth' (וַיֵּשְׁבוּ לְפָנָיו הַבְּכֹר כִּבְכֹרָתוֹ וְהַצָּעִיר כִּצְעִרָתוֹ; Gen. 43.33). In this setting, Joseph leads the feast in front of his brothers (וַיֵּשְׁבוּ לְפָנָיו), the same way as Belshazzar presides before his thousand guests in Dan. 5.1b (וְלָקֳבֵל אַלְפָּא). Portions are then distributed among the brothers, and Benjamin's share is five times as big as anyone else's (וַיִּשָּׂא מַשְׂאֹת מֵאֵת פָּנָיו אֲלֵהֶם וַתֵּרֶב מַשְׂאַת בִּנְיָמִן מִמַּשְׂאֹת כֻּלָּם חָמֵשׁ יָדוֹת; Gen. 43.34). Noteworthy is that, in the Vulgate, Jerome translated Gen. 43.33 as follows: *sederunt coram eo primogenitus iuxta primogenita sua et minimus iuxta aetatem suam* ('they sat in front of [Joseph], the firstborn in accordance with his birthright, and the smallest in accordance with his age'). His way of rendering כִּצְעִרָתוֹ ('according to his youth') with *iuxta aetatem suam* ('in accordance with his age') here departs from the original sense in a way that matches his translation of לָקֳבֵל in Vulg. Dan. 5.1 (*secundum suam aetatem*); it agrees even more with the wording of his paraphrase of Vulg. Dan. 5.1 in *Comm. Dan.* 5.1 (*iuxta suam aetatem*).[477] As a result, there is even more intertextuality between the banquet scenes of Gen. 43 and Dan. 5 in the Vulgate version than there is in the Hebrew original. If Dan. 5.1 seemed unclear to Jerome—all the more because he was not as familiar with Aramaic as he was with Hebrew—the recourse to the translation technique of interpolation could allow him to derive the meaning of לָקֳבֵל from

---

[477] Jerome's translation of כִּצְעִרָתוֹ does not match any of the known versions.

other banquet episodes, provided that the context matched that of Dan. 5.1.

In summary, in Vulg. Dan. 5.1, Jerome omitted the word for 'wine' in his translation of חַמְרָא שְׁתֵה so as to avoid lexical repetitions; he then construed אַלְפָּא as the subject of an independent clause introduced by the conjunction 'and' in וְלָקֳבֵל and ending before Vulg. Dan. 5.2a; he finally may have been led to think that לָקֳבֵל functioned as an adverb and consequently sought inspiration from other banquet scenes of the Bible in order to find an appropriate object (*suam aetatem*) to supply and to harmoniously expand on the verse.[478] To be sure, his translation of Dan. 5.1 was produced independently of other sources.

2.5. The Rendering *collega* in Vulg. Dan. 4.5: A Case of Departure in the Vulgate Caused by Jerome's Exclusive Reliance on the *recentiores*' Version

In Dan. 4, king Nebuchadnezzar has a dream that unsettles him. He therefore decides to summon the wisest men of Babylon and to have them interpret the dream (Dan. 4.1–3). As he tells them the dream and realises that they are not capable of interpreting it, Daniel makes his entrance.

---

[478] The translation process which I propose is a hypothesis: for lack of a more straightforward answer, it may pave the way for future attempts to solve the case of Vulg. Dan. 5.1, which has received almost no attention in modern scholarship.

3. The Translation of the Book of Daniel

MT Dan. 4.4b–5a

וְחֶלְמָא אָמַר אֲנָה קָֽדָמֵיהוֹן וּפִשְׁרֵהּ לָא־מְהוֹדְעִין לִי: וְעַד אָחֳרֵין עַל קָֽדָמַי דָּנִיֵּאל

And I was telling the dream before them but they could not (lit., did not) make its interpretation known to me. / And eventually Daniel entered before me…

In Jerome's translation of this verse, Daniel is called 'a partner':

Vulg. Dan. 4.4b–5a

Et somnium narravi in conspectu eorum et solutionem eius non indicaverunt mihi / donec collega ingressus est in conspectu meo Danihel

And I told the dream in front of them but they did not disclose its solution to me / until a partner, Daniel, walked in in front of me…

In the commentary, the lemma that corresponds to Dan. 4.5a matches the Vulgate version of the verse. Jerome commented as follows:

If we put aside the Seventy translators, who have omitted [Dan. 4.3–6] (I do not know for which reason), the three remaining ones (*tres reliqui*, i.e., the *recentiores*) have rendered 'partner' (*collegam*) [here]. This is why (*unde*) their version (i.e., the LXX), by the decision of the heads of the church (*iudicio magistrorum ecclesiae*), was repudiated in this volume (i.e., the Book of Daniel), and that of Theodotion, which agrees both with the Hebrew and the other translators (i.e., the *recentiores*), is commonly read (*editio* [...] *Theodotionis vulgo legitur, quae et Hebraico et ceteris translatoribus congruit*).[479]

---

[479] *Comm. Dan.* 4.5a (p. 220).

As Jerome said, Dan. 4.3–6 are verses missing in the LXX; they are not attested in the VL either. This circumstance enabled Jerome to assert that the process whereby the LXX gradually fell into disuse in favour of Theodotion's version was the result (*unde*) of 'a repudiation' dictated by "the heads of the church." He also claimed that the three *recentiores* had unanimously rendered *collega* 'partner', which corresponds to their translation of what appears as אָחֳרֵין in our edition of the MT of Dan. 4.5a. He finally added that Theodotion agreed not only with "the other translators," that is, the *recentiores*, but also "with the Hebrew," i.e., with the Aramaic here. Later in the commentary he justified the rendering *collega* in light of Dan. 4.6a, in which Nebuchadnezzar calls Daniel 'chief of the magicians' (רַב חַרְטֻמַיָּא) in reference to his feats of wisdom:

> It is no wonder that [Daniel] was appointed as 'chief of all the soothsayers' (*princeps hariolorum omnium*), he who at the king's command learned the wisdom of the Chaldeans and was found ten times wiser than everyone. [...] [Therefore,] Daniel himself, who according to them no doubt represents a holy force (*sancta fortitudo*), is here appointed by Nabuchodonosor as his chief of soothsayers and he is called a partner (*collega*).[480]

If we turn our attention to our edition of Theodotion's version, Dan. 4.4b–5a reads as follows:

καὶ τὸ ἐνύπνιον εἶπα ἐγὼ ἐνώπιον αὐτῶν, καὶ τὴν σύγκρισιν αὐτοῦ οὐκ ἐγνώρισάν μοι, / ἕως οὗ ἦλθεν Δανιηλ

---

[480] *Comm. Dan.* 4.6a (pp. 220–22).

> And I told the dream in front of them, and they could not (lit., did not) make its interpretation known to me, / until the [moment] when Daniel came.

This version does not contain an equivalent for *collega*, which reading Jerome attributed to the *recentiores*, including Theodotion. Indeed, it says 'until the [moment] when Daniel came' (ἕως οὗ ἦλθεν Δανιηλ), which agrees in meaning with Dan. 4.5a as reflected in our edition of the MT (וְעַד אָחֳרֵין עַל קָדָמַי דָּנִיֵּאל 'and eventually Daniel entered before me'). The discrepancy between the MT, Jerome's interpretation, and our edition of Theodotion's version can be explained with a good deal of certainty. In order to do so, we shall reconstruct the course of action followed by Jerome.

The only occurrence of the phrase וְעַד אָחֳרֵין in the Aramaic portion of the Hebrew Bible is here, in Dan. 4.5a; moreover, the word אחרין is a *hapax legomenon* only attested in this construction. As אחרין has been associated with the word אחרית 'end' (as in Dan. 2.8 בְּאַחֲרִית יוֹמַיָּא 'at the end of the days'), the phrase וְעַד אָחֳרֵין has come to be construed as meaning 'and at last', 'and eventually'. It is now noteworthy that the apparatus of BHS records several manuscripts in which Dan. 4.5a reads אחרן instead of אחרין. The term אחרן means 'another' in the masculine; it occurs on various occasions in the Book of Daniel (in Dan. 2.11 and 5.17, for example, it refers to Daniel, albeit implicitly). It is significant in this regard that certain textual witnesses also attest to a variant reading in Theodotion Dan. 4.5, one that agrees with אחרן: ἕως οὗ ἕτερος εἰσῆλθεν ἐνώπιον μου Δανιήλ ('until the [moment] when another one, Daniel, came in in front of me').[481] By means of an emendation of this variant reading, a Greek equivalent of *collega* has long been reconstructed by several scholars: their hypothesis that the word ἕτερος 'another' was mistranscribed by Greek scribes as ἑταῖρος 'companion' has stood the test of time. Migne summarised as follows:

> The ancients—Chrysostom and Theodoret, to be specific[482]—did not read 'partner' (*collegam*) but 'another' (*alterum*), that is, not ἑταῖρος but ἕτερος. Furthermore, the former interpretation, that is, the one that proposes 'friend' or 'partner', is very far from the Aramaic truth: this is why it has seemed to scholars that Jerome used poorly corrected manuscripts and that he consequently understood 'partner' instead of 'another', i.e., he read ἑταῖρος instead of ἕτερος in the Greek. In fact, Nabuchodonosor could have wanted to call Daniel by the name of 'partner', as he [Daniel] was [like] 'another self' (*alter ipse*) [to him] and was second [only] to him. Actually, in the second century, this was a well-known saying by Clement of Alexandria: 'I, another one, am a companion' (ὁ δὲ ἑταῖρος ἕτερος ἐγώ). Then

---

[481] See Field, *Hexapla*, II, p. 917, fn. 5; and the apparatus in Ziegler's edition. The fact that the variant reading אחרן is attested in Aramaic manuscripts tends to invalidate Courtray's theory that the existence of two Greek versions, one with ἕτερος and one without, stemmed from a misreading of אחרין (*Prophète*, p. 89). An investigation of the relationship of the two Theodotion texts with one another and with the two Aramaic versions (אחרן and אחרין) could shed light on the textual history of the Book of Daniel; such an undertaking, however, does not fall within the purview of this monograph.

[482] See the apparatus under Dan. 4.5 in Haelewyck, *Danihel*, p. 232.

3. The Translation of the Book of Daniel

> Origen in Homily 18 on Numbers wrote: 'Let us go through this [passage] again which is written in [the Book of] Daniel about *Daniel and his three friends* (ἑταίροις in Greek)'.[483]

The graphic proximity of ἕτερος and ἑταῖρος no doubt misled Jerome into arguing that *collega* was the translation of the *recentiores*. Courtray agrees with the view that he most likely relied on a Greek manuscript in which ἕτερος had been mistranscribed as ἑταῖρος,[484] but he also suggests that Jerome may have been the one responsible for misreading ἕτερος as ἑταῖρος in a *Vorlage* that was not corrupt.[485] Who misread the Greek is not important here: what matters to us in this case study is that Jerome incorporated the reading *collega* into the Vulgate and argued that it agreed with the Aramaic in his commentary. This interpretation of Dan. 4.5a indeed reflects a process whereby Jerome necessarily employed a Greek version in which he read ἑταῖρος, without consulting the Aramaic at all. Had he checked the Aramaic, his *Vorlage* would have exhibited the *lectio facilior* אחרן or the *lectio difficilior* אחרין: either way he could not have come to the rendering *collega*, since neither the former nor the latter Aramaic term signified 'a partner'. As it was more convenient for him to skip the Aramaic and to rely on the Greek, he claimed that *collega* agreed with the Aramaic, thus blindly trusting the reading that he had ascribed

---

[483] My translation of Migne's comments on *collega* in *Comm. Dan.* 4.5a, in his edition of Jerome's commentary on Daniel (PL 25, pp. 513–14, fn. c). See also Field's observation in *Hexapla*, II, p. 917, fn. 6; and Ziegler's remark on Dan. 4.5 in his part of the LXX apparatus.

[484] Courtray, *Prophète*, pp. 88–89.

[485] Courtray, *Comm. Dan.*, pp. 220–21, fn. 2; 'Jérôme traducteur', p. 116.

to the *recentiores*. In short, he did not read the Aramaic text in this passage.

It has been demonstrated throughout this chapter that Jerome often relied on the *recentiores* in his treatment of the Hebrew-Aramaic Book of Daniel. His way of employing their translations—that of Theodotion in particular—showed that they represented a storehouse of exegesis to him. In our last case study (section 2.5), Jerome argued that the word *collega*, which he found in the *recentiores*' translation of Dan. 4.5a, conformed with the Aramaic; he had accordingly incorporated this reading into Vulg. Dan. 4.5a, as though it reflected the *hebraica veritas*. As explained above, this case of departure from the Aramaic indicates that he blindly trusted the Greek. On the whole, if he generally exploited the interpretation of the *recentiores* to make sense of the Hebrew-Aramaic of Daniel, he could also give precedence to their versions over the original text, to the detriment of the original sense. The theory that, for the sake of convenience, he occasionally followed Theodotion's translation without checking his Hebrew-Aramaic *Vorlage*, may be best illustrated here, in his translation of Dan. 4.5a.

4. THE TRANSLATION OF THE BOOK OF ESTHER

1.0. Textual History

While the Book of Esther is composed of ten chapters in the MT, the two extant Greek traditions, the LXX and the A-Text, contain six major additional passages.[486] According to Haelewyck, a third Greek version that is now lost underlies the most ancient VL form of the book: indeed, the Old Latin texts can differ, in their structure and in certain aspects of the narrative, from the LXX and the A-Text.[487] Greek readings attested in multiple manuscripts—ones

---

[486] According to Cavalier, the *terminus a quo* of the LXX of Esther can be dated to the first century BCE. The so-called 'Lucianic' text or 'A-Text' (Cavalier and Moore have dismissed the former term as unsuited) is believed to represent a tradition that took form after the LXX, probably in the middle of the first century CE. See Cavalier, *Esther*, pp. 24–26, pp. 28–37, and pp. 43–44; and Moore, *Daniel, Esther, and Jeremiah*, pp. 162–65, and 'A Greek Witness'. Torrey contends that the LXX and A-Text of Esther (apart from two of their expansions which he considers original in Greek) and the Hebrew version represent independent translations of two different Aramaic *Vorlagen*: one of them split into the LXX and the A-Text, and the other gave birth to the Hebrew (see Torrey, 'The Older Book of Esther', pp. 5–7, p. 9, p. 27, pp. 30–39). The theory that the two Greek versions of Esther are not translations of the Hebrew text (at least not as reflected in the MT) is compelling. For a different view, see Kalimi's summary of the scholarly discussions of this matter in *The Book of Esther*, pp. 27–28.

[487] Haelewyck, *Hester*, pp. 68–69 and pp. 77–95. See also Cavalier, *Esther*, pp. 26–27, p. 31, and pp. 33–64. For a recent overview of the VL

that generally agree with the Hebrew where the LXX departs from it—arguably represent Origen's revision of the latter towards the former (see section 1.2.2).[488] In his *Jewish Antiquities*, Josephus also presented an extensive paraphrase of the story.[489] The core of the narrative common to the Hebrew and two main

version of Esther, see Haelewyck, 'Esther'; on the VL form of the additional episodes, see also Haelewyck, 'Latin', pp. 405–6.

[488] See Cavalier, *Esther*, p. 25; Haelewyck, *Hester*, pp. 70–71; Bickerman, 'The Colophon of the Greek Book of Esther', p. 341 and 'Notes on the Greek Book of Esther', p. 102, fn. 4. When revising the LXX, Origen relied on the *recentiores*' versions (and mostly on Theodotion's): he did not directly consult the Hebrew (on Origen's relationship with his Hebrew sources, see de Lange's remarks in *Origen and the Jews*, pp. 51–52 and p. 58; and Kamesar, 'Rabbinic Midrash and Church Fathers', pp. 30–31, and ibid. fn. 42). Therefore, if his revision is attested in the case of Esther, one or several *recentiores* versions of the book must have existed. It is striking, however, that almost no scholar mentions, let alone discusses, to my knowledge, the fact that there is no attestation of *recentiores* translations of the Book of Esther. Cavalier touches on this matter very briefly (*Esther*, p. 25); so do Haelewyck (*Hester*, p. 70) and McClurg ('Esther', p. 438). Hanhart—who ascribed to Aquila a rendering of Est. 1.6 found in a nineteenth-century edition of a Midrash of Esther—argues that that is the only extant reading attributable to one of the *recentiores* (see Hanhart's introduction to his edition of Esther, *Esther*, p. 63 and fn. 2; see also Field's remarks at the end of his edition of the Hexapla, II, in *Auctarium ad Origenis Hexapla*, p. 5, fn. 1). McClurg has further attempted to identify two Aquila readings in Origen's edition of the LXX of Esther ('Esther', p. 438). The subject of the hypothetical *recentiores* translations of the Book of Esther is addressed below in section 4.1.4.

[489] See Haelewyck, *Hester*, pp. 72–74.

Greek versions probably "reached its final form in either the late Persian or early Hellenistic Period,"[490] that is, around the second half of the fourth century BCE. On the other hand, the composition of the additional episodes found in the Greek versions is generally dated to the second century BCE, and to the first in the case of the later ones.[491] According to the chronology reconstructed by Canellis, the Book of Esther is one of the last books of the Hebrew Bible translated by Jerome, alongside Joshua, Judges and Ruth, as the Vulgate version was completed around 404–405.

---

[490] Moore, *Esther*, p. LIX; see also *Daniel, Esther, and Jeremiah*, p. 161. The date is disputed: for a survey of the scholarly views on this matter, see Cavalier, *Esther*, pp. 23–24. Cavalier argues for a late *terminus ad quem* of the Hebrew text—around the first century CE—as it is found in the MT. Likewise, in Torrey's view, the Hebrew text in its final form is an abbreviated version of the Aramaic source text from which it was translated, one that was edited after Josephus' time (see Torrey, 'The Older Book of Esther', pp. 38–39).

[491] See Moore, *Daniel, Esther, and Jeremiah*, pp. 12–13, p. 161 and pp. 165–66, and 'On the origins'; Wills, *Introduction to the Apocrypha*, pp. 28–29. The last paragraph of the LXX version of Esther has been read by many as a colophon providing an author, Lysimachus, a place, Jerusalem, and an approximate date, between the end of the second century BCE and the beginning of the first: "In the fourth year of the reign of Ptolemy and Cleopatra, [...] Lysimachus, son of Ptolemy, one of those in Jerusalem, translated [the present letter of the *Phrourai*, i.e., Purim])" (my translation of LXX Est. F.11). According to Cavalier, this paragraph is not a colophon: rather, it should be read as the last sentence of the LXX version of the story, that is, in context, not as an external unit (Cavalier, *Esther*, pp. 28–29). See also Torrey, 'The Older Book of Esther', pp. 25–27; Moore, *Daniel, Esther, and Jeremiah*, p. 161, fn. 16, and pp. 250–52; Bickerman, 'The Colophon of the Greek Book of Esther'.

1.1. The *sensus de sensu* and the *verbum e verbo* in the Vulgate of Esther

To our knowledge, Jerome did not write a commentary on Esther. Direct citations of the book, or even mentions of the name of Esther, are scarce in his letters (between five and ten altogether).[492] On the other hand, certain linguistic remarks in his preface to the Vulgate version, as well as in the annotations that he added at the end of his translation to introduce those of the passages that he did not find in his Hebrew *Vorlage*, cast light on the nature of his work and on his way of treating his sources. In his preface, he compared his translation, which he described as a *verbum e verbo* rendering of the Hebrew, with a "corrupted" version of the book presented as the *editio vulgata*:

> The Book of Esther has obviously been corrupted by various translators (*Librum Hester variis translatoribus constat esse vitiatum*).[493] For my part, after picking it up from the

---

[492] The verses of Esther that Jerome cited in his correspondence tended to come from the episodes missing from the Hebrew. See, for example, *Epist.* 49.14 (II, p. 137) and 130.4 (VII, p. 169): in both letters, he adduced material from the episode placed in the Greek versions between MT Est. 4.17 and 5.3 (= LXX Est. C.1–D.16 and A-Text Est. 4.12–5.12). By contrast, in QHG 12.15–16 (p. 20), he quoted a passage present in the Hebrew text (Est. 2.12–13). For a discussion of some of Jerome's quotations of the Book of Esther in his letters and commentaries, see Haelewyck's preface, *Hester*, pp. 34–36.

[493] Canellis (*Préfaces*, p. 378, fn. 3) and Haelewyck ('Latin', p. 407) discerned Greek translators behind this remark. However, it is not clear whether Jerome here actually meant the Greek, the Old Latin, or both groups of translators.

archives of the Hebrews (*quem ego de archivis Hebraeorum elevans*), I have translated it word for word, very accurately (*verbum e verbo pressius transtuli*). The common edition stretches (*editio vulgata* [...] *trahit*)[494] this book here and there with convoluted narrative threads (*laciniosis hinc inde verborum funibus*), as it adds things that could have been said and heard over time (*addens ea quae ex tempore dici poterant et audiri*). [...] As for you, Paula and Eustochium, since you have endeavoured to engage with the Hebrews' libraries and you have vetted the disputes of the interpreters (*interpretum certamina conprobastis*),[495] with the Hebrew Book of Esther at hand, [please] inspect our translation through each and every word (*per singula verba nostram*

---

[494] In Jerome, the mention of the *editio vulgata* generally points to the LXX, not to the VL (see Haelewyck, *Hester*, p. 19, especially fn. 11 [Haelewyck repeats this point in 'The Relevance of the Old Latin', p. 452]; and Courtray, 'Jérôme face au livre d'Esther', p. 30 and *Prophète*, pp. 67–68). Jerome implied it to some extent in the first Vulgate annotation introducing the Greek episodes of Esther, at the end of Vulg. Est. 10.3, as he indicated that he found these portions in the *editio vulgata* "in the tongue and characters of the Greeks" (see my translation below). At the same time, there may have been exceptions, too. For instance, in the Vulgate preface to the so-called Books of Solomon (see my fn. 114), Jerome first mentioned the Greek title of the Book of Proverbs (*Parabolae*), and then went on to specify that the *vulgata editio* was called *Proverbia* (i.e., a Latin name) (Vulg., p. 957). On Jerome's way of employing the expression *editio vulgata* and its possible variations, see Sutcliffe's discussion in 'The Name "Vulgate"', pp. 345–47.

[495] Here, again, one cannot infer whether Jerome meant just the Greek interpreters or both the Greek and the Old Latin ones (Paula and Eustochium knew Latin as well as Greek [see Cavallera, *Saint Jérôme*, I, p. 89 and p. 291, fn. 2]). Tantalising is the hypothesis that he sometimes put the LXX and the VL in the same basket (see section 1.7).

> *translationem aspicite*), so as to acknowledge that I have not lengthened it by adding even a single thing (*me nihil etiam augmentasse addendo*), but that I have simply rendered the Hebrew story into the Latin tongue, in a faithful account, just as it is in Hebrew (*sed fideli testimonio simpliciter, sicut in hebraeo habetur, historiam hebraicam latinae linguae tradidisse*).[496]

As a general rule, Jerome rejected the *verbum e verbo* translation method; he preferred and advocated for the *sensus de sensu* one, which consisted of rendering the overall meaning of a unit, rather than the exact wording of the original text: "In fact, not only do I confess it, but I profess it loud and clear: I do not render word for word (*non verbum e verbo*) [...] but sense for sense (*sed sensum exprimere de sensu*)."[497] As Jerome's translation of Esther was not meant to be an exception to this rule, the point that he had made in his preface, namely, that the Vulgate of Esther is a word-for-word translation of the Hebrew (*verbum e verbo pressius transtuli; per singula verba*), was an overstatement and should not be taken literally. First, when arguing that additional 'narrative threads' had been scattered across the common edition (*laciniosis hinc inde verborum funibus*), Jerome was clearly referring to large portions altering the structure of the book, not simply to the wording of certain verses. As a matter of fact, the two main Greek versions and the extant Old Latin ones attest to the existence of very different forms of the narrative. The fact that Jerome employed the phrase *fideli testimonio* further suggests that he conceived of the

---

[496] Vulg., p. 712. See Canellis' remarks in *Préfaces*, pp. 378–82.

[497] *Epist.* 57.5 (III, p. 59). See section 1.8.

Hebrew text as a whole ("I have simply rendered the Hebrew story [...] in a faithful account"). In accordance with his translation theory, indeed, an accurate rendering of a text was to transcend the wording so as to better capture the substance: the translation could thus be "faithful" without being *verbum e verbo*. Accordingly, by insisting that the Vulgate of Esther was a *verbum e verbo* translation, Jerome sought above all to reinforce the idea that, as opposed to his predecessors, he had neither mistranslated the original narrative, nor added material that modified its structure. On the contrary, his readers should be assured that, unlike the *editio vulgata*, his version would faithfully follow the structure of the original.[498] On a formal level, however, the claim that the *verbum e verbo* method was employed in the Vulgate of Esther did not correspond at all to reality: as shall be demonstrated in this chapter, Jerome's translation is in fact composed to a large extent of *sensus de sensu* renderings.

1.2. The Structure of the Vulgate Version, the Additional Episodes, and the Status of the Book

Despite Jerome's assertions, the structure of the Vulgate version of Esther does not completely agree with that of the Hebrew. Indeed, the annotations in the book, which provide essential infor-

---

[498] By all means, Jerome's condemnation of the *editio vulgata* of Esther is reminiscent of his rejection of the LXX version of Daniel ('it is very much at variance with the [Hebrew] truth' [*multum a veritate discordet*]), whose removal from the churches he lauded (see Vulg., p. 1341; and section 3.1.2.1).

mation on Jerome's relationship with versions other than the Hebrew text, introduce the reader to the episodes missing from the Hebrew. While they are found within the narrative in the Greek texts,[499] in the Vulgate translation they appear at the end, appended to the portion corresponding to the Hebrew version, compiled in a consecutive manner.[500] As a result of this operation, the structure of Esther in the Vulgate has taken a hybrid form (one that resembles the form of the Vulgate of Daniel). The annotations that Jerome added before each of the additional episodes read as follows:

> I have expressed (*expressi*) what is in the Hebrew with absolute reliability (*plena fide*); but, as for what follows (*haec*

---

[499] For the specific order of these episodes and their variations in each version, see Cavalier, *Esther*, pp. 37–39 and pp. 45–64.

[500] In contrast with this treatment of the additional episodes in Esther, Jerome left the Prayer in the same place in the Vulgate of Daniel as in the Greek *Vorlage* (see section 3.1.2.2). That he himself was responsible for placing the episodes missing in the Hebrew of Esther at the end of the Vulgate version is possible but not certain. Another preface that was appended, in some textual witnesses, to the preface that Jerome wrote for the Vulgate of Esther, and whose content suggests that it was initially meant to introduce an Old Latin version of the book, could indicate—provided that Jerome is the author of this preface, too (which is disputed)—that he indeed placed them himself there. A third preface known through three manuscripts and attributed to Cassiodorus explicitly ascribes this decision to Jerome. See Haelewyck, *Hester*, pp. 19–22, 'The Relevance of the Old Latin', pp. 452–53, and 'Latin', p. 407; and Cavalier, *Esther*, pp. 42–43.

4. The Translation of the Book of Esther   249

autem quae sequuntur), I have found it written (*scripta repperi*) in the common edition (*editio vulgata*):[501] it is preserved

---

[501] It should be noted that Jerome never actually said that he was the translator of the episodes appended to the Vulgate of Esther. In Courtray's view, it is reasonable to assume that he is ('Jérôme face au livre d'Esther', p. 31). Likewise, while acknowledging that in theory these could be the versions of an Old Latin translator ('The Relevance of the Old Latin', p. 452, fn. 44), Haelewyck attempts to demonstrate that they were produced by Jerome from an Origenic edition of the LXX (see *Hester*, pp. 19–21 and pp. 64–65, and 'Latin', pp. 406–7; on Origen's edition of the additional episodes, see Hanhart's comments in *Esther*, pp. 75–77). According to Haelewyck, Jerome's claim, in the annotation placed after Vulg. Est. 10.3, that he 'found' (*repperi*) these Greek writings is evidence, *inter alia*, that he is indeed the author of those translations. The way Sutcliffe defines Jerome's use of the verb *reperio*, albeit in a different context, as meaning 'to ascertain', 'to learn', tends to contradict Haelewyck, however (see Sutcliffe, 'St Jerome's Hebrew Manuscripts', pp. 201–2). On the whole, it is interesting that, while Jerome repeatedly specified, in his prefaces and in the annotations interspersed in his translations, which portions of the Books of Esther and of Daniel he did not find in the Hebrew scrolls, he never explicitly promoted the Vulgate versions of these episodes as his own translations: for Esther, see Vulg., p. 712, pp. 724–26, p. 728; for Daniel, see Vulg., pp. 1341–42, p. 1348, p. 1351, p. 1368 (see also *Comm. Dan.*, pp. 128–32; 3.23 [p. 198]; 3.91a [p. 206]; 13 [p. 530]; 13.54b–55 and 58b–59 [p. 542]; 14.17 [p. 546]). By contrast, that he himself translated the portion that corresponds to the Hebrew of Esther is couched in clear terms through the use of the verbs *transtuli* 'I have translated' in the Vulgate preface (Vulg., p. 712), and *expressi* 'I have expressed' in the annotation appended to Vulg. Est. 10.3. One cannot determine beyond doubt, at least not on the basis of Jerome's statements, whether the Vulgate versions of the episodes missing from the Hebrew are translations that he himself produced from the Greek. As in the Vulgate of Daniel, the additional

in the tongue and characters of the Greeks. However, this chapter (*hoc capitulum*) appeared after the end of the book and, as is our wont, we have prefixed it with the obelus, that is, with a broach.[502] (after Vulg. Est. 10.3)

This was also the beginning in the common edition; neither in Hebrew nor in any of the translators does it appear (*nec apud ullum fertur interpretum*).[503] (between Vulg. Est. 11.1 and 11.2)

The proem [reads] up to here. [The verses] that follow in this passage were located where it is written in the scroll 'And they plundered their goods' or 'their riches' (i.e., Est. 3.13). We have found them in the common edition only. (between Vulg. Est. 12.6 and 13.1)

A copy of the letter [reads] up to here. As for [the verses] that follow after this passage, I have found them written where it reads 'And carrying on, Mordecai did all that Esther had ordered him [to do]' (i.e., Est. 4.17). These [verses], however, appear neither in the Hebrew, nor in any of the translators altogether (*apud nullum penitus feruntur interpretum*).[504] (after Vulg. Est. 13.7)

I have found these [verses] also added in the common edition. (before Vulg. Est. 15.1)

As well as those that have been placed below. (after Vulg. Est. 15.3)

---

episodes in the Vulgate of Esther would require in-depth stylistic and comparative analyses.

[502] On the obelus, see sections 1.2.2 and 3.1.2.2.

[503] According to Haelewyck, by 'the translators', Jerome could only mean the *recentiores* (*Hester*, p. 19, fn. 10). This matter is addressed below.

[504] Same remark as in fn. 503.

> A copy of King Artaxerxes' letter, which he dispatched in favour of the Jews to all the provinces of his realm. This is not contained in the Hebrew scroll either. (before Vulg. Est. 16.1)

It is shown here that, whereas the Vulgate of Esther was supposed to represent the Hebrew text, Jerome added to his translation the portions that belonged to the Greek versions of the book. Inasmuch as the structure of the Vulgate disagreed with that of the Hebrew, it disagreed with the *hebraica veritas* agenda, too. Jerome's stance on what should have been considered canon is not clear, all the more because this matter is nowhere addressed in the annotations that he wrote to introduce the episodes missing from the Hebrew text (although he extensively discussed the additional episodes in the Book of Daniel, his view on their canonicity remained confusing, too).[505] The fact that, in his *œuvre*, Je-

---

[505] See section 3.1.2.2. The way the Latin community dealt with Jerome's treatment of the episodes missing from the Hebrew of Esther seems very different from the way they dealt with his treatment of the episodes missing from the Hebrew-Aramaic of Daniel. Indeed, Jerome's treatment of Daniel and of the additional episodes triggered a long-lasting quarrel with Rufinus, and probably more accusations from other detractors, to which Jerome was still referring in his 407 commentary on Daniel: 'And I am astonished that certain faultfinders may revile me, as though I had abridged the book' (*Et miror quosdam* μεμψιμοίρους *indignari mihi, quasi ego decurtaverim librum*) (*Comm. Dan.*, p. 130). On the other hand, the Vulgate translation of Esther, in 404–405, does not seem to have received these criticisms, and it consequently did not call for the same defence on the part of Jerome. As argued in this chapter, the lower status of the Book of Esther in the Christian tradition no doubt

rome very rarely engaged with Esther on a hermeneutic or exegetical level most likely has to do with the transmission history of the book. Indeed, in the time of Jerome, Esther enjoyed little popularity among Christians, who seem to have contested its status, or at least questioned it (in a somewhat analogous manner to the way Jews treated the book).[506] Jerome responded to the lower status of Esther by being as expeditious as possible in his treatment of the text: as shall be demonstrated in this chapter, this came at the cost of precision. His use of the word *historia* in the Vulgate preface—"I have simply rendered the Hebrew story (*historiam hebraicam*) into the Latin tongue" (see above)—may be revealing in this regard. That term was rather rare to find employed in a Vulgate preface:[507] in those of the Pentateuch and of

---

led him as a translator and a commentator not to devote much time to the book.

[506] On the reception of the Book of Esther in the Christian tradition, see Cavalier, *Esther*, pp. 120–21 and p. 126; Moore, *Esther*, pp. XXV–XXXI; Kalimi, *The Book of Esther*, pp. 235–42; and Canellis, *Préfaces*, pp. 130–31. On its reception in the Jewish tradition, see Moore, *Esther*, pp. XXI–XXV and pp. XXX–XXXIV; and Kalimi, *The Book of Esther*, pp. 164–72.

[507] Interestingly, among Jerome's translations of the Hebrew Bible, apart from one occurrence in the Vulgate of Ezra (Vulg. Ezra 4.15), the word *historia* only appears in the Vulgate of Esther (Vulg. Est. 2.23, 6.1, 9.32, 16.7), and it always translates the word ספר 'book' with respect to the Persian kings' 'book' of chronicles. In Vulg. Est. 16.7, which corresponds to LXX Est. E.7 and to A-Text Est. 7.24, *ex veteribus historiis* 'from the ancient stories' stands for ἐκ τῶν παλαιοτέρων ἱστοριῶν 'from the more ancient inquiries / accounts'.

4. The Translation of the Book of Esther

the Book of Isaiah, Jerome meant it in the sense of 'history';[508] in that of the Book of Daniel, with regard to the story of Susanna, he equated it to *fabula* 'fable';[509] in that of the Book of Kings, he used it in reference to the Book of Ruth and to the Book of Chronicles;[510] in that of the Book of Judith, he noted with surprise that Judith, though numbered 'among the *historiae*', had been accepted as a holy book by the Council of Nicaea.[511] That he referred to the Book of Esther as a *historia* probably indicated, too, that he regarded it as of lesser importance than most books, much like Susanna or Judith: he may have consequently taken the liberty of translating it less meticulously.

1.3. Jerome's Treatment of the Book

Jerome's own assessment of his work could show that he was wont to translate particularly fast in certain cases. Indeed, he argued in the Vulgate prefaces to the Book of Tobit and to that of Judith that he had rushed his job "in one day," in the case of the former, and "in one tiny night," in that of the latter:

---

[508] Vulg., p. 4 and p. 1096, respectively.

[509] Vulg., p. 1341 (and *Comm. Dan.*, p. 130). See my fn. 370.

[510] Vulg., pp. 364–65. See also Jerome's preface to his revision of the VL of Chronicles (edited by Canellis in *Préfaces*, p. 344).

[511] "[The Book of Judith] is considered to be among the stories / the historical accounts (*inter historias*). But since (*sed quia*) the Nicene Synod is reported to have considered [it] as part of the Holy Scriptures, I have assented to your request (i.e., I have agreed to translate it)!" (Vulg., p. 691). On Jerome's view on the Book of Judith, see also section 3.1.2.2 of this monograph, especially fn. 376.

You demand that I translate a book composed in the Aramaic tongue with a Latin style (*ut librum chaldeo sermone conscriptum ad latinum stilum traham*)—the Book of Tobias by all means—which the Hebrews, after removing it from the catalogue of the Divine Scriptures (*de catalogo divinarum Scripturarum secantes*), have transferred (*manciparunt*) to [the section] that they call Hagiographa (*Agiografa*).[512] [...] I have persisted as I could, and since the Chaldeans' language is close to the Hebrew tongue, I have met with a speaker most proficient in both languages and it took me one day of work (*unius diei laborem arripui*): whatever this [man] communicated to me in Hebrew words, I, with [the help of] a summoned scribe (*accito notario*), set forth in Latin terms.[513]

Since the Nicene Synod is reported to have considered the Book [of Judith] as part of the Holy Scriptures, I have assented to your request—to your demand, rather!—and, once set aside the activities in which I was eagerly engrossed, I devoted one tiny night's work to it (*huic unam lucubratiunculam dedi*), and I rendered sense for sense more so than word for word (*magis sensus e sensu quam ex verbo verbum transferens*). I have edited out the most corrupted variants (lit., diversity) [found] in the many manuscripts (*multorum codicum varietatem vitiosissimam amputavi*); I have only expressed in Latin words what I could find perfectly

---

[512] Canellis opts for the reading *Apocrypha*, rather than *Agiografa*, in her edition of the preface (*Préfaces*, p. 368). See my fn. 376.

[513] Vulg., p. 676. For a discussion of Jerome's reliance on tachygraphs, see Arns, *La technique du livre*, pp. 51–62; Courtray, *Prophète*, pp. 131–35; Williams, *The Monk and the Book*, pp. 201–21; and Canellis, *Préfaces*, p. 371, fn. 6.

intelligible in Aramaic (*sola ea quae intellegentia integra in verbis chaldeis invenire potui, latinis expressi*).[514]

In both prefaces, Jerome underlined the rapidity of his undertaking and openly stated that he spent as little time as possible on these translations.

In the preface to the Vulgate of Esther, he felt the need to remind the reader that his translation was an exact representation of the Hebrew version (*verbum e verbo pressius transtuli*): it would have been more correct to say that the portion that ran from Vulg. Est. 1.1 to 10.3 corresponded to the Hebrew text, while the rest followed episodes that were not in the Hebrews' scrolls. Furthermore, our investigation will show that even the portion corresponding to the Hebrew text is not an exact representation of the Hebrew, but an approximate one. The Christian view on the status of the Book of Esther surely accounts for this phenomenon. Jerome's age at the time when he translated the book—he was at least in his late fifties in 404–405—could also explain why he may not have been as thorough as he would have liked in his rendering of the Hebrew. Indeed, no more than ten years later, in his commentary on the Book of Ezekiel, he argued the following:

---

[514] Vulg., p. 691. Although Jerome argued in that preface that the Book of Judith was in Aramaic, he did not mention the help of an assistant who translated his Aramaic *Vorlage* into Hebrew so that he might, in turn, translate it into Latin, as in the case of Tobit. Gallagher suggests, however, that the same linguistic expert rendered Judith from Aramaic into Hebrew for Jerome ('Why Did Jerome', p. 373). See also section 1.3.

> As my eyes have grown dim from old age [...] I am by no means capable of going through the scrolls of the Hebrews again by nocturnal light. These [texts] are also obscure (lit., blinded) in daylight and by sunbeams, given how small the letters are to me. As for the commentaries of the Greek brothers, I am only exposed to them orally.[515]

While in 404–405 Jerome's vision might still have been good enough to read from scrolls, it is probable that it had already begun to deteriorate after decades spent translating and commenting on Scripture. His capacity, and perhaps his willingness, to be as meticulous as he once had been would have arguably been affected as a result.

1.4. Jerome and the *recentiores*

Jerome's relationship with his sources in the translation of Esther can be difficult to establish. As indicated above, he openly condemned the additions of the *editio vulgata*, many of which are presumably still found in the two extant Greek versions and in the Old Latin ones. Although there is no attested form of a *recentiores* version of the Book of Esther (see fn. 488), the hypothesis that Aquila, Symmachus and Theodotion once produced translations of the book which are now lost is reasonable. It is all the more plausible since Greek readings attributed to Origen's revision of the LXX are attested: if there is an Origen version of Esther, there is a *recentiores* translation that underlies it.

---

[515] Jerome's preface to the seventh book of *Comm. Ezech.* (CCSL 75, p. 278). Jerome completed this commentary in 414 (Kelly, *Jerome*, p. 306), a few years before his death.

In the present study, we ought to wonder whether Jerome ever had access to *recentiores* versions. The lack of evidence makes it difficult to prove it: the fact that he did not write a commentary on Esther, and that his citations of the book, or his mentions of the character of Esther, are particularly infrequent in his letters, might suggest that he did not have as much material to work with as usual (or at least that he did not take the time to consult all available sources). At the same time, the lesser importance of Esther among Christian communities explains well in itself why it received little attention from Jerome. Furthermore, some of his expansions in the Vulgate of Esther are actually reminiscent of readings found in Origen's revision of the LXX (which he seems to have used, as shown below in section 2.4). Finally, it is striking that on two occasions—in the annotation interspersed between Vulg. Est. 11.1 and 11.2 and in the one appended to Vulg. Est. 13.7—Jerome seems to have referred to the work of the *recentiores* with the phrase *nec apud ullum / apud nullum interpretum* ('not in any / in none of the translators'): "This was also the beginning in the common edition; neither in Hebrew nor in any of the translators does it appear;" "These [verses], however, appear neither in the Hebrew, nor in any of the translators altogether" (see above). It is therefore possible that Jerome had access to a translation hypothetically produced by Theodotion, or by one of the two other *recentiores*, on top of Origen's edition.

2.0. The Case Studies

Jerome stated on multiple occasions that he rendered the Hebrew of Esther 'word for word, very accurately' (*verbum e verbo pressius*), 'literally' (*per singula verba*), 'with absolute reliability' (*plena fide*), 'just as it is in Hebrew' (*sicut in hebraeo habetur*), without "lengthening it" or "adding even a single thing."[516] In this chapter, we demonstrate that it is precisely not the *verbum e verbo* but the *sensus de sensu* method that Jerome employed. More than just a *sensus de sensu* rendering of the Hebrew, the Vulgate of Esther is arguably one of the Vulgate translations that departs the most from the original wording of the Hebrew. The *sensus de sensu* was pushed to an extreme, as it were, as Jerome paraphrased most of the text, often in a very approximate way; he also relied less on his usual sources and worked more independently than in his other Vulgate translations. Indeed, the vast majority of his paraphrases do not match any of the known versions. These paraphrases can either curtail the Hebrew or expand on it: in the former case, they attest to the reality that Jerome worked particularly fast; in the latter, they tell us that he also enjoyed literary creativity as a translator. In the first section, we deal with paraphrases of the Hebrew that either fully or partly agree with the Greek and Old Latin versions of Esther (sections 2.1.1 and 2.1.2): while most of the Vulgate of Esther reflects Jerome's stylistic independence, these two examples shed light on certain exceptions. We then turn to paraphrases of the Hebrew that are mostly, but not entirely, independent of the other versions: we first investigate

---

[516] Find all these citations above.

Jerome's rendering of a verse (section 2.2.1) and then his responses to the syntagm משתה היין and to the word משתה (section 2.2.2). Following this section, we explore his rendering of two verses (sections 2.3.1 and 2.3.2): these paraphrases, which he produced without consulting the other versions, are representative of the majority of his renderings in the Vulgate of Esther. We then address a Vulgate expansion on a syntagm which seems to have been inspired by a reading attributed to Origen's edition of the LXX (section 2.4).[517]

2.1. Paraphrases Reflecting Some Reliance on the Greek and Old Latin Versions in the Vulgate

2.1.1. Vulg. Est. 3.9: A *sensus de sensu* Rendering Syntactically and Lexically Inspired by the Greek and Old Latin Versions

MT Est. 3.9

אִם־עַל־הַמֶּלֶךְ טוֹב יִכָּתֵב לְאַבְּדָם וַעֲשֶׂרֶת אֲלָפִים כִּכַּר־כֶּסֶף אֶשְׁקוֹל עַל־יְדֵי עֹשֵׂי הַמְּלָאכָה לְהָבִיא אֶל־גִּנְזֵי הַמֶּלֶךְ׃

If it is good to the king, let it be written, in order to destroy them, and I shall pay ten thousand talents of silver into the hands of those who deal with (lit., those who do) the administration to bring into the king's treasury.

---

[517] These categories are meant to enable us to investigate Jerome's sources and translation technique in the Vulgate of Esther. This translation is probably one of the least studied Vulgate translations, on a stylistic level, in modern scholarship: a variety of other approaches are therefore still to be defined and explored (see, for instance, Skemp's stylistic analyses of Vulg. Est. in 'Learning by Example', pp. 276–78, and in 'Vulgate').

Vulg. Est. 3.9

Si tibi placet decerne ut pereat et decem milia talentorum adpendam arcariis gazae tuae

If it pleases you, decree [it], that [this people] perish,[518] and I shall pay ten thousand talents to the bursars of your treasury.

The discrepancy between the Hebrew verse and the Latin one is manifest here; yet Jerome's translation does not disagree in meaning with the original. Indeed, his way of rendering וַעֲשֶׂרֶת אֲלָפִ֜ים כִּכַּר־כֶּ֗סֶף אֶשְׁקוֹל֙ עַל־יְדֵי֙ עֹשֵׂ֣י הַמְּלָאכָ֔ה לְהָבִ֖יא אֶל־גִּנְזֵ֥י הַמֶּֽלֶךְ as *et decem milia talentorum adpendam arcariis gazae tuae* represents a paraphrase through which he abbreviated עַל־יְדֵי֙ עֹשֵׂ֣י הַמְּלָאכָ֔ה לְהָבִ֖יא אֶל־גִּנְזֵ֥י הַמֶּֽלֶךְ 'into the hands of those who deal with (lit., those who do) the administration to bring into the king's treasury' to an indirect object (*arcariis*) governing a genitive (*gazae tuae*): *arcariis gazae tuae* 'to the bursars of your treasury'. As the Hebrew was formulated in a periphrastic way, Jerome decided to compress its structure, which allowed him to make progress more rapidly without altering the sense of the original. It is very likely, though, that the *sensus de sensu* rendering *arcariis gazae tuae* was inspired by the technique of the Greek translators:

LXX Est. 3.9

εἰ δοκεῖ τῷ βασιλεῖ, δογματισάτω ἀπολέσαι αὐτούς, κἀγὼ διαγράψω εἰς τὸ γαζοφυλάκιον τοῦ βασιλέως ἀργυρίου τάλαντα μύρια

---

[518] The subject *populus* 'the [Jewish] people' is implied here (it was last expressed in Vulg. Est. 3.8).

If it seems [good] to the king, let it be decreed to destroy them, and I shall distribute ten thousand talents of silver to the king's treasury.

A-Text Est. 3.9

εἰ δοκεῖ οὖν τῷ βασιλεῖ, καὶ ἀγαθὴ ἡ κρίσις ἐν καρδίᾳ αὐτοῦ, δοθήτω μοι τὸ ἔθνος εἰς ἀπώλειαν, καὶ διαγράψω εἰς τὸ γαζοφυλάκιον ἀργυρίου τάλαντα μύρια

If therefore it seems [good] to the king, and it is the right decision in his heart, let this nation be handed over to me for [their] destruction, and I shall distribute ten thousand talents of silver to the treasury.

The Greek way of paraphrasing the periphrastic turn of the Hebrew construction—εἰς τὸ γαζοφυλάκιον τοῦ βασιλέως 'to the king's treasury' in the LXX, εἰς τὸ γαζοφυλάκιον 'to the treasury' in the A-Text—no doubt influenced Jerome in his paraphrase (*arcariis gazae tuae*).[519] Unlike the Greek translators, though, who only referred to a 'treasury' (τὸ γαζοφυλάκιον), Jerome did not remove the agents in charge (עֹשֵׂי הַמְּלָאכָה) from his translation, as he spoke of 'bursars' (*arcariis*). However, the word *arcariis* still echoes the Greek to some extent. Indeed, the adjective *arcarius* 'pertaining to a money-box' is derived from the noun *arca* 'a safe', 'a box', which is related to the verb *arceo* 'to keep away', 'to enclose': *arcarius*, which as a noun points to the keeper of a box that contains money, i.e., to a treasurer, is closer to the semantic field of τὸ γαζοφυλάκιον than to that of עֹשֵׂי הַמְּלָאכָה, which is more ge-

---

[519] The fact that Jerome employed a singular (*gazae tuae*), as in the Greek versions (τὸ γαζοφυλάκιον), to represent what was a plural in Hebrew (גִּנְזֵי) may be meaningful too (see below).

neric. The rendering *arcariis gazae tuae* ultimately reflects a translation process whereby Jerome conflated the Greek and the Hebrew: the compound τὸ γαζοφυλάκιον—which is composed of the noun γάζα 'treasure' or 'treasury' and of the verb φυλάσσω 'to keep', 'to watch'—was split into two distinct elements (*arcariis* for -φυλάκιον and *gazae* for γαζο-) and then adjusted to the Hebrew portrayal of the scene, in which people (עֹשֵׂי הַמְּלָאכָה), not just a treasury (τὸ γαζοφυλάκιον), were introduced.[520] The use of the word *gaza* 'treasury' is interesting, too. The root γαζ- in the word γαζοφυλάκιον is phonetically close to גִּנְזֵי: Jerome probably appreciated this effect in the Greek and therefore employed the word *gaza* in his own translation. In this sense, he aligned his translation of Est. 3.9 not only with the syntax but also, to some extent, with the lexicon of the Greek versions. Noteworthy is that, by calquing the compound γαζοφυλάκιον with *gazophilatium / gazofilacium*,[521] the VL translators also resorted to a rendering that contained the root *gaz-*:

---

[520] It is interesting that, when a similar phrase occurred in Est. 9.3 (וְעֹשֵׂי הַמְּלָאכָה אֲשֶׁר לַמֶּלֶךְ 'and they who deal with [lit., who do] the administration pertaining to the king'), Jerome paraphrased the Hebrew in a way that differed not only from his rendering in Vulg. Est. 3.9, but also from that of the Greek translators, who translated the whole phrase with two words: (Vulg. Est. 9.3) *omnisque dignitas quae singulis locis et operibus praeerat* 'and every authority that was in charge of each place and operation' / (LXX Est. 9.3 and A-Text Est. 7.42 [= Est. 9.3]) οἱ βασιλικοὶ γραμματεῖς 'the royal secretaries'.

[521] These Latin terms reflect two different spellings of the same word.

VL Est. 3.9

Si ergo tibi placet rex et optimum est (/ videtur) sensui tuo detur mihi genus hoc in perditionem et describam (/ exhibebo / conferam) in gazophilatio tuo (/ gazofilacium tuum) talenta decem milia (/ talenta argenti decem milia).[522]

So if it pleases you, [O] King, and it is (/ seems) best in your view, let this race be handed over to me for [their] destruction and I shall distribute (/ offer / grant) ten thousand talents (/ ten thousand talents of silver) to your treasury.

While in the two Greek versions and in the MT the king is referred to in the third person, it should be observed that, like the VL translators (*tibi placet rex, sensui tuo, in gazophilatio tuo*), Jerome used the singular second-person pronoun (*tibi placet, gazae tuae*). On the whole, it is clear that his relationship with his sources was somewhat inconsistent with his radical condemnation of the *editio vulgata* of Esther (see my introduction above). In Vulg. Est. 3.9, he no doubt drew on the translation of his Greek predecessors, and potentially on the Old Latin version, too.[523]

---

[522] Different VL traditions have been recorded by Haelewyck. I have added here, in parentheses, those of the readings that were relevant to our study. Much of the VL verse conforms with the A-Text of Est. 3.9 against the LXX version.

[523] One should be mindful of Origen's version, too. In the case of Est. 3.9, for instance, a variant reading recorded in Hanhart's apparatus and attributed to his revision of the LXX agrees with the syntax of the Hebrew: μυρια ταλαντα αργυριου παραστησω επι χειρας των ποιουντων τα εργα εισαγαγειν 'I shall place ten thousand talents of silver into the hands of those who manage (lit., those who do) the affairs to bring into...' It is therefore noteworthy that, where the Vulgate phrasing follows the LXX

Further analysis of Jerome's lexical choices shows that he could also be autonomous in his treatment of the syntagm גִּנְזֵי הַמֶּלֶךְ. Indeed, גִּנְזֵי הַמֶּלֶךְ occurred in Est. 4.7, too, and his response differed from that of Vulg. Est. 3.9:

MT Est. 4.7

וַיַּגֶּד־לוֹ מָרְדֳּכַי אֵת כָּל־אֲשֶׁר קָרָהוּ וְאֵת ׀ פָּרָשַׁת הַכֶּסֶף אֲשֶׁר אָמַר הָמָן לִשְׁקוֹל עַל־גִּנְזֵי הַמֶּלֶךְ בַּיְּהוּדִיִּים לְאַבְּדָם

And Mordechai informed him of everything that had happened to him and of the sum of money that Haman said that he would pay to the king's treasury for the Jews, to destroy them.

Vulg. Est. 4.7

Qui indicavit ei omnia quae acciderant quomodo Aman promisisset ut in thesauros regis pro Iudaeorum nece inferret argentum

[Mordechai] who disclosed to him all the things that had happened, how Haman had promised that he would bring money into the king's treasuries for [the sake of] the Jews' ruin.

LXX Est. 4.7

ὁ δὲ Μαρδοχαῖος ὑπέδειξεν αὐτῷ τὸ γεγονὸς καὶ τὴν ἐπαγγελίαν, ἣν ἐπηγγείλατο Αμαν τῷ βασιλεῖ εἰς τὴν γάζαν ταλάντων μυρίων, ἵνα ἀπολέσῃ τοὺς Ἰουδαίους

And Mordechai indicated to him what happened and the promise that Aman made (lit., promised) the king of ten

---

and A-Text syntax, it is at odds not only with the Hebrew but also with Origen's version.

thousand talents for the treasury, so that he might destroy the Jews.[524]

In LXX Est. 4.7, the syntagm עַל־גִּנְזֵי הַמֶּלֶךְ 'to the king's treasury' is represented by τῷ βασιλεῖ εἰς τὴν γάζαν '[the promise] to the king for the treasury'. The word גִּנְזֵי is therefore rendered by τὴν γάζαν. On the other hand, Jerome translated עַל־גִּנְזֵי הַמֶּלֶךְ as *in thesauros regis* 'into the king's treasuries': this matches the Hebrew construction against the LXX wording. Also noteworthy is that, while τὴν γάζαν here is singular (like *gazae tuae* in Vulg. Est. 3.9, which followed τὸ γαζοφυλάκιον in the LXX and A-Text versions), the plural *thesauros* agrees with גִּנְזֵי in number.[525] Jerome ultimately resorted to a different word—*thesauros* instead of *gaza*—which attests to his penchant for lexical variation. Therefore, as opposed to Vulg. Est. 3.9, Vulg. Est. 4.7 does not conform with the LXX, neither syntactically nor lexically.

2.1.2. A New Structure and Abbreviations Potentially Inspired by the Greek: Vulg. Est. 10.2

MT Est. 10.2

וְכָל־מַעֲשֵׂה תָקְפּוֹ וּגְבוּרָתוֹ וּפָרָשַׁת גְּדֻלַּת מָרְדֳּכַי אֲשֶׁר גִּדְּלוֹ הַמֶּלֶךְ הֲלוֹא־הֵם כְּתוּבִים עַל־סֵפֶר דִּבְרֵי הַיָּמִים לְמַלְכֵי מָדַי וּפָרָס:

And [as for] every deed of [King Ahasuerus'] power and his might, and the account of the greatness of Mordechai

---

[524] A-Text Est. 4.7 is not attested and the VL verse does not contain a rendering for 'treasury'.

[525] In their apparatus, Weber and Gryson mention the existence of the variant reading *thesauro* 'treasury', in the singular, in four textual witnesses.

whom the king promoted, are they not written in the book of the chronicles (lit., in the book of everyday matters / of the words of the days) of the kings of Media and Persia?

Vulg. Est. 10.2

Cuius fortitudo et imperium et dignitas atque sublimitas qua exaltavit Mardocheum scripta sunt in libris Medorum atque Persarum

[King Ahasuerus'] (lit., whose) strength and reign and dignity, as well as the grandeur through which he elevated Mordechai, have been written in the books of the Medes and of the Persians.

Parsing Vulg. Est. 10.2 is necessary to understand the course of action that Jerome followed in his translation of the Hebrew verse; in general, it seems that he either modified or removed certain turns and words so as to simplify the structure of the sentence. In rendering וְכָל־מַעֲשֵׂה תָקְפּוֹ 'And [as for] every deed of [King Ahasuerus'] power' as *cuius fortitudo et imperium* '[King Ahasuerus'] strength and reign', he appears to have elided וְכָל־ and to have read מַעֲשֶׂה in the absolute (as though וְכָל־מַעֲשֵׂה had not formed a construct chain with תָקְפּוֹ); *et dignitas* 'and [his] dignity' would then correspond to his translation of וּגְבוּרָתוֹ 'and his might'.[526] The unit וּפָרָשַׁת גְּדֻלַּת מָרְדֳּכַי אֲשֶׁר גִּדְּלוֹ הַמֶּלֶךְ 'and the account of the greatness of Mordechai whom the king promoted'

---

[526] It may also be that the entire phrase וְכָל־מַעֲשֵׂה was elided in Jerome's translation. In that case, *cuius fortitudo* could stand for תָקְפּוֹ and *et imperium* for וּגְבוּרָתוֹ (which would mean that *et dignitas* does not represent anything in the Hebrew); or *cuius fortitudo* and *imperium* could represent two renderings for תָקְפּוֹ and *et dignitas* one for וּגְבוּרָתוֹ. Either way, what

was rewritten in the Vulgate as *atque sublimitas qua exaltavit Mardocheum* 'as well as the grandeur through which [the king] elevated Mordechai'; the particle הֲלוֹא in הֲלוֹא־הֵם (which I translated as 'are they not') was not expressed; and the unit עַל־סֵפֶר דִּבְרֵי הַיָּמִים לְמַלְכֵי מָדַי וּפָרָס 'in the book of the chronicles (lit., the book of everyday matters / of the words of the days) of the kings of Media and Persia' was abbreviated to *in libris Medorum atque Persarum* 'in the books of the Medes and of the Persians'. In theory, Jerome could have applied these modifications without consulting the Greek versions. It is however likely that he relied on them here, as many of his abbreviations match or echo the wordings found in the LXX and in the A-Text:

LXX Est. 10.1a and 10.2

Ἔγραψεν δὲ ὁ βασιλεὺς [...] / καὶ τὴν ἰσχὺν αὐτοῦ καὶ ἀνδραγαθίαν, πλοῦτόν τε καὶ δόξαν τῆς βασιλείας αὐτοῦ· ἰδοὺ γέγραπται ἐν βιβλίῳ βασιλέων Περσῶν καὶ Μήδων εἰς μνημόσυνον.

And the king recorded (lit., wrote) [...] / his strength and virtue, and both the wealth and the glory of his kingdom; behold, they have been written in the book of the kings of the Persians and of the Medes as a memorial.

A-Text Est. 7.50a and 7.51 (= Est. 10.1a and 10.2)

Καὶ ἔγραψεν ὁ βασιλεὺς [...] καὶ τὴν ἰσχὺν αὐτοῦ, πλοῦτόν τε καὶ δόξαν τῆς βασιλείας αὐτοῦ. / καὶ ἐδόξασε Μαρδοχαῖος καὶ ἔγραψεν ἐν τοῖς βιβλίοις Περσῶν καὶ Μήδων εἰς μνημόσυνον.

---

matters to us is that, as shown below, the Vulgate verse reflects a structure similar to that of the Greek versions, against the Hebrew.

And the king recorded (lit., wrote) [...] his strength, and both the wealth and the glory of his kingdom. And Mordechai extolled [him] and wrote [it] in the books of the Persians and of the Medes as a memorial.

In the LXX, the phrase וְכָל־מַעֲשֵׂה תָקְפּוֹ וּגְבוּרָתוֹ is represented by two nouns (καὶ τὴν ἰσχὺν αὐτοῦ καὶ ἀνδραγαθίαν 'his strength and virtue') governed by the same verb (Ἔγραψεν 'he wrote'), without genitival relation to one another,[527] which indicates that the translators did not read—or that they operated as though there were not—a long construct chain in the original (וְכָל־מַעֲשֵׂה תָקְפּוֹ).[528] Jerome may have been inspired by this translation technique in rendering the Hebrew with three nominatives (*cuius fortitudo et imperium et dignitas*). In the Hebrew, the "account of Mordechai's greatness" is mentioned among the matters that have been written down in the kings' book of chronicles. Jerome turned 'the account of the greatness of Mordechai whom the king promoted' (וּפָרָשַׁת גְּדֻלַּת מָרְדֳּכַי אֲשֶׁר גִּדְּלוֹ הַמֶּלֶךְ) into 'the grandeur through which [the king] elevated Mordechai' (*sublimitas qua exaltavit Mardocheum*): in his version, the 'greatness / grandeur' therefore seems to be that of the king (*qua*), not Mordechai's anymore.[529] This

---

[527] This excludes the genitive pronoun αὐτοῦ, which represents, like *cuius* in Jerome, the singular third-person pronouns suffixed to תָקְפּוֹ and וּגְבוּרָתוֹ.

[528] In the A-Text, וְכָל־מַעֲשֵׂה תָקְפּוֹ וּגְבוּרָתוֹ is represented by a single noun: καὶ τὴν ἰσχὺν αὐτοῦ 'and his strength'.

[529] If *quomodo* 'how' was meant to render פָּרָשַׁת in Vulg. Est. 4.7, as the word order suggests (אֵת כָּל־אֲשֶׁר קָרָהוּ וְאֵת ׀ פָּרָשַׁת הַכֶּסֶף אֲשֶׁר אָמַר הָמָן / *omnia quae acciderant quomodo Aman promisisset*; see my translation above in section 4.2.1.1), then *qua* could stand for וּפָרָשַׁת in Vulg. Est. 10.2,

departure from the Hebrew version of the narrative strongly echoes the two Greek texts, in which not only is there no "account," but what was described as Mordechai's greatness in the MT seems to have been rendered as 'both the wealth and the glory of [the king's] kingdom' (πλοῦτόν τε καὶ δόξαν τῆς βασιλείας αὐτοῦ);[530] in the A-Text, it is even Mordechai who 'extolled' the king (καὶ ἐδόξασε

---

thus introducing a type of account, too. This reading of the verse would ascribe the *sublimitas* to the king even more clearly: "[King Ahasuerus'] strength, reign, dignity, and grandeur, insofar as (*qua*) he elevated Mordechai, have been written..." On the other hand, should we read *quae* instead of *qua* (which variant is attested in four textual witnesses according to Weber and Gryson's apparatus), the sense of Vulg. Est. 10.2 could seem to agree more with the Hebrew: "[King Ahasuerus'] strength and reign and dignity, as well as the grandeur which (*quae*) elevated Mordechai..." In theory, it would also be grammatically possible to render *sublimitas qua exaltavit Mardocheum* as 'the grandeur in which [the king] elevated Mordechai', in which case *sublimitas* could correspond to Mordechai's new rank. Noteworthy are the VL forms of Est. 4.7 and 10.2, in which *quoniam* 'since' and *quemadmodum /sicut* 'in which way / just as', respectively, seem to be echoed by *quomodo* in Vulg. Est. 4.7 and *qua* in Vulg. Est. 10.2.

[530] This rendering, which is found both in the LXX and the A-Text, may be a case of interpolation. Indeed, the phrasing πλοῦτόν τε καὶ δόξαν τῆς βασιλείας αὐτοῦ is reminiscent of the Greek translations of Est. 1.4: בְּהַרְאֹתוֹ אֶת־עֹשֶׁר כְּבוֹד מַלְכוּתוֹ וְאֶת־יְקָר תִּפְאֶרֶת גְּדוּלָּתוֹ 'when he displayed the wealth of his glorious kingdom and the splendour of his magnificent greatness' / (LXX) μετὰ τὸ δεῖξαι αὐτοῖς τὸν πλοῦτον τῆς βασιλείας αὐτοῦ καὶ τὴν δόξαν τῆς εὐφροσύνης τοῦ πλούτου αὐτοῦ 'after showing them the wealth of his kingdom and the glory of the celebration of his wealth' / (A-Text) εἰς τὸ ἐπιδειχθῆναι τὸν πλοῦτον τῆς δόξης τοῦ βασιλέως 'for the wealth of the king's glory to be displayed'.

Μαρδοχαῖος).⁵³¹ The particle הֲלוֹא, which has the function of a presentative (as reflected by ἰδοὺ 'behold' in the LXX), is not expressed in the A-Text or in the Vulgate. Jerome's abbreviation of עַל־סֵפֶר דִּבְרֵי הַיָּמִים (*in libris* 'in the books') also perfectly matches the A-Text, in which the translators wrote 'in the books' (τοῖς βιβλίοις), too; in the LXX, the syntagm is represented by ἐν βιβλίῳ 'in the book', in the singular.⁵³² Finally, while the word for 'kings' (לְמַלְכֵי מָדַי וּפָרָס) was retained in the LXX (βασιλέων Περσῶν καὶ Μήδων), it was omitted in the A-Text and in the Vulgate. In summary, Vulg. Est. 10.2 paraphrases the Hebrew in a way that can agree with one or both Greek versions. Noteworthy is that Jerome's translation here differs a great deal from the attested VL versions:

VL Est. 10.2

Et adnuntiata est gloria Mardochei quemadmodum illum rex honorificaverat (/ sicut illum honorificavit rex) in regno suo sicut (/ et ecce / hoc enim) scriptum est in libro regis (/ in

---

⁵³¹ The reading attributed to Origen in Hanhart's apparatus is noteworthy: μαρδοχαιω (-χαιου) οσα εμεγαλυνεν αυτον '[the glory] of Mordechai, which made him / which [was] so [great] that [the king] made him / insofar as [the king] made him powerful / great'. It is striking that in VL Est. 10.2, which seems to reflect Origen's version of the LXX here, the king also "honoured" Mordechai: *gloria Mardochei quemadmodum illum rex honorificaverat / sicut illum honorificavit rex* (see below). In the MT and probably in the Vulgate (see my fn. 529), the king is the one who 'promoted / elevated' Mordechai, too.

⁵³² Hanhart records a variant reading attributed to Origen—a calque of דִּבְרֵי הַיָּמִים—in the apparatus of the LXX: λογων των ημερων '[in the book] of the words of the days'.

libro dierum) Persarum et Medorum in memoriam (/ tamquam in memoriam testamenti)

And Mordechai's glory has been announced the way the king had honoured him (/ just as the king honoured him) in his own reign, just as it (/ and behold it / this indeed) was written in the book of the king (/ in the book of the days) of the Persians and of the Medes for [the sake of] remembering (/ in memory of a testament, as it were).

2.2. Paraphrases of the Hebrew that Jerome Produced Mostly Independently of the Other Sources

The first two case studies of this chapter have illustrated how Jerome could rely on the Greek and, to some extent, on the Old Latin (section 2.1.1), or solely on the Greek (section 2.1.2). These examples should be considered as exceptions, though, as a comparison of the Vulgate of Esther with the Hebrew, the Greek versions, and the Old Latin ones, shows that Jerome mostly avoided employing other sources when paraphrasing the Hebrew. Although we cannot ascertain to what extent he consulted hypothetical *recentiores* versions of Esther, paraphrase as a translation technique is, in principle, incompatible with the strict translation method that generally characterises Aquila's, Symmachus', and Theodotion's styles: each of them endeavoured to render, in his own way, the Hebrew text of his time as accurately, and sometimes as literally as possible, in response to the LXX. Accordingly, where the Vulgate departs significantly from the wording of the

Hebrew, it presumably does not reflect the version of one of the *recentiores*.[533]

Again, the recourse to paraphrase also disagreed with the statements that Jerome made in his preface, in which he both strongly dismissed the *editio vulgata* of Esther as filled with additions and insisted that he himself had done no more than translate the 'story' (*historia*) from Hebrew into Latin.[534] His age at the time when he translated the book, the fact that he considered it a *historia*, and more generally the lower status of Esther in Christian communities (see my introduction above), are what led him to adopt a looser approach than usual in his stylistic treatment of the text. Sections 2.1.1 and 2.1.2 showed that he had abbreviated certain Hebrew constructions in his translation. However, his approximate way of rendering the Hebrew text did not only take the form of abbreviations: it entailed additions and expansions, too. The following case studies (sections 2.2.1 and 2.2.2) reflect this translation technique and demonstrate, at the same time, how Jerome could paraphrase the Hebrew in a manner that was mostly, though not completely, independent of the Greek and the Old Latin.

---

[533] This rule comes with its exceptions. Indeed, as argued below in section 4.2.4, it is likely that Jerome's long paraphrase of a Hebrew syntagm represents an expansion inspired by Origen's edition and, therefore, by a *recentiores* version.

[534] Vulg., p. 712.

2.2.1. Independent Adjustments and a Case of Departure from the Hebrew Potentially Motivated by the Greek: Vulg. Est. 1.8

MT Est. 1.8

וְהַשְּׁתִיָּה כַדָּת אֵין אֹנֵס כִּי־כֵן ׀ יִסַּד הַמֶּלֶךְ עַל כָּל־רַב בֵּיתוֹ לַעֲשׂוֹת כִּרְצוֹן אִישׁ־וָאִישׁ:

And the drinking [went] according to the law, no one [was] compelling: for [it was] so, the king had established that / for the king had thus established that all the leaders of his house should act as per the will of each and every man.

The Hebrew is elliptical here, and the way the Greek translators rendered this verse shows that they had difficulties interpreting it. Indeed, the LXX and the A-Text propose two different readings, both of which depart from the Hebrew:

LXX Est. 1.8

ὁ δὲ πότος οὗτος οὐ κατὰ προκείμενον νόμον ἐγένετο, οὕτως δὲ ἠθέλησεν ὁ βασιλεὺς καὶ ἐπέταξεν τοῖς οἰκονόμοις ποιῆσαι τὸ θέλημα αὐτοῦ καὶ τῶν ἀνθρώπων.

But this was no drinking according to the established custom / law, but the king had wanted [it] so and he ordered the stewards to execute (lit., to do) his wish as well as [that] of the men.

A-Text Est. 1.8

καὶ πότος κατὰ τὸν νόμον· οὕτως γὰρ ἐπέταξεν ὁ βασιλεὺς ποιῆσαι τὸ θέλημα τῶν ἀνθρώπων.

And the drinking [went] according to the custom / law; for so the king ordered that the men's wish be executed (lit., done).

In both versions, the translators adapted the sense of the verse so as to fix what they probably regarded as illogical in the Hebrew. In the LXX, the negation οὐ was added: the banquet did not take place in accordance with the law (οὐ κατὰ προκείμενον νόμον),[535] whereas it did in the MT (כַּדָּת). It was also made explicit that it was because 'the king wanted so' (οὕτως δὲ ἠθέλησεν ὁ βασιλεὺς), which rendering expands on כִּי־כֵן 'for [it was] so / for [...] thus' through the addition of the verb ἠθέλησεν. The phrase אֵין אֹנֵס was not translated. On the other hand, in the A-Text, the banquet took place as per the law (κατὰ τὸν νόμον), as in the MT. Furthermore, unlike the LXX translators, the A-Text ones did not expand on כִּי־כֵן (οὕτως γὰρ); however, as in the LXX, they left אֵין אֹנֵס untranslated. Relevant is Josephus' paraphrase of the verse in *Jewish Antiquities*:

Josephus, *Ant.*, 11.188–89

προσέταξε δὲ καὶ τοῖς διακόνοις μὴ βιάζεσθαι πίνειν, τὸ ποτὸν αὐτοῖς συνεχῶς προσφέροντας, ὡς καὶ παρὰ Πέρσαις γίνεται, ἀλλ' ἐπιτρέπειν αὐτοῖς καὶ πρὸς ὃ βούλεται τῶν κατακειμένων ἕκαστος φιλοφρονεῖσθαι.

But [the king] also commanded the servants not to force [anyone] to drink by continuously bringing them beverages (as is indeed [the case] with the Persians), but to let them enjoy themselves, too, in accordance with what each of the guests (lit., of those lying down) wants.[536]

---

[535] Hanhart notes that the negation οὐ is absent in certain manuscripts.

[536] The passage where Josephus wrote that the servants should not 'force' the guests 'to drink by continuously bringing them beverages' (μὴ βιάζεσθαι πίνειν, τὸ ποτὸν αὐτοῖς συνεχῶς προσφέροντας) is an expansion

Josephus' portrayal of the scene agrees with the LXX translators' to the extent that the banquet was described as not following the Persian custom; in an analogous way to the LXX version too (οὕτως δὲ ἠθέλησεν ὁ βασιλεὺς), if the banquet was not going as per the custom, Josephus made it clear that it was thanks to the king's instruction 'to let the guests enjoy themselves' (ἐπιτρέπειν αὐτοῖς [...] φιλοφρονεῖσθαι).[537] In his version, the king is the one who orders 'not to compel' (אֵין אֹנֵס / προσέταξε [...] μὴ βιάζεσθαι).

---

meant to expound the content of the Persian custom (ὡς καὶ παρὰ Πέρσαις γίνεται) to which the Hebrew only seems to allude (כְּדָת).

[537] As argued by Moore, Est. 1.8 was "a troublesome verse [in Hebrew] for versions and commentators alike." In his view, the Hebrew contradicts itself: "on the one hand, the drinking *was* 'according to law (sic) (*kdt*)' of the king, that is, whenever the king drank, everyone drank (cf. Herodotus I. 33; Xenophon, *Cyropaedia* VIII. 8, 10; Josephus, *Antiquities* XI. 188); on the other hand, 'no one was compelling ('ên 'ōnēs)', that is, one could drink as much, or as little, as he wanted" (Moore, *Esther*, pp. 7–8). Like Moore, Cavalier argues that there is a contradiction in the Hebrew verse: she cites, also on the basis of Herodotus, *Hist.*, 1.33, a Persian custom according to which guests had to drink as much as the king (Cavalier, *Esther*, p. 144). If this was the law implied in כְּדָת, then the fact that 'no one [was] compelling' (אֵין אֹנֵס) and that "all the leaders of [the king's] house should act as per the will of each and every man" is indeed at odds with it. However, the custom that Moore claims to adduce from Xenophon, Herodotus, and Josephus—and which Cavalier also allegedly cited from Herodotus—is not found in any of these sources: in *Cyr.*, 8.8.10, Xenophon only said that Persians drank in excess at banquets (τοσοῦτον δὲ πίνουσιν); in *Hist.*, 1.33, Herodotus did not deal with this matter at all (in *Hist.*, 1.133, he famously addressed the Persians' strong proclivity for wine [οἴνῳ δὲ κάρτα προσκέαται] and the

The interpretation of Est. 1.8 was probably arduous for Jerome, too, who, like his predecessors, attempted to clarify the meaning of the verse and to make it more coherent. However, his rendering did not exactly follow the LXX translators' interpretation; it did not conform with the A-Text treatment either.

> Vulg. Est. 1.8
>
> *Nec erat qui nolentes cogeret ad bibendum sed sic rex statuerat praeponens mensis singulos de principibus suis ut sumeret unusquisque quod vellet*
>
> And there was no one who would pressure those who did not want to into drinking, but the king, who assigned every one of his noblemen to the tables, deliberated in such a way that each [of the guests] might take what he wanted.

Jerome's stylistic adjustments were produced, for the most part, independently. In the Vulgate, as the phrase כְּדָת was removed, the two elements וְהַשְּׁתִיָּה 'and the drinking' and אֵין אֹנֵס 'no one

---

custom according to which they deliberated about the most serious matters only when drunk [μεθυσκόμενοι δὲ ἐώθασι βουλεύεσθαι τὰ σπουδαιέστατα τῶν πρηγμάτων]); and in *Ant.*, 11.188, Josephus did seem to bring up a practice that consisted of forcing guests to drink continuously, but not "whenever the king drank," as argued by Moore. On the whole, it does not seem necessary to identify the exact law or custom that was being referred to in the Hebrew in order to understand the Greeks' interpretations. Either the banquet conformed with a certain law (כְּדָת) but was also without constraints (אֵין אֹנֵס), which contradiction could be solved by the addition of a negation (LXX and Josephus); or the phrase כְּדָת introduced the content of the law in question, namely, that no one may compel anyone to drink more or less than they should wish (אֵין אֹנֵס), in which case the king accordingly ordered that the wishes of his guests "be executed" (A-Text).

[was] compelling' were combined and paraphrased through a single syntactical unit: *nec erat qui nolentes cogeret ad bibendum* 'and there was no one who would pressure those who did not want to into drinking'. While *nec erat qui* [...] *cogeret* renders אֵין אֹנֵס and *ad bibendum* corresponds to וְהַשְּׁתִיָּה, *nolentes* ('those who did not want to') is an addition that represents Jerome's evaluation of the situation based on what אֵין אֹנֵס implies. The unit כִּי־כֵן ׀ יִסַּד הַמֶּלֶךְ עַל כָּל־רַב בֵּיתוֹ לַעֲשׂוֹת כִּרְצוֹן אִישׁ־וָאִישׁ was translated with two units in the Vulgate: *praeponens mensis singulos de principibus suis* '[the king] who assigned every one of his noblemen to the tables', and *sed sic rex statuerat* [...] *ut sumeret unusquisque quod vellet* 'but the king deliberated in such a way [...] that each [of the guests] might take what he wanted'. The former paraphrases יִסַּד הַמֶּלֶךְ עַל כָּל־רַב בֵּיתוֹ: unlike the LXX translators (τοῖς οἰκονόμοις 'the stewards') and Josephus (τοῖς διακόνοις 'the servants'),[538] Jerome interpreted כָּל־רַב בֵּיתוֹ as noblemen from the king's entourage (*singulos de principibus suis*), not as chamberlains; he further added the mention of dining tables (*mensis*). In the latter unit, *sed sic rex statuerat* translates כִּי־כֵן with the addition of a verb (*statuerat*); *unusquisque* 'each [of the guests]' stands for אִישׁ־וָאִישׁ 'each and every man'; the phrase *ut sumeret* [...] *quod vellet* 'that [each of the guests] might take what he wanted' expands on כִּרְצוֹן 'as per the will of' by adding *ut sumeret*. Finally, לַעֲשׂוֹת was elided. In the Vulgate, the guests (*unusquisque*) are the subject (*ut sumeret* [...] *quod vellet*), while in the Hebrew the 'leaders of the house' (כָּל־רַב בֵּיתוֹ) are those who perform the action (לַעֲשׂוֹת כִּרְצוֹן אִישׁ־)

---

[538] The phrase כָּל־רַב בֵּיתוֹ was omitted in the A-Text translation.

וְאִישׁ). Most of Jerome's renderings are not matched in any of the other known versions: they attest to his independence in the translation process. On the other hand, when adding a verb in his rendering of כִּי־כֵן (*sed sic rex statuerat*), he may have followed the LXX translators' technique (οὕτως δὲ ἠθέλησεν ὁ βασιλεὺς).[539] Reminiscent of the LXX and A-Text translators' method too is his removal of a key element of the verse in his translation: instead of deleting אֵין אֹנֵס though, as in the two Greek versions, he chose to leave כַּדָּת unrendered. It should finally be observed that the Vulgate seems to owe nothing to the Old Latin:

VL Est. 1.8

Et cum convenissent multitudines ad praesti[tu]tum diem secundum legem praecepti dedit rex libertatem procurantibus convivium ut omissa disciplina domus regiae omnes recumbentes facerent voluntatem suam (/ et praecepit actoribus domus suae nemini vim fieri sed facere voluntate / secundum voluntatem recumbentium) et quousque vellent protraherent

---

[539] As shown in my translation of the Vulgate verse, *praeponens* governs *mensis singulos de principibus suis* the same way as יִסַּד takes the prepositional phrase עַל כָּל־רַב בֵּיתוֹ לַעֲשׂוֹת as its complement. However, semantically, the verb *statuerat*, unlike ἠθέλησεν in the LXX, could stand for יִסַּד, too. Therefore, Jerome may have translated יִסַּד with both *praeponens* and *statuerat*, i.e., through a double rendering (in which case כִּי־כֵן was simply translated as *sed sic*). A similar translation technique was employed in the First Targum to Esther: ארום כן שם טעם מלכא על כל דאיתמנא אפיטרופוס על ביתיה 'For the king had thus made a decree (שם טעם) over everyone who had been appointed (דאיתמנא) as administrator over his house' (First Targum to Est. 1.8; p. 7). There are two extant Targumim to the Book of Esther; scholars have dated their composition to the early Middle Ages (see Damsma, 'The Targums to Esther').

> *bibendi iocunditatem (/ ad iocunditatem ut biberent secundum legem)*
>
> And as crowds gathered on the prescribed day, in accordance with the law of the precept, the king granted a release (lit., the king gave liberty) to those in charge of the banquet so that, once the custom of the royal palace neglected, all the guests (lit., all those lying down) might act [as per] their will (/ and he ordered the managers of his house that there be no force exerted on anyone but to act by the will of / in accordance with the will of the guests [lit., of those lying down]) and, as long as they wished, protract the joy of drinking (/ so that they might drink, in accordance with the law, for [their own] enjoyment).

On the whole, many of Jerome's renderings in Vulg. Est. 1.8 were achieved without relying on the Greek (cf. the addition of *nolentes*; the translation of כִּרְצוֹן אִישׁ־וָאִישׁ as *ut sumeret unusquisque quod vellet*; the additional mention of 'tables' [*mensis*]). Rendering כָּל־רַב בֵּיתוֹ as *singulos de principibus suis* 'every one of his noblemen' may have been an attempt to accurately reflect the Hebrew against the LXX reading (τοῖς οἰκονόμοις) and the omission of that element in the A-Text: it would represent a *hebraica veritas* translation in this sense. Furthermore, two departures from the Hebrew in the Vulgate potentially arose either by analogy with the Greek or in response to it. First, if Jerome rendered the phrase כִּי־כֵן with an additional verb (*sed sic rex statuerat*) (see fn. 539), his elaboration on the Hebrew echoes the LXX translators' technique (οὕτως δὲ ἠθέλησεν ὁ βασιλεύς). Secondly, the removal of כָּדָת in the Vulgate may represent a diplomatic translation meant not to contradict the Hebrew or the LXX. Indeed, Jerome could have wanted to create a version halfway between the Hebrew verse, where the banquet was taking place 'as per the law', and the LXX one, where it was 'not according to the established custom / law'. With this translation technique he could resolve the disagreement, and to some extent the tension, between the two versions. However, this compromise necessarily came at the expense of the *hebraica veritas* principle, too.

2.2.2. The Banquet in the Vulgate of Esther

Jerome's way of representing the banquets in the Book of Esther reveals important aspects of his translation technique. In Vulg. Est. 5.6, for instance, his translation of the phrase בְּמִשְׁתֵּה הַיַּיִן 'at the wine banquet' as *postquam vinum biberat abundanter* 'after [the king] had drunk wine plentifully' reflects three features of his method: a tendency to introduce an evaluation of the passage through a paraphrase (section 2.2.1), a fondness for lexical variation (section 2.2.2), and stylistic independence (section 2.2.3).

2.2.2.1. Jerome's Evaluation of the Context in Vulg. Est. 5.6

MT Est. 5.6

וַיֹּאמֶר הַמֶּלֶךְ לְאֶסְתֵּר בְּמִשְׁתֵּה הַיַּיִן מַה־שְּׁאֵלָתֵךְ וְיִנָּתֵן לָךְ וּמַה־בַּקָּשָׁתֵךְ עַד־חֲצִי הַמַּלְכוּת וְתֵעָשׂ׃

And the king said to Esther at the wine banquet: "What is your request? Let it (lit., and let it) be given to you. And what is your demand? Up to half of the kingdom, let it (lit., and let it) be done."

4. The Translation of the Book of Esther

Vulg. Est. 5.6

Dixitque ei rex postquam vinum biberat abundanter quid petis ut detur tibi et pro qua re postulas etiam si dimidiam partem regni mei petieris inpetrabis

And the king said to her, after he had drunk wine plentifully: "What do you ask, that it be given to you? And whatever you demand, even if you should ask for half of my kingdom, you shall obtain."

It has been established a couple of times in this monograph that Jerome could expand on a Hebrew verse so as to introduce his evaluation of a passage.[540] Here his paraphrase of בְּמִשְׁתֵּה הַיַּיִן corresponds to the same type of expansion: in the Hebrew it is only said that the king is addressing Esther 'at the wine banquet'; Jerome, on the other hand, specified that the king 'had drunk wine plentifully' before doing so (*postquam vinum biberat abundanter*). This expansion emphasises a particular aspect of banquet scenes. The figure of the ruler in the Book of Esther and in other books, such as that of Daniel or in the Joseph story, is characterised to a large extent by fits of rage and by harshness and ruthlessness. By contrast, banquet scenes can serve as a backdrop against which the ruler may show the opposite side of his personality by displaying his wealth and his lavish ways (see for instance Est. 1.3–8, 2.18, 7.2). More specifically, in Est. 5, the point of the banquet is to portray a situation in which the king is being shown in a festive, and therefore merciful, light: this is what the extreme magnanimity of the offer made to Esther of 'up to half of the

---

[540] See sections 2.2.5.2 and 4.2.2.1.

kingdom' is meant to illustrate. Here Jerome endeavoured to present this exceptional behaviour as being provoked by the excess of drinking: he therefore translated בְּמִשְׁתֵּה הַיַּיִן as *postquam vinum biberat abundanter*. A similar translation technique was employed in Vulg. Dan. 5.2: indeed, by rendering בִּטְעֵם חַמְרָא as *iam temulentus* 'just inebriated', Jerome tried to stress that, when Belshazzar suddenly decided to use, at his own banquet, all the gold vessel and the silverware acquired from the looting of the Temple of Jerusalem, it was in a fit of drunkenness (see my fn. 462).

2.2.2.2. The Translator's Fondness for Lexical Variation

In the Vulgate of Esther, in most cases, Jerome rendered משתה 'drinking-bout', 'banquet', 'feast', with the word *convivium* 'social gathering', 'banquet', 'feast' (Vulg. Est. 1.3,[541] 1.5, 1.9, 2.18, 5.4, 5.5, 5.8, 5.12, 5.14, 6.14, 9.19).[542] On a couple of occasions he employed a synonym of *convivium*: *epulae* (Vulg. Est. 9.18, 9.22).

---

[541] It is interesting that in Vulg. Est. 1.3 Jerome expanded on the Hebrew עָשָׂה מִשְׁתֶּה 'he made a feast' in adding that the king had 'made a great feast' (*fecit grande convivium*): this rendering perfectly matches his translation of עֲבַד לְחֶם רַב 'he made a great feast' as *fecit grande convivium* in Vulg. Dan. 5.1. Jerome may have remembered or consulted the banquet episode in Vulg. Dan. 5 as he was translating Est. 1. Also possible is that he followed one of the Greek versions against the Hebrew. Indeed, while LXX Est. 1.3 reads δοχὴν ἐποίησεν 'he gave (lit., made) a reception' and A-Text Est. 1.3 καὶ ἐποίησεν ὁ βασιλεὺς πότον 'and the king gave (lit., made) a drinking party', Hanhart records the variant reading δοχὴν μεγαλην 'a great reception', which is also found in the Peshitta.

[542] It is noteworthy that, where Jerome employed *convivium*, either one, several or all attested VL traditions exhibit this word, too, in the following verses: VL Est. 1.3, 1.5, 1.9, 2.18, 5.4, 5.12.

4. The Translation of the Book of Esther

In two other verses, he resorted to a double rendering, through the use of both *convivium* and *epulae*. Indeed, in Vulg. Est. 8.17, he translated שִׂמְחָה וְשָׂשׂוֹן לַיְּהוּדִים מִשְׁתֶּה וְיוֹם טוֹב 'joy and gladness to the Jews, a banquet and a good day' as *mira exultatio epulae atque convivia et festus dies* 'an extraordinary joy, feasts as well as banquets and a holiday'. The word order of Vulg. Est. 9.17— where the three terms *epulis gaudio atque conviviis* 'with feasts, joy as well as banquets' translate יוֹם מִשְׁתֶּה וְשִׂמְחָה 'a day of feasting and joy'—might suggest that *epulis* corresponds to יוֹם מִשְׁתֶּה; more likely, though, is that יוֹם מִשְׁתֶּה was rendered twice here, with both *epulis* and *conviviis*, as in Vulg. Est. 8.17. In Est. 2.18, מִשְׁתֶּה occurs twice: the first time Jerome translated it with *convivium*; he then translated the phrase אֵת מִשְׁתֵּה אֶסְתֵּר as *pro coniunctione et nuptiis Hester* 'for the union and marriage / wedding of Esther', i.e., by means of a double rendering:

MT Est. 2.18a

וַיַּעַשׂ הַמֶּלֶךְ מִשְׁתֶּה גָדוֹל לְכָל־שָׂרָיו וַעֲבָדָיו אֵת מִשְׁתֵּה אֶסְתֵּר

And the king made a great feast for all his princes and his servants: Esther's feast.

Vulg. Est. 2.18a

Et iussit convivium praeparari permagnificum cunctis principibus et servis suis pro coniunctione et nuptiis Hester

And [the king] ordered that a most sumptuous feast be prepared for all his princes and servants in honour of (lit., for) the union and marriage / wedding of Esther.

In interpreting מִשְׁתֵּה אֶסְתֵּר as Esther's wedding (or marriage), Jerome was following the Greek description of the scene (and, more specifically, the LXX one, in which the first מִשְׁתֶּה was also treated as a normal feast):

> LXX Est. 2.18a
>
> καὶ ἐποίησεν ὁ βασιλεὺς πότον πᾶσιν τοῖς φίλοις αὐτοῦ καὶ ταῖς δυνάμεσιν ἐπὶ ἡμέρας ἑπτὰ καὶ ὕψωσεν τοὺς γάμους Εσθηρ
>
> And the king gave (lit., made) a drinking party for all his friends and for the forces [of the kingdom] for seven days, and he exalted (i.e., celebrated) the wedding of Esther.
>
> A-Text Est. 2.18a
>
> καὶ ἤγαγεν ὁ βασιλεὺς τὸν γάμον τῆς Εσθηρ ἐπιφανῶς
>
> And the king brilliantly celebrated the wedding of Esther.

Jerome may also have been inspired by the VL version on a lexical level. Indeed, where Vulg. Est. 2.18 displays the words *convivium* and *nuptiae*, the Old Latin verse does too:

> VL Est. 2.18a
>
> *Et fecit rex convivium (/ et facto convivio) omnibus amicis suis et omni virtuti suae ad nuptias Hester (/ et universis virtutibus egit nuptias eius praeclare / et omni exercitui suo diebus septem et exaltavit nuptias Hester)*
>
> And the king made a feast (/ and as the feast took place) for all of his friends and for his entire force, in support of the marriage / wedding of Esther (/ and for all the forces he brilliantly celebrated her wedding / and for his entire army for seven days and he exalted [i.e., celebrated] the marriage / wedding of Esther).

4. The Translation of the Book of Esther   285

While it is clear that Jerome aligned his translation of Est. 2.18 with the LXX, and perhaps to some extent with the VL, too,[543] his recourse to the double rendering *pro coniunctione et nuptiis*, through the addition of the word *coniunctio* 'union', is unmatched: it attests to his taste for lexical variation and to a certain stylistic independence and flexibility in his way of employing his sources.

In LXX and A-Text Est. 2.18, the introduction of a 'wedding' (γάμος) reflects the translators' interpretation of the verse based on the context of the passage. In Est. 1.19–20, it is said that the king will start looking for a new queen across the entire kingdom; then, after choosing Esther as his new queen in Est. 2.17, he immediately decides to give what is presented as 'a great feast' (מִשְׁתֶּה גָדוֹל) and as 'the feast of Esther' (מִשְׁתֵּה אֶסְתֵּר) in the Hebrew of Est. 2.18. As shown above, the Greek translators saw in this an allusion to the king's wedding with Esther.[544] The Hebrew, the LXX and the Vulgate version of Est. 1.5 are also relevant to compare in this regard:

---

[543] On a stylistic level, following the LXX / VL in Est. 2.18 could have also been a convenient way to avoid repeating the word *convivium* in the same verse, as the Hebrew contained מִשְׁתֶּה twice. However, this was not necessarily Jerome's priority. Indeed, in Vulg. Est. 1.5, the word *convivium* was used twice, although מִשְׁתֶּה occurred once (see below).

[544] Josephus also referred to a wedding four times in his version of Est. 2.17–18: νομίμως αὐτὴν ἄγεται γυναῖκα καὶ γάμους αὐτῇ ποιεῖται 'he made her [his] lawful wife and organised (lit., made) their (lit., her) wedding'; ἑορτάζειν τοὺς γάμους 'to celebrate the wedding'; ὑπὲρ τῶν γάμων 'for the wedding' (*Ant.*, 11.202–3).

MT Est. 1.5

וּבִמְלֹואת ׀ הַיָּמִ֣ים הָאֵ֗לֶּה עָשָׂ֣ה הַמֶּ֡לֶךְ לְכָל־הָעָ֣ם הַנִּמְצְאִים֩ בְּשׁוּשַׁ֨ן הַבִּירָ֜ה לְמִגָּד֧וֹל וְעַד־קָטָ֛ן מִשְׁתֶּ֖ה שִׁבְעַ֣ת יָמִ֑ים בַּחֲצַ֕ר גִּנַּ֖ת בִּיתַ֥ן הַמֶּֽלֶךְ׃

And when these days were fulfilled, the king made, for the entire people to be found in the fortress of Susa, from the great to the small, a feast, for seven days, in the court of the garden of the king's palace.

LXX Est. 1.5

ὅτε δὲ ἀνεπληρώθησαν αἱ ἡμέραι τοῦ γάμου ἐποίησεν ὁ βασιλεὺς πότον τοῖς ἔθνεσιν τοῖς εὑρεθεῖσιν εἰς τὴν πόλιν ἐπὶ ἡμέρας ἓξ ἐν αὐλῇ οἴκου τοῦ βασιλέως

But when the days of the wedding were fulfilled, the king gave (lit., made) a drinking party for the nations that were found towards the city, for six days, in the court of the king's house.

Vulg. Est. 1.5

Cumque implerentur dies convivii invitavit omnem populum qui inventus est Susis a maximo usque ad minimum et septem diebus iussit convivium praeparari in vestibulo horti et nemoris quod regio cultu et manu consitum erat

And when the days of feasting were fulfilled, [the king] invited the entire people that was found in Susa, from the greatest one to the smallest one, and he commanded that a feast be organised for seven days on the forecourt of the garden and of the grove which had been planted with royal care and by hand.

Where the MT reads וּבִמְלֹואת ׀ הַיָּמִים הָאֵלֶּה 'and when these days were fulfilled', in the LXX it is said ὅτε δὲ ἀνεπληρώθησαν αἱ ἡμέραι τοῦ γάμου 'but when the days of the wedding were fulfilled', and in the Vulgate *cumque implerentur dies convivii* 'and when the days of feasting were fulfilled'.[545] The word *convivii* is an addition here, as a feast is not mentioned in this part of the Hebrew verse: the phrase הַיָּמִים הָאֵלֶּה 'these days' does point to a feast, though, that is, to the first one that the king gave for the entire kingdom in Est. 1.3–5. On the other hand, in the LXX, the 'days' in question are said to be those of a 'wedding': while there was a contextual explanation for that interpretation in LXX Est. 2.18, there does not seem to be one here. The Vulgate rendering *dies convivii* is therefore rooted in the Hebrew version of the narrative; it may have been meant as a response to the LXX version, according to which it was not a feast but a wedding that had taken place: *convivii* would represent as such a *hebraica veritas* addition. Noteworthy is that, in the version attributed to Origen, the mention of a 'drinking party' (πότος) was added, too (instead of γάμος); it could be that Jerome followed Origen in adding *convivii*.[546] To be sure, his translation technique in Vulg. Est. 1.5a seems to be the opposite of the one employed in Vulg. Est. 2.18a, where he adopted the Greek reading 'wedding' with *pro coniunctione et nuptiis Hester* against מִשְׁתֵּה אֶסְתֵּר.

---

[545] The A-Text verse contains a reading that is not matched by any version: ἕως ἀνεπληρώθησαν αἱ ἡμέραι ἃς ἐποίησεν ὁ βασιλεὺς [...], πότον [...] ἄγων τὰ σωτήρια αὐτοῦ 'until the[se] days were fulfilled, which the king had turned into (lit., made) [...] a drinking-party [...] [during which] he celebrated his deliverance'. See Cavalier's comments on A-Text Est. 1.5 in *Esther*, p. 142.

[546] Jerome's reliance on Origen in the Vulgate translation of Est. 1.5 is further investigated in section 4.2.4.

Wherever the phrase משתה היין 'the wine banquet' occurs (Est. 5.6, 7.2, 7.7, 7.8), Jerome's responses differ not only from his treatment of the word משתה when it is used on its own, but also from one another. As seen above, in Vulg. Est. 5.6, he rendered בְּמִשְׁתֵּה הַיַּיִן as *postquam vinum biberat abundanter*. In Est. 7.2, where the king repeats the question that he asked Esther in Est. 5.6 (the two verses are almost identical), Jerome rendered וַיֹּאמֶר הַמֶּלֶךְ לְאֶסְתֵּר גַּם בַּיּוֹם הַשֵּׁנִי בְּמִשְׁתֵּה הַיַּיִן 'and the king said to Esther, also on the second day, at the wine banquet' with *dixitque ei rex etiam in secundo die postquam vino incaluerat* 'and the king said to her, also on the second day, after he had grown passionate (lit., hot) from the wine'.[547] Here, he expanded on the original, as in Vulg. Est. 5.6, by explicitly presenting the king as intoxicated with wine. However, with *postquam vino incaluerat*, he resorted to a more colourful verb than the one employed in Vulg. Est. 5.6—*incalesco* instead of *bibere*—and he did not add an adverb like *abundanter*. In Vulg. Est. 7.7, after Esther denounces Haman to the king as the one who seeks to destroy her people, the king gets angry and leaves the feasting hall: וְהַמֶּלֶךְ קָם בַּחֲמָתוֹ מִמִּשְׁתֵּה הַיַּיִן

---

[547] Jerome's expansion on the Hebrew echoes his translation of כְּטוֹב לֵב־הַמֶּלֶךְ בַּיָּיִן 'as the heart of the king [felt] good from the wine' (Est. 1.10) as *cum rex esset hilarior et post nimiam potionem incaluisset mero* 'as the king was most merry and grew passionate (lit., hot) with pure wine after too much drinking': the same verb as in Vulg. Est. 7.2 was employed (*incalesco* 'to grow hot'). Also interesting here is that, in his expansion on the Hebrew in Vulg. Est. 1.10, Jerome resorted to the opposite translation technique to that of Josephus in his paraphrase of the verse: in the Vulgate, the king's drunkenness is emphasised; in Josephus, it is disregarded (*Ant.*, 11.190).

4. The Translation of the Book of Esther 289

אֶל־גִּנַּת הַבִּיתָן 'and the king rose in his wrath [and went] from the wine banquet to the palace garden'. Jerome translated this as *rex autem surrexit iratus et de loco convivii intravit in hortum arboribus consitum* 'but the king furiously (lit., furious) stood up and from the banquet hall (lit., place of feasting) he went into the garden planted with trees'.[548] With this translation, Jerome paraphrased the Hebrew, as *de loco convivii* omits the word for 'wine' and adds the word for 'place' (*loco*). Furthermore, here, as opposed to his expansions in Vulg. Est. 5.6 and 7.2, his rendering of מִמִּשְׁתֵּה הַיַּיִן is not indicative of the king's state, but puts emphasis on the spatial configuration of the scene through the addition of *loco*: 'from the banquet hall (lit., place of feasting)'. As shown above, *convivium* is a standard rendering for משתה in the Vulgate of Esther: the addition of the word *locus* as part of the genitival construction *loco convivii* therefore served to express more clearly what was elliptically formulated in the Hebrew.[549] It also seems that in

---

[548] It is interesting that, of all versions, Greek and Old Latin, it is Josephus' way of representing בַּחֲמָתוֹ 'in his wrath' with ταραχθέντος 'troubled' (*Ant.*, 11.265)—the aorist passive participle of ταράσσω—that Jerome's translation *iratus* 'furious'—the perfect participle of *irascor*—matches best grammatically. In the A-Text, בַּחֲמָתוֹ is represented by ἔκθυμος […] γενόμενος […] καὶ πληθεὶς ὀργῆς '[he] who was spirited and filled with anger'; in the VL by *correptus furore* 'carried away with rage'; in the LXX it is omitted (a variant attributed to Origen reads εν οργη αυτου 'in his anger'). Jerome's translation of גִּנַּת הַבִּיתָן 'the palace garden' as *hortum arboribus consitum* 'the garden planted with trees' in this verse and elsewhere is investigated below (see section 4.2.4).

[549] The Hebrew syntax is elliptical, but the prepositions מִן 'from' and אֶל 'to' indicate that the king is going from one place to another (as reflected by '[and went]' in my translation). Accordingly, Jerome also added the

adding *locus* Jerome aligned his translation of מִמִּשְׁתֵּה הַיַּיִן in Vulg. Est. 7.7 with the wording of Est. 7.8. Indeed, in Est. 7.8, as the king retraces his steps, the reverse route is described: וְהַמֶּלֶךְ שָׁב מִגִּנַּת הַבִּיתָן אֶל־בֵּית | מִשְׁתֵּה הַיַּיִן 'and the king returned from the palace garden to the house of wine feasting'. Here, instead of משתה היין, the Hebrew reads בֵּית | מִשְׁתֵּה הַיַּיִן 'the house of wine feasting', which construct chain Jerome also rendered with *convivii locus*: *qui cum reversus esset de horto nemoribus consito et intrasset convivii locum* 'he who, once he had returned from the garden planted with groves and had entered the banquet hall (lit., the place of feasting)...'[550] The phrase מִמִּשְׁתֵּה הַיַּיִן was therefore treated the same way in Vulg. Est. 7.7 as בֵּית | מִשְׁתֵּה הַיַּיִן in Vulg. Est. 7.8. Only, in the former verse, the word *locus* is an addition, while in the latter it stands for בֵּית. Apart from the fact that the word for 'wine' was omitted, in Vulg. Est. 7.8, the phrase *convivii locus* can

---

verb that was implied in the Hebrew: *intravit* 'he went into'. He added *intrasset* again in Vulg. Est. 7.8 for the same reason (see below).

[550] The fact that Jerome rendered the two Hebrew phrases in Est. 7.7 and 7.8 the same way is reminiscent of the LXX version, in which the construct chains מִמִּשְׁתֵּה הַיַּיִן and בֵּית | מִשְׁתֵּה הַיַּיִן are represented by the same word, συμπόσιος 'drinking party'. Also worthy of attention is the lexical choice of the Old Latin translators in VL Est. 7.7 and 7.8: *de loco suo* 'from his place' and *ad locum suum* 'to his place', respectively. Jerome's employment of the word *locus* where the Hebrew reads מִמִּשְׁתֵּה הַיַּיִן, but also for בֵּית | מִשְׁתֵּה הַיַּיִן, may have been inspired by the Old Latin. Comparatively, there is no rendering for the Hebrew phrase in A-Text Est. 7.9 (= Est. 7.7), although ἐπὶ τὸ συμπόσιον occurs in A-Text Est. 7.11 (= Est. 7.8); a variant reading attributed to Origen's edition, εις τον οικον του ποτου του οινου 'to the house of the wine drinking party', is attested in the apparatus of LXX Est. 7.8.

be considered a *verbum e verbo* rendering of בֵּית ׀ מִשְׁתֵּה הַיָּיִן; in Vulg. Est. 7.7 the same phrase reflects a *sensus de sensu* treatment of מִמִּשְׁתֵּה הַיָּיִן which stemmed by analogy with Est. 7.8.

In summary, Jerome treated the phrase משתה היין in different ways across the Vulgate of Esther: twice he expanded on the phrase in two different, though synonymous, manners (Vulg. Est. 5.6, 7.2); once, while omitting the word for 'wine', he produced a *verbum e verbo* translation of בֵּית ׀ מִשְׁתֵּה הַיָּיִן (Vul. Est. 7.8); in Vul. Est. 7.7, he rendered משתה היין by means of an interpolation, as though it were בֵּית ׀ מִשְׁתֵּה הַיָּיִן. The fact that he rendered משתה with synonyms, *convivium* and *epulae*, that he translated מִשְׁתֵּה אֶסְתֵּר in Vulg. 2.18 in a way that departed from the Hebrew and agreed with the Greek—by means of a double rendering (*pro coniunctione et nuptiis Hester*) unique to the Vulgate version—and that he translated משתה היין with paraphrases and expansions, ultimately reflects his attachment to lexical variation. How stylistically independent he was in his treatment of משתה can now be further established.

2.2.2.3. Jerome's Stylistic Independence in the Translation of משתה

It was demonstrated above that the Vulgate translation of מִשְׁתֵּה אֶסְתֵּר in Est. 2.18a followed the Greek versions; furthermore, Jerome's recourse to the words *convivium* and *nuptiae* conformed with the lexical choices of the Old Latin translators. It is also possible that the equal treatment of משתה היין in Vulg. Est. 7.7 and בֵּית ׀ מִשְׁתֵּה הַיָּיִן in Vulg. Est. 7.8 was inspired by the other versions: the translation technique of the Greek translators, as well as the lexical choices of the Old Latin ones, may have played a part in Jerome's way of translating the two Hebrew phrases with *convivii locus* (see fn. 550). Nevertheless, in general, examples that reflect a correspondence between the Vulgate of Esther and the Greek and Old Latin sources in the treatment of משתה are less common than those that do not. First, a comparative analysis shows that, when Jerome followed a version other than the Hebrew, he freely selected among his sources which of the readings that they offered he would introduce in the Vulgate. Secondly, his recourse to lexical variation did not depend on the Greek versions: the passages where he varied in his response to משתה do not match those where the Greek translators varied in theirs. In other words, they did not dictate Jerome's use of *epulae, convivium,* or both.[551] That he used *convivium* in verses where the Old Latin translators had, too (see fn. 542), is not evidence either that he depended on their version; if anything, it shows that he followed it when he pleased and illustrates as such the flexibility of his technique. Likewise, as he introduced, in Vulg. Est. 2.18a, a notion foreign to the Hebrew verse and inspired by the Greek—a wedding—he also added the word *coniunctio*: by employing an unmatched double rendering (*pro coniunctione et nuptiis Hester*), he showed his

---

[551] The Greek translators could opt for words that conveyed a slightly different meaning. They rendered משתה as follows: πότος 'drinking party' (LXX Est. 1.5, 1.9, 2.18, 6.14; A-Text Est. 1.3, 1.5, 5.14 [= Est. 5.4], 6.23 [= Est. 6.14]); δοχή 'reception' (LXX Est. 1.3, 5.4, 5.5, 5.8, 5.12, 5.14; A-Text Est. 1.9, 5.15 [= Est. 5.5], 5.18 [= Est. 5.8]); γάμος 'wedding' or 'marriage' (LXX Est. 2.18, 9.22; A-Text Est. 2.18); χαρά 'joy' (LXX Est. 9.17, 9.18); and κώθων 'carousal' (LXX Est. 8.17).

stylistic independence. His translation of the phrase בְּמִשְׁתֵּה הַיַּיִן 'at the wine banquet' as *postquam vinum biberat abundanter* in Vulg. Est. 5.6 represents an original expansion, too, as none of the other extant versions reflects an equivalent phrasing: the LXX reads ἐν [...] τῷ πότῳ 'at the drinking party',[552] the phrase is elided in the A-Text,[553] and there is no VL version attested for this verse. Similarly, where Vulg. 7.2 reads *postquam vino incaluerat*, neither the LXX (ἐν τῷ πότῳ 'at the drinking party') nor the A-Text (ὡς δὲ προῆγεν ἡ πρόποσις 'but as the pre-[dinner] cocktail went on') could have motivated Jerome's phrasing. The VL version, *factum est autem in bona propinatione* 'but it happened during a good toasting'—which expands on the A-Text through the addition of the adjective *bona* 'good'—proposes a reading that suggests, to some extent, the drunkenness of the king. However, the fact that a king is likely to get drunk at his own banquet is a conventional idea; at any rate, Jerome's phrasing in the Vulgate, which unlike the VL explicitly establishes the king's intemperance due to excessive drinking (*incaluerat*), differs too much from the Old Latin reading to have been inspired by it stylistically: with *postquam vinum biberat abundanter* and *postquam vino incaluerat*, Jerome produced

---

[552] Two variant readings recorded in Hanhart's LXX apparatus read as follows: εν τω ποτω του οινου 'at the wine drinking party' (which reflects Origen's revision) and ως δε εγενηθη επι της αριστευουσης προποσεως 'but as he was at an excellent pre-[dinner] cocktail'. Although the latter reading implies to some extent that the king was enjoying himself, it does not seem that it could have inspired Jerome, stylistically speaking, in his portrayal of the scene (*postquam vinum biberat abundanter*).

[553] The A-Text reading εν τω ποτω του οινου 'at the wine drinking party' is attested in one manuscript (see Hanhart's apparatus).

unique versions of these Esther verses. Once again, here and elsewhere, the introduction of expansions, whether inspired by extant versions or created independently, was fundamentally at odds with the claim that the Vulgate book would not "lengthen [the story] by adding even a single thing" and that it would "simply render the Hebrew into the Latin tongue."[554]

2.3. Two Verses Representative of the Most Common Type of Paraphrase in Vulg. Est.

The two verses investigated below may serve as representative examples of the most common type of paraphrase found in the Vulgate version of Esther: indeed, these case studies illustrate best the translation process whereby Jerome operated independently of all other versions in the application of the *sensus de sensu* method. That he creatively paraphrased the Hebrew without stylistically relying on the Greek or on the Old Latin versions does not mean that his renderings did not arise in response to them. In fact, Jerome did not lose sight of his agenda, that of the *hebraica veritas*, in the translation of the Hebrew of Esther. Our first case study (section 2.3.1), for instance, shows that where the Vulgate emphasises particular aspects of the Hebrew verse, the Greek and the Old Latin texts contain a completely different narrative: beyond Jerome's creativity, this is likely to reflect his attempt to correct his predecessors' versions. In the second case study (section 2.3.2), however, the Vulgate expansion on the Hebrew does not aim at correcting anything in the Greek: rather, it

---

[554] Vulg., p. 712.

corresponds to Jerome's own elaboration on a point implied in the Hebrew, one that the LXX translators seem to have intended to exploit before him, albeit in a very minor way.

2.3.1. Stylistic Departures from the Hebrew that Still Reflect the *hebraica veritas* Against the Other Versions in Vulg. Est. 9.4

MT Est. 9.4

כִּי־גָדוֹל מָרְדֳּכַי בְּבֵית הַמֶּלֶךְ וְשָׁמְעוֹ הוֹלֵךְ בְּכָל־הַמְּדִינוֹת כִּי־הָאִישׁ מָרְדֳּכַי הוֹלֵךְ וְגָדוֹל׃

For Mordechai was powerful (lit., great) in the king's house, and his reputation went forth throughout all the provinces, for the man Mordechai grew more and more powerful (lit., went and grew great).

Vulg. Est. 9.4

Quem principem esse palatii et plurimum posse cognoverant fama quoque nominis eius crescebat cotidie et per cunctorum ora volitabat

He whom they had known to be the leader / prince of the palace, and to be capable of [doing] a lot: the fame of his name was also growing by the day and flying around through everyone's mouth.

The entire Hebrew verse makes it clear that Mordechai is held in high regard by the king and that he reached a status of choice in his entourage (see Est. 8). The Vulgate version emphasises the portrayal of this ascent to power: where the Hebrew simply described Mordechai as 'great in the king's house' (כִּי־גָדוֹל מָרְדֳּכַי בְּבֵית הַמֶּלֶךְ), Jerome made him a 'leader / prince of the palace, capable of [doing] a lot' (*quem principem esse palatii et plurimum posse* cognoverant).⁵⁵⁵ In the Vulgate, the sequence of events is also reversed: Mordechai's reputation 'grows by the day' and then 'flies around through everyone's mouth', while in the Hebrew it first 'goes forth throughout all the provinces' before Mordechai is said to 'grow more and more powerful'. Furthermore, here, much of the Vulgate language is figurative in its way of paraphrasing the Hebrew: instead of presenting Mordechai as the one 'growing more and more powerful' (כִּי־הָאִישׁ מָרְדֳּכַי הוֹלֵךְ וְגָדוֹל), Jerome referred to the 'fame of his name growing by the day' (*fama quoque nominis eius crescebat cotidie*); this fame is not 'going forth throughout all the provinces' (וְשָׁמְעוֹ הוֹלֵךְ בְּכָל־הַמְּדִינוֹת) in the Vulgate but it is 'flying around through everyone's mouth' (*et per cunctorum ora volitabat*). Neither the Greek nor the Old Latin versions of Est. 9.4 contain similar phrasings: Jerome's modifications are original and attest to his literary creativity. However, that he was independent in his stylistic treatment of the Hebrew does not mean that he was not, at the same time, responding to the work of his predecessors. Indeed, in the present case, his Latin emphasises points in the Hebrew verse which the Greek and Old Latin versions seem to either misrepresent, or to represent on the basis of a different text:

LXX Est. 9.4

προσέπεσεν γὰρ τὸ πρόσταγμα τοῦ βασιλέως ὀνομασθῆναι ἐν πάσῃ τῇ βασιλείᾳ

---

⁵⁵⁵ Analogous to the Vulgate translation is the First Targum to Esther in Est. 9.4 (p. 32): כי ארום אפיטרופוס ורב סרכן מרדכי בבית מלכא 'For Mordechai [had become] the administrator and the chief-officer in the king's house'.

4. The Translation of the Book of Esther

For it [just so] happened that / For [news] came that the king's ordinance was cited (lit., named) in the entire kingdom.

A-Text Est. 7.43 (= Est. 9.4)

καὶ προσέπεσεν ἐν Σούσοις ὀνομασθῆναι Αμαν καὶ τοὺς ἀντικειμένους ἐν πάσῃ βασιλείᾳ

And it [just so] happened that / And [news] came that, in Susa, Haman['s] and the opponents[' names] were cited (lit., named) in the entire kingdom.

VL Est. 9.4

Praeceptum enim erat timorem regis nominari (/ Quoniam praeceptum erat regis imperium nominari) in omni civitate eius (/ et erat nominabilis in omnem civitatem)

Indeed, it was a principle that / it had been ordered that the fear of the king be celebrated (lit., named) (/ Since it was a principle that / it had been ordered that the authority / the reign of the king be celebrated [lit., named]) in his entire city (/ and it was celebrated across the entire city).

These translations of Est. 9.4 all disagree on what is to be 'named' (ὀνομασθῆναι / *nominari* / *nominabilis*): while in the LXX the 'king's ordinance' is cited (τὸ πρόσταγμα τοῦ βασιλέως),[556] in the A-Text

---

[556] According to Cavalier, it is Mordechai who is 'named' here, in LXX Est. 9.4 (*Esther*, p. 225). More specifically, 'the fear of Mordechai' (that is, the fear that he inspires), which is the last subject expressed in the preceding LXX verse (ὁ γὰρ φόβος Μαρδοχαίου), is what should supposedly be named. In order to reach this understanding, Cavalier construed LXX Est. 9.4 as follows: "For the king's ordinance had circulated (προσέπεσεν γὰρ τὸ πρόσταγμα τοῦ βασιλέως), so that [he] (i.e., Mordechai) might be named in the entire kingdom (ὀνομασθῆναι ἐν πάσῃ τῇ βασιλείᾳ)." This

Haman is presented as a public enemy, as it were, along with his militia. In the first of the three VL versions, the fact that the king should be feared (*timorem regis*) is to be celebrated, whereas in the second one it is his authority or his reign (*regis imperium*). It could be—although elements may be missing from the extant VL fragment—that, in the third form cited here (*et erat nominabilis in omnem civitatem*), the fear that Mordechai inspired, last mentioned in the previous VL verse (*timor enim Mardocei*), is being celebrated. All these versions of Est. 9.4 seem to share, against the Vulgate and the Hebrew, the following characteristic: Mordechai's fame is never mentioned. Even though Jerome endeavoured to translate the Hebrew of Esther in an expeditious way, there is no doubt that he kept an eye on the Greek and Old Latin versions. Therefore, by stressing Mordechai's new status in his paraphrase of Est. 9.4 (*quem principem esse palatii et plurimum posse cognoverant*), it is likely that he meant to correct what he perceived as a major departure in the Greek and Old Latin texts.

2.3.2. Meaningful Additions in Vulg. Est. 9.18

In Est. 8.11, Jews are authorised by royal decree 'to muster, to stand up for their lives, to exterminate, and to slay and destroy' their enemies. It is then repeated throughout Est. 9 that they have been acting on this decree. While the Jews from the provinces, after putting an end to their fight on the thirteen of the month of

---

construal, though not impossible, is less straightforward and grammatically plausible than my translation (see above). A VL tradition, however, may have supported Cavalier's interpretation to some extent (see below).

Adar, begin to rest on the fourteenth (Est. 9.16–17), those from the city of Susa are said to fight both on the thirteenth and on the fourteenth, so as to rest on the fifteenth (Est. 9.18). In the Vulgate, Jerome paraphrased Est. 9.18 and expanded on it:

MT Est. 9.18

וְהַיְּהוּדִיים אֲשֶׁר־בְּשׁוּשָׁן נִקְהֲלוּ בִּשְׁלֹשָׁה עָשָׂר בּוֹ וּבְאַרְבָּעָה עָשָׂר בּוֹ וְנוֹחַ בַּחֲמִשָּׁה עָשָׂר בּוֹ וְעָשֹׂה אֹתוֹ יוֹם מִשְׁתֶּה וְשִׂמְחָה

And the Jews who [were] in Susa mustered on the thirteenth [of the month] (lit., of it) and on the fourteenth (lit., of it), and they rested on the fifteenth (lit., of it) and made it a day of feasting and joy.

Vulg. Est. 9.18

At hii qui in urbe Susis caedem exercuerant tertiodecimo et quartodecimo eiusdem mensis die in caede versati sunt quintodecimo autem die percutere desierunt et idcirco eandem diem constituere sollemnem epularum atque laetitiae

But those who had been carrying out the slaughter in Susa City engaged in the slaughter on the thirteenth and on the fourteenth day of the same month; however, they stopped striking on the fifteenth day and for this reason they established the same day as a yearly / as an appointed [time] of banqueting and of joy.

In the Hebrew verse, it is simply said that the Jews 'gathered' (נִקְהֲלוּ), without direct reference to their fight; in context, however, it is clear that they mustered in order to go to battle (see Est. 9.13–15). Jerome chose to put emphasis on this implication and to leave aside the literal sense of נִקְהֲלוּ, i.e., the gathering itself. Indeed, his first modification consisted of specifying that the Jews of the city had been busy with the killing of their enemies (*hii qui in urbe Susis caedem exercuerant*). After omitting the part where they mustered (נִקְהֲלוּ), he highlighted the battle again by further adding that they 'engaged in the slaughter' (*in caede versati sunt*). Then, where the Jews are said in the Hebrew to have started resting (נוֹחַ), the Vulgate paraphrases 'they stopped striking' (*percutere desierunt*); the causality between the cessation of hostilities and the establishing of a holiday (*eandem diem constituere sollemnem*) also becomes more explicit through the addition of the adverb *idcirco* 'for this reason'. Before Jerome, the LXX translators seem to have also felt the need, albeit to a much lesser extent, to rewrite the Hebrew verse in a way that might stress the Jews' state of unrest:[557]

> LXX Est. 9.18
>
> οἱ δὲ Ἰουδαῖοι οἱ ἐν Σούσοις τῇ πόλει συνήχθησαν καὶ τῇ τεσσαρεσκαιδεκάτῃ καὶ οὐκ ἀνεπαύσαντο· ἦγον δὲ καὶ τὴν πεντεκαιδεκάτην μετὰ χαρᾶς καὶ εὐφροσύνης
>
> But the Jews, those in Susa City, were also brought together on the fourteenth and they did not rest; but they also celebrated the fifteenth with joy and merriment.

Rather than a series of additions that would directly refer to the battle, as in the Vulgate, the LXX translators introduced a subtle modification to address it. Here, the fourteenth is portrayed as the day when the Jews of Susa, who were 'brought together' again, 'did not rest' (συνήχθησαν καὶ τῇ τεσσαρεσκαιδεκάτῃ καὶ οὐκ ἀνεπαύσαντο); in the Hebrew, on the fourteenth, they were only brought together (נִקְהֲלוּ בִּשְׁלֹשָׁה עָשָׂר בּוֹ וּבְאַרְבָּעָה עָשָׂר בּוֹ). Furthermore, in the Greek, the fifteenth is celebrated as a holiday (ἦγον δὲ καὶ τὴν πεντεκαιδεκάτην μετὰ χαρᾶς καὶ εὐφροσύνης), but it is not

---

[557] Neither the A-Text nor the VL version is attested.

formally presented as a rest day, while in the Hebrew it is both a day of rest and a holiday (וְנוֹחַ בַּחֲמִשָּׁה עָשָׂר בּוֹ וְעָשֹׂה אֹתוֹ יוֹם מִשְׁתֶּה וְשִׂמְחָה). The fact that the fifteenth was celebrated was probably sufficient in the Greek translators' eyes to imply what the Hebrew said explicitly, namely, that the Jews also rested then.[558] Jerome's way of rendering the Hebrew obviously differs from the LXX version; however, both in the Vulgate and the LXX, the gathering of the Jews was interpreted, and exploited, as a metonymy for the fight: in the Latin, the verb נִקְהֲלוּ was elided and explicit references to the Jews' slaughtering their enemies were added instead; in the Greek, the battle was hinted at by the moving of וְנוֹחַ to the preceding day, that is, to the fourteenth, and through the addition of a negation (τῇ τεσσαρεσκαιδεκάτῃ καὶ οὐκ ἀνεπαύσαντο). Jerome's expansion was somewhat analogous to the LXX translators' interpretation in this sense. Again, the sheer fact that he introduced expansions in his translation is at odds with his criticism of the *editio vulgata*, which "adds things that could have been said and heard over time," and with the assertion that he produced a word-for-word translation of the Hebrew.[559] On the other hand, this translation technique conforms with the *sensus de sensu*

---

[558] In Josephus' version, the fact that the Jews rest is also implicitly communicated through their feasting: ὁμοίως δὲ καὶ οἱ ἐν τοῖς Σούσοις Ἰουδαῖοι τὴν τετράδα καὶ δεκάτην καὶ τὴν ἐχομένην τοῦ αὐτοῦ μηνὸς συναθροισθέντες εὐωχήθησαν 'And similarly, the Jews in Susa fared sumptuously as they had gathered together on the fourteenth and on the following [day] of the same month' (*Ant.*, 11.292).

[559] See Vulg., p. 712.

method, which could involve additions as long as the overall rendering conveyed the ideas of the original text: this was the case with Jerome's paraphrase of Est. 9.18.

2.4. A Paraphrase of Origen's Edition of the LXX: The Royal Garden in the Vulgate of Esther

In this final case study, we analyse the Vulgate representation of the king's garden in Esther. The syntagm גנת הביתן 'the garden of the palace' occurs in Est. 1.5, 7.7 and 7.8. In his treatment of the Hebrew, Jerome seems to have consistently paraphrased Origen's edition against all other versions, including the Hebrew text.

> MT Est. 7.7a
>
> וְהַמֶּלֶךְ קָם בַּחֲמָתוֹ מִמִּשְׁתֵּה הַיַּיִן אֶל־גִּנַּת הַבִּיתָן
>
> And the king rose in his wrath [and went] from the wine banquet to the palace garden.
>
> Vulg. Est. 7.7a
>
> *rex autem surrexit iratus et de loco convivii intravit in hortum arboribus consitum*
>
> But the king furiously (lit., furious) stood up and from the banquet hall (lit., the place of feasting) he went into the garden planted with trees.

In the Hebrew the king is said to go to the 'palace garden' (גִּנַּת הַבִּיתָן), without further descriptive details. In the Vulgate, the palace is not mentioned, and the garden is portrayed with embellishments as a 'garden planted with trees' (*hortum arboribus consitum*). A comparison between the LXX, the A-Text, the VL, Josephus and the Vulgate shows that Jerome's expansion is not rooted in any of those Greek or Old Latin versions. The variant reading attributed to Origen in Hanhart's apparatus is, on the other hand, revealing:

LXX Est. 7.7a

ὁ δὲ βασιλεὺς ἐξανέστη ἐκ τοῦ συμποσίου εἰς τὸν κῆπον

But the king stood up from the drinking party [and went] to the garden.

A-Text Est. 7.9 (= Est. 7.7a)

ἔκθυμος δὲ γενόμενος ὁ βασιλεὺς καὶ πλησθεὶς ὀργῆς ἀνεπήδησε καὶ ἦν περιπατῶν

But the king, who was spirited and filled with anger, leaped up and [started] pacing around.

VL Est. 7.7a

Et audito hoc correptus furore rex exilivit de loco (/ rex autem surrexit de loco suo) proiciens calicem (/ mappam / calicem meri) et cum exiret in hortum

And, as soon as the king heard this (lit., as this was heard), carried away with rage, he sprung out of the hall (lit., out of the place) (/ but the king stood up from his hall [lit., from his place]), flinging away a cup (/ the tablecloth / a cup of wine) and as he went away to the garden...

Josephus, *Ant.*, 11.265

Ταραχθέντος δὲ πρὸς τοῦτο τοῦ βασιλέως καὶ ἀναπηδήσαντος εἰς τοὺς κήπους ἐκ τοῦ συμποσίου

But as the king was troubled with this and leaped up towards the gardens from the drinking party...

Origen Est. 7.7a

τὸν κῆπον τον συμφυτον

[To] the wooded / leafy garden

The esthetical touch that the reading found in Origen adds to the depiction of the garden seems to have inspired Jerome in his rendering of גִּנַּת as *hortum arboribus consitum* 'the garden planted with trees'. Indeed, the adjective σύμφυτος is a compound based on the noun φυτόν 'a plant' prefixed with the preposition σύν 'with': it portrays the garden (τὸν κῆπον) as rich with foliage, i.e., 'wooded' or 'leafy'. Likewise, in the phrase *hortum arboribus consitum*, the word *consitum* is the perfect (passive) participle of *consero*, a compound made of *sero* 'to plant' to which the preposition *cum* 'with' has been prefixed: it stands for συμφυτον. If the participle *consitus* can be employed on its own,[560] a noun or an adverb is often added: therefore, here, Jerome expanded on Origen's portrayal of the garden by enriching it with trees (*arboribus*). Further analysis of his treatment of גנת הביתן across the Vulgate of Esther bears out the hypothesis that the adjective σύμφυτος underlies his translation. In Vulg. Est. 7.8, for instance, a rendering close to *hortum arboribus consitum* was employed to translate the Hebrew: *horto nemoribus consito* ('the garden planted with groves'). Again, neither the LXX, nor the A-Text, the VL, or Josephus could have motivated this choice:

MT Est. 7.8a

וְהַמֶּ֡לֶךְ שָׁב֩ מִגִּנַּ֨ת הַבִּיתָ֜ן אֶל־בֵּ֣ית ׀ מִשְׁתֵּ֣ה הַיַּ֗יִן

And the king returned from the palace garden to the house of wine feasting.

---

[560] See for instance Quintilian, *Institutio Oratoria*, 5, 10, 37: *Spectatur* […] *montanus an planus, maritimus an mediterraneus, consitus an incultus* 'We check (lit., it is examined) […] whether [the place] is hilly or flat, by the sea or inland, cultivated or untilled…'

4. The Translation of the Book of Esther

Vulg. Est. 7.8a

Qui cum reversus esset de horto nemoribus consito et intrasset convivii locum

He who, once he had returned from the garden planted with groves and had entered the banquet hall (lit., the place of feasting)…

LXX Est. 7.8a

ἐπέστρεψεν δὲ ὁ βασιλεὺς ἐκ τοῦ κήπου

But the king returned from the garden.

A-Text Est. 7.11a (= Est. 7.8a)

καὶ ὁ βασιλεὺς ἐπέστρεψεν ἐπὶ τὸ συμπόσιον

And the king returned to the drinking party.

VL Est. 7.8a

Reversus est autem rex (/ et reversus est rex) de horto ad locum suum

But the king came back (/ and the king came back) from the garden to his hall (lit., to his place).

Josephus, *Ant.*, 11.265

ἐπεισελθὼν ὁ βασιλεὺς καὶ πρὸς τὴν ὄψιν ἔτι μᾶλλον παροξυνθεὶς

When the king walked back in, and as he was even more irritated at that sight…

Origen Est. 7.8a

κήπου του συμφυτου εις τον οικον του ποτου του οινου

[From the] wooded / leafy garden to the house of the wine party.

Even more noteworthy is Jerome's expansion in his rendering of Est. 1.5. In Est. 1.5, a banquet is said to be taking place 'in the court of the garden of the king's palace' (בַּחֲצַר גִּנַּת בִּיתַן הַמֶּלֶךְ). Here, the syntagm differs slightly from גנת הביתן in Est. 7.7 and 7.8, as it forms a construct chain with בַּחֲצַר 'in the court of' and הַמֶּלֶךְ 'of the king'. In the Vulgate, this long chain was translated as *in vestibulo horti et nemoris quod regio cultu et manu consitum erat* 'on the forecourt of the garden and of the grove which had been planted with royal care and by hand'.[561] The LXX reads ἐν αὐλῇ οἴκου τοῦ βασιλέως 'in the court of the king's house'; the A-Text ἔνδον ἐν τῇ αὐλῇ τοῦ βασιλέως 'within the king's court'; the VL *in aula / in atrio regis* 'at the court / in the king's hall'.[562] On the other hand, Origen's variant, which is recorded as οἴκου + συμφυτου in Hanhart's apparatus, without the word κῆπος, may have read as follows: οἴκου συμφυτου τοῦ βασιλέως 'of the king's wooded / leafy house'.[563] The Vulgate representation of בַּחֲצַר גִּנַּת בִּיתָן הַמֶּלֶךְ could therefore be analysed as follows: *in vestibulo horti* ('on the forecourt of the garden') represents a *verbum e verbo* rendering of בַּחֲצַר גִּנַּת and *et nemoris quod regio cultu et manu consitum erat* ('and of the grove which had been planted with royal care and by hand') a *sensus*

---

[561] The First Targum to Esther contains an expansion that partly echoes the embellishments of the Vulgate translation: בדרת גינתא גואה דלמלכא דהות נציבא אילני עבדין פירין ובושמנין כבישין עד פלגותהון דהב טב ושלימין באשלמות אבן טבא ומטללין עילויהון 'In the court of the king's inner garden, which had been planted with fruit-bearing trees and with spices plated with fine gold up to their middle and finished with a fine gem setting and casting shade over them' (First Targum to Est. 1.5; p. 6). See also the description of the royal garden in the Second Targum to Est. 1.5 (p. 37).

[562] There is no description of the location of the banquet in Josephus' version of Est. 1.5.

[563] Of all versions of Est. 1.5, Vulg. Est. 1.5 is the only one that contains a rendering for גִּנַּת (*horti*).

de sensu expansion on συμφυτου and הַמֶּלֶךְ / τοῦ βασιλέως.[564] As in Vulg. Est. 7.7 and 7.8, the word בִּיתָן was elided. On the whole, Jerome's translation technique tells us here that, instead of translating the Hebrew, he rendered Origen's version and expanded on it: more importantly, he did so in a passage where it departed from his Hebrew *Vorlage* (provided that it contained ביתן and that

---

[564] According to Hanhart, the rendering σύμφυτος, which may be attributable to Aquila, reflects an erroneous etymological construal of the rare word ביתן (which only occurs in Est. 1.5, 7.7 and 7.8). See Hanhart, *Esther*, pp. 74–75, fn. 1. I would rather argue that the *recentiores* translator whose version of Est. 1.5, 7.7 and 7.8 is found in Origen's edition did not manage to understand what ביתן meant and consequently expanded on גנת / κῆπος with σύμφυτος to make up for it. Besides, in LXX Est. 1.5, the word οἴκου 'house' already seemed to stand for ביתן (see fn. 565). Also plausible is that σύμφυτος represents a reading of בֶּחָצֵר in Est. 1.5, and that this reading was incorporated into Est. 7.7 and 7.8. Indeed, the *qal* passive participle of the verb בצר 'to cut off', 'to make inaccessible', 'to enclose', is graphically close to בֶּחָצֵר: in LXX Zech. 11.2 for example הַבָּצוּר is represented by ὁ σύμφυτος (the Hebrew reads יַעַר הַבָּצוּר 'the dense [lit., inaccessible] forest', but the Masoretes suggested הבציר as the *qere*, in which case the Hebrew means 'the forest of vintage'; however, the LXX followed the *qetiv* and translated the Hebrew as ὁ δρυμὸς ὁ σύμφυτος 'the leafy thicket'). Furthermore, the term בצור could conceivably be imagined in the context of Est. 1.5: it would point to the 'dense garden' of the king's palace. Therefore, if the *recentiores* translator who employed σύμφυτος read the *qal* passive participle of בצר instead of בֶּחָצֵר in Est. 1.5, he may have continued to use this adjective in Est. 7.7 and 7.8—even though בצור / בחצר was not present in these verses— through a process of interpolation.

there was no equivalent for σύμφυτος).[565] His way of treating his sources was at variance with the postulate of the Hebrew text's supremacy, which underlay the Vulgate project. If he relied on Origen where it differed from the Hebrew, he must have thought that it would enrich his translation on a stylistic level without impairing the meaning of the Hebrew: this was indeed the advantage of the *sensus de sensu* translation method.[566]

---

[565] It is noteworthy that, of all translations of Est. 1.5, 7.7 and 7.8, LXX Est. 1.5 (as well as Origen's version) seems to be the only one in which there is a word for 'palace': οἴκου arguably stands for בִּיתָן (and ἐν αὐλῇ for בַּחֲצַר). It could also be that בית (οἶκός) was read instead of בִּיתָן.

[566] Further comparative analysis of the Vulgate of Esther could help in identifying similar cases of agreement with Origen's edition (see also above, section 4.2.2.2.2); it would also shed light on the overall transmission history and on the content of the hypothetical *recentiores* version, or versions, of the Book of Esther.

5. CONCLUSION

1.0. A Summary of Jerome's Sources

A remark that Jerome made in his preface to the commentary on the Book of Isaiah is repeatedly quoted in modern scholarship: 'The ignorance of the Scriptures is the ignorance of the Christ' (*ignoratio scripturarum, ignoratio Christi est*).[567] As explained before, Jerome believed that Scripture, and more specifically the style in which Scripture was composed, that is, its wording, embodied the 'mystery' (*mysterium*), and that the mystery embodied the divine.[568]

Jerome promoted the idea that the Hebrew Bible represented the original version of Scripture: according to him, since the Septuagint translation existed in different forms, from which had stemmed a variety of Old Latin texts, and as these translations could differ from one another, the accurate sense, or the 'truth' rather, of the Old Testament was to be drawn from the Hebrew Bible (*hebraica veritas*). As he regarded it as the supreme textual authority, he set out to translate it into Latin and, where necessary, to do so against other versions. That he generally endeavoured to impose, through his translations, the meaning conveyed by the Hebrew text, when the Bibles employed by Christians differed from it, cannot be denied: *hebraica veritas* renderings are easy to identify in this respect (sections 2.2.1 and 3.2.3).

---

[567] Preface to *Comm. Isa.* (CCSL 73, p. 1).

[568] See section 1.8.

As shown in this monograph, however, this goal was not always achievable: for example, when the meaning of a Hebrew phrase was obscure, Jerome followed the interpretations that he found in other versions, which he also conflated (sections 2.2.3 and 2.2.4). More striking, he could decide, even when the Hebrew was intelligible, to reproduce LXX or VL readings that differed from it (sections 2.2.5.1, 4.2.1 and 4.2.2.2.2): this is likely to have been a politically motivated approach designed not to overly surprise or offend the Christian audience.

On a strictly technical level, Jerome also translated more comfortably from Greek than from Hebrew: his faith in the *recentiores* sometimes led him, as a result, to make uncritical choices by incorporating renderings that did not reflect the Hebrew (sections 3.2.2.2, 3.2.5 and 4.2.4). By all means, the *recentiores*' translations were one of his main sources in the treatment of the Hebrew (sections 2.2.3, 2.2.4 and 3.2.2.1). He ultimately showed his flexibility and creativity by routinely introducing his own interpretations in his translation, even though they could depart from the wording of the Hebrew (sections 2.2.2, 2.2.5.2, 3.2.4, 4.2.2.1, 4.2.2.2.1, 4.2.2.2.3 and 4.2.3). In section 3.2.1.1 and in the annotations interspersed in the Vulgate of Esther,[569] the sources to which Jerome referred could not be identified beyond doubt. On the whole, he was often pulled in different directions, notwithstanding his effort to generally remain faithful to the *hebraica veritas*. Consequently, the Vulgate, which was supposed to be a Latin vehicle for the Hebrew Bible, ended up representing a

---

[569] See section 4.1.4.

translation of the Hebrew, but also of various Greek and Old Latin versions.

2.0. Jerome's Techniques of Translation and Some Concluding Remarks

It has been established that Jerome could introduce his own evaluation of a passage of the Hebrew Bible in his translation, i.e., with no parallel in any of the extant versions: the examples studied in sections 2.2.5.2, 4.2.2.1, 4.2.2.2.1 and 4.2.2.2.2 illustrated this type of response. An analogy could perhaps be drawn with the technique of the authors of Midrashim and of the Targumim, who frequently elaborated on a passage with a series of explanatory details. Two instances of interpolation (sections 3.2.4 and 4.2.2.2.2) were also detected as part of Jerome's techniques of translation: the recourse to interpolation was meant to clarify or elaborate on a passage in a contextually harmonious way. Through the double rendering, which was addressed in sections 2.2.3, 2.2.4, 4.2.2.1 (see fn. 539), and 4.2.2.2.2, Jerome meant to offer alternatives in his translation. This technique proved useful when the meaning of the Hebrew was obscure: in sections 2.2.3 and 2.2.4, the Vulgate contains different readings for the same term, all of which are technically possible. However, Jerome also employed it when the Hebrew could have been translated in a straightforward way: in section 4.2.2.2.2, for example, the double rendering matched the Greek against the *hebraica veritas*. He often incorporated different traditions into his work, the novelty of which is that he alone decided which traditions, among all the texts that he had at hand, he would select, and where he would use them.

Jerome's method has also exhibited a significant amount of lexical variation, as seen in sections 3.2.1, 3.2.2, 3.2.4 and 4.2.2.2. The recourse to synonymous words or phrases allowed him to avoid the repetitions that could occur in the original; nevertheless, whether there were repetitions in the Hebrew or not, that technique attested above all to his fondness for variation. It was indeed a way for him to express his literary creativity. His use of certain extreme paraphrases in the translation of the Book of Esther (chapter 4), more than in any other books, further reflected that creativity: he was ultimately more stylistically conservative earlier in his life, when translating Daniel around 393 and Genesis in the late 390s, than in 404–405 when rendering Esther. At the same time, he was much more dependent on his sources in the translation of Daniel and of Genesis than in that of Esther.

Jerome firmly asserted that the translator's goal was to express the ideas of the original text without being hampered by the idioms of the source language. The *sensus de sensu*, which permitted artistic licence in this regard, was his way of expressing his freedom as a translator. The application of this method also confirms that his translations were not meant as glosses for the Christian audience to read and learn Hebrew: to be sure, when Jerome referred a Latin addressee who he knew could not engage with Hebrew material to the "Hebrews" ("Go ask the Hebrews!"), so as to put an end to a linguistic argument over his rendering of

5. Conclusion

a text, he did not actually mean it.[570] He was indeed well aware that only an elite circle among his Latin-speaking Christian associates, like Paula and Eustochium (see section 4.1.1), could engage with Hebrew sources. The motivation behind the Vulgate project was therefore to create an autonomous Latin version of Scripture. Besides, Jerome claimed that his translation would convey the 'true' meaning of Scripture in accordance with the Hebrew text. This monograph has shown how his sources in the translation of the Hebrew Bible could be other than the Hebrew Bible.

Little is written on Jerome's sources in general, considering what could be found by further exploring his work. Vulgate studies are modest, too, in comparison with Septuagint studies, for example. The misconception that the Vulgate is not worthy of investigation, in the context of comparisons with other Bible versions but also on a literary level, has prevented modern scholarship from benefitting from valuable findings. This monograph has also aspired to demonstrate that, if the Vulgate is given more attention, new discoveries can be made in the field of Bible studies.

---

[570] See section 1.6.

BIBLIOGRAPHY

1.0. Primary Sources

Catenae on Genesis = *La chaîne sur la Genèse: Édition intégrale,* edited by Françoise Petit. 4 vols. Traditio Exegetica Graeca. Leuven: Peeters, 1991–1996.

Gen. Rab. = *Midrash Bereshit Rabba,* edited by Julius J. Theodor and Chanoch Albeck. 3 vols. Jerusalem: Wahrmann Books, 1965.

Genizah Manuscripts = *Genizah Manuscripts of Palestinian Targum to the Pentateuch,* edited and translated by Michael L. Klein. 2 vols. Cincinnati: Hebrew Union College Press, 1986.

Jerome, *Against Jovinian* = Jérôme. *Contre Jovinien: Livre I,* edited and translated by Luce Savoye. SC 637. Paris: Les Éditions du Cerf, 2023.

———, *Chron.* = Saint Jérôme. *Chronique: Continuation de la Chronique d'Eusèbe, années 326–378,* edited by Rudolf Helm, translated and annotated by Benoît Jeanjean and Bertrand Lançon. Collection « Histoire ». Rennes: Presses Universitaires de Rennes, 2004.

———, *Comm. Dan.* = Jérôme. *Commentaire sur Daniel,* edited and translated by Régis Courtray. SC 602. Paris: Les Éditions du Cerf, 2019.

———, *Comm. Jon.* = Jérôme. *Commentaire sur Jonas,* edited and translated by Yves-Marie Duval. SC 323. Paris: Les Éditions du Cerf, 1985.

———, *Comm. Matt.* = Saint Jérôme. *Commentaire sur S. Matthieu*, edited and translated by Émile Bonnard. 2 vols. SC 242 and 259. Paris: Les Éditions du Cerf, 1977–1979.

———, *Divina Bibliotheca* = *Sancti Eusebii Hieronymi Stridonensis presbyteri Divina bibliotheca antehac inedita*, edited by Jean Martianay and Antoine Pouget, and by the monks of the Order of Saint Benedict from the Congregation of Saint Maur. 5 vols. Paris: Coustelier (vols. 1–2); Paris: Rigaud (vols. 3–5), 1693–1706.

———, *Epist.* = Saint Jérôme. *Correspondance*, edited and translated by Jérôme Labourt. 8 vols. Collection des Universités de France. Paris: Belles Lettres, 1949–1963.

———, *QHG* = *Hieronymi quaestiones hebraicae in libro Geneseos*, edited by Paul de Lagarde. Leipzig: Teubner, 1868.

———, *Ruf.* = Saint Jérôme. *Apologie contre Rufin*, edited and translated by Pierre Lardet. SC 303. Paris: Les Éditions du Cerf, 1983.

———, *Vir. ill.* = *Hieronymus und Gennadius: De viris inlustribus*, edited by Carl Albrecht Bernoulli. Freiburg and Leipzig: Akademische Verlagsbuchhandlung von J. C. B. Mohr, 1895.

———, Vulgate and Its Prefaces = *Biblia sacra: Iuxta Vulgatam versionem*, edited by Robert Weber and Roger Gryson. Stuttgart: Deutsche Bibelgesellschaft, 2007.

Jos. Asen. = *Le Livre de la Prière d'Aseneth*, edited by Pierre Batiffol. Studia Patristica: Études d'ancienne littérature chrétienne 1. Paris: Ernest Leroux Éditeur, 1889.

Justinian, *Nov.* 146 = '146: Peri Hebraion'. In *Corpus Juris Civilis*, edited by Rudolf Schöll and Wilhelm Kroll, vol. 3, 714–18. Berlin: Weidmann, 1895.

Leqaḥ Ṭov = Ṭovyah ben ʾEliʿezer. מדרש לקח טוב המכונה פסיקתא זוטרתא על חמשה חומשי תורה, edited by Salomon Buber. 5 vols. Wilna: Wittwe & Gebrüder Romm, 1880.

Letter of Aristeas = *Aristeas to Philocrates: Letter of Aristeas*, edited and translated by Moses Hadas. Jewish Apocryphal Literature. New York: Harper & Brothers for Dropsie College, 1951.

LXX

Book of Daniel (LXX and Theodotion's version) = *Susanna. Daniel. Bel et Draco*, edited by Joseph Ziegler, Olivier Munnich and Detlef Fraenkel. Vetus Testamentum Graecum 16, 2. Göttingen: Vandenhoeck & Ruprecht, 1999.

Book of Esther (LXX and A-Text) = *Esther*, edited by Robert Hanhart. Vetus Testamentum Graecum 8, 3. Göttingen: Vandenhoeck & Ruprecht, 1966.

Gen. 37–50 (the Joseph story) = *Genesis*, edited by John William Wevers. Vetus Testamentum Graecum 1. Göttingen: Vandenhoeck & Ruprecht, 1974).

Septuagint = *Septuaginta: Id est Vetus Testamentum graece iuxta LXX interpretes*, edited by Alfred Rahlfs and Robert Hanhart. Stuttgart: Deutsche Bibelgesellschaft, 2006.

MT = *Biblia Hebraica Stuttgartensia*, edited by Karl Elliger, Wilhelm Rudolph et al. Stuttgart: Deutsche Bibelgesellschaft, 1997.

Onomastica sacra = *Onomastica sacra: Untersuchungen zum Liber interpretationis nominum hebraicorum des Hl. Hieronymus,* edited by Franz Wutz. 2 vols. Texte und Untersuchungen zur Geschichte der Altchristlichen Literatur. Leipzig: J. C. Hinrichs, 1914–1915.

Origen, *Comm. Matt.* = *Origenes Matthäuserklärung I,* edited by Erich Klostermann and Ernst Benz. Die griechischen christlichen Schriftsteller der ersten drei Jahrhunderte 40. Leipzig: J. C. Hinrichs, 1935.

———. *Ep. Afr.* = Origène. *Philocalie, 1–20: Sur les Écritures,* edited and translated by Marguerite Harl; and *La Lettre à Africanus sur l'Histoire de Suzanne,* edited and translated by Nicholas de Lange. SC 302. Paris: Les Éditions du Cerf, 1983.

———, Hexapla = *Origenis Hexaplorum quae supersunt: Sive veterum interpretum graecorum in totum Vetus Testamentum fragmenta,* edited by Frederick Field. 2 vols. Oxford: Clarendon Press, 1875.

———, *Hom. Num.* = *Homilien zum Hexateuch in Rufins Übersetzung,* edited by Wilhelm A. Baehrens. Die griechischen christlichen Schriftsteller der ersten drei Jahrhunderte 7. Leipzig: J. C. Hinrichs, 1921.

Tanḥuma Buber = מדרש תנחומא על חמשה חומשי תורה, edited by Salomon Buber. 3 vols. Wilna: Wittwe & Gebrüder Romm, 1885.

Tanḥuma Yelammedenu = מדרש תנחומא הנקרא ילמדנו והוא מדרש על חמשה חומשי תורה, edited by Menahem Mann ben Solomon ha-Levi Amelander. Amsterdam: Solomon ben Joseph Proops Press, 1733.

Targum Neofiti of Genesis = *Neophyti 1: Targum Palestinense*; *MS de la Biblioteca Vaticana*, vol. 1, edited by Alejandro Díez Macho. Textos y estudios "Cardenal Cisneros" 8. Madrid: Consejo Superior de Investigaciones Científicas, 1968.

Targum Onkelos of Genesis = *The Bible in Aramaic Based on Old Manuscripts and Printed Texts*, vol. 1, edited by Alexander Sperber. Leiden: Brill, 1959.

Targum Pseudo-Jonathan of Genesis = תרגום יונתן בן עוזיאל על התורה דנעתק מכתב יד שהיה טמון וצפון בעיר לונדון, edited by Moshe Ginsburger. Berlin: S. Calvary, 1903.

Targumim of the Book of Esther

First Targum = *The First Targum to Esther: According to the MS Paris Hebrew 110 of the Bibliothèque Nationale*, edited and translated by Bernard Grossfeld. New York: Sepher-Hermon Press, 1983.

Second Targum = The Targum Sheni to the Book of Esther: A Critical Edition Based on MS. Sassoon 282 with Critical Apparatus, edited by Bernard Grossfeld. New York: Sepher-Hermon Press, 1994.

The Acts of the Scillitan Martyrs = 'The Acts of the Scillitan Martyrs'. In *The Acts of the Christian Martyrs*, edited and translated by Herbert Musurillo, 86–89. Oxford Early Christian Texts. Oxford: Clarendon Press, 1972.

The Fragment-Targums of the Pentateuch According to Their Extant Sources, edited and translated by Michael L. Klein. 2 vols. Rome: Biblical Institute Press, 1980.

VL

Bibliorum Sacrorum Latinæ versiones antiquæ, seu vetus Italica, edited by Pierre Sabatier and Vincent de La Rue. 3 vols. Remis: Apud Reginaldum Florentain, 1743.

Book of Daniel = *Danihel*, edited by Jean-Claude Haelewyck. VL 14/1. Freiburg: Verlag Herder, 2021.

Book of Esther = *Hester*, edited by Jean-Claude Haelewyck. VL 7/3. Freiburg: Verlag Herder, 2003–2008.

Book of Genesis = *Genesis*, edited by Bonifatius Fischer. VL 2. Freiburg: Verlag Herder, 1951–1954.

Book of Isaiah = *Esaias*, edited by Roger Gryson. 2 vols. VL 12. Freiburg: Verlag Herder, 1987–1997.

2.0. Secondary Sources

Aberbach, Moses, and Bernard Grossfeld, eds and trans. *Targum Onqelos on Genesis 49*. Aramaic Studies 1. Missoula, MT: Scholars Press for the Society of Biblical Literature, 1976.

Aitken, James K. 'The Jewish Use of Greek Proverbs'. In *Jewish Reception of Greek Bible Versions*, edited by Nicholas R. M. de Lange, Julia G. Krivoruchko, and Cameron Boyd-Taylor, 53–77. Texts and Studies in Medieval and Early Modern Judaism 23. Tübingen: Mohr Siebeck, 2009.

———. 'The Social and Historical Setting of the Septuagint: Palestine and the Diaspora'. In *The Oxford Handbook of the Septuagint*, edited by Alison G. Salvesen and Timothy Michael Law, 73–80. Oxford: Oxford University Press, 2021.

Alexander, Philip S. 'The Cultural History of the Ancient Bible Versions: The Case of Lamentations'. In *Jewish Reception of Greek Bible Versions*, edited by Nicholas R. M. de Lange, Julia G. Krivoruchko, and Cameron Boyd-Taylor, 78–102. Texts and Studies in Medieval and Early Modern Judaism 23. Tübingen: Mohr Siebeck, 2009.

Amara, Dalia. 'Septuagint'. In *Textual History of the Bible*, edited by Armin Lange and Emanuel Tov, 542–54. The Hebrew Bible 1C. Leiden: Brill, 2017.

Andrist, Patrick. 'La structure des codex *Vaticanus*, *Alexandrinus*, et *Sinaiticus*: Questions ouvertes sur le canon, la fabrication et la circulation de ces Bibles'. In *Comment le Livre s'est fait livre: La fabrication des manuscrits bibliques (IVe–XVe siècle)—Bilan, résultats, perspectives de recherche*, edited by Chiara Ruzzier and Xavier Hermand, 11–37. Bibliologia 40. Turnhout: Brepols, 2015.

Antin, Paul. '"Simple" et "simplicité" chez saint Jérôme', *Revue Bénédictine* 71 no. 3–4 (1961): 371–81.

Arns, Paulo Evaristo. *La technique du livre d'après saint Jérôme*. Paris: E. de Boccard, 1953.

Bardy, Gustave. 'Les traditions juives dans l'œuvre d'Origène', *Revue Biblique* 34 no. 2 (1925): 217–52.

———. 'Saint Jérôme et ses maîtres hébreux', *Revue Bénédictine* 46 (1934): 145–64.

Barr, James. 'St Jerome and the Sounds of Hebrew', *Journal of Semitic Studies* 12 no. 1 (1967): 1–36.

———. 'St. Jerome's Appreciation of Hebrew', *Bulletin of the John Rylands University Library of Manchester* 49 no. 2 (1967): 281–302.

Barr, Jane. 'The Vulgate Genesis and St. Jerome's Attitude to Women', *Studia Patristica* 17 no. 1 (1982): 268–73.

Barthélemy, Dominique. *Les Devanciers d'Aquila*. Supplements to Vetus Testamentum 10. Leiden: Brill, 1963.

———. 'La Place de la Septante dans l'Église'. In *Aux Grands Carrefours de la Révélation et de l'Exégèse de l'Ancien Testament*, edited by Charles Hauret, 13–28. Recherches Bibliques 8. Bruges: Desclée de Brouwer, 1967.

———. 'Origène et le texte de l'Ancien Testament'. In *Epektasis: Mélanges patristiques offerts au Cardinal Jean Daniélou*, edited by Jacques Fontaine and Charles Kannengiesser, 247–61. Paris: Beauchesne, 1972.

———. 'Pourquoi la Torah a-t-elle été traduite en grec?'. In *On Language, Culture, and Religion in Honor of Eugene A. Nida*, edited by Matthew Black and William Alley Smalley, 23–41. Approaches to Semiotics 56. The Hague: Mouton, 1974.

———. 'Qui est Symmaque?', *Catholic Biblical Quarterly* 36 no. 4 (1974): 451–65.

Bickerman, Elias J. 'The Colophon of the Greek Book of Esther', *Journal of Biblical Literature* 63 no. 4 (1944): 339–62.

———. 'Notes on the Greek Book of Esther', *Proceedings of the American Academy for Jewish Research* 20 (1951): 101–33.

Billen, Albert Victor. *The Old Latin Texts of the Heptateuch*. Cambridge: Cambridge University Press, 1927.

Binder, Stéphanie Élodie, and Thomas Villey. 'Jewish Communities in North Africa'. In *The Routledge Handbook of Jews and Judaism in Late Antiquity*, edited by Catherine Hezser, 527–46. Abingdon: Routledge, 2024.

Blondheim, David Simon. *Les parlers judéo-romans et la Vetus Latina: Étude sur les rapports entre les traductions bibliques en langue romane des Juifs au moyen âge et les anciennes versions*. Paris: Librairie Ancienne Édouard Champion, 1925.

Blum, Erhard, and Kristin Weingart. 'The Joseph Story: Diaspora Novella or North-Israelite Narrative?', *Zeitschrift für die alttestamentliche Wissenschaft* 129 no. 4 (2017): 501–21.

Bogaert, Pierre-Maurice. 'Septante et versions grecques'. In *Dictionnaire de la Bible: Supplément*, edited by Louis Pirot, André Robert, Jacques Briend, and Édouard Cothenet, vol. 12, 536–95 (538–59 written in collaboration with Bernard Botte). Paris: Letouzey & Ané, Éditeurs, 1996.

———. 'De la *vetus latina* à l'hébreu pré-massorétique en passant par la plus ancienne Septante: Le livre de Jérémie, exemple privilégié', *Revue théologique de Louvain* 44 (2013): 216–43.

———. 'The Latin Bible'. In *The New Cambridge History of the Bible*, edited by James Carleton Paget and Joachim Schaper, vol. 1, 505–26. Cambridge: Cambridge University Press, 2013.

———. 'The Vetus Latina (Old Latin)'. In *The Oxford Handbook of the Septuagint*, edited by Alison G. Salvesen and Timothy

Michael Law, 623–38. Oxford: Oxford University Press, 2021.

Booth, Alan D. 'The Date of Jerome's Birth', *Phoenix* 33 no. 4 (1979): 346–53.

Boustan, Ra'anan. 'Afterword: Rabbinization and the Persistence of Diversity in the Jewish Culture in Late Antiquity'. In *Diversity and Rabbinization: Jewish Texts and Societies between 400 and 1000 CE*, edited by Gavin McDowell, Ron Naiweld, and Daniel Stökl Ben Ezra, 427–49. Cambridge Semitic Languages and Cultures 8. Cambridge: Open Book Publishers, 2021.

Boyd-Taylor, Cameron. 'Afterlives of the Septuagint: A Christian Witness to the Greek Bible in Byzantine Judaism'. In *The Jewish-Greek Tradition in Antiquity and the Byzantine Empire*, edited by James K. Aitken and James Carleton Paget, vol. 3, 135–51. New York: Cambridge University Press, 2014.

Braverman, Jay. *Jerome's 'Commentary on Daniel': A Study of Comparative Jewish and Christian Interpretations of the Hebrew Bible*. Catholic Biblical Quarterly Monograph Series 7. Washington, DC: Catholic Biblical Association of America, 1978.

Burkitt, Francis Crawford. *The Old Latin and the Itala*. Texts and Studies: Contributions to Biblical and Patristic Literature 4. Cambridge: Cambridge University Press, 1896.

Burstein, Eitan. 'La compétence de Jérôme en hébreu: Explication de certaines erreurs', *Revue d'Études Augustiniennes et Patristiques* 21 (1975): 3–12.

Cameron, John S. 'The *Vir Tricultus*: An Investigation of the Classical, Jewish and Christian Influences on Jerome's translation of the Psalter *Iuxta Hebraeos*'. PhD dissertation, University of Oxford, 2006.

———. 'The Rabbinic Vulgate?'. In *Jerome of Stridon: His Life, Writings, and Legacy*, edited by Andrew Cain and Josef Lössl, 117–29. Burlington, VT: Ashgate, 2009.

Cañas Reíllo, José Manuel. 'Latin'. In *Textual History of the Bible*, edited by Frank Feder, Matthias Henze, and Mika Pajunen, 153–57. The Deuterocanonical Scriptures 2B. Leiden: Brill, 2019.

———. 'The Latin Bible and the Septuagint'. In *The Oxford Handbook of the Latin Bible*, edited by Hugh A. G. Houghton, 19–36. New York: Oxford University Press, 2023.

Canellis, Aline. *Préfaces aux livres de la Bible.* Sources Chrétiennes 592. Paris: Les Éditions du Cerf, 2017.

Capelle, Paul. *Le Texte du psautier latin en Afrique.* Collectanea Biblica Latina 4. Rome: F. Pustet, 1913.

Cavalier, Claudine, ed. and trans. *Esther.* La Bible d'Alexandrie 12. Paris: Les Éditions du Cerf, 2000.

Cavallera, Ferdinand. *Saint Jérôme: Sa vie et son œuvre*, 2 vols. Leuven: "Spicilegium Sacrum Lovaniense" Bureaux, Édouard Champion, 1922.

Ceulemans, Reinhart. 'Greek Christian Access to "the Three," 250–600 CE'. In *Greek Scripture and the Rabbis*, edited by Timothy Michael Law and Alison G. Salvesen, 165–91. Contributions to Biblical Exegesis and Theology 66. Leuven: Peeters, 2012.

———. 'Greek Church Fathers'. In *Textual History of the Bible*, edited by Armin Lange and Emanuel Tov, 755–58. The Hebrew Bible 1C. Leiden: Brill, 2017.

Collins, John J. *Daniel*. Hermeneia: A Critical and Historical Commentary on the Bible. Minneapolis: Fortress Press, 1993.

Condamin, Albert. 'L'influence de la tradition juive dans la version de Saint Jérôme', *Recherches de science religieuse* 5 (1914): 1–21.

Courtray, Régis. 'Jérôme, traducteur du Livre de Daniel', *Pallas* 75 (2007): 105–24.

———. *Prophète des temps derniers: Jérôme commente Daniel*. Théologie Historique 119. Paris: Beauchesne, 2009.

———. 'Porphyre et le livre de Daniel au travers du Commentaire sur Daniel de Jérôme'. In *Le Traité de Porphyre contre les chrétiens: Un siècle de recherches, nouvelles questions—Actes du colloque international organisé les 8 et 9 septembre 2009 à l'Université de Paris IV–Sorbonne*, edited by Sébastien Morlet, 329–56. Collection des Études Augustiniennes, Série Antiquité 190. Paris: Institut d'Études Augustiniennes, 2011.

———. 'Saint Jérôme et la conversion à l'Écriture'. In *La Conversion chez les Pères de l'Église*, edited by Daniel Vigne, 203–17. Paris: Éditions Parole et Silence, 2014.

———. 'Jérôme face au livre d'Esther', *Cahiers Évangile: Supplément* 190 (2019): 30–32.

Damsma, Alinda. 'The Targums to Esther', *European Judaism: A Journal for the New Europe* 47 no. 1 (2014): 127–36.

Davies, Philip R. *Daniel*. Old Testament Guides 4. Sheffield: JSOT Press, 1985.

Davis Bledsoe, Amanda M. 'The Relationship of the Different Editions of Daniel: A History of Scholarship', *Currents in Biblical Research* 13 no. 2 (2015): 175–90.

de Bruyne, Donatien. 'Une nouvelle préface de la traduction hexaplaire de Saint Jérôme', *Revue Bénédictine* 31 (1919): 229–36.

De Crom, Dries. 'The *Letter of Aristeas*'. In *The Oxford Handbook of the Septuagint*, edited by Alison G. Salvesen and Timothy Michael Law, 121–34. Oxford: Oxford University Press, 2021.

de Lange, Nicholas R. M. *Origen and the Jews: Studies in Jewish-Christian Relations in Third-Century Palestine*. University of Cambridge Oriental Publications 25. Cambridge: Cambridge University Press, 1978.

———. 'The Letter to Africanus: Origen's Recantation?', *Studia Patristica* 16 (1985): 242–47.

———. 'The Revival of the Hebrew Language in the Third Century CE', *Jewish Studies Quarterly* 3 no. 4 (1996): 342–58.

———. 'The Greek Bible Translations of the Byzantine Jews'. In *The Old Testament in Byzantium*, edited by Paul Magdalino and Robert Nelson, 39–54. Washington, DC: Dumbarton Oaks Research Library and Collection, 2010.

———. *Japheth in the Tents of Shem: Greek Bible Translations in Byzantine Judaism*. Texts and Studies in Medieval and Early Modern Judaism 30. Tübingen: Mohr Siebeck, 2015.

———. 'Hebraists and Hellenists in the Sixth-Century Synagogue: A New Reading of Justinian's Novel 146'. In *"Let the Wise Listen and Add to Their Learning" (Prov 1:5): Festschrift for Günter Stemberger on the Occasion of His 75th Birthday*, edited by Constanza Cordoni and Gerhard Langer, 217–26. Studia Judaica 90. Berlin: De Gruyter, 2016.

de Sainte-Marie, Henri. 'Le Psaume 22 (21) dans le *iuxta Hebraeos*'. In *Richesses et déficiences des anciens psautiers latins*, edited by Pierre Salmon, 151–87. Collectanea Biblica Latina 13. Rome: Abbaye Saint-Jérôme, 1959.

De Troyer, Kristin. 'The Septuagint'. In *The New Cambridge History of the Bible*, edited by James Carleton Paget and Joachim Schaper, vol. 1, 267–88. Cambridge: Cambridge University Press, 2013.

den Dulk, Matthijs. *Between Jews and Heretics: Refiguring Justin Martyr's Dialogue with Trypho*. Routledge Studies in the Early Christian World. London: Routledge, 2018.

Di Lella, Alexander A. Introduction, and Commentary on Chapters 10–12 in *The Book of Daniel*, by Louis F. Hartman and Alexander A. Di Lella. The Anchor Bible 23. Garden City, NY: Doubleday, 1978.

———. 'The Textual History of Septuagint-Daniel and Theodotion-Daniel'. In *The Book of Daniel: Composition and Reception*, edited by John J. Collins and Peter W. Flint, vol. 2, 586–607. Supplements to Vetus Testamentum 83. Leiden: Brill, 2001.

Dorival, Gilles. 'L'Apport des Pères de l'Église à la question de la clôture du canon de l'Ancient Testament'. In *The Biblical*

Canons, edited by Jean-Marie Auwers and Henk Jan de Jonge, 81–110. Bibliotheca Ephemeridum Theologicarum Lovaniensium 163. Leuven: Presses Universitaires de Louvain, 2003.

———. 'Les Hexaples d'Origène'. In *Lieux de Savoir 2: Les mains de l'intellect*, edited by Christian Jacob, 521–35. Paris: Albin Michel, 2011.

Ehlers, Widu-Wolfgang, Michael Fieger, and Wilhelm Tauwinkl. 'Some Notes about Jerome and the Hexameters in the Book of Job', *Vulgata in Dialogue* 2 (2018): 47–51.

Ehrensvärd, Martin. 'Why Biblical Texts Cannot Be Dated Linguistically', *Hebrew Studies* 47 (2006): 177–89.

Estin, Colette. *Les Psautiers de Jérôme: A la lumière des traductions juives antérieures*. Collectanea Biblica Latina 15. Rome: San Girolamo, 1984.

Fernández Marcos, Natalio. *Introducción a las versiones griegas de la Biblia*, 2nd edition. Textos y estudios "Cardenal Cisneros" 64. Madrid: Consejo Superior de Investigaciones Científicas, 1998.

———. '*Non placet Septuaginta:* Revisions and New Greek Versions of the Bible in Byzantium'. In *Jewish Reception of Greek Bible Versions*, edited by Nicholas R. M. de Lange, Julia G. Krivoruchko, and Cameron Boyd-Taylor, 39–50. Texts and Studies in Medieval and Early Modern Judaism 23. Tübingen: Mohr Siebeck, 2009.

Gallagher, Edmon L. 'Why Did Jerome Translate Tobit and Judith?' *Harvard Theological Review* 108 no. 3 (2015): 356–75.

———. 'The Latin Canon'. In *Textual History of the Bible*, edited by Frank Feder, Matthias Henze, and Mika Pajunen, 166–90. The Deuterocanonical Scriptures 2A. Leiden: Brill, 2020.

Gentry, Peter J. 'Pre-Hexaplaric Translations, Hexapla, Post-Hexaplaric Translations'. In *Textual History of the Bible*, edited by Armin Lange and Emanuel Tov, 211–35. The Hebrew Bible 1A. Leiden: Brill, 2016.

———. 'Origen's Hexapla'. In *The Oxford Handbook of the Septuagint*, edited by Alison G. Salvesen and Timothy Michael Law, 553–71. Oxford: Oxford University Press, 2021.

Golka, Friedemann W. 'Genesis 37–50: Joseph Story or *Israel*-Joseph Story?', *Currents in Biblical Research* 2 no. 2 (2004): 153–77.

Gordon, Cyrus H. 'Rabbinic Exegesis in the Vulgate of Proverbs', *Journal of Biblical Literature* 49 no. 4 (1930): 384–416.

Grabbe, Lester L. 'Aquila's Translation and Rabbinic Exegesis', *Journal of Jewish Studies* 33 (1982): 527–36.

Grafton, Anthony, and Megan Williams. *Christianity and the Transformation of the Book: Origen, Eusebius, and the Library of Caesarea*. Cambridge, MA: The Belknap Press of Harvard University Press, 2006.

Graves, Michael. *Jerome's Hebrew Philology: A Study Based on His Commentary on Jeremiah*. Supplements to Vigiliae Christianae 90. Leiden: Brill, 2007.

———. 'Midrash-Like Word Plays in Aquila's Translation of Genesis'. In *Greek Scripture and the Rabbis*, edited by Timothy Michael Law and Alison G. Salvesen, 65–86. Contributions to Biblical Exegesis and Theology 66. Leuven: Peeters, 2012.

———. 'Vulgate'. In *Textual History of the Bible*, edited by Armin Lange and Emanuel Tov, 278–89. The Hebrew Bible 1A. Leiden: Brill, 2016.

———. 'The Septuagint in the Latin World'. In *The Oxford Handbook of the Septuagint*, edited by Alison G. Salvesen and Timothy Michael Law, 605–20. Oxford: Oxford University Press, 2021.

———. 'Latin Texts: Antiquity and Late Antiquity'. In *Textual History of the Bible*, edited by Russell E. Fuller and Armin Lange, 231–46. A Companion to Textual Criticism 3A. Leiden: Brill, 2023.

Gray, George Buchanan. *The Forms of Hebrew Poetry Considered with Special Reference to the Criticism and Interpretation of the Old Testament*. London: Hodder and Stoughton, 1915.

Gribomont, Jean. 'The Translations: Jerome and Rufinus', *Patrology* 4 (1986): 195–254.

Gzella, Holger. *A Cultural History of Aramaic: From the Beginnings to the Advent of Islam*. Handbook of Oriental Studies 111. Leiden: Brill, 2015.

Hadas-Lebel, Mireille. 'Qui utilisait la LXX dans le monde juif?'. In *La Bible des Septante: Le Pentateuque d'Alexandrie*, edited by Cécile Dogniez and Marguerite Harl, 42–49. Paris: Les Éditions du Cerf, 2001.

Haelewyck, Jean-Claude. 'The Relevance of the Old Latin Version for the Septuagint, with Special Emphasis on the Book of

Esther', *Journal of Theological Studies*, New Series 57 no. 2 (2006): 439–73.

———. 'Esther'. In *Textual History of the Bible*, edited by Armin Lange and Emanuel Tov, 459–61. The Hebrew Bible 1C. Leiden: Brill, 2017.

———. 'Latin'. In *Textual History of the Bible*, edited by Frank Feder, Matthias Henze, and Mika Pajunen, 405–8. The Deuterocanonical Scriptures 2B. Leiden: Brill, 2019.

Hardy, Nicholas. *Criticism and Confession: The Bible in the Seventeenth Century Republic of Letters*. Oxford-Warburg Studies. Oxford: Oxford University Press, 2017.

Harl, Marguerite, ed. and trans. *La Genèse*. La Bible d'Alexandrie 1. Paris: Les Éditions du Cerf, 1986.

Hartman, Louis F. A New Translation with Notes and Commentary on Chapters 1–9 in *The Book of Daniel*, by Louis F. Hartman and Alexander A. Di Lella. The Anchor Bible 23. Garden City, NY: Doubleday, 1978.

Hayward, Charles Thomas Robert. 'Saint Jerome and the Aramaic Targumim', *Journal of Semitic Studies* 32 no. 1 (1987): 105–23.

———. *Saint Jerome's 'Hebrew Questions on Genesis'*. Oxford Early Christian Studies. Oxford: Clarendon, 1995.

Hendel, Ronald, and Jan Joosten. *How Old Is the Hebrew Bible? A Linguistic, Textual, and Historical Study*. The Anchor Yale Bible Reference Library. New Haven, CT: Yale University Press, 2018.

Henze, Matthias. 'Textual History of the Additions to Daniel'. In *Textual History of the Bible*, edited by Frank Feder, Matthias

Henze, and Mika Pajunen, 133–42. The Deuterocanonical Scriptures 2B. Leiden: Brill, 2019.

Hornkohl, Aaron. 'Biblical Hebrew: Periodization'. In *Encyclopedia of Hebrew Language and Linguistics*, edited by Geoffrey Khan, vol. 1, 315–25. Leiden: Brill, 2013.

Houghton, Hugh A. G. *The Latin New Testament: A Guide to Its Early History, Texts, and Manuscripts*. Oxford: Oxford University Press, 2016.

———. 'Scripture and Latin Christian Manuscripts from North Africa'. In *The Bible in Christian North Africa, Part I: Commencement to the "Confessiones" of Augustine (ca. 180 to 400 CE)*, edited by Jonathan P. Yates and Anthony Dupont, 15–50. Handbooks of the Bible and Its Reception 4, 1. Berlin, Boston: De Gruyter, 2020.

———. 'The Earliest Latin Translations of the Bible'. In *The Oxford Handbook of the Latin Bible*, edited by Hugh A. G. Houghton, 1–18. New York: Oxford University Press, 2023.

Jay, Pierre. 'La datation des premières traductions de l'Ancien Testament sur l'hébreu par saint Jérôme', *Revue d'Études Augustiniennes et Patristiques* 28 nos. 3–4 (1982): 208–12.

———. *L'Exégèse de Saint Jerôme: D'après son 'Commentaire sur Isaïe'*. Paris: Études augustiniennes, 1985.

Jobes, Karen H., and Moisés Silva. *Invitation to the Septuagint*, 2nd edition. Grand Rapids, MI: Baker Academic, 2015.

Joosten, Jan. 'The Linguistic Dating of the Joseph Story', *Hebrew Bible and Ancient Israel* 8 no. 1 (2019): 24–43.

Joubert, François. *Explication des principales prophéties de Jérémie, d'Ezéchiel, et de Daniel, Disposées selon l'ordre des Tems*, 4 vols. Avignon: Chez Alexandre Girard, 1749.

Juster, Jean. *Les Juifs dans l'Empire romain: Leur condition juridique, économique et sociale*, 2 vols. Paris: Librairie Paul Geuthner, 1914.

Kalimi, Isaac. *The Book of Esther between Judaism and Christianity: The Biblical Story, Self-identification, and Antisemitic Interpretation*. Cambridge: Cambridge University Press, 2023.

Kamesar, Adam. *Jerome, Greek Scholarship, and the Hebrew Bible: A Study of the 'Quaestiones Hebraicae in Genesim'*. Oxford Classical Monographs. Oxford: Clarendon Press, 1993.

———. 'Rabbinic Midrash and Church Fathers'. In *Encyclopaedia of Midrash: Biblical Interpretation in Formative Judaism*, edited by Jacob Neusner and Alan Avery-Peck, vol. 1, 20–40. Leiden: Brill, 2005.

———. 'Jerome'. In *The New Cambridge History of the Bible*, edited by James Carleton Paget and Joachim Schaper, vol. 1, 653–75. Cambridge: Cambridge University Press, 2013.

———. 'Jerome and the Hebrew Scriptures'. In *The Oxford Handbook of the Latin Bible*, edited by Hugh A. G. Houghton, 49–64. New York: Oxford University Press, 2023.

Kato, Teppei. 'Hebrews, Apostles, and Christ: Three Authorities of Jerome's *Hebraica Veritas*', *Vigiliae Christianae* 73 no. 4 (2019): 420–39.

Kedar-Kopfstein, Benjamin. 'Divergent Hebrew Readings in Jerome's Isaiah', *Textus* 4 no. 1 (1964): 176–210.

———. 'The Vulgate as a Translation: Some Semantic and Syntactical Aspects of Jerome's Version of the Hebrew Bible'. PhD dissertation, The Hebrew University of Jerusalem, 1968.

———. 'Textual Gleanings from the Vulgate to Jeremiah', *Textus* 7 no. 1 (1969): 36–58.

Kelly, John N. D. *Jerome: His Life, Writings and Controversies*. London: Duckworth, 1975.

Khan, Geoffrey. *A Short Introduction to the Tiberian Masoretic Bible and Its Reading Tradition*, 2nd edition. Gorgias Handbooks 28. Piscataway, NJ: Gorgias Press, 2013.

King, Daniel. '*Vir Quadrilinguis?* Syriac in Jerome and Jerome in Syriac'. In *Jerome of Stridon: His Life, Writings, and Legacy*, edited by Andrew Cain and Josef Lössl, 209–23. Burlington, VT: Ashgate, 2009.

Kratz, Reinhard. 'The Joseph Story: Diaspora Novella—Patriarchal Story—Exodus Narrative. Part II: Historical Reflections'. In *The Joseph Story between Egypt and Israel*, edited by Konrad Schmid, Thomas Römer, and Axel Bühler, 23–33. Archaeology and Bible 5. Tübingen: Mohr Siebeck, 2021.

Kraus, Matthew. 'Hebraisms in the Old Latin Version of the Bible', *Vetus Testamentum* 53 no. 4 (2003): 487–513.

———. *Jewish, Christian, and Classical Exegetical Traditions in Jerome's Translation of the Book of Exodus*. Supplements to Vigiliae Christianae 141. Leiden: Brill, 2017.

———. 'Rabbinic Traditions in Jerome's Translation of the Book of Numbers', *Journal of Biblical Literature* 136 no. 3 (2017): 539–63.

Krauss, Samuel. 'The Jews in the Works of the Church Fathers', *The Jewish Quarterly Review* 5 no. 1 (1892): 122–57.

———. 'Jerome (Eusebius Hieronymus Sophronius)'. In *The Jewish Encyclopedia*, edited by Isidore Singer et al., vol. 7, 115–18. New York: Funk and Wagnalls Company, 1924.

Kreuzer, Siegfried. 'Old Greek, *kaige* and the *trifaria varietas*—A New Perspective on Jerome's Statement', *Journal of Septuagint and Cognate Studies* 46 (2013): 74–85.

Lange, Armin. 'The Canonical Histories of the Jewish Bible and the Christian Old Testament with Special Attention to the Deuterocanonical Books: A Synthesis'. In *Textual History of the Bible*, edited by Frank Feder, Matthias Henze, and Mika Pajunen, 5–112. The Deuterocanonical Scriptures 2A. Leiden: Brill, 2020.

Lapin, Hayim. *Rabbis as Romans: The Rabbinic Movement in Palestine, 100–400 CE*. New York: Oxford University Press, 2012.

Le Bohec, Yann. *Les Juifs dans l'Afrique romaine*. Saint Macaire: Memoring Éditions, 2021.

Lee, John A. L. *A Lexical Study of the Septuagint Version of the Pentateuch*. Septuagint and Cognate Studies 14. Chico, CA: Scholars Press, 1983.

McClurg, Andrew. 'Esther'. In *Textual History of the Bible*, edited by Armin Lange and Emanuel Tov, 437–39. The Hebrew Bible 1C. Leiden: Brill, 2017.

Millar, Fergus. 'Jerome and Palestine', *Scripta Classica Israelica* 29 (2010): 59–79.

Moore, Carey A. 'A Greek Witness to a Different Hebrew Text of Esther', *Zeitschrift für die alttestamentliche Wissenschaft* 79 no. 3 (1967): 351–58.

———. 'On the Origins of the LXX Additions to the Book of Esther', *Journal of Biblical Literature* 92 no. 3 (1973): 382–93.

———. *Daniel, Esther, and Jeremiah: The Additions—A New Translation with Introduction and Commentary*. The Anchor Yale Bible 44. New Haven, CT: Yale University Press, 2010.

———. *Esther: A New Translation with Introduction and Commentary*. The Anchor Yale Bible 7A. New Haven, CT: Yale University Press, 2011.

Morin, Jean. *Exercitationes biblicae: De Hebraei Graecique Textus sinceritate*. Paris: Antonius Vitray, Linguarum Orientalium Regius Typographus, 1633.

Munnich, Olivier. 'Origène, éditeur de la *Septante* de *Daniel*'. In *Studien zur Septuaginta: Robert Hanhart zu Ehren—Aus Anlaß seines 65. Geburtstages*, edited by Detlef Fraenkel, Udo Quast, and John William Wevers, 187–218. Mitteilungen des Septuaginta-Unternehmens 20. Göttingen: Vandenhoeck & Ruprecht, 1990.

———. 'Les révisions juives de la Septante: Modalités et fonctions de leur transmission—Enjeux éditoriaux contemporains'. In *La Bible juive dans l'Antiquité*, edited by Rémi Gounelle and Jan Joosten, 141–90. Histoire du texte biblique 9. Lausanne: Éditions du Zèbre, 2014.

———. 'Daniel, Susanna, Bel and the Dragon: Old Greek and Theodotion'. In *The Oxford Handbook of the Septuagint*, edited by Alison G. Salvesen and Timothy Michael Law, 291–305. Oxford: Oxford University Press, 2021.

Nautin, Pierre. *Origène: Sa vie et son œuvre*. Christianisme antique 1. Paris: Beauchesne, 1977.

———. 'L'Activité littéraire de Jérôme de 387 à 392', *Revue de Théologie et de Philosophie* 115 no. 3 (1983): 247–59.

———. 'Hieronymus', *Theologische Realenzyklopädie* 15 (1986): 304–15.

———. 'Le "De Seraphim" de Jérôme et son appendice "Ad Damasum"'. In *Roma Renascens: Beiträge sur Spätantike und Rezeptiongeschichte—Ilona Opelt von ihren Freunden und Schülern zum 9.7.1988 in Verehrung gewidmet*, edited by M. Wisseman, 257–93. Frankfurt am Main: Verlag Peter Lang, 1988.

Newman, Hillel. 'Jerome and the Jews' (היירונימוס והיהודים). PhD dissertation, The Hebrew University of Jerusalem, 1997. [Hebrew].

———. 'Jerome's Judaizers', *Journal of Early Christian Studies* 9 no. 4 (2001): 421–52.

———. 'The Normativity of Rabbinic Judaism: Obstacles on to the Path to a New Consensus'. In *Jewish Identities in Antiquity: Studies in Memory of Menahem Stern*, edited by Lee I. Levine and Daniel R. Schwartz, 165–71. Texte und Studien zum antiken Judentum 130. Tübingen: Mohr Siebeck, 2009.

Millar, Fergus. 'Jerome and Palestine', *Scripta Classica Israelica* 29 (2010): 59–79.

Moore, Carey A. 'A Greek Witness to a Different Hebrew Text of Esther', *Zeitschrift für die alttestamentliche Wissenschaft* 79 no. 3 (1967): 351–58.

———. 'On the Origins of the LXX Additions to the Book of Esther', *Journal of Biblical Literature* 92 no. 3 (1973): 382–93.

———. *Daniel, Esther, and Jeremiah: The Additions—A New Translation with Introduction and Commentary*. The Anchor Yale Bible 44. New Haven, CT: Yale University Press, 2010.

———. *Esther: A New Translation with Introduction and Commentary*. The Anchor Yale Bible 7A. New Haven, CT: Yale University Press, 2011.

Morin, Jean. *Exercitationes biblicae: De Hebraei Graecique Textus sinceritate*. Paris: Antonius Vitray, Linguarum Orientalium Regius Typographus, 1633.

Munnich, Olivier. 'Origène, éditeur de la *Septante* de *Daniel*'. In *Studien zur Septuaginta: Robert Hanhart zu Ehren—Aus Anlaß seines 65. Geburtstages*, edited by Detlef Fraenkel, Udo Quast, and John William Wevers, 187–218. Mitteilungen des Septuaginta-Unternehmens 20. Göttingen: Vandenhoeck & Ruprecht, 1990.

———. 'Les révisions juives de la Septante: Modalités et fonctions de leur transmission—Enjeux éditoriaux contemporains'. In *La Bible juive dans l'Antiquité*, edited by Rémi Gounelle and Jan Joosten, 141–90. Histoire du texte biblique 9. Lausanne: Éditions du Zèbre, 2014.

———. 'Daniel, Susanna, Bel and the Dragon: Old Greek and Theodotion'. In *The Oxford Handbook of the Septuagint*, edited by Alison G. Salvesen and Timothy Michael Law, 291–305. Oxford: Oxford University Press, 2021.

Nautin, Pierre. *Origène: Sa vie et son œuvre*. Christianisme antique 1. Paris: Beauchesne, 1977.

———. 'L'Activité littéraire de Jérôme de 387 à 392', *Revue de Théologie et de Philosophie* 115 no. 3 (1983): 247–59.

———. 'Hieronymus', *Theologische Realenzyklopädie* 15 (1986): 304–15.

———. 'Le "De Seraphim" de Jérôme et son appendice "Ad Damasum"'. In *Roma Renascens: Beiträge sur Spätantike und Rezeptiongeschichte—Ilona Opelt von ihren Freunden und Schülern zum 9.7.1988 in Verehrung gewidmet*, edited by M. Wisseman, 257–93. Frankfurt am Main: Verlag Peter Lang, 1988.

Newman, Hillel. 'Jerome and the Jews' (הייירונימוס והיהודים). PhD dissertation, The Hebrew University of Jerusalem, 1997. [Hebrew].

———. 'Jerome's Judaizers', *Journal of Early Christian Studies* 9 no. 4 (2001): 421–52.

———. 'The Normativity of Rabbinic Judaism: Obstacles on to the Path to a New Consensus'. In *Jewish Identities in Antiquity: Studies in Memory of Menahem Stern*, edited by Lee I. Levine and Daniel R. Schwartz, 165–71. Texte und Studien zum antiken Judentum 130. Tübingen: Mohr Siebeck, 2009.

Norris, Oliver W. E. 'The Latin Psalter'. In *The Oxford Handbook of the Latin Bible*, edited by Hugh A. G. Houghton, 65–76. New York: Oxford University Press, 2023.

Olariu, Daniel. 'Textual History of Daniel'. In *Textual History of the Bible*, edited by Armin Lange and Emanuel Tov, 517–27. The Hebrew Bible 1C. Leiden: Brill, 2017.

———. 'From Suspicion to Appreciation: The Change of Perception Regarding Theodotion's Version of Daniel in Patristic Literature'. In *The Oxford Handbook of The Bible in Orthodox Christianity*, edited by Eugen J. Pentiuc, 52–68. Oxford: Oxford University Press, 2022.

Parker, David C. 'The New Testament Text and Versions'. In *The New Cambridge History of the Bible*, edited by James Carleton Paget and Joachim Schaper, vol. 1, 412–54. Cambridge: Cambridge University Press, 2013.

Rajak, Tessa. 'Theological Polemic and Textual Revision in Justin Martyr's *Dialogue with Trypho the Jew*'. In *Greek Scripture and the Rabbis*, edited by Timothy Michael Law and Alison G. Salvesen, 127–40. Contributions to Biblical Exegesis and Theology 66. Leuven: Peeters, 2012.

Rebenich, Stefan. 'Jerome: The "vir trilinguis" and the "hebraica veritas"', *Vigiliae Christianae* 47 (1993): 50–77.

Redford, Donald B. *A Study of the Biblical Story of Joseph (Genesis 37–50)*. Supplements to Vetus Testamentum 20. Leiden: Brill, 1970.

Remley, Paul. 'The Latin Textual Basis of *Genesis A*', *Anglo-Saxon England* 17 (1988): 163–89.

Römer, Thomas. 'How to Date Pentateuchal Texts: Some Case Studies'. In *The Formation of the Pentateuch: Bridging the Academic Cultures of Europe, Israel, and North Africa*, edited by Jan C. Gertz, Bernard M. Levinson, Dalit Rom-Shiloni, and Konrad Schmid, 357–70. Forschungen zum Alten Testament 111. Tübingen: Mohr Siebeck, 2016.

———. 'The Role of Egypt in the Formation of the Hebrew Bible', *Journal of Ancient Egyptian Interconnections* 18 (2018): 63–70.

———. 'How "Persian" or "Hellenistic" Is the Joseph Narrative?' In *The Joseph Story between Egypt and Israel*, edited by Konrad Schmid, Thomas Römer, and Axel Bühler, 35–55. Archaeology and Bible 5. Tübingen: Mohr Siebeck, 2021.

Salmon, Pierre. 'Introduction'. In *Richesses et déficiences des anciens psautiers latins*, edited by Pierre Salmon, 5–21. Collectanea Biblica Latina 13. Rome: Abbaye Saint-Jérôme, 1959.

Salvesen, Alison G. 'Did Aquila and Symmachus Shelter under the Rabbinic Umbrella?' In *Greek Scripture and the Rabbis*, edited by Timothy Michael Law and Alison G. Salvesen, 107–25. Contributions to Biblical Exegesis and Theology 66. Leuven: Peeters, 2012.

Schaper, Joachim. 'The Origin and Purpose of the Fifth Column of the Hexapla'. In *Origen's Hexapla and Fragments: Papers Presented at the Rich Seminar on the Hexapla, Oxford Centre for Hebrew and Jewish Studies, 25th [July]–3rd August 1994*, edited by Alison G. Salvesen, 3–15. Texte und Studien zum antiken Judentum 58. Tübingen: Mohr Siebeck, 1998.

Scheck, Thomas P. *St. Jerome: Commentary on Ezekiel*. Ancient Christian Writers 71. New York: The Newman Press, 2017.

Scheetz, Jordan. 'Daniel's Position in the Tanach, the LXX-Vulgate, and the Protestant Canon', *Old Testament Essays* 23 no. 1 (2010): 178–93.

Schipper, Bernd U. 'Joseph, Ahiqar, and Elephantine: The Joseph Story as a Diaspora Novella', *Journal of Ancient Egyptian Interconnections* 18 (2018): 71–84.

Schmid, Konrad. 'How Old Is the Hebrew Bible? A Response to Ronald Hendel and Jan Joosten', *Zeitschrift für die alttestamentliche Wissenschaft* 132 no. 4 (2020): 622–31.

Schulman, Alan R. 'On the Egyptian Name of Joseph: A New Approach', *Studien zur Altägyptischen Kultur* 2 (1975): 235–43.

Schwartz, Seth. 'Language, Power and Identity in Ancient Palestine', *Past & Present* 148 no. 1 (1995): 3–47.

———. 'Rabbinization in the Sixth Century'. In *The Talmud Yerushalmi and Graeco-Roman Culture*, edited by Peter Schäfer, vol. 3, 55–69. Texte und Studien zum antiken Judentum 93. Tübingen: Mohr Siebeck, 2002.

Schwarz, Werner. *Principles and Problems of Biblical Translation: Some Reformation Controversies and Their Background*. Cambridge: Cambridge University Press, 1955.

Segal, Michael. *Dreams, Riddles, and Visions: Textual, Contextual, and Intertextual Approaches to the Book of Daniel*. Beihefte zur Zeitschrift für die alttestamentliche Wissenschaft 455. Berlin: De Gruyter, 2016.

Severino Croatto, José. ''Abrek „Intendant" dans Gén. XLI 41, 43', *Vetus Testamentum* 16 no. 1 (1966): 113–15.

Simon, Richard. *Histoire critique du Vieux Testament*. Rotterdam: Reinier Leers, 1685.

Skemp, Vincent T. M. 'Learning by Example: *Exempla* in Jerome's Translations and Revisions of Biblical Books', *Vigiliae Christianae* 65 (2011): 257–84.

———. 'Vulgate'. In *Textual History of the Bible*, edited by Armin Lange and Emanuel Tov, 441–46. The Hebrew Bible 1C. Leiden: Brill, 2017.

Smelik, Willem F. 'Justinian's Novella 146 and Contemporary Judaism'. In *Greek Scripture and the Rabbis*, edited by Timothy Michael Law and Alison G. Salvesen, 141–63. Contributions to Biblical Exegesis and Theology 66. Leuven: Peeters, 2012.

———. *Rabbis, Language and Translation in Late Antiquity*. Cambridge: Cambridge University Press, 2013.

Soggin, Jan Alberto. 'Dating the Joseph Story and Other Remarks'. In *Joseph: Bibel und Literatur—Symposion Helsinki, Lathi 1999*, edited by Friedemann W. Golka and Wolfgang Weiß, 13–24. Oldenburgische Beiträge zu Jüdischen Studien 6. Oldenburg: Bis-Verlag, 2000.

Speiser, Ephraim A. ed. and trans. *Genesis. The Anchor Yale Bible* 1. New Haven, CT: Yale University Press, 2008.

Stemberger, Günter. 'Exegetical Contacts between Christians and Jews in the Roman Empire'. In *Hebrew Bible / Old Testament: The History of Its Interpretation*, edited by Magne Sæbø, vol. 1, 569–86. Göttingen: Vandenhoeck & Ruprecht, 1996.

Sutcliffe, Edmund F. 'St. Jerome's Pronunciation of Hebrew', *Biblica* 29 nos. 1–2 (1948): 112–25.

———. 'St Jerome's Hebrew Manuscripts', *Biblica* 29 no. 3 (1948): 195–204.

———. 'The Name "Vulgate"', *Biblica* 29 no. 4 (1948): 345–52.

Swete, Henry Barclay. *An Introduction to the Old Testament in Greek.* Cambridge: Cambridge University Press, 1914.

Thibaut, André. 'La révision hexaplaire de saint Jérôme'. In *Richesses et déficiences des anciens psautiers latins*, edited by Pierre Salmon, 107–49. Collectanea Biblica Latina 13. Rome: Abbaye Saint-Jérôme, 1959.

Tkacz, Catherine Brown. '*Labor tam utilis*: The Creation of the Vulgate', *Vigiliae Christianae* 50 no. 1 (1996): 49–72.

Torrey, Charles C. 'The Older Book of Esther', *Harvard Theological Review* 37 no. 1 (1944): 1–40.

Tov, Emanuel. 'The Evaluation of the Greek Scripture Translations in Rabbinic Sources'. In *Hebrew Bible, Greek Bible, and Qumran*, edited by Peter Schäfer, Annette Y. Reed, Seth Schwartz, and Azzan Yadin, 365–77. Texte und Studien zum antiken Judentum 121. Tübingen: Mohr Siebeck, 2008.

———. *Textual Criticism of the Hebrew Bible*, 3rd edition. Minneapolis, MN: Fortress Press, 2012.

———. 'The Septuagint Translation of Genesis as the First Scripture Translation'. In *Textual Criticism of the Hebrew Bible, Qumran, Septuagint*, edited by Emanuel Tov, vol. 3, 504–20. Supplements to Vetus Testamentum 167. Leiden: Brill, 2015.

———. *The Text-Critical Use of the Septuagint in Biblical Research*, 3rd edition. Winona Lake, IN: Eisenbrauns, 2015.

Veltri, Giuseppe. *Libraries, Translations, and 'Canonic' Texts: The Septuagint, Aquila and Ben Sira in the Jewish and Christian Traditions*. Supplements to the Journal for the Study of Judaism 109. Leiden: Brill, 2006.

———. 'The Septuagint in Disgrace: Some Notes on the Stories on Ptolemy in Rabbinic and Medieval Judaism'. In *Jewish Reception of Greek Bible Versions*, edited by Nicholas R. M. de Lange, Julia G. Krivoruchko, and Cameron Boyd-Taylor, 142–54. Texts and Studies in Medieval and Early Modern Judaism 23. Tübingen: Mohr Siebeck, 2009.

Vergote, Jozef. *Joseph en Égypte: Genèse chap. 37–50 à la lumière des études égyptologiques récentes*. Leuven: Publications Universitaires, 1959.

Wasserstein, Abraham, and David J. Wasserstein. *The Legend of the Septuagint: From Classical Antiquity to Today*. Cambridge: Cambridge University Press, 2006.

Weigert, Sebastian. *Hebraica Veritas: Übersetzungsprinzipien und Quellen der Deuteronomiumübersetzung des Hieronymus*. Beiträge zur Wissenschaft vom Alten und Neuen Testament 207. Stuttgart: Verlag W. Kohlhammer, 2016.

Weill, Julien. 'Notes de littérature judéo-hellénistique', *Revue des études juives* 82 nos 163–64 (1926): 125–31.

Wilhite, David E. *Ancient African Christianity: An Introduction to a Unique Context and Tradition*. London: Routledge, 2017.

Williams, Megan Hale. *The Monk and the Book*: *Jerome and the Making of Christian Scholarship*. Chicago: The University of Chicago Press, 2006.

Wills, Lawrence M. *Introduction to the Apocrypha: Jewish Books in Christian Bibles*. New Haven, CT: Yale University Press, 2021.

Young, Ian. 'Biblical Texts Cannot Be Dated Linguistically', *Hebrew Studies* 46 (2005): 341–51.

Young, Ian, Robert Rezetko, and Martin Ehrensvärd. *Linguistic Dating of Biblical Texts*, 2 vols. BibleWorld. London: Equinox, 2008.

Zelzer, Klaus. 'La *Vetus Latina*'. In *L'Âge de transition: De la littérature romaine à la littérature chrétienne de 117 à 284 après J.-C.*, edited by Klaus Sallman, translated into French by François Heim, 398–415. Nouvelle histoire de la littérature latine 4. Turnhout: Brepols, 2000.

Zilverberg, Kevin. *The Textual History of Old Latin Susanna*. Opusculum ad lectionem coram. Rome: Pontifical Biblical Institute, 2017. (unpublished research)

———. *The Textual History of Old Latin Daniel from Tertullian to Lucifer*. Textos y estudios "Cardenal Cisneros" 85. Madrid: Consejo superior de investigaciones científicas, 2021.

———. 'The Greek Loan Word Presbyteri in Vetus Latina and Vulgate Susanna (Vulg. Dan. 13): Reception by Cyprian, Lucifer, and Jerome'. In *Varietate delectamur: Multifarious Approaches to Synchronic and Diachronic Variation in Latin—Selected Papers from the 14th International Colloquium on Late and Vulgar Latin (Ghent, 2022)*, edited by Giovanbattista

Galdi, Simon Aerts, and Alessandro Papini. Turnhout: Brepols, forthcoming.

INDEX

Personal Names

Ambrose, 19
Apollinaris, 24, 73 n. 187, 128
Aquila, 6, 11 n. 32, 12–14, 15 nn. 43–44, 17 n. 47, 32, 34–35, 38, 40, 52, 57, 58 n. 145, 65, 72 n. 186, 73 n. 189, 75, 86 n. 216, 88, 103, 115–20, 120 n. 284, 121, 125, 127 n. 296, 128, 130, 132, 134–35, 136 n. 313, 137–38, 142–43, 145, 164 n. 356, 184–87, 193, 196, 201, 203–6, 208 n. 439, 210 n. 441, 211 n. 444, 212, 226, 227 n. 470, 242 n. 488, 256, 271, 307 n. 564
Augustine, 19 n. 52, 22, 23 n. 59, 48, 69–71, 74 n. 189, 76 n. 198, 126 n. 294, 144–45, 148 n. 328
Baranina, 25, 66
Basil of Caesarea, 19
Cicero, 19 n. 52, 32 n. 85, 85, 91, 174
Cyprian, 21, 157 n. 338, 217 n. 456
Damasus, 27, 28, 34, 36, 46
Epiphanius, 60 n. 150

Eusebius, 19 n. 52, 31, 32 n. 85, 60 n. 150, 68 n. 178, 72 n. 186, 86 n. 216, 87, 92 n. 228
Eustochium, 41 n. 102, 112 n. 268, 245, 313
Horace, 32, 92
Josephus, 33, 57, 84, 110 n. 267, 159 n. 348, 242, 243 n. 490, 274–75, 276 n. 537, 277, 285 n. 544, 288 n. 547, 289 n. 548, 301 n. 558, 302–5, 306 n. 562
Justin, 7–8, 51–52
Justinian, 12, 60 n. 150
Marcella, 191, 216 n. 452
Origen, 14–17, 18 n. 49, 30, 31 n. 84, 33, 38, 39, 40 n. 102, 41 n. 102, 54, 55 n. 134, 56 n. 136, 62 n. 160, 68 n. 178, 73 n. 189, 86 n. 216, 97 n. 240, 117 nn. 278–79, 123 n. 289, 133–35, 136 n. 313, 155 n. 335, 164 n. 356, 165, 166, 167 n. 362, 169 n. 369, 170–71, 172 n. 376, 173 n. 376, 177–79, 184 n. 391, 194, 202, 206, 239, 242, 249 n. 501, 256–57, 259, 263 n. 523, 264 n. 523, 270

nn. 531–32, 272 n. 533, 287, 289 n. 548, 290 n. 550, 293 n. 552, 302–8
Pammachius, 74 n. 191, 191, 216 n. 452
Pamphilius, 86 n. 216
Paul, 20, 56 n. 135, 67, 100
Paula, 41 n. 102, 112 n. 268, 245, 313
Philo, 10 n. 30, 68, 120 n. 282, 130 n. 300, 140 n. 320, 194
Porphyry, 168–69
Ptolemy, 3, 56 n. 137, 78, 95, 243 n. 491
Rufinus, 19 n. 52, 46 n. 113, 76, 77 n. 199, 159, 163, 168–69, 251 n. 505
Symmachus, 6, 12, 13 nn. 38–39, 14, 15 nn. 43–44, 32, 38, 40, 52, 57, 58 n. 145, 72 n. 186, 73 n. 189, 75, 88, 103, 117, 120–21, 122 n. 286, 125, 128, 130, 138, 142, 164 n. 356, 184, 196 n. 419, 201, 204–8, 226, 227 n. 470, 256, 271
Tertullian, 20–21, 44 n. 110
Theodotion, 14, 15 n. 44, 16 n. 46, 17, 32, 39, 40, 52, 57, 65, 72 n. 186, 73 n. 189, 75, 88, 103, 105, 117, 127 n. 296, 128 n. 296, 138 n. 317, 155–57, 161–66, 169 n. 368, 177–79, 182–84, 187 n. 399, 188 n. 400, 189, 191–92, 193 n. 412, 201–9, 210 nn. 440–41, 212–14, 216–19, 222–27, 230, 235–37, 238 n. 481, 240, 242 n. 488, 256–57, 271
Theophilus, 188–91, 201
Virgil, 32 n. 85, 175 n. 380

Place Names

Africa *Proconsularis*, 18
Alexandria, 2, 84, 86 n. 216, 95, 188, 238
Antioch, 24, 86 n. 216
Bethlehem, 25, 27, 30, 47 n. 115, 57, 58 n. 146, 65–66, 153
Carthage, 19–20, 157 n. 338
Chalcis, 24–26, 47 n. 115, 57, 63
Constantinople, 12–13, 27, 86 n. 216
Egypt, 9–10, 18, 86 n. 216, 108 n. 265, 139–40, 232
Jerusalem, 2, 32 n. 85, 57, 66, 220, 243 n. 491, 282
Oea, 69–70
Palestine, 9, 11, 27 n. 75, 55 n. 133, 59 n. 147, 63 n. 162, 175 n. 382

Rome, 25, 27, 32 n. 85, 57, 58 n. 146, 216 n. 452

General Terms

apocrypha, 27 n. 76, 50, 172, 243 n. 491, 254 n. 512

Apostle, 32 n. 85, 39, 40 n. 100, 48–49, 50–52, 53 n. 125, 56 n. 135, 67–68, 83, 85, 97–100, 103 n. 258, 112–13, 196 n. 419

calque, 20 n. 54, 120 n. 284, 220 n. 462, 262, 270 n. 532

canon, 158, 159 n. 348, 161, 168–73, 178, 251

Christ, 7–8, 32 n. 85, 40, 49, 50, 51 n. 122, 52, 56 n. 137, 57 n. 142, 66–68, 78, 83, 85, 94–95, 99, 159, 163–64, 165 n. 357, 218–19, 309

double rendering, 136, 278 n. 539, 283, 285, 291–92, 311

evaluation, 10 nn. 28–29, 10–11 n. 31, 152, 277, 280–81, 311

Evangelist, 48–50, 51, 99, 103 n. 258

fountainhead, 37–38, 77, 86, 87 n. 217

hebraica veritas, 37, 47, 50 n. 121, 54–55, 58 n. 146, 63 n. 162, 68 n. 178, 71, 76, 89–90, 101, 103, 108–10, 112, 116, 119, 128, 160, 166, 169 n. 369, 173, 180, 187–88, 196, 201, 212, 215, 219, 240, 251, 279–80, 287, 294–95, 309–11

Hebrew truth, 37, 69, 77, 85, 90, 100, 111, 122, 158, 161, 165, 170 n. 370, 173 n. 378, 177, 202

Hebrews, 1, 38, 42, 48–49, 50, 51 n. 122, 55–58, 62–69, 74–75, 76, 86, 89, 103 n. 258, 104, 110, 112, 115–16, 132–33, 137, 143, 158, 161, 167–69, 171, 172 n. 376, 173, 177–78, 185–87, 201, 245, 254–56, 312

Hexapla, 14–15, 16 n. 46, 17, 30 nn. 81–82, 40, 71–72, 73 n. 186 and 188, 86, 103, 117 n. 278, 120 n. 283, 122 n. 286, 125, 134 n. 310, 184 n. 391, 185 nn. 392 and 394, 194 n. 415, 206, 208 n. 439, 227 n. 470, 238 n. 481, 239 n. 483, 242 n. 488

informant, 55, 58 n. 146, 65, 69, 133–34, 195

interpolation, 133 n. 308, 180, 219, 231 n. 475, 233, 269 n. 530, 291, 307 n. 564, 311

lexical variation, 181, 200–1, 204 n. 431, 205–6, 209, 211 n. 444, 212, 228–29, 265, 280, 282, 285, 291–92, 312
Mishna, 60–61, 96
mystery, 40, 78, 93–96, 309
New Testament, 18 n. 52, 19–20, 21 n. 55, 27, 38, 43 n. 108, 48–49, 50 n. 121, 52–53, 74, 98 n. 243, 108–13, 196 n. 419
Old Testament, 1, 5, 8, 14, 29, 31 n. 84, 35–36, 38–39, 42, 43 n. 108, 46, 49, 51–53, 56 n. 137, 67, 75, 78 nn. 202–3, 94, 110, 112–13, 144, 160, 161 n. 351, 194, 309
paraphrase, 46, 89, 91, 100, 130 n. 300, 137, 149–50, 152, 179, 189–91, 201, 226–27, 229, 242, 258–61, 270–72, 274, 277, 280–81, 288 n. 547, 291, 294, 298, 300, 302, 312
Pharisee, 59, 66, 171
recentiores, 14, 15 n. 44, 16 n. 46, 17, 38, 40, 42, 57, 59, 72 n. 186, 73 n. 188, 75, 94, 102, 109, 116 n. 277, 117, 122, 124–28, 134 n. 311, 135, 142, 151, 158, 165, 180, 184, 199 n. 421, 204–5, 208 n. 439, 209, 210 n. 441, 212, 226, 227 n. 470, 234–37, 239–40, 242 n. 488, 250 n. 503, 256–57, 271–72, 307 n. 564, 308 n. 566, 310
sensus de sensu, 89, 91–92, 94 n. 231, 96, 98–100, 120, 126, 137, 146, 152, 189, 244, 246–47, 258–60, 291, 294, 301, 308, 312
teacher, 25, 49, 56 n. 137, 58–59, 62, 64 nn. 163–64, 65, 67, 74, 135
translation technique, 1, 91, 104, 106, 125, 128, 137, 149, 152, 180, 206, 212, 225, 228 n. 472, 259 n. 517, 268, 271–72, 278, 280, 282, 287, 291, 301, 307
verbum e verbo, 91, 93 n. 231, 244–47, 255, 258, 291, 306
word order, 93, 138, 141, 199, 218 n. 457, 268 n. 529, 283

About the Team

Alessandra Tosi and Geoffrey Khan were the managing editors for this book and provided quality control.

Krisztina Szilagyi performed the copyediting of the book in Word.

The fonts used in this volume are Charis SIL, SBL Hebrew and SBL Greek.

Annie Hine created all of the editions — paperback, hardback, and PDF. Conversion was performed with open source software freely available on our GitHub page at https://github.com/OpenBookPublishers.

Jeevanjot Kaur Nagpal designed the cover of this book. The cover was produced in InDesign using Fontin and Calibri fonts.

www.ingramcontent.com/pod-product-compliance
Lightning Source LLC
Chambersburg PA
CBHW051535230426
43669CB00015B/2605